The Severed Alliance

By the same author:

Timeless Flight: The Definitive Biography Of The Byrds
Neil Young: Here We Are In The Years
Roxy Music: Style With Substance
Van Morrison: A Portrait Of The Artist
The Kinks: The Sound And The Fury
Wham! (Confidential) The Death Of A Supergroup
Starmakers And Svengalis: The History Of British Pop Management
The Football Managers
Timeless Flight Revisited

MORRISSEY & MARR

The Severed Alliance

Johnny Rogan

OMNIBUS PRESS

LONDON · NEW YORK · SYDNEY

Exclusive distributors:

Book Sales Limited,
8/9 Frith Street,
London W1V 5TZ.

Music Sales Corporation,
225 Park Avenue South,
New York, NY 10003, USA.

Music Sales Pty Ltd.,
120 Rothschild Avenue,
Rosebery, NSW 2018, Australia.

To the Music Trade only:
Music Sales Limited,
8/9 Frith Street,
London W1V 5TZ, UK.

Typeset on Quark XPress 3.0

Printed and bound in Great Britain by
Mackays of Chatham PLC, Chatham, Kent

Every effort has been made to trace the copyright holders
of the photographs in this book but one or two were
unreachable. We would be grateful if the photographers
concerned would contact us.

A catalogue record for this book is available from the
British Library.

CONTENTS

For DEBORAH RILEY

ACKNOWLEDGEMENTS

FIRSTLY, I WOULD LIKE TO THANK Vini Reilly who arrived about a third of the way through this project, and connected me with both Morrissey and Marr. This proved crucially important in the development of the book. On reflection, I am especially grateful to Johnny for allowing me to exhaust us both with some hard questions, and latterly to Mike Joyce for inviting me to his house for a similarly lengthy session.

The foundations of this book are based on numerous interviews conducted over a three-and-a-half year period. I am grateful to the following for their cooperation and willingness to speak: Rob Allman, John Barratt, Andrew Berry, Danny Betesh, Richard Boon, Bruno X, Peter Cassan, Steve Cassan, Patricia Corrigan, John Cotcher, Ann Courtney, Tommy Courtney, David Crosby, Gary Curley, Jimmy Curley, Tony (TJ) Davidson, Noel Devaney, Howard Devoto, Andy Dog, Bobby Durkin, Mike Ellis, Andy Farley, Gary Farrell, Rita Flynn, Mike Foley, John Fox (Foxy), Ken Friedman, Seamus Gilsenan, Rob Gretton, Dave Haslam, Fred Hood, Paddy Jacobs, Stuart James, Bob Johnson, Matt Johnson, Danny Kelly, Kevin Kennedy, Nick Kent, Harvey Lisberg, Nils Lofgren, Chris Lukes, Steve Mardy, Elliot Marks, Dennis Matthews, Ellen McArdle, Oz McCormick, Annette Messenger, Eddie Messenger, Eddie Messenger Jnr, Mick Middles, Mike Moore, Peter Morrissey, Ann, Ellen and Patricia Morrissey, Joe Moss, Ian Moss (Moey), John Muir, Nora Nolan, Paddy Nolan, John O'Brien, Larry Parnes, Ivor Perry, Scott Piering, Graham Pink, JL Pooley, John Porter, Julie Porter, Chris Power, Patrick Quinn, Paul Riley, Margaret Roe, Michael Roe, Mike Roe, Beryl Roche, Beryl Ryan, Grant Showbiz, Patrick Smith, Steve Smythe, Matthew Sztumpf, Geoff Travis, Will Trotter, James Verrechia, Michele Weaver, Tony Wilson and Simon Wolstencroft.

Special hellos to Billy Bragg, Hettie Church, Martha Defoe, Peter Doggett, Billy Duffy, Shaun Duggan, Peter Frame, Paul Garvey, Wally Hammond, Michael Herbert, Gordon King, Rachel King, Linder, Angie Marr, Per McEvoy, Alan McGee, Ann-Marie McVeigh, Vanessa Potter, Phil Powell, Karl Quinlan, Old John Robertson, Shelley Rohde, Marcus Russell, Bob Searle, George Sweeney, Troy Tate, Mark Taylor, Paul Whittall, Mark Wood and Brendan Wyse.

Additional thanks to my sister Anne, Greg Acton, Denise Alexander, Peter 'Bardy' Barden, Colin Larkin, Sean Morris, Cathy Shea, Teresa Walsh,

and everyone in Manchester, Dublin, London and elsewhere for their help.
For valuable editorial feedback and proof-reading on the book in progress:
Chris Charlesworth and Peter Doggett.

   Rob Allman, Mike Joyce, Steve Mardy, Eddie Messenger, John Muir, Julie
Porter, Vini Reilly, Grant Showbiz, Steve Smythe and Morrissey's aunts,
Patricia and Ann, entrusted me with photographic/archive material or live
tapes, which were much appreciated. Remarkably, at the time of writing,
there is no definitive news source or fanzine on the activities of Morrissey
and Marr. However, the redoubtable Mark Taylor is about to launch a peri-
odical on Steven Patrick, the first issue of which should be available by the
time this book goes to the printers. Details available (with SAE/IRC) from
132, Sylvia Avenue, Bristol, BS3 5BZ, UK. Anyone wishing to communicate
with me about either this book or projected sequels years hence is welcome
to write via the publisher.

Johnny Rogan

FOREWORD

MORRISSEY & MARR: The Severed Alliance is the first volume of a long-term trilogy documenting the histories of two of the most famous and important figures in contemporary popular music. This book covers the lives and careers of Morrissey and Marr up until the end of their partnership, with an extended epilogue chronicling their more recent work. In the succeeding volumes, assuming the authorial zeal remains, I intend to cover Morrissey's solo career in even greater detail, taking a closer look at his development as a writer and recording artiste as well as examining the musicianship of Johnny Marr extend from The Smiths, through The Pretenders, The The, Electronic and beyond. Such an undertaking will necessarily involve at least five years' additional research, and much can happen to us all in that period. However, if Morrissey and Marr continue to produce work anywhere near as interesting as their output between 1982-87, then this is a labour devoutly to be wished. At present, I find it difficult to imagine undertaking anything else. The rest looks strangely anti-climactic by comparison, which says much for how this particular project has dominated my life in recent years.

People often ask me at what point I decide to write a book and it's never an easy question to answer. As I don't write commissioned biographies as a rule, and rely on my own ideas rather than those of publishers, a project usually germinates in my mind for quite some time before I finally make the big artistic and financial plunge. In the case of Morrissey and Marr, the first flickerings go back to 1986. At that time, they had long established themselves as my favourite UK group, but other matters were on my mind. I was staggering towards the conclusion of the original 300,000 word manuscript of *Starmakers & Svengalis*. It was a period of severe austerity, sleeping on floors, living on £18 per week and stretching time beyond reason to cover word lengths. Many hours were spent at Camden Library, reading the papers and rock books and taking advantage of the free electricity in order to write for part of the day in comparative warmth. A regular visitor to the music section was none other than Nick Kent, probably my all-time favourite music writer. He was living in conditions arguably worse than mine, with a diet equally poor. We chatted frequently about The Byrds, the state of pop and, on one occasion, The Smiths. Kent seemed genuinely excited that I had even seen the group and was pleased that I regarded *Meat Is Murder* and *The Queen Is Dead* so highly. We didn't stay for long on The Smiths and I cannot now recall what we said, except that the conversation leaped extravagantly back to Larry Parnes, forward to The Beatles and The Rolling Stones, back to The Byrds, on to the concept of the svengali and, finally, to a dissection of Malcolm McLaren.

One year later, I was on the road promoting my latest book, a ludicrously serious study of the phenomenon called Wham! It was actually an outtake from the *Svengalis* tome, deliberately expanded to book size and written as a commentary on the cynical pop process of the eighties. Wham! seemed the perfect subject matter. In Manchester, I was interviewed by, of all people, Mick Middles, who turned out to be charmingly self-effacing. We chatted about Wham!, as arranged, but I was more interested to hear his troubled dealings with The Smiths. The next day, at BBC Liverpool, I was booked to appear on a programme called *Street Life*. The young interviewer reeled off the usual questions before completely disarming me by asking what I thought of The Smiths. How could he have known? It was a weird coincidence. We spent about 15 minutes talking about the group, which was infinitely preferable to another Wham! radio regurgitation. "Why don't you write a book about The Smiths?" he asked pointedly. I deflected the question with the pedestrian, "It's too early in their career", but I secretly thought to myself, "Maybe one day..." A few weeks later, The Smiths split and, some time afterwards on the *South Bank Show*, that same interviewer was hailed as a special fan and passing witness. His name was Shaun Duggan.

The demise of The Smiths initially put me off the idea of a book. I fully expected the market to be flooded with posthumous tomes but nothing appeared except Middles' slim volume and *Morrissey In His Own Words* collated by the pseudonymous John Robertson (who not only shared my initials, but took his pen name from a Byrds song. Needless to say, it *wasn't* me!). Finally, after immense consideration and a visit to Eire to mull over the implications, I decided to write a serious book either on The Smiths, Morrissey alone, or Morrissey & Marr (who contractually *were* The Smiths).

What followed were three-and-a-half years of tough research and considerable expense. About a quarter of the way in, I signed with a publisher. All the advance quickly went on travelling alone. During numerous trips to Manchester I saw more pubs than I care to remember, from Fonzo in the Midland and Mike Roe at the Cornbrook, down to Bobby Durkin's exploits in the Royal Oak and Pear Tree, and beyond. I have nothing but good memories of this period and wouldn't have missed it for the world. You always know when a book has you in its grip. It dominates your days and continually invades your dreams, night after night. And what dreams I had. In one, Peter Morrissey was exposed as the secret identity of Eamon de Valera; in another, a crippled Morrissey besieged by fans met me outside a funfair; in a third, Marr sang a version of 'Ask' for the next Electronic single and also announced his intention to manufacture a range of Johnny Marr sweatshirts. The genesis of the dreams are no doubt subliminally revealed in the text.

The majority of the characters I interviewed are listed in the Acknowledgements section. After the interviews began to approach the 100 mark, even I felt it was time to call a halt. My publishers were no doubt much relieved by this, but kept the faith in spite of the necessary extended deadlines. They had hoped that the book could be completed within a year, but two more followed as the bank balance dwindled. My own faith was demonstrated by an attempt to return their advance cheque in full as self-punishment for my absolutely necessary tardiness. The noble Frank Warren tore it up, thereby underlining his complete belief in the book too. That's what I call a good author/publisher relationship. Now that this volume is over, it's pleasing to report that I still love The Smiths' work and, surprisingly to some, Marr and Morrissey's solo excursions too. I play this stuff all the time to the exclusion of much else, which is the greatest compliment any author can offer to his subject.

Johnny Rogan

INTRODUCTION

The Severed Alliance

23 APRIL 1991

JOHNNY MARR SITS IN HIS CAR considering his diary of commitments. In a couple of days' time, he will be travelling to Kildare for the funeral of his grandmother. Ireland looms large in the background of Marr, as it does for all the ex-members of The Smiths. The first generation sons of Irish emigrants, they have various links with the country through a network of extended family and friends. It is Manchester, however, that is regarded as home and, significantly, all four Smiths have remained there, resisting the convenient temptation of London or the lure of America.

Marr's future, even more than that of his illustrious former songwriting partner, resembles an open book. He has long fulfilled his original ambition to be respected as a guitarist, as opposed to "The Smiths' guitarist". His recent career and present attitude remind me very much of David Crosby after he left The Byrds. Weary of the pressures and claustrophobic role-play engendered by a brand name, he embarked on a series of recordings with "friends". It is interesting to note that Marr visited Crosby after leaving The Smiths. According to David, they even wrote a song together, but it remains only half-completed. Johnny recalls Crosby re-tuning a guitar as though it were a Rubrik cube and presenting it to him with the words: "Play that!" To his lasting pride, Marr obliged and passed the test.

The "playing with friends" philosophy that Crosby promoted in the late Sixties was never fully accepted or understood by the public. Instinctively, people prefer identifiable groups and labels by which they can gauge and chart a performer's progress. When Crosby worked with Stills, Nash & Young they were usually perceived as a fully-fledged group. The lesser permutations, like Crosby & Nash, the Stills-Young Band, or Crosby solo, were perceived as incomplete or aberrant by comparison. Even Neil Young, who fashioned a prolific and formidable body of solo work over 20 years, was frequently asked when CSN&Y would reconvene. Groups have a way of capturing the public's imagination in an intangibly powerful way. The gang mentality of the group, which The Smiths personified more than any comparable unit of their decade, is a burdensome legacy. In his new role as a member of no "real group", Marr will always be open to accusations of playing the dilettante or super sessioner. It is no coincidence that the two major ventures in which he has involved himself since The Smiths betray an air of impermanence. The The has always been Matt Johnson's concept and remains the classic example of an individual masquerading under a group monicker. Electronic, at least as far as the public are concerned, is merely a temporary offshoot from New Order.

Marr is aware of the popular aversion to casual projects, even ones as intense, committed and long in the making as Electronic. Even so, he is unlikely ever to return to a set-up similar to The Smiths. "I've got a healthy respect for certain traditions in pop music," he observes, "and The Smiths were brought up on a lot of those, like the group as a single entity. As much as I loved those traditions, I'm quite excited about the climate now. I think it's very open-minded and a little bit more progressive. A really important philosophy that The Smiths was built on was Leiber/Stoller, the Brill Building and Phil Spector. He's been more of an influence on me than anyone else. That's the way I feel about doing different projects. It's not like the way I was working with The Pretenders, being a fan of Nils Lofgren and a famous sideman. When I met Joe Moss [The Smiths' first manager] I thought I was Phil Spector with a guitar, running around with mastertapes. I had quite an irreverent attitude really. Playing a guitar was always a means to an end for me".

The end that Marr envisages is having the chance to proceed at his own speed on projects whose needs create their own personnel. At present, he is content to veer between Electronic, with whom he is scheduled to tour America, and The The, whose follow-up to *Mind Bomb* will be issued in 1992. What lies beyond that is anybody's guess, but Marr hints at a "nucleus of myself, Dave Palmer, James Eller and a singer and a couple of other musicians thrown in, exploring a kind of Mancunian Sly And The Family Stone. If I work towards anything, that's the group set-up I'd use, with a couple of singers and maybe multi-racial stuff and a different attitude towards technology. That's the way I see the future."

Marr's life has been remarkably stress free since the demise of The Smiths. He has retained a strikingly low media profile, rarely emerging, apart from a concentrated series of interviews to promote Electronic. "I think the older Johnny is getting, he doesn't really care about the impressions people have of him," Matt Johnson suggests. "He's better off not doing interviews, but just doing his work. His work speaks louder. When he wasn't doing interviews, he was more in the paper than people who were talking every week. He's got so much energy and ideas and always wants to work." Another area of Marr's career that has altered significantly is his attitude towards business. During The Smiths' days, both he and Morrissey attempted to control so much of their empire that they often fell victim to their own autonomy. Their apparent aversion to written contracts and an inability to decide upon a suitable manager all too frequently proved their undoing. The result was a series of minor skirmishes and threatened court battles, which continue to this day. Marr, at least, has learned his lesson from those unhappy sagas and has since appointed a long-term manager in Marcus Russell. Without the burden of self-administration, Marr has been able to work at his own pace and avoid the arrows of aggrieved litigants. "All you've got to do is ask anybody who's ever worked with me since the end of The Smiths what the score is with me paying people," he stresses. "You'll get your answer then." Indeed, there is no shortage of people who will testify to Marr's integrity, and the respect he commands in the music business is considerable. "He's true to himself and there's no act with him," Matt Johnson testifies. "He's a genuine guy and you don't get many of them in the music business, unfortunately. He's one of the most generous and loyal people that I've met, which is why I really like him. He's a very genuine person. He's gone through quite a lot in his life. You tend to find that people who have lived a lot, it enriches their spirit. He's been a good friend to me."

Of course, Marr's career has not represented a series of uninterrupted accolades. Marr's public image has ranged from that of the aspiring guitar star to the upmarket session player and studio bound recluse. There are elements of truth in all these caricatures but the key to his personality lies in a desire to expand his knowledge and horizons. Marr was always willing to move on and stay one step ahead of outmoded fashions. His respect for the past has taught him not to be consumed by its cosy familiarity. The fight to reach his present standing in the business has often brought some hard decisions and tough compromises, which are unflinchingly detailed in the text. As his first songwriting partner, Rob Allman, carefully considered: "Johnny *could* step on your toes, but he was *never* a hurtful person".

20 JULY 1991

On the day of Morrissey's return to the London stage I receive a bundle of photographs of the Morrissey clan, stretching back to the beginning of the twentieth century. Hours before setting out for the concert, I spread the striking black-and-white photos across the kitchen table and marvel at the period detail and family resemblances. It is an eerie feeling to see, for the first time, a shot of Steven's late grandfather, Peter Morrissey. There he stands imperiously on his wedding day back in the early twenties, quiff in flight, a full 70 years ahead of his time. In another cameo shot, the legendary grandfather is playing with a cigarette in his mouth, as if imitating an American movie gangster. Later this evening, his grandson will send a shiver through me by striking that same pose, while singing: 'Give us a cigarette'. The gap between Dublin 1921 and London 1991 suddenly dissolves.

Five years have passed since Morrissey last played London and expectations about his concert comeback are high. The trains leading to Wembley abruptly reach a halt at Neasden, where an intrusive Ryder Truck Rentals vehicle reminds passers-by of the usurping Happy Mondays. This unhappy augur results in tiresome delays which, combined with the decision to start the show early, cause a last-minute rush towards the Arena. Outside, ticket touts, defeated by Morrissey's unexpectedly early appearance, have called it a day and are asking a mere £3-a-ticket. The singer, unaware of the vagaries of London transport, is already on stage. Inside, Wembley officials strap yellow-coloured wrist bands on the arena dwellers, as though they were mental hospital patients. The same sense of spine-tingling drama that attended most Smiths concerts is discernible, even in this vast edifice. If anything, it is stronger than ever due to the tensions provoked by Morrissey's long absence from live performance. What strikes the observer most forcibly throughout this tour is the preponderance of youth among Morrissey's following. The audience actually looks younger than it did during The Smiths' heyday. Morrissey must feel like Dorian Gray in reverse; while he slowly ages, his audience remains young. There is a spattering of Smiths T-shirts among the hordes, but it is the Morrissey monicker that dominates. Eavesdropping on conversations and chatting to the faithful, it is evident that those around me never even saw The Smiths. It is to that name, however, that most observations continue to turn. The Smiths are the great institution that is no more, and it is with reverence, rather than nostalgia, that these concert-goers refer to the Morrissey/Marr collaboration. For Morrissey's new fans, seeing The Smiths seems the equivalent of having witnessed Elvis Presley in the Fifties or The Beatles in the Sixties. The sense of distance is overwhelming.

Although the Morrissey/Marr union is regarded as sacrosanct, it is surprisingly hard to find that undoubted small core that still follows and appreciates the exploits of both artistes. Since the severing of the alliance there has been no contact and little common ground between this once great partnership. Their post-Smiths exploits represent an ongoing epilogue rather than a continued chapter, and increasingly demand separate treatments. Morrissey and Marr now resemble Lennon and McCartney *apart* and in later years each will require independent books detailing their post-alliance career. Thus, the over-ambitious crazy concept of the ten-year trilogy as time forges new careers. And how worthy will their standing be in the late Nineties?

Such thoughts are scattered by the compelling nature of Morrissey's performance. He oozes charisma, offering that peculiar combination of gauche vulnerability and athleticism that characterized his gait during previous concert evenings. The rockabilly backing group are dynamic to a manic degree and bring a much-needed animation to some of the understated work on his recent *Kill Uncle* collection. The decision not to include Smiths material is wise - not so much as a statement of policy, but as a matter of artistic pride. Morrissey needs to establish his present work and look to the future for inspiration and relevance. For a performer whose oeuvre, indeed his very philosophy, seems based on endlessly re-examining a lost, painful past, this is a brave and arguably necessary move.

The "relaunched" live Morrissey displays a power onstage which I have seldom seen from any other artiste of his generation. He revels in the messianic adoration and transforms the audience by his sheer presence. Looking around me, I am reminded of the words of Vini Reilly, who summed up Morrissey's appeal in an eloquent flourish. "Morrissey is a star," he proclaimed quietly. "Stardom is being in love. It's like a transference that exists between a psychoanalyst and his patient. I've watched

Morrissey onstage - he has charisma and people sense it. The audience transfers its ideals and adoration on to him, and he reflects it back. He becomes something other than mere mortal, and that is the essence of stardom. Morrissey is genuinely a phenomenon and a star, and there aren't many of those around. 'Morrissey' is not an invented thing. It's real. There's not a moment of untruth in his life."

Morrissey's power as a performer lies in his unorthodox manipulation of sound and movement: the abandon in dance, the unpredictability of gesture, the wayward microphone technique and the unbridled love of eccentric phrasing. Onstage, his tattered garments resemble a shredded Richard Hell. Morrissey looks as though he has just squeezed through a gauntlet of frenzied, grasping fans. Mid-song, he stops to adopt a *Carry On* camp hand-on-hip pose; he creases his brow, traces his chin with his fingers and becomes Rodin's Thinker. While the group soar past him like exploding comets, Morrissey is abruptly transformed into life. Suddenly, he is the deranged stripper, already half-topless, and restlessly tugging at his scanty top. He flails his inexhaustible compatriots into further action by using the microphone as a whip, falls to his knees, then collapses across a monitor. In a single motion he arises, arches an eyebrow and continues. This is a movement of Chaplinesque simplicity that appears to question, condone and vindicate his unique theatricalism. The sounds that emerge from his mouth are pure Morrisseyspeak. Single syllables are stretched to breaking point and merge with otherworldly gargles, close microphone kisses and indecipherable phrases which, in their own way, probably say more than can be gleaned from any lyric sheet. The star's relationship with his audience is effectively summed up in that wonderful finale, 'Disappointed'. Every night he can promise to sing his last ever song, only to announce that he has changed his mind again and thereby provoke an uproar. The song also serves as an invitation to invade the stage against impossible odds. Remarkably, one youth evades the security guards and, in a desperate feat of athletic prowess, lands onstage, where he clings to Morrissey like a limpet. This is much more impressive than those easy ceremonial hugs performed for the video shoot at Wolverhampton back in 1988. Morrissey smiles with satisfaction and appears to enjoy being clung to so lovingly. Finally, he waves farewell to his friendly assailant as a bouncer prises him free. Stage left, another interloper crashes through the mixing desk and is buried beneath three guards; it takes three more to subdue him. The singer looks on askance and announces: "Goodnight, and thank you". It is a consummate performance.

This is the Morrissey of the Nineties and he looks as though he has only begun.

4 OCTOBER 1991

After a season of Morrissey performances at which audiences marvel at his new-found power, the final London gig of the year promises much. The sound system at Hammersmith Odeon is the most impressive I have heard on the tour, but such considerations are soon dwarfed by more dramatic events. Not surprisingly, the show commences with everybody on their feet, as Morrissey lunges his way through the pulsating 'The Last Of The Famous International Playboys'. A surge to the front of the stage is intercepted by zealous security guards, whose collected muscle seems likely to be in constant need this evening. Gradually, however, the crowd settles, and the excitable fans seem content to stay in their allotted places. Morrissey, sensing frustration among his more expressive enthusiasts, quizzically enquires whether we are feeling fettered. Almost inviting a display of athletic, stage-invading worship, he suggests that "it only takes one", before adding "I will forgive you". At the beginning of the poignant 'Driving Your Girlfriend Home', at least one youth takes him at his word, and can be seen desperately clambouring onstage, only to be brutally beaten back by a barrel-bodied security guard. While the group plays on, Morrissey hovers uneasily at the side of the stage, questioning the need for such security and demanding: "Why does it have to be so UGLY?" Seconds later, he signals for the group to stop and leaves the stage, claiming that he will sort out the security problem. It is at this point that an already promising performance is utterly transformed.

Over five minutes pass, while we wait expectantly. The backstage scenes must be extraordinary, but they can hardly match what is occurring in the theatre. The atmosphere is electric. The audience voice their antipathy towards the security guards with a stream of abuse that grows louder and more insistent as the minutes creep by. One beer-bellied, burly bouncer crouches at the front of the stage looking uncannily like an unleashed Rottweiler. The unstoppable cries of "You fat bastard" reverberate around the auditorium. One playful fan takes this opportunity to run across the stage and back, much to the appreciation of us all. By now, it seems clear that Morrissey is absolutely adamant about neutering the security, even at the cost of abandoning the show. The tension is tangible.

Finally, the singer re-emerges with a look of victory on his face. Even before he announces the lifting of the draconian security measures, many of us realize that the spattering of overweight guards has already retreated on to the stage. The scenes that follow are amazing. Having spotted the signals, I immediately join the first wave of invaders, hurtling down the aisle to within a couple of feet of the stage. This is where opportunities are seized and territory claimed. I quickly find myself the perfect niche by climbing atop the back seats of row c and spreadeagling my legs onto row b. To my grateful surprise, I find it is possible to dance, or sway in an unencumbered clockwise fashion, while still straddled across two rows. The soft seat beneath me serves as a safety net and trampoline from which to springboard back into position in the event of a fall. The new song 'I've

Changed My Plea To Guilty' proves a particularly effective accompaniment, as does 'Interesting Drug'. A fellow interloper beside me is not so fortunate. Suddenly, I detect a wrenching sound, and look on stunned as the seat literally disintegrates under him and he spirals Humpty-Dumpty fashion into the blackness. The stage is now under constant invasion, but in such a gentle, organized fashion that the bouncers need only serve as polite ushers, should they choose. One ugly scene ensues at the end when an over-eager youth is pushed from the stage and comes spinning backwards towards us. For those like myself, precariously perched nine foot in the air atop the wooden backs of seats, his approach is akin to a cannon ball. Several of us tumble like dominoes but, after hitting the floor, rapidly reassemble to reclaim our lost mountainous peaks. By the end of the show, having spent an hour bouncing across and off seat tops, my knees, thighs and shins are covered in dark and light coloured bruises. Thankfully, there are no cuts or abrasions. I see no other injuries around me, and even that flying cannonball looked unharmed on landing. Throughout the show, the audience are incredibly solicitous, not only towards Morrissey, who is greeted by unintrusive hugs or quick handshakes, but also to those jostling in their midst. The usual one-off flare-ups and sudden displays of violence that some concerts produce are conspicuous by their absence. This is, in fact, a far gentler and more tolerant audience than that attracted by The Smiths during their final phase in late 1986.

The evening ends with the excited realization that Morrissey has single-handedly transformed an enjoyable performance into an event. The show also underlines his acute appreciation of audience psychology, as well as revealing his own desires and needs. Contrary to his actions, he does not seek to break down the gap between star and audience, but to strengthen its power through the notion of possibility. Morrissey's strength lies in his simultaneous remoteness and availability. The message he conveys to his followers is that he can be seen, can be reached, can be touched... but only for an instant. Soon he will return to Altrincham, to a house surrounded by security cameras, to a telephone whose (061) 941 **** number is known only to a select few, to tastefully laid-out Chinese rugs, to a grand piano that he will never properly learn to play and to a solitary but orderly life whose introspective moments are already enshrined in an ever-expanding list of songs. In one sense, this is just another concert on the tour but many people will remember this evening for the remainder of their lives. At moments such as these, the money problems, abandoned friendships, frustrated outbursts and contractual conundrums that have dogged the performer's career fade into relative insignificance. At his best, Morrissey can still transform event into myth. This is why so many believe he is worthy of pop godhead like no other among his generation. Strangely, there is a phrase that I find myself uttering again and again as we shuffle through the night - "this is the last pop star".

16 OCTOBER 1991

For the past fortnight the names of Electronic and Morrissey have domi-nated the news pages. Marr has announced his intention to play his first London performance at Wembley in December, while Morrissey has been cascading across the stages of the capital, but declining all interviews. It's been a tough week for the *NME*. Editor Danny Kelly longs to have Morrissey's photograph back on the cover, but knows he has no hope of obtaining an interview. However, the singer's name continues to emblazon the front page, enticing eager readers. Last week, a concert reviewer in the paper bemoaned the absence of the priceless Johnny Marr, complained sadly about the singer's supposed loss of dignity, and concluded: "I hasten away from the carnage. Come on Morrissey, *let go.*" That, of course, is the last thing that the *NME* really wants to happen. They still hang on his every word, even if this takes the form of a handful of phrases scrawled in crayon. Today, the paper runs a three page photo spread of Morrissey in Japan, which the star has reluctantly agreed to caption. This is regarded as a major scoop, and was evidently not won lightly. "To arrange that, I had to prostrate myself," the editor moans. "For some reason Morrissey thinks I'm out to get him the whole time because I did write in a Christmas issue that he'd had a terrible year. Of course, he's been a source of endless great crack for us over the years, so it's a two-way street. The point I'm making is, I'm almost tired of the intricacies, the byzantine web that he weaves." If the *NME* have at last grown weary of Morrissey's determined aloofness, then there is little evidence of that in their news features or letters columns, which endlessly debate his every creative move or utterance. In a media world where artistes barter for front covers in return for exclusive interviews, Morrissey secures the accolade without having to say a word.

After digesting the *NME* photo supplement during the afternoon, I decide to speak to Morrissey this evening about his reasons for actively avoiding media coverage. His responses prove instructive. "I don't want anything written, which must sound strange, but I just don't," he explains. Far from "weaving intricate webs", his attitude towards the music press is one of tired detachment and guarded isolation. His innocent photo caption-ing is a means of satisfying the Morrissey-fixated *NME* without the need to open his mouth. For such an articulate pop star this self-imposed silence seems all the more frustrating. Many believe that Morrissey is merely continuing pop's grand tradition of creating a mystique through unavail-ability. Like Presley, Bowie and Prince, the dictum "less press means more spreads" seems an easy conclusion in the circumstances. With Morrissey, however, the desire to escape music press scrutiny is neither an affectation, nor a career master plan, nor an egotistical assertion of his own importance, but, rather, a genuine need. "I find it, on a personal level, encroaching enough as it is without things appearing in print", he tells me. "Thus, this week's *NME*. I feel pretty fatigued to be honest. Not by music, or by mak-ing music, but by people who write about music or, rather, write about the people who make music. I'd rather just, as much as I can, stay in a cupboard at the end of the foot of the stairs." Morrissey continues in this vein, ably articulating his ambivalence towards the business of fame. It is an underlying theme that runs throughout this book. "People don't seem to be aware of the terrible paradox of being fêted all over the place, given all kinds of credibility, with people hanging on to your every word and feeling incredibly popular, yet being completely isolated and lonely," notes Morrissey's friend Vini Reilly. "He has a few close friends, but he's constantly surrounded by people who don't really understand him. The more successful he became, rather than not being lonely anymore, he became more lonely. Now, he can't go out. We try to go out. I've been to the theatre with him and the whole place is aware that he's there. It's really uncomfortable and he has to leave, even though we've made arrangements with security, who smuggle him in and out. It's unbelievable. He's attempted to shop on a weekday in Manchester or Bristol, with a couple of people with him, and he can't get very far down the road before two people will be walking behind him and every shop he goes in, they'll watch everything he does. You have to be there to see it. If you try going in a pub or café, it's not possible. He's had this constant urge to find somewhere to exist just to be left alone and go about his business. He touches nerves other people don't touch. He's had to accept that he can't live like a normal person, and it's a drag. He has realized that there are certain people he can trust and, over a period of time, he's established a trust with them. He's strengthened his circle, but it's still very small. I think it always will be."

Morrissey acknowledges this sense of isolation. "I exist in a vacuum,"he notes. "I make records and I'm very grateful to this faithful public that continues to buy them." Morrissey has, at times, cultivated his own pop godhead by empathizing so strongly with his fans, but even that cannot fully explain the reverence which he continues to command. It has become both a blessing and a curse. When you assure Morrissey of the need to keep his whereabouts strictly confidential, he wearily scoffs: "I think everybody already knows."

1

November Spawned A Morrissey

1ST NOVEMBER 1935

IT WAS ALL SAINTS' DAY, a Holy Day of Obligation, when Peter Aloysius Morrissey was born at 12 Fumbally Lane, several streets north of Dublin's River Liffey. His father, who shared his Christian name, was a stoker on the city railway, while his mother, Ellen, like most of the women of the period, worked at home. The Morrisseys were a large family, though not huge by the standards of the time. Peter was the sixth in line, preceded by Thomas, Mary Bridget, Patricia, Ellen and Christina. Three more children would follow in later years. When Peter was only eight days old, the family moved from their northside tenement to one of the government's new housing settlements in Clonard Road, Crumlin. "I was a stone's throw away from Christy Brown, who lived a few roads away," Peter remembers.

The Browns were a sprawling family and the severely handicapped Christy was one of 22 children, a figure which made the Morrissey clan seem sparse by comparison. Despite having no control over his body, apart from his left foot, Christy emerged as one of Crumlin's and Ireland's most impressive and original novelists and his autobiography, *My Left Foot*, was later made into an award-winning film. Another celebrated literary figure who lived near to the Morrisseys was Brendan Behan, whose chequered career saw him join the IRA and serve a sentence in an English borstal (recalled in *Borstal Boy*) for possession of explosives. Although the late Thirties were a period of great change for Ireland, nationalism was rife, and the future uncertain.

The years immediately preceding Peter's birth had been dominated by turmoil, grief and tragedy in equal measure. Indeed, recent history had been so full of contradiction and irony as to seem almost fictional. The land had been successively torn asunder by revolution, guerrilla warfare against the British, and a bloody civil war, culminating in the emergence of the Irish Free State and suspended dreams of a Republic. The fate of the Irish Republican movement and the strange reversals of fortune suffered by its leading members were embodied in the paradoxical figure of the man whose name was on the lips of the nation: Eamon de Valera.

De Valera had been the last of the Irish Volunteer commanders to surrender after the 1916 Easter uprising. Sentenced to death, he was later reprieved and assumed the presidency of Sinn Fein and the Irish Volunteers from 1917. Imprisoned the following year, he escaped and became a leading figure in the Anglo-Irish War of 1919-21. It was a spirited campaign, egged on by the traditional Irish battle cry: "A rush and a charge and the land is ours". The intelligence network, masterminded by Michael Collins, had proven so effective throughout this phase of guerilla activity that the British were discussing the possibility of sending in 250,000 troops.

By 1921, the English invaders were forced to the negotiating table, though not before Lloyd George had effectively partitioned the island by setting up the Parliament of Northern Ireland at Stormont, Belfast. Partition was a highly emotive issue, guaranteed to complicate long term discussions on Ireland's future. Home Rule for the entire island had been tantalizingly close since the days of Charles Stewart Parnell and, less than a decade before, John Redmond had seen the bill through the House of Commons. While Conservative leader Bonar Law was fomenting violence in Northern Ireland and threatening to sever Ulster from Home Rule, Redmond passionately declared: "The two nation theory is to us an abomination and blasphemy." This view was reiterated with increasing rhetoric by such republicans as Arthur Griffith, who alluded to a higher authority in insisting, "Ireland cannot shift her frontiers. The Almighty traced them beyond the currency of men to modify." In the wake of the 1916 Easter uprising and its attendant executions, the ideal of a united Ireland was written in blood by the doomed poet/schoolteacher Padraic Pearse, who prophesied that the man who accepted a final settlement of anything less than total separation from England would be guilty of such a crime against the Irish nation "that it would be better for that man... that he had not been born."

De Valera opposed Partition ("Ulster cut from Ireland would leave her without her head - her heart"), yet recognized that the outcome of the Treaty negotiations were likely to fall short of the 32 county ideal.

There is little doubt among contemporary historians that de Valera was pushing along a road towards an acceptance of Partition as an inevitable temporary measure. Both in the private sessions of Dail Eireann, and in the first draft of his famous Document No. 2, he revealed a pragmatic approach to the Ulster question. Indeed, in the leaked, unamended version of Document No. 2, he included all the Ulster clauses contained in the Treaty.

Partition, of course, was not the only obstacle facing the Treaty delegation. A more important and emotive matter to many Republicans was the vexed question of sovereignty to the English king. The British delegation was willing to offer Ireland dominion status which, as chairman Michael Collins rightly realized, would enable the Free State to declare itself a Republic at a later date. Although the Oath proclaiming allegiance to monarchical authority was largely perfunctory, it remained anathema to hard-core nationalists.

Reconciling the contradictory demands of militant Republicans, Ulster Unionists and the British Government was a political impossibility, so some compromise was inevitable. The Irish delegation, from which de Valera was conspicuously absent, laboriously modified the Oath and removed the intractable "Ulster question" from the agenda by accepting the findings of a vaguely concocted Boundary Commission, which was expected to annex Tyrone and Fermanagh to the Free State. Collins was not alone in believing that the remaining four counties of Protestant Ulster would thereafter be unable to survive as political and economic entities. Finally, under duress from Lloyd George, and with the settlement in jeopardy, the Treaty was signed. The previous weekend, at a Cabinet meeting held in Dublin, de Valera sided with the "irreconcilables" and voted against the London agreement. Collins understood the implications all too well and, echoing the curse of Padraic Pearse, declared: "I have signed my own death warrant."

On 7 January 1922, Dail Eireann ratified the Treaty by a small majority and, five months later, the people of the Irish Free State supported that decision in their first General Election. By that time, attempts to forestall conflict between pro-and anti-Treatyites had foundered. De Valera reluctantly aligned himself with the militants and the country was soon ravaged by civil war. By the time the Republicans had accepted a cease-fire, Ireland had lost some of its most influential rebels and politicians, including the executed Erskine Childers and the tragically assassinated Michael Collins. Any hopes of eroding Partition by assimilating Tyrone and Fermanagh were dashed when the British and Unionists took advantage of the Free State's parlous condition and rendered the Boundary Commission farcical. The Unionists retained the six counties and the sacrilegious Partition was established.

The Civil War ended with imprisonment for de Valera, who had escaped a warrior's death for the second time in six years. A master strategist, he rose from the political wilderness and, in 1926, announced that he was forming a new party: Fianna Fail (Soldiers of Destiny). Within six years, the party had achieved a narrow victory in the 1932 General Election, with an increased majority the following year. These results were to have profound implications for the Constitution of Ireland as de Valera's avowed intention was to fulfil the dreams of 1921 by hastening the break with imperialist Britain and establishing a genuine Republic. One of his first actions as the new Taoiseach was to release IRA prisoners and ensure that those who had fought in the Civil War were rewarded with military pensions. The honeymoon with IRA Irregulars, however, was to prove short-lived. Their public drilling parades and refusal to disarm soon provoked de Valera to declare the organization unlawful. Further sweeping changes were to follow.

By 1937, two years after the birth of Peter Morrissey, the Oath of Fidelity to the King had been removed from the Constitution, the role of Governor General rendered irrelevant, and the draconian Land Annuities paid to the British Exchequer suspended. The Irish Free State had also passed away and the country was renamed Eire. The new Constitution claimed sovereignty over the entire island, including the whole of Ulster, in what was a highly symbolic and platonic realization of the ultimate Republican goal. As the triumphant de Valera later declared, with some exaggeration: "*Our eyes have seen the glory* which Parnell and his comrades longed for, and strove for but did not see".

Peter Morrissey's childhood in the newly-named Eire could hardly have had a more dramatic backdrop of social, political and economic upheaval. Living conditions in Dublin remained essentially the same as before the Civil War, when James Connolly had described the city with acerbity as an Alsatian den of "high rents, slum tenements, rotten staircases, stinking yards, high death rates, low wages, corporation jobbery and margarine wrapped in butter paper". The Dublin scandal was strikingly unveiled in a 1938 survey which found that 60 per cent of tenements (6,554 of 11,039) were unfit for human habitation. Within these squalid warrens, a staggering 64,940 people suffered inadequate sanitation, disease and the grim prospect of an early death. The government had responded to Dublin's problems by funding a substantial rehousing programme in which families were moved to the outskirts of the city. During the Thirties, new estates of semi-detached and terraced dwellings appeared in areas such as Crumlin, Cabra, Drimnagh, Raheny, Artane and Inchicore.

The Morrissey family moved to Crumlin at a time when de Valera's rebuilding scheme was still in its infancy. Rows of identical houses offered identical facilities: a parlour, kitchen, bathroom, two bedrooms and a front and back garden. It was reasonably comfortable for small families but if you happened to have six or more children, as many did, then bed space was at a premium. The district was beginning to swell with a steady influx of young families, but conditions were far from ideal. A report on the local community of the time outlined some of the basic problems: "The new settlements in Crumlin and Drimnagh are without any of the essential amenities. There are no parks, no playing fields, no town halls... no factories, no technical schools, no secondary schools, no football grounds. A fine police barracks has been provided to control the unruly crowds of workless adolescents."

Although the scores of families from the decaying tenements were pleased to acquire new homes, the location left a lot to be desired. Dubliners were notoriously proud of their urban upbringing and many regarded Crumlin as the back of nowhere. When Stephen Behan was informed that his family were moving just a few miles from the city centre, he exploded, "Sure, they eat their dead out there!" His son Brendan was equally uncomplimentary and accused de Valera of relocating the cream of the city out into a bog. "They could've built flats in the centre of town for us and kept reservations like this for them that come from the country," he remarked with playful bigotry. "The only grass we ever saw, we were asked to keep off it," was his proud rejoinder to the invading culchies.

Crumlin was certainly bleak in the mid-Thirties, with the trams only travelling as far as Dolphin's Barn, after which there was a long walk along the roads. Situated on the slopes of the Dublin mountains, it seemed so cold and windy that many of the settlers nicknamed the place Siberia. When Brendan Behan first set foot in the area in search of his parents' new corporation house, he was accosted by a local and advised, "Turn back before it's too late!"

Peter Morrissey Snr. did not share the acerbic view of the Behans. By a remarkable coincidence, he was reared in Poddle Park, a street away from his new corporation house in Clonard Road. Moreover, his wife Ellen (McDonnell) had grown up in nearby Kimmage Road. Having moved a few streets north of the Liffey after their marriage, they regarded the return to Crumlin as something of a homecoming. For the Morrisseys' new neighbours, the settling-in period was considerably more difficult, with mass unemployment and hunger causing hardship in equal measure. Infant mortality was also alarmingly high and nine of Christy Brown's 22-strong family died during birth or childhood. The Morrisseys also suffered their share of grief. After Peter's birth, Ellen had a fifth daughter, Ann, and two more sons, both of whom died as infants. Their names were Patrick and Steven. "I was only a kid myself and didn't know what was going on," Peter recalls. "I remember being in the house and my mother started screaming. Patrick was in the pram and he was turning a different colour. Although I was only six or seven, I can vividly remember those incidents." When he later came to have children of his own, the names Steven and Patrick would be revived to honour the tragic dead.

Before long, Peter joined his brother Thomas at St Agnes School; the boys were taught by Christian brothers, while Mary, Patricia, Ellen, Chrissie and Ann received their education from the Sisters of Charity. One of Patricia Morrissey's earliest memories is traipsing across fields to attend Sunday Mass at St Agnes Church. "It was all fields then," she remembers. Despite the bleakness, Crumlin gradually evolved over the next few years. Peter was happy enough to live three-and-a-half miles from O'Connell Street and, as a teenager, he took frequent advantage of the playing fields in spacious Phoenix Park. The youngsters' capacity to find their own entertainment was unquenchable. A favourite pastime among the older boys was picking cinders from the tipheads on the main road, which they sold for a princely 1/6d per sack. Skirmishes between rival gangs would erupt occasionally over a favoured patch, usually ending in a cloud of cinder dust. Bicycles were in sufficient supply for jaunts into the city centre or country, and most families possessed a radio. The novelty value of a Marconi was emphasized by Peter's surprised reaction upon hearing his brother Thomas correctly identifying the distinctive croon of Bing Crosby. "The song hadn't finished and I was amazed that he actually knew who was singing!"

Shows such as *Hospitals' Requests, Question Time* and *Take The Floor* (with the redoubtable Dinjo) were popular on Radio Eireann and during the evenings listeners often tuned to the BBC Home Service and Light Programme. For the youngsters, Radio Luxembourg (founded in 1933) offered some exotic late night listening. A threepenny bit was sufficient to gain access to the flea pit palace, otherwise known as the Sundrive Cinema in nearby Sundrive Road. Every Saturday morning at half-past ten, throngs of youngsters would congregate outside, eager to sample the latest Western cliff-hanger. Inside the dark picture-house, they sat on wooden benches, loudly engrossed in the adventures of such Western heroes as Roy Rogers and Hopalong Cassidy. All too often, the humorous gibes and catcalls from the audience were more entertaining than the actual movie. As a special treat, some kids were allowed to accompany their elders to the Classic Cinema in Turenure to see a major motion picture, but many had to wait until they began work at 14 before enjoying such luxuries.

For Crumlin's "unruly crowds of workless adolescents" the best chance to dissipate surplus energy was with the crack of a hurling stick or the kick of a football. Many of the players proved brilliant street footballers, whose paucity of facilities could not quench their natural skills. Peter Morrissey would soon line up amongst them.

The outbreak of World War II in 1939 had little effect on the Morrissey family. The previous year, de Valera, in one of his finest political coups, had secured the return of the Irish ports retained by Britain under the terms of the 1921 Treaty. This enabled Eire to remain neutral for the entirety of the Second World War and fulfil the Taoiseach's promise that "small states must not become the puppets of the larger powers". De Valera was well-schooled in the rhetoric of sacrifice and preached austerity as a national virtue. There were lots of shortages during wartime but a crippling duty on exported cattle meant that the public had an abundant supply of meat, which was cheaply available. While the economic war dragged on, beef, streels of sausages and lots of black and white pudding were the order of the day. A weekend roast and daily stews, topped off with apple pie and custard, was typical Crumlin cuisine. For the Morrisseys, meat was murphy.

De Valera's determination to reinforce Eire's independence extended far beyond neutrality and meat consumption. Like his predecessors in the opposing Cumann na nGaedheal party, he was intent on reviving the Irish language. His doomed Gaelicization policy would not reverse the natural decline of the language but the new stress on cultural autonomy would seriously effect the next generation of school children. By the time Peter Morrissey took his place at school, Irish was a compulsory subject on the national syllabus. The new secondary school examinations, the Intermediate and the Leaving Certificate, could not be awarded to any candidate who had failed to pass the Irish paper. This meant that a disproportionate amount of school time was spent studying the national language to the detriment of other subjects. In most areas, all subjects were taught in both English and Irish, even though the majority of teachers were ill-equipped for the task and expressed dissatisfaction with the policy.

The quest for a national identity was further exemplified through the work of the Gaelic Athletic Association, which determined to replace "foreign" games with Irish sports. A ban was imposed on any member who even watched a game of soccer or rugby. Although association football was popular among the working class of Dublin, the game was vetoed by the Christian Brothers. Peter Morrissey was particularly annoyed by this ruling and offered his own subtle protest during the school's trial matches for the GAA. "I just refused to catch the ball," he explained. "I'd head it or chest it like a soccer player, so I was never chosen for the Gaelic teams."

The government also recognized the importance of religious instruction in education and appeared to accept the Catholic Clerical Managers' recommendation that "... the only satisfactory system of education for Catholics is one wherein Catholic children are taught in Catholic schools by Catholic teachers under Catholic control." De Valera, a devout Catholic himself, acknowledged the role of the Church in moral, as opposed to political, matters and encouraged the clergy to take on teaching duties. The public was equally supportive of the Catholic Church as a socializing agent and also accepted the post-colonial hunger for cultural autonomy. Although there was no national Church in Eire, religion and nationalism seemed inextricably linked.

While Peter Morrissey pored over his Catechism and attended St Agnes Church in preparation for his confirmation, Tomas Derrig, the Minister of Education, displayed the zeal of a Jesuit in championing the Gaelicization process and urging "a most intense war against English and against human nature itself for the life of the language." De Valera amplified such rhetoric, arguing that the language revival was an even more crucial issue than Partition. While supporting the Republican view that Irish unity was inevitable, he believed that the language would die unless drastic educational measures were established during his term of office. In one of his stranger flights of fantasy, he even claimed that the language revival would spread across Northern Ireland.

The essential "Irishness" that de Valera promoted so effectively was never better exemplified than in his memorable radio duel with Winston Churchill at the end of World War II. The British Prime Minister (whose diseased father Randolph had previously attempted to scupper Home Rule by playing on Orange fears in the North) severely censured Eire's neutrality throughout the conflict. While paying only passing reference to the "thousands of southern Irishmen who had hastened to the battlefield", he accused the Taoiseach of frolicking with the Germans and Japanese and, in a remarkable display of imperialist arrogance, suggested that it would have been quite natural to violate Eire's neutrality with force. It was a characteristically self-righteous attack from Churchill, who knew that Eire had entered into secret intelligence liaisons with Britain and the United States and realized that de Valera had come close to coaxing a guarantee of a united Ireland *and* neutrality. Churchill clearly had no sympathy with the theory that Irish neutrality may have been the best possible consequence, since the protection of Eire would probably have stretched the Allies' resources to breaking point. He also neglected to acknowledge Eire's despatch of fire brigades to the Unionist North when the British province had been bombed. Nor was there any reference to de Valera's willingness to allow Eire to be used as an advertising board and recruiting base for their ancient neighbours. Throughout the War, the Labour Exchanges of this "neutral" state displayed posters urging civilians to join the British forces or, more euphemistically, "Come To England And See The World". The vast number of people who had accepted the invitation, and whom de Valera had made no attempt to dissuade, underlined the degree of pro-British neutrality.

The Irish public fully expected de Valera to reply to Churchill in equally scathing terms, but, instead, the Taoiseach provided a diplomatic display of restrained magnanimity. "I know the kind of answer I am expected to make," he began, before unexpectedly excusing Churchill's belligerent insensitivity in a speech whose cordial humility exhibited a startling political maturity. The real victor for de Valera was Eire herself, "... a small nation that stood alone not for one year or two, but for several hundred years against aggression: that endured spoilations, was clubbed many times into insensitivity, but each time on returning consciousness took up the fight anew; a small nation that could never be got to accept defeat and has never surrendered her soul". After concluding his broadcast, de Valera was greeted by cheering crowds in the streets of Dublin.

The nationalist euphoria that had gripped Dublin in 1945 reached its apogee four years later when Eire was declared a Republic. Such pride soon evaporated as the country slouched towards economic recession and a crisis in the balance of payments. As ever, the city was a monument of picturesque Georgian splendour couched in poverty. For many, it remained the carnivore capital of Europe and affluent tourists, weary of rationing and lusting for meat, would ferry across the channel to sample the succulent steaks available at restaurants like the Dolphin and Jammets. Ironically, the occupants of this meat-eating mecca would soon emulate their forefathers of the famine by emigrating *en masse*. For the Morrisseys, as for all Dublin, the problem was obtaining work and reasonable wages. Competition for jobs was fierce in Dublin and the situation was worsened by massive rural depopulation and internal migration. The Morrisseys had to travel in order to earn. Every morning, Peter Morrissey Snr cycled over to Inchicore where he was employed as a railway stoker. Thomas, the eldest boy, secured a job as a messenger for the grocers Jacobs in Rathmines; Patricia found a post as a domestic, while Mary and Ellen worked at a laundry in Turenure. With nearly one-fifth of the population of Eire living in Dublin, employment of any description was a blessing.

By the late Forties, Crumlin had built up from its humble beginnings, and contained a number of shops, factories and facilities that increased its popularity among residents. Although money was still scarce and families were still large, there was at least a growing, healthy, young population, eager for entertainment. Dances were tremendously popular and the Silver Slipper, at the top of the Long Mile, was a favourite among Crumlin's youth. Peter's sister, Ellen, was already an accomplished ballroom dancer, while Thomas and Mary had their own distinctive jitterbug routine. Christina preferred ceilis. Although Peter insists that he never attended dances, his sister Ann recalls accompanying him to St Pauls on Mount Angus Road. On Sundays, the light-footed ventured into Dublin for an afternoon ceili or modern dancing session at the Mansion House. Most of the smaller nearby towns had their own halls which were converted into instant ballrooms or theatres. For 1/6d you could see a variety concert with musical sketches and comedy, followed by a dance, often sponsored by

Fianna Fail, Fine Gael or Clann na Poblachta. The political fund raising by rival parties seldom bothered the dancers, who were there for the fun and romance. Sons and daughters felt obliged to hand over their small wage packets to their parents and those with sufficient pocket-money might be lucky enough to attend one of the city's more expensive evening dances. In Dublin, big band orchestras, conducted by such major names as Mick Delahunty, Maurice Mulcahy and Gay McIntyre, dominated the scene. The dances usually lasted from 9pm-2am and the entrance fee was a hefty five shillings. Even by the standards of the day, they were fairly staid affairs in which musicians generally remained seated for the entire performance. Showbands had yet to come into existence and the word "teenager" was still a neologism.

The influence of the Catholic Church in social matters remained pervasive. The censorship board had banned many books, films and even songs, while over-vigilant parish priests kept a watchful eye on the public behaviour of courting couples. The two local pubs in Crumlin, Floods and the Halfway House, were frequented by a predominantly older crowd of married men. Virtually all Crumlin's youth had taken the pledge during their confirmation year and a sizeable number remained teetotallers until well into their twenties. The wearing of the pioneer's pin was not merely a symbol of sobriety, but the sign of a good Catholic. As Peter Morrissey's contemporary Rita Flynn recalled: "If a boy wasn't a pioneer, you wouldn't be allowed to go out with him."

With his interest in playing football and keeping fit, Peter was not tempted by the drink. He was a striking, upstanding youth, who seemed a likely candidate for early marriage. After leaving school, he found work at a button factory in nearby Stannaway Avenue. A handful of small factories had sprung up in Crumlin and with a hungry, young population eager for work, they could keep their gates open 24 hours a day. Morrissey worked a five day/five night shift and received seven pounds and one shilling per week, which was good money then. "I liked that job," he recalls. "I made ash trays and lamp shades." On the shop floor there was an alluring line of young girls, busily sewing buttons on to cards. Peter briefly went out with a couple of them - Maud Nuene and, later, Annie Gilsenan, who lived in nearby Ballymount. However, it was another young teenager from the button factory with whom he would form a lasting relationship.

Elizabeth Ann Dwyer originally hailed from the impoverished tenements of central Dublin. The daughter of Patrick and Bridget Dwyer (née McInerney), she was born on 13 November 1937 at Holles Street Hospital. The family was living at 97 Pearse Street at the time and briefly moved near South Gt George's Street before securing their corporation house in Crumlin. Betty, as she was popularly known, attended St Agnes School, adjacent to the Christian Brothers, and was in the same year as Peter's sister Ann, who also worked at the button factory. While Ann was the youngest member of the Morrissey family, Betty was the second eldest girl in her household. The Dwyers was something of a matriarchal stronghold with a formidable line-up of sisters - Dorothy, Betty, Patti, Jeane, Mary and

Rita. Young Ernie Dwyer was the only boy. In common with Peter Morrissey Snr, Betty's father, Patrick, was employed by CIE, where he worked as a bus conductor. Although Peter Jnr did not date Betty until long after she had left school at 14, he had often seen her walking home to Captain's Road, only a few minutes from his house. She was a petite, attractive girl, with long fair hair, striking features and a quiet disposition. In a different era, she might well have settled in Dublin, but these were difficult times. Like so many young women of her generation, she would soon find herself caught in the irresistible maelstrom of mass exodus from her homeland.

Female emigration from Eire was abnormally high in the immediate post-war period as women outnumbered men in the search for new jobs. Nationalist aspirations were temporarily forgotten amid growing concern about inflation and unemployment. Even de Valera had been swept from power and Fianna Fail increasingly found itself part of a coalition government. The initial haemorrhage of emigration had little effect on unemployment which, paradoxically, multiplied each year. For those on the jobless register, poverty perenially threatened. A proposed Welfare State system based on UK lines had been put forward by the Clann na Poblachta party but met steely resistance from the Catholic Church, jealous of its traditional role as social arbiter. As the jobless queues increased, there were public demonstrations and heated debates, but the cold exodus to England continued. A spiral of emigration saw entire families systematically uprooted and replanted in such cities as Liverpool, London, Birmingham and Manchester. Between 1951-56, over 200,000 people made the journey and even more followed in the second half of the decade. A large proportion of these new emigrants were teenagers, many of whom had only recently left school.

The Morrisseys had already begun the inevitable drift across the channel, with Mary, Patricia and Ellen leading the way. Patricia Morrissey journeyed to London in January 1952 and, two months later, married fellow Dubliner Richard Corrigan. The following year the couple returned home, where Patricia gave birth to her son, Anthony. With her mother Ellen in poor health, the dutiful daughter decided to settle in Crumlin for awhile. When she next returned to England, her new destination was Manchester.

The Manchester connection had come about through the eldest daughter Mary Bridget, whose husband's brother was based there. Seeking a fresh start, Mary and her spouse had decided to open a pet shop in Moss Lane, Moss Side. With the Manchester-Dublin link established, Patricia and Richard followed, temporarily leaving their infant son at Clonard Road. "It's a very mixed-up family history," Patricia cautions. "Mary is my sister, but she's also my aunt by marriage. She married my husband's uncle!"

Unable to settle happily in Manchester without her baby, Patricia again returned to Crumlin and it was during this period that her husband Richard worked at the local button factory. Often, he would regale Peter with stories about life in Manchester and soon persuaded him to seek work there. "I was quite happy in Dublin," Peter recalled, "but if you've got a brother-in-law who is four years older, you look upon him as a man and listen when he advises you." Ferries leaving from Dun Laoghaire were regularly overbooked at the time, and Morrissey was one of the more reluctant passengers. "Richard talked him into it," Patricia confirms. "Sure, he'd have to blame somebody, that Peter! He wanted to see what it was like on the other side." Unfortunately, initial impressions of the city were far from pleasing. "When I did get to Manchester I thought I'd made a mistake for the first couple of weeks," he remembers. "It was arranged that Betty would follow me over in six weeks, so I stuck it out. I didn't want to look bad coming home. Betty was quite anxious to get over and see England."

The first trip was something of a reconnaissance mission during which they stayed with Patricia. After a spell, they returned to Dublin, but the draw of Manchester proved too great. In 1955, both Ellen and Ann were married there and, during the same period, Peter and Betty emigrated permanently. What they left behind was an Eire still arguing and mourning the loss of its sons and daughters. The Bishop of Clonfert summed up the contemporary malaise in a simple, yet acute political analysis: "The capital sin of our Irish state is our failure to provide for our young people an acceptable alternative to emigration. Our version of history has tended to make us think of freedom as an end in itself and of independent government - like marriage in a fairy story - as the solution to all our ills."

If there was a fairy godfather of Irish nationalism, then it was undoubtedly de Valera himself, now reduced to sharing power with his rivals and still espousing self-sacrifice ("We have to tighten our belts") as the only panacea for the country's ills. For many, his dream of a Gaelic, rural, Irish utopia now seemed outdated, chimerical and tarnished by poor economic decisions, unemployment and unprecedented emigration. Towards the end of the Fifties, the population had fallen to an all-time low of 2.8 million and there were even wild and whirling statements about the imminent extinction of the Irish race. By the early Sixties, however, with Sean Lemass in power, tax free incentives and foreign investments from multi-national companies would reverse the recession, cease the haemorrhage and usher in a new era of prosperity for Eire. By that time, though, most of the young emigrants of the previous decade had already made a new life for themselves in England. They would not return.

2

The Feast Of Humility

MANCHESTER, IN COMMON with the rest of England during the Fifties, welcomed the Irish grudgingly and all too frequently betrayed a brutally undisguised racism. Advertisements for accommodation and employment announced their prejudices boldly in such humiliating prohibitions as 'No Irish Need Apply' and 'No Irish, No Coloureds, No Dogs'. Newly-arrived foreigners relied on relatives, old friends or advice from the Catholic Church and Counties Associations to direct them to suitable lodgings.

Peter Morrissey again stayed with his sister Patricia at 20 Stockton Street, Moss Side, while Betty was conveniently situated only a few minutes away at 112 Tamworth Street, M15. The teenage girl was fortunate to come under the wing of an elder couple, Mr and Mrs Grant, who treated her like a daughter. "They were really lovely people and pampered her a bit," Peter recalled. Despite securing reasonable accommodation, the new immigrants had their share of culture shock. Manchester was a world far removed from Dublin, in a strange country that had no knowledge of such small luxuries as brak, boxty, soda bread, colcannon, Cidona, dulse, red lemonade or Kimberley biscuits. Employment prospects for unskilled Irish men of the period usually meant labouring, which the diminutive Morrissey was determined to avoid. Accordingly, he wasted no time in finding a suitable post at the Johnson, Clapham and Morris warehouse in Trafford Park, which offered him the opportunity to work as a fork-lift truck driver, for £7 a week.

In theory, Elizabeth Dwyer had a better chance of securing a worthwhile job. The prospects for Irish working women were rather more attractive than those offered to men, and the Fifties had seen a steady female influx into nursing, the social services, domestic and clerical work. Unfortunately, the better jobs usually required a stoical tolerance of initially low wages or a period of training leading to promotion. Such deferred gratification was unacceptable to Betty who instead took on an undemanding but reasonably-paid post as a packer at a blanket makers. This at least ensured that she and Peter had sufficient money between them to save a small amount every month. It was no easy life, however, for Eire's children felt obliged to contribute a slice of their hard-earned income to those left behind in the mother country. In the Fifties alone, net remittances from emigrants represented over £12 million of Eire's gross national product.

Given their financial restrictions, Morrissey and Dwyer had an unsurprisingly quiet courtship, going on the occasional outing and visiting the cinema. They kept close links with the Irish community in Stretford as more and more people arrived from Dublin. Through his footballing interest and infrequent appearances at local pubs, Peter met some of the new arrivals, a large proportion of whom seemed to marry English girls. Among them was a former Irish Volunteer named Harry Denton, who arrived in search of Patsy Gilsenan, the brother of the Ballymount girl whom Peter had once dated. Gilsenan directed Denton to the hospitable Mrs Sheedy of Parks Road, who miraculously found beds in her lodgings for nearly a score of Irish workmen. After a hard week's slog, the labourers would tour the pubs in the vicinity, taking in the Eagle, the Wellington and the Stretford Park Hotel, all of which were renowned for their singing sessions. Morrissey made cameo appearances at certain weekends, but he was virtually a teetotaller at the time whose favourite drink was a timid bitter shandy. The Dublin crowd, including Gilsenan, Denton and Mikey Roe, enjoyed his company, mainly because he was always laughing or joking and seemed perpetually in good spirits. Most noticeably, he was the man without vices: Peter Morrissey didn't gamble, smoke or drink. He was also disappointed to see any evening spoiled by an argument or impromptu scrap. "I got into a fight with my brother Bernard," Harry Denton recalls, "and Peter calmed me down. He'd try and pacify you. He was a peaceful person and didn't like to see violence."

By the end of 1956, Morrissey had adjusted to Manchester ways and was about to enter a new stage in his life. That November was a time of treble celebration. Peter was 21, Betty was 19, and their marriage was not far away. As the couple toasted their respective birthdays and continued courtship, a radio announcer on the BBC Light Programme congratulated vocalist Johnnie Ray who, that very month, had topped the Hit Parade with 'Just Walkin' In The Rain'. The singer was the last of the pre-rock 'n' roll pop idols with a talent measured in immoderate emotion and boyish vulnerability. They called him the 'Prince of Wails' and the 'Nabob of Sob', while diligently noting that he wore a hearing-aid. That alone was enough to make him unique in pop history, at least up until as late as 1983. Only then would another singer, complete with dangling hearing-aid, dare to combine that same sense of onstage melodrama and wreak similar pandemonium throughout the concert halls of Britain.

On 16 March 1957, the marriage of Peter Morrissey and Elizabeth Dwyer was celebrated at the Chapel of Our Lady of Perpetual Succour in Moss Side. It was the eve of St Patrick's Day, and therefore a good excuse for the more patriotic guests to extend the nuptial celebrations at Stockton Street for a further 24 hours. Soon after the wedding, the couple moved to 17 Harper Street in Hulme, and within a year Betty gave birth to their first child, Jacqueline. Bringing up a baby meant that she had to forego packing blankets while Peter increased the family income by accepting overtime as a cotton worker at the Johnson, Clapham and Morris warehouse. Remarkably, he had sufficient surplus energy to devote most of his leisure time to playing football. He was a keen fan of Manchester United and like the rest of the city was deeply shocked and saddened by the events of 6 February 1958 when the team's charter plane crashed in Munich. There were a horrifying 24 deaths, including eight star players from the first eleven. It would take years to replenish the side and Morrissey was frequently rebuked by his Dublin pals for neglecting to put his name forward as a likely second team candidate. He had, in fact, already passed trials at Bury, where manager Bert Head had been alerted to his superb striking ability. Morrissey was frustratingly modest about his footballing skills, however, and found it difficult to take the two evenings off every week for training. Since football clubs neglected to pay expenses in those days, the financial pinch proved a further impediment. Instead, Morrissey contented himself playing park football at the weekend.

Every Sunday after morning Mass, a bunch of Irish lads would congregate outside the Northumberland pub and walk to the croft on Stretford Road, just across from the library. A collection of half-crowns would be taken, some coats would be thrown down as surrogate goal posts, and for the next couple of hours, Ginger Crowe, Harry Denton, Peter Morrissey and the rest would contest their own version of the FA Cup Final. The opposition usually consisted of the denizens of the Talbot, a rival Dublin pub frequented by the garrulous Mikey Roe. As the afternoon progressed, the players, many of them still in crumpled Sunday suits, would re-organize their teams to accommodate late arrivals. Often the numbers grew to an unwieldy 15-a-side and the more eager competitors would play on till after 5pm, missing their dinner in the process. The elder pub sages were impressed by the youngsters' lively talent and, eager to sample some vicarious glory, persuaded them to fund a series of friendlies. Eventually, enough money was collected to purchase some proper kit and hire a bus for away outings. The team manager, Frank McGuire, assembled a formidable side, which even included a couple of English players, Billy Warnock and the publican's goalkeeping son, Eddie Messenger. After contesting some tough friendlies, both the Northumberland and the Talbot were admitted to the Chorlton League. Their progress thereafter was remarkable. During their first season, the Northumberland won the League Championship while the Talbot finished runners-up. One year later, their positions were reversed and the twin Dublin domination continued into the early Sixties. Morrissey emerged as the leading league goal-scorer and soon had enough miniature trophies to clog up the sitting-room sideboard in Harper Street. The indomitable Harry Denton, intoxicated by romantic generosity, presented his Championship medal to his latest love, Erica Gilsenan, another of the beauteous Ballymount clan.

As the Northumberland celebrated its footballing pre-eminence, Morrissey was infrequently taken aside by well-meaning team mates and told that he should be playing in the First Division of the national Football League. "He seriously was *that* good," Harry Denton enthuses. "Peter was a brilliant footballer and should have gone places. He lived and breathed the game and was the best player in the team by a long way. He wasn't a drinker and always looked fit. He had the style of George Best combined with the powerful shot of Bobby Charlton. But if you ever said he should play for Manchester United, he'd feel embarrassed and just laugh it off."

Instead, Peter farmed himself out to other minor leagues and became the star player in the Johnson, Clapham and Morris works team. The Northumberland captain, Seamus Gilsenan, and fellow Dubliner Harry Denton, were drafted into the side and soon found themselves chasing another Championship in the Saturday afternoon fixture lists. JCM ended the season unbeaten but their superb record was matched by rivals Red Star, who shared the same points total. A play-off, arranged at Moss Fields, attracted about 100 people, eager to relish the match of the season. The pundits in the crowd agreed that the play-off would be a tense affair and the exceptionally strong defence of each side suggested that a single goal might prove decisive. If anything, the odds were marginally in Red Star's favour as JCM were fielding a weakened team due to holiday absenteeism. In the event, the deadlock was broken by a characteristic Morrissey flourish, which Seamus Gilsenan still recalls with wide-eyed enthusiasm. "Peter won the League for us," he stresses. "They just couldn't get the ball off him. It was impossible. They kept trying to bring him down but finally he just ran through the entire team like Georgie Best and scored an absolutely fantastic goal. It was out of this world. Even the other team applauded."

Following JCM's victory, Morrissey was more sought after than ever, but resisted the advances of pub poachers with his usual self-effacing laugh. Seamie continued to chide, "You've lost your way, you!" but the Northumberland's favourite forward could never take such praise seriously. By now, he was a settled family man and Betty was pregnant for the second time in two years.

The parents agreed that if the child was a boy then he should take part of his name from his maternal grandfather. Peter also wanted to honour the memory of his deceased infant brothers by christening his first son with both their names. Soon after being admitted to the Park Hospital in Davyhulme, the young mother gave birth to Steven Patrick. The date was 22 May 1959, a great day for ex-truck drivers and iconographical pop stars alike. Peter Morrissey had sired a male heir and Elvis Presley was number one in the charts with 'A Fool Such As I'. It was also the Feast of Humility, the austere thirteenth-century nun who had chosen to live entombed, sleeping on her knees with her head resting on a wall. During her self-imposed imprisonment, she survived on a starvation diet of bread and water. Steven Patrick Humility would have been a great pop name, but it was not to be. For a time, however, the humble May child lay in social limbo, unrecorded by the authorities. Nearly two months elapsed before the Registrar of Births finally documented the details of the elusive babe.

With all the Championship medals, births, christenings and celebrations, it was not surprising that Peter infrequently succumbed to his friends' admonitions to have a pint. On such occasions, the results were comically calamitous. As Harry Denton observed: "He'd conk out, more or less!" After one session, in which the over-sociable Morrissey exceeded the deadly three-pint mark, he had to be bodily escorted home. Even after two pints he seemed noticeably woozy and usually fell victim to the giggles, which was somehow in keeping with his jovial manner. In the Northumberland, Morrissey's name was synonymous with affability and good humour. He was also known for his generosity of spirit. When Seamus Gilsenan complained about the state of his digs, Peter had no hesitation in offering him a room in Harper Street. Seamus stayed for 18 months and was occasionally called upon to babysit when Peter and Betty had a night out at the pictures. He remembers Steven as an exceptionally quiet child who, even then, betrayed a noticeable resemblance to his father.

In the years immediately after Steven's birth, Peter was seen less and less in the pub and spent most of his evenings at home. It was all Seamus could do to drag him out on a Friday night. Betty seemed equally unconcerned about outings and the family unit was solidly insular. Peter was regarded as steady, dependent, always in work and willing to suffer longer hours for improved pay. Steven and his sister Jacqueline therefore had a reasonably secure upbringing with young, solicitous parents who ensured that their children were well turned out and wanted for nothing.

The occasional babysitter, Seamus, had left Harper Street by 1962 and married, though he continued to work with Peter at Tillotsons' Containers, a box manufacturers in Worsley Street. In order to ease the tedium of the long night shift, Peter would amuse his colleague by displaying elaborate and seemingly impossible feats of footballing skill, using blocks of wood and printed targets on a wall. A working pattern had now been established for Peter Morrissey which ensured that he would always accept late shifts. Although this meant that he could spend more time with his family during alternate weeks off, he was often unavailable during daylight hours and the kids had to learn to stay quiet while he slept upstairs. With time on her hands during the day, Betty would read magazines and the occasional book, although the Morrissey household was as impoverished of literature as most other working-class homes in the area.

The period between 1962-66 may well have been the happiest days of Steven Morrissey's life. He had the additional security of an extended family, as various close relations relocated to the area. Peter's brother Thomas had belatedly followed his younger sibs across the water and secured a job at Manchester Central as a ticket collector. Like his parents, he had a reasonably big family, siring four daughters and three sons. The existence of male cousins on the Morrissey side ensured that Steven did not represent "the end of the family line". The Morrissey family tree would continue, irrespective of his lack of progeny.

Among the other emigrants were Betty's parents, who gamely left their two-bedroomed house in Captain's Road. Patrick Dwyer had long since given up his original occupation as a bus conductor for the more lucrative pay offered by labouring and, like his children, had adapted to the challenge of a new life in Manchester. Family solidarity was noticeably strong. From an early age, Steven was surrounded by women, as a veritable battalion of aunts descended on Harper Street. Auntie Mae Bridget, Auntie

Patricia, Auntie Ellen, Auntie Chrissie, Auntie Ann, Auntie Dorothy, Auntie Patti, Auntie Jeane, Auntie Mary, Auntie Rita... it was a feat to remember them all, let alone their husbands, plus the aunts by marriage and the growing legion of baby cousins. Loneliness was not merely unlikely, but impossible.

Sunday was often the occasion of family visits and usually the day that Peter's body clock readjusted itself after a week of night work. There was something ineffably special and reassuring about Sunday. During the afternoon, homely kitchen aromas wafted through the air and the Light Programme provided an appetizing soundtrack of popular music and comedy: *Two-Way Family Favourites* linked homesick servicemen with exiled sweethearts and devoted mothers via an impossibly eclectic selection of chestnut standards and topical tunes; in *The Clitheroe Kid* the magically-ageless Jimmy Clitheroe pitted his juvenile wits against a snobbish sister, with the unwitting assistance of her gormless boyfriend; in later years, the Kid was followed by the outrageous and incomprehensibly camp Julian and Sandy, who exposed a secret fantasy netherworld of innocent homosexuality in the centrepiece of *Round The Horne*; finally, as afternoon turned to evening, the senatorial Alan Freeman dramatized the contrasting fortunes of the pop élite in his *Pick Of The Pops* chart rundown.

During the winter of 1962-63 the younger children in Harper Street prayed for their first glimpse of a white Christmas and they were not to be disappointed. Before long, a blanket of fathomlessly deep snow had stretched across Britain, driven inexorably by blinding blizzards and a numbing coldness that had already succeeded in freezing rivers, demobilizing public transport, raising the unemployment rate to a staggering 3.9 per cent, marooning a family on a Dartmoor farm for 60 days, escalating the tragic incidences of hypothermia among the poor, aged and infirm, and encouraging eccentric religious prophets and failed meteorologists to herald the imminent arrival of an apocalyptic Ice Age.

That winter seemed to symbolize the death of the Fifties and presage the emergence of a new era that became known in tabloid journalese as the "Swinging Sixties". It was a strange accident of history that saw Britain's sepulchral isle consumed by a dramatic and rapid series of social, political and cultural changes that would transform the decade more completely than any turning of a calendar. Across the world, in the racially-torn United States, the beatific Martin Luther King announced that he had a dream and inspired a new generation of kids to demonstrate publicly against institutionalized injustices which threatened the heart of American democracy. Meanwhile, that other contemporaneous champion of the oppressed, John Fitzgerald Kennedy, made his famous freedom speech at the Berlin Wall. Within a matter of months he was killed by an assassin's bullet in an American city already renowned for its ostentatious wealth and barely disguised bigotry.

The day after the Kennedy assassination left an eerie feeling, as though time itself had been abruptly severed. Even the kids watching the first episode of a new television series named *Dr Who* could not escape the feeling that something was amiss. The sadness was particularly strong in Irish communities, where the Catholic president was most favoured. Those too young to comprehend the full implications of such a tragedy accepted the news, as children often do, unfazed and resigned. In Manchester, a lad named John Kilbride spent the afternoon at the cinema watching an adventure film called *The Moguls* before taking his ritual weekly wander round the open market in Ashton-under-Lyme. Within days, posters appeared in the area with the message: "Have You Seen This Boy?" He was never seen again.

The mystery of the missing boy, like that of a similarly-aged missing girl earlier in the year, remained a parochial issue. Tributes to Kennedy were still pouring into newspaper offices and, as 1963 reached its close, there was time to reflect on Britain's own political climate. "Sensation" was the word most frequently coined, though it was scandal rather than tragedy that characterized the Profumo affair. The embarrassing spectacle of a Cabinet Minister's sordid liaison with a prostitute might normally have passed unnoticed were it not for her exclusive clientèle, which included Captain Evgeni Ivanov, a prominent naval attaché from the Russian Embassy. Profumo at first denied the charge but under scrutiny from the Secret Service later confirmed his discretion and promptly resigned. The scandal proved sufficient to focus attention on the Tory Party as a whole and the newspapers were full of wild stories concerning a network of organized prostitutes busily servicing various Members of Parliament, wealthy landowners and High Court judges. Such highly publicized outrage reinforced the view among foreign settlers and British youth that their hosts and elders were not necessarily their equals or betters. The vestiges of Victorian respect for politicians and statesmen who hid private vices behind cant denouncements of juvenile delinquency and adolescent promiscuity gradually gave way to an insidious cynicism as harbingers of the cult of youth mercilessly exposed the inadequacies of the old order. It was the age of the instant event when incidents and trends converged upon and replaced each other with extraordinary rapidity. Arctic winter, papal death, presidential assassination and even a preposterously executed Great Train Robbery flashed past in a blur of evanescent headlines.

Cultural and stylistic changes proved equally incandescent. Young designers like Mary Quant were busily brushing aside the conservatism of Fifties dress with such youth-orientated styles as the radically revealing mini-skirt. Furniture became tastelessly garish, bizarrely geometric and unashamedly non-utilitarian, with formica replacing natural wood. At the cinema, the latest box-office hero was James Bond, a peculiarly British Secret Agent whose lascivious amorality, suave cynicism and obsession with new technology and gimmicky gadgetry was an apt comment on the times. The great British class conflict, so prevalent in the work of such working-class writers of the Fifties as John Braine, Keith Waterhouse, Alan Sillitoe, Shelagh Delaney and David Storey, was now making the transition to the big screen. *Look Back In Anger, A Taste Of Honey, Saturday Night And Sunday Morning, The L-Shaped Room, This Sporting Life* and *The Family Way* were almost all glimpses of the proletariat from the inside, written by the children of manual workers, many of them from northern factory towns and cities. A surprise new hit television series, *Coronation Street* originated from, of all places, Manchester. Even the London-based top-rated comedy shows such as *Steptoe And Son* and *Till Death Us Do Part* broke with tradition by showing ungentrified working-class families unafraid to reveal their vulgarity and prejudices. For many impressionable youngsters, the cultural clashes of the Sixties would have a profound effect on their tastes and attitudes and mould the remainder of their lives.

In many respects, the most significant changes for Steven Morrissey were those in the area of popular music. A young, mop-haired musical quartet from Liverpool had exploded on to the scene with a chirpy effervescence and melodious infectiousness that had captured the imagination of a new generation of teenagers. The Beatles arrived at the perfect psychological moment, reinforcing a working-class assault on fashion, music, cinema and the peripheral arts. Having dominated the number one chart position during 1963, they went on to reap extraordinary success in the United States, a continent that had previously seemed immune to the vagaries of British pop. Suddenly, Liverpool was the pop capital of the world and in the wake of The Beatles came a plethora of new Merseybeat chart toppers including Gerry And The Pacemakers, Billy J Kramer And The Dakotas and The Searchers. Amid their chart domination, there was even room for a Merseybeat girl, Cilla Black, who enjoyed two of the biggest number one hits of 1964 with 'Anyone Who Had A Heart' and 'You're My World'. On *Pick Of The Pops*, Alan Freeman speculated theatrically: "Can Cilla hang on for another two weeks with 'You're My World' and reign in the glory of 'Anyone Who Had A Heart'?" Such a question might have appealed to Steven Morrissey but it was probably far from the mind of 12-year-old Keith Bennett, a short-sighted youth from distant Longsight, who was passing his time by teasing a couple of female class-mates. His mother watched him cross the busy Stockport Road seemingly out of trouble and danger. He too was never seen again.

Steven Morrissey's first year at school coincided with ever-accelerating shifts in the pop scene as a veritable kaleidoscope of colourful new names and fresh styles fought for short-lived domination on the evanescent landscape of the charts. Within two weeks of Steven passing through the gates of St Wilfred's Primary School, Herman's Hermits became the first Manchester beat group to hit number one. On *Top Of The Pops*, their baby-faced buck-toothed lead singer Peter Noone warbled the sparkling 'I'm Into Something Good' savouring every syllable of its title. Noone was replaced at the top by a barefoot girl from Dagenham named Sandra Goodrich, who chose the alliterative pun Sandie Shaw for her stage monicker. Although her name conjured up a seaside ambience, her début chart topper was the distinctly urban '(There's) Always Something There To Remind Me', a Burt Bacharach/Hal David composition that detailed a neurotically nostalgic trip through city streets in which every physical object served as a painful reminder of all that had been lost in a relationship.

Shaw was not alone in her melancholy. An even darker mood permeated the recordings of Lynn Ripley, alias Twinkle, whose long, blonde hair and diminutive stature contrasted with Sandie's brown tresses and imposing height. In November 1964, Twinkle charted with 'Terry', a death song similar in theme to the Shangri-Las' contemporaneous biker anthem, 'Leader Of The Pack'. Young Steven was quite taken by these stories in song, with their crashing motor cycles, doomed heroines and aggrieved lovers. His class-mate Chris Lukes remembers him during the very early days at St Wilfreds as a sensitive and imaginative child who would be moved to near tears by a particularly sad story read in class. It was the one unusual trait of a lad who mixed well with the other boys and girls, both in the classroom and the playground.

The lower school was run by the bespectacled Mother Peter, whom the kids perceived as a remote but vaguely benevolent presence; her omniscient reputation was enough to keep them in order. The waspish Miss Illan seemed a more intimidating figure and certainly was not to be crossed. Predictably, there were also the angelic, mother substitutes, such as Sister Aloysius and Miss Cosgrove, who smiled frequently and seemed blessed with endless patience and bounty. Occasionally, they would dispense a star prize, such as a Dinky car or chocolate bar, to the pupil of the moment. Term ended on a positive note with the school engendering a festive atmosphere that augured well for the holidays. The Beatles hogged the Christmas number one spot, as recent tradition demanded, with their latest million seller, 'I Feel Fine'. Christmas Day was the usual flurry of eagerly-opened presents, plentiful food and day-long available television, including the *Top Of The Pops* round-up of the year's chart toppers. Boxing Day was a time to wind down the excitement by taking a trip to one of the busy fun fairs, which were particularly popular in Manchester. Rusholme ruffians represented only a small proportion of the teeming masses that were attracted by the mesmerizing bright lights, exotic smells and whirling sounds of the fair in full swing. In nearby Ancoats, a girl named Lesley Ann had spent her last penny on the rides at Miles Platting, but dallied longer than her bored brothers who went home for their tea. She was last observed by a school friend enviously watching screaming riders careering recklessly on the dodgems. She too would never be seen again.

During the second term of Steven's first school year, Manchester unexpectedly hit the world map as the premier city in the pantheon of pop. The man responsible for this phenomenon was a chartered accountant turned pop entrepreneur named Danny Betesh. His Manchester-based agency Kennedy Street Enterprises promoted several local acts including Freddie And The Dreamers, Wayne Fontana And The Mindbenders and Herman's Hermits, and it was this trio that spearheaded the US invasion. For six consecutive weeks they occupied the coveted number one spot in the American charts and during an incredible week at the end of April were one, two and three in the Hot 100. This was a feat previously matched only by The Beatles and momentarily caused Betesh to be spoken of in the same breath as the Liverpudlian svengali Brian Epstein. For at least a month, Manchester was unquestionably the most celebrated pop city in the world.

Back in England, Manchester's Easter triumph met a steely challenge from the representatives of other major cities as groups like The Rolling Stones, The Animals, The Yardbirds, The Who, Unit 4 Plus 2 and The Moody Blues kept the beat boom alive. Yet, throughout this delightfully democratic period of pop, there was a simultaneous upsurge in the fortunes of female performers whose ranks now included Cilla Black, Dusty Springfield, Sandie Shaw, Petula Clark, Lulu, Twinkle, Françoise Hardy and Jackie Trent. Among this congregation was a former convent girl named Marianne Faithfull whom manager Andrew Loog Oldham had selected as a virginal antidote to the indecent behaviour of his much-publicized bad boys The Rolling Stones. Faithfull had long, straight, blonde hair, just like Steven's mother and sister, and although her voice seemed weak, there was a certain seductive innocence about her persona which proved mysteriously enticing. Steven was entranced enough to persuade his parents to purchase a copy of her latest disc, 'Come And Stay With Me'. By the time the 6/8d had been handed over the counter at Paul Marsh Records in Alexander Road, his other flame Sandie Shaw was back at number one with 'Long Live Love'. Interestingly, it was at this point that Steven first recalled seeing James Dean in *Rebel Without A Cause*. It was almost as if his heroes and heroines were marshalling themselves in a single time period to chisel out a chunk of childhood happiness that would be recollected ceaselessly in his moribund teenage years.

The summer of 1965 was one of the best ever in pop music. Folk-rock was in vogue and both Bob Dylan and The Byrds had made their presence felt and expanded pop's vocabulary in the process. For the Morrisseys, however, it was time to leave Harper Street and move across to Queens Square, near Moss Side, where they purchased a house. Hulme was already a decaying area, which the town planners had transformed into a concrete wasteland. Even St Wilfreds had found itself surrounded by rubble, literally in the middle of nowhere. At least the family retained some links with Harper Street as Peter had offered the house to Seamus Gilsenan and his wife. This innocent exchange of tenancy was greeted with indignation by bureaucratic Town Hall staff, but after chastening Gilsenan, they grudgingly allowed him to stay at his new home.

The second year at St Wilfreds passed smoothly, but there was more local drama in October 1965 when the body of Edward Evans was found battered to death. The murderer was Ian Brady, the son of a former meat porter at Smithfield Market. After moving from Glasgow to Moss Side, Brady had first taken a job at a meat market before securing a clerical post at Millwards, a chemical company in Levenshulme Road. Within weeks his work colleagues were commenting on his moodiness and quick temper. His insularity was deep and he appeared to spend most of his time and money on books, whose subject matter ranged from Naziism to the works of Marquis de Sade. In spite of his taciturnity, Brady found a willing disciple and lover in a work-mate named Myra Hindley, who participated willingly in his abduction and murder of children. It was Brady's attempt to extend that evil to a third party which proved his undoing. David Smith, the brother-in-law of Hindley, had witnessed the slaying of Evans and, after consulting his wife, duly informed the police. Evidence linking Brady and Hindley with the disappearance of Lesley Ann Downey emerged soon afterwards and a witness directed the authorities to a bleak spot on Saddleworth Moor where a corpse was exhumed from a shallow grave. Among Lesley Ann's naked remains was a string of white beads that had been given to her as a Christmas present on the eve of her fateful visit to the fun fair. On 6 December 1965, committal proceedings were opened against Brady and Hindley. While separated, they sent each other a message in code, which threatened: 'SMITH WILL DIE'.

Feelings about the Moors murders ran high in Manchester and relations of the victims vented their wrath outside the magistrate's court. The trial took place the following spring, amid an atmosphere of shock, tension and suppressed violence. Even as a child, Morrissey was unusually aware of the drama and remembers the conspiratorially hushed conversations between worried mothers outside school gates. "At times, it was like living in a soap opera," he recalled. In his imagination, there seemed an inexplicably evil presence on the streets of Manchester that he could barely articulate, let alone define.

By an odd coincidence, the prosecution lawyer for the Brady/Hindley case was William Mars-Jones, who would later win a place in the annals of pop legal history by judging the multi-million pound dispute between Gilbert O'Sullivan and Gordon Mills. Back in 1966, his task was decidedly more gruesome. In open court, the full horrors of Downey's ordeal were relayed to the nation, for the murderers had chosen to tape the final tortured moments of her life for posterity. The verdict was never in doubt but the guilty pair escaped the hangman's noose due to the recent abolition of capital punishment. Throughout the proceedings, their attitude had betrayed silent resignation rather than visible remorse. During the interrogation, Myra had offered the defiant refrain: "Whatever Ian has done, I have done."

In May 1966, Hindley was imprisoned in Holloway, north London, a bleak Victorian gaol that housed 950 women prisoners. There, she suffered the ostracism and violence that seem reserved for "sex offenders". Fellow inmates took to whispering "Suffer little children to come unto me" whenever she walked by. Others were less solemnly dramatic and beat her up. Initially, she remained aloof and openly contemptuous of her media labelling as the 'Moors Murderess'. Her macabre humour was revealingly captured in a letter to her jailed lover in which she flippantly complained: "I didn't murder any moors, did you?"

Hindley and Brady remain imprisoned and have clearly changed radically during their 25-year incarceration. Brady accepted that there was no hope of parole and finally succumbed to diagnosable mental illness. The steely Hindley later found successive salvation in lesbianism, feminist literature and religion. But such character changes seemed scarcely relevant in the eyes of the grieving families and a sizeable proportion of the British public. Horrific crimes had left the murderers immutably captured in time. The survivors paid an arguably heavier price; the scarred lives of the victims' relatives represent a catalogue of immeasurable despair. Others suffered too, including the murderers' innocent relatives. Maureen Hindley, despite having "shopped" her sister to the police, was ceaselessly hounded by a vindictive public and died a few years later from a brain haemorrhage. Even her funeral was brutally disrupted. The bitterness and horror produced by these unfathomable murders contaminated the futures of countless individuals and their children throughout the city of Manchester.

The Moors murderers had accomplished the dubious distinction of transforming tragic event into myth. Hindley herself recognized this in a periodic blast against her home town: "The Mancunians in particular are rooted in the myth, right up to their heads; they're narrow-minded, conventional people, who believe everything they read, see or hear - and they're vengeful." The frustrated need for appeasement was mirrored in a shocked silence, which the child Morrissey duly noted. "It was too horrific for people to think about and discuss," he concluded. Like so many events and characters from this period, the murders were thoroughly assimilated into Morrissey's personal mythical landscape. "I did have a fixation on the Moors murders as a potential victim," he confessed. Years later, he would find himself drawn into the saga for very different reasons.

While the Moors controversy raged, Steven was taking his first communion at St Wilfreds Church. It was an eventful morning for the class of '66, who turned out in their best clothes to receive the Host. Afterwards, they were treated to a post-Mass boiled-egg breakfast which tasted unexpectedly wondrous following their long fast. A commemorative photograph of that day captures Steven looking assured in his white shirt and tie, smack in the centre of the line-up. After Easter, the next major religious festival was Whit Sunday, a time for Manchester to show off its love of parades. There was usually a touch of rivalry between the local religious factions with the Catholics walking on Friday and the Protestants on Monday. The mischievous or bigoted would delight in taunting "cat licks", a phrase guaranteed to provoke the learned response, "proddy dogs". Whitsun generally meant more fairs and a chance for children to call on beneficent relations and receive some eagerly-anticipated half-crowns.

As summer approached, the mood of the nation seemed decidedly optimistic. Carnaby Street fashions were in vogue and visiting American singer Roger Miller was glorifying Blighty with the condescending tribute 'England Swings'. It was the year of the Anglophiliacs. Even in the area of international sport, England emerged as global champions, audaciously lifting soccer's 1966 World Cup in a parodic equivalent of real wars past. And so it went on. Callow youths were awarded prestigious political honours, *enfant terrible* entrepreneurs infiltrated the stuffy boardrooms of British industry, and piratical broadcasters in garish, floral shirts and psychedelic ties invaded the hallowed corridors and sanctified airwaves of the BBC. Everyone, or so it seemed, was paying gratuitous homage at the apparently inviolable altar of youth. The soundtrack to this period continued to reveal a healthy democracy in pop: Dusty Springfield enjoyed her first and only chart topper with 'You Don't Have To Say You Love Me', The Rolling Stones continued their dark, nihilistic musings on 'Paint It Black', Nancy Sinatra percolated a comic sexuality on 'These Boots Are Made For Walkin'', and her stately father Frank bridged the generation gap with the instant standard 'Strangers In The Night'. Even the pre-teens were catered for thanks to The Beatles' nursery rhyme 'Yellow Submarine' and Napoleon XIV's 'They're Coming To Take Me Away, Ha! Haaa!' with its novelty backwards-playing B-side.

The first week of September 1966 saw Steven promoted to the juniors. There were a number of new faces, most notably the headmaster, John Coleman, and some trainee teachers including Mr Slavin and Mr Deacon, whose youth and affability made them more approachable than the elder, established members of staff. Steven seemed particularly well-adjusted and was one of the most popular kids in his class. Fellow pupils remember him as neither extrovert nor shy but blessed with a quick wit and likeable personality. He enjoyed talking about pop music and took considerable satisfaction from watching England win the Eurovision Song Contest for the first time on 8 April 1967 with Sandie Shaw's 'Puppet On A String'. For Morrissey, her victory was akin to a personal triumph.

While Steven was settling in well, there was no disputing the star of Junior 1. Frances Ellis effortlessly finished top of the class, prematurely booking herself the post of future head girl in the process. Her competitive class-mate Steve Smythe was aggrieved at finishing an anti-climactic second and thereafter kept a close eye on potential academic rivals. Regrettably, the engaging Steven Morrissey would not be among them. "Academically, he never made much of a mark," Smythe recalls. "We used to have exams every year and if you didn't finish in the top six, there wasn't going to be much chance afterwards. And I can never remember Steven Morrissey doing well." Another ex-pupil recalls Morrissey stumbling in a reading lesson, in which he pronounced island as "is-land", much to the private amusement of those who knew better. Despite such lapses, he remained in the middle-range ability of the top class and those who appreciated his imaginative wit agreed that he was "a good kid".

Significant changes took place during Junior 2, including a substantial influx of new pupils from nearby St Lawrence's school. Among their number was Michael Roe, the son of Peter Morrissey's footballing rival. Arriving in J2 was something of a baptism of fire, for the new form teacher was Miss Dudley, a formidable Irish mistress, who was not afraid to use the strap. An upstanding Catholic herself, she had the serious responsibility of overseeing her charges during their confirmation year. Much of the teaching centred on the nature of sin in its various forms from Original to venial and mortal. The meaning of confession and the mystery of transubstantiation unfolded week by week and the importance of the sacraments was regularly stressed. One pupil, the gangling Chris Lukes, had the temerity to interrupt Miss Dudley on a particular religious point and

received an incredulous, "Why?! You ask, why?" for his apparently heretical impertinence. He soon rebelled by deliberately missing Mass, but was
devious enough to check the colour of the priest's vestments prior to
Monday morning assembly. Miss Dudley was punctilious about pupils
attending Mass and did not waver from punishing those who had lapsed.
According to Morrissey, the attitude was, "We'll sever your head for your
own good. You'll learn, my son."

Confirmation preparation was completed by the visiting Father Clarke,
who ensured that the class understood its Catechism and could recite the
Ten Commandments, Seven Deadly Sins and Seven Cardinal Virtues. Many
hours were spent laboriously learning the correct response for the Mass,
including the lengthy Credo with its mysterious references to "all things
visible and invisible". The Catechism encompassed those amazingly
cosmological concepts of limbo and purgatory, in which the souls of gener-
ations past awaited their ultimate salvation. This was a lot more dramatic
than anything Steven had ever heard in a Twinkle song, but for some
reason it instilled unease rather than awe. For the first time, Morrissey's
world was revealing its darker aspects. Even his parents' marriage seemed
less concrete than in earlier times and prompted the child to consider the
likely impermanence of all human relationships. His Aunt Patricia noted
the change in the boy, who seemed strangely quiet. "He had a good life
when he was very young," she recalled. "I don't know what it was but he
became very shy and didn't want to mix. He was a lovely child but too
quiet and very reserved."

To his class-mates, Steven remained lively and amusing, but he remembers that confirmation year as a moment in time when his morbidity
achieved consciousness. Conscience doth make cowards of us all and
Morrissey was no exception. Strangely, it was the concept of eternal life and
a place in heaven that most filled the boy with irrational dread. "Can you
imagine living this life without end?" he later joked. It was Morrissey's sad
error that he perceived heavenly immortality in a corporeal rather than
spiritual sense, equating its regenerative grace in inappropriately worldly
currency. His faith would prove neither strong nor lasting.

Apart from confirmation preparation, J2 had been dominated by boys'
football talk. Manchester United had finished top of the League the previous season and were continuing their immemorial quest for the European
Cup. Peter Morrissey was naturally intrigued by their progress and his
enthusiasm rubbed off on young Steven, who was displaying superficial
signs of following in his father's footsteps. On 29 May 1968, Manchester
United appeared at Wembley Stadium to contest the final against the
talented Benfica. With striker Denis Law absent through injury, United
elected to build patiently from the back and wisely employed the ferocious
Nobby Stiles to mark the brilliant Eusebio out of the game. The deadlock
remained unbroken until the 65th minute when Bobby Charlton made
novel use of his head by glancing the ball into the net. Manchester grimly
hung on until 10 minutes from full time when Milan dramatically equal-
ized. Soon after, Eusebio broke free but, with history at his mercy, failed to

score the killer goal. In extra time, the sensational young forward George Best weaved past several opponents, including the keeper, and arrogantly deposited the ball into Milan's goal. Brian Kidd and Bobby Charlton completed the scoring to put the tie beyond doubt at 4-1. It was a joyous occasion for Manchester, the fulfilment of a dream that had seemed irrevocably destroyed on a Munich airfield in 1958.

The wayward soccer genius George Best had captured the imagination of the nation and his superb footballing skills, pop star looks and unpredictable behaviour made him a super hero to a legion of youngsters. A cursory resemblance between George Best and Peter Morrissey was later commented on by several class mates, which must have made an impression on young Steven. For a time, he accompanied his father to United's home matches at Old Trafford and even took some interest in playing the game. Yet there was something half-hearted in his approach, which struck the observant Chris Lukes: "He was capable and could kick a ball, unlike some, but he didn't seem very motivated." Indeed, even before the end of his primary school years, Morrissey's soccer skills were in danger of waning from insufficient practise.

The fascination for pop music would not be quenched so easily. During the first term of Junior 3, Morrissey was commenting on chart positions and new records with the enthusiasm of a young zealot. The Beatles had just topped the Hit Parade with 'Hey Jude' which at 7 minutes, 11 seconds was the longest single ever to achieve such a feat. The Fab Four's new label Apple had also found its first star in the chaste Mary Hopkin whose 'Those Were The Days' impertinently displaced The Beatles from the number one spot.

While nostalgic ballads dominated the autumn airwaves, the eyes of J3 were firmly set on the future. The new form mistress turned out to be Miss Redmond, a paragon who had taught several of the children's mothers, including those of Chris Lukes and Steve Smythe, the tallest and brightest boys in the class. Among Redmond's many roles was deputizing as a music teacher, where she displayed her considerable skills playing hymns on the piano. One of her favourites, the festive 'We Three Kings', caught Morrissey's attention and he adapted the lyrics to create his own witty version retitled 'We Four Stevens' after several mates in his class.*

Morrissey's scribbles and doodlings passed unnoticed by the other pupils, but he enjoyed the thrill of putting pen to paper. On bath nights, he would insist on putting a plank across a tub so that he could continue to read a comic or write some notes. "When my mother put me in the bath, I shut myself away," he recalled nostalgically. At school, he was content to fade into a predominantly pleasant atmosphere.

"St Wilfreds was a happy place", reminisced Michael Roe, expressing a

* The humorously immortalized quartet comprised himself, Steve Smythe, Steve Pratt and Steve Usher (who transferred to English Martyrs in Chorlton soon after). Another candidate, the vowelless Maths swot Steve Vhgh, was inadvertently omitted from Morrissey's singing roll call and also left the following year.

view with which the majority of the alumni wholeheartedly concurred. "There was no fighting or outcasts and Morrissey was a perfectly normal child." Nevertheless, the entire class was to experience some disruptive changes in their final year. The decision to demolish blocks of terraced houses in the area caused many families to move home and the Morrisseys were relocated to a council house at 384 Kings Road, Stretford. In September 1969, a replacement school building was opened, adjacent to the old St Wilfreds, and the pupils had to adapt to a different routine. There was also a new class teacher, the no-nonsense Mr Ajas, a Maltese-born immigrant whose most distinctive feature was an extraordinarily prominent Adam's apple. The boys had already experienced his regimented ways during the previous year's woodwork class as well as on the school yard football pitch, where he displayed judicial fastidiousness backed by a woeful lack of soccer skill. The unfortunate Chris Lukes crossed swords with his new form teacher after involving himself in a football game in which another boy broke his leg. While arguing his case, Lukes was asked, "Did you break his leg on purpose?" and promptly burst into tears. "He was the first man to make me cry and it seemed terribly unjust," Lukes now recalls. Morrissey, from the sidelines, was happy enough to be a soccer has-been at the age of 10.

The major problem facing the pupils of J4 was correctly reading their teacher's apparently unpredictable temperament. He was often quite humorous and made the class laugh a lot, yet he seemed quick to take offence and frequently created a mood of hushed uncertainty. His religious lessons evoked the atmosphere of a Jesuit sermon with detailed descriptions of hellish damnation which unnerved several of his charges. "It used to petrify me," recalls Morrissey who had been unsettled enough by the prospect of heaven, long before hearing about the intimidating alternative. Ajas took his role as a moral instructor very seriously. His pet hate was petty vandalism, which had briefly broken out at the beginning of the first term. The newly-built school was a wrecker's delight and although no serious damage had been done, a PVC chair was slashed and the statue of Our Lady badly chipped. Ajas was appalled by such behaviour and promised to unmask the culprits. The high-spirited boys in the year, including Billy O'Shea, Vincent O'Rourke and Stephen Meehan were paraded in front of the class and systematically interrogated until they had proven their innocence. Further likely suspects were then lined-up, but all to no avail. Ajas evidently enjoyed playing the chief prosecutor and his investigative stamina seemed inexhaustible. As Steve Smythe recollects: "These Perry Mason court-room dramas used to go on for days". Unfortunately, the results were rarely conclusive and the successive post-mortems ultimately proved time-consuming and counter productive. With the dreaded 11-plus examination looming only months ahead, Junior 4's prospects already seemed decidedly ominous.

During their final days at St Wilfreds, pupils were expected to act responsibly and therefore received some authority themselves. Chris Lukes, despite his secret avoidance of Sunday Mass, was appointed head boy while Frances Ellis, whose academic reputation had diminished since J1, became head girl. A number of other pupils were recruited as prefects, including Steve Smythe, Sarah Stapleton and Morrissey. This was a time when maturity was reflected in the acquisition of a girlfriend, even though such friendships seldom extended beyond the school gates. Unlike many of the boys, Morrissey was surprisingly confident in the presence of females and had already become acquainted with several friends of his sister Jacqueline. At school, he was seen frequently alongside Kathleen Geoghan, a pale, freckle-faced Irish girl with an engaging personality and outgoing confidence. They spent much of their prefect duty together, patrolling the forbidden zone between the old and new blocks.

At Christmas, their cosy relationship was publicly displayed as a result of some fortuitous casting in the school nativity play. Chris Lukes had already secured what he assumed was the plum part - narrating the play from the sidelines in his finest reading voice. He hardly expected to be upstaged, least of all by Steven Morrissey, who had been cast as dull, old Joseph. During rehearsals, however, Morrissey, astonished the class by his capacity to *ad lib*. While Kathleen Geoghan luxuriated in her role as Joseph's pregnant, virgin wife Mary, Morrissey fawned over her with such amusingly-inappropriate lines as, "Sit down, love, and put your feet up!" It was Morrissey's peculiar achievement to transform the nativity play with naturalistic dialogue more suited to a kitchen-sink drama. On the day of the performance, he was relaxed and confident enough to repeat his rehearsal triumph and charmed the audience with his unselfconscious paternal kindheartedness. As Lukes acknowledged: "He was very good, very funny, and I felt a bit envious because I had to read from a set text."

At the end of term the class was allowed to bring in records and enjoy a supervised afternoon disco in the school hall. On the 166 bus, Lukes and Morrissey agreed to select their favourites and the results were predictably contrasting. Heavily influenced by his elder brother's tastes, Lukes came armed with a cache of Motown and Stax classics. He even had the audacity to play Max Romeo's risque 'Wet Dream', which caused considerable comment among the more knowledgeable boys. Morrissey, meanwhile, contributed a baffling assortment of singles by Twinkle, Sandie Shaw and his favourite of the moment - Susan Maughan's 1962 hit, 'Bobby's Girl'. "I assumed that came from Jackie," observed Lukes, forgetting that Morrissey's sister would only have been five at the time of the disc's original release. Even in 1970, Morrissey's tastes were eclectic and traversed into his parents' era with no sense of incongruity. His enjoyment of girl singers was constant, but he was aware that even Sandie Shaw had become unfashionable. By the end of the decade, her chart career seemed on the rocks. Her latest single, 'Heaven Knows I'm Missing Him Now' had flopped miserably, but Morrissey liked the title and would adapt it for his own use years later. His tastes were naturally most influenced by the charts, though he showed considerable interest in Lukes' Tamla/ soul collection, which included recordings by Fontella Bass and The Marvelettes. In the background, meanwhile, the disco blared out a haphazard selection of ska and pop, ranging from Desmond Dekker's 'The Israelites' and Harry J And The All Stars' 'The Liquidator' to Bob And Marcia's 'Young, Gifted And Black'. The dance class show-offs attempted elaborate back-flips in the hope of impressing the girls who studiously feigned disinterest. Morrissey observed, somewhat detached, hungrily assimilating what was to be the closing soundtrack of his happiest days.

The remainder of the school year was anti-climactic and passed in a whirl. The 11-plus, so important to the futures of all the children, crept up unnoticed and was taken under regrettable conditions. Denied the comfort of their own school building, the class was shipped *en masse* to the imposing St Gregorys Grammar in Ardwick, where they spent two days in an unfamiliar environment answering questions that would determine their educational future. The unlucky few who lived outside the catchment area were forced to sit the examination with strangers from other schools. The final results were an all too familiar indictment of the tripartite educational system. Only three St Wilfreds pupils from the class of 1970 passed the 11-plus: Steve Smythe, Chris Lukes and Sarah Stapleton. While they headed for St Gregorys, Stretford Grammar and St Josephs, the majority of the form enrolled at nearby St Ignatius.

Three of the boys, however, had a very different destination. For the next five years, Noel Devaney, Michael Roe and Steven Morrissey would be the guests of St Marys Secondary Modern in Stretford.

3

The Headmaster Ritual

STEVEN MORRISSEY WAS DOOMED before he even passed the gates of St Marys. Although no academic, he had at least left primary school with a healthy interest in reading, music, drama and writing stories. Remarkably, there was little or no outlet for any of these activities in his new school. Music and drama were not on the syllabus, no languages were taught and there was no librarian. Throughout his five-year stay, there was never a school concert, play, nor even a school magazine to display extra-curricular work. As one of his teachers curtly observed: "The school was dying on its feet while he was there!" For an adolescent like Morrissey, with vaguely cultural aspirations, the place of learning was a perverse anathema whose prevailing philistinism threatened to cudgel his artistic expression into a regimented stream of incoherent banality. He could hardly have encountered a worse institution and would later curse his school days with a venom unequalled by any songwriter of his generation.

The real target, however, was not the school or the teachers but the moribund system that had allowed St Marys to live on in its parlous, anachronistic state. The notion that a secondary modern, with all its inherent inequality, could still exist in the enlightened early Seventies was a terrible indictment of Trafford's political and egalitarian impotence. Worse still was the realization that, far from improving its teaching and pastoral facilities, St Marys seemed irretrievably locked on a reverse path towards the educational dark ages. Its best days remained in a recent past that most of the teachers recollected with a mixture of nostalgia, suppressed bitterness and defeated resignation.

During the early Fifties, St Marys had been a mixed institution that offered a watered-down grammar school curriculum, marginally weighted in favour of the arts. The tripartite system had ensured that the intellectual cream was whisked off to Stretford Grammar, but the teachers strove, with some success, to establish a stable, caring atmosphere. Although the staff was poorly qualified in many subjects, and university graduates were practically non-existent, they at least offered the virtues of consistency and continuity. Loyalty, or lack of prospects, ensured that staff changes were minimal and the organization of the school was far from unimpressive.

By the early Sixties, a modest number of pupils were leaving with O-level passes and could look back upon a tough but tolerable six years in which they had defied the academic odds stacked against them. The majority of the boys may have been heading for the construction trade but, even for them, the St Marys years contained some happy memories. The presence of girls in the school ensured that immature behaviour was less prevalent and provided a welcome social mix, as well as having a beneficial effect on classroom dynamics and academic standards. Many of the teachers seemed genuinely enthusiastic, and, drama lessons, school productions, choir practises and trips abroad were commonplace. "It was a thriving place and a nice atmosphere," recalled one teacher from the period.

An enduring testament to the lively contributions of the pupils at St Marys can be found in the school magazines of the era. A rare promotional photograph of The Beatles was included in the 1963 issue and the previous year the most significant British pop star of his day had sent a splendid portrait shot signed, "Best Wishes to St Marys, Stretford, from Cliff Richard". One can only imagine how profoundly enthused Morrissey would have been at the prospect of writing to his favourite stars, securing their autographs and having his pop theories expounded in print. That possibility, along with many more, was extinguished at the end of 1963, when the entire female population of the school was removed and transplanted to the newly-created Cardinal Vaughans Secondary Modern For Girls. "It was one of the worst things that ever happened," lamented Graham Pink, then head of English. Indeed, the evacuation of the girls irrevocably altered the atmosphere and ethos of the school, which never fully recovered.

The headmaster that emerged from the sex purge was Vincent Morgan, "an army officer and a gentleman", who was left with the unenviable task of leading his school into its next era. Demoralized staff were already leaving in droves as the full implications of the new St Marys brutally sank in. With the brightest pupils and the best teachers now gone, there was a rapid decline in academic attainment, a discernible increase in hooliganism and the introduction of draconian punishments to keep the new offenders in line. Suddenly, the ethos of St Marys became custodial rather than pastoral, and respect was measured less in educational aspirations than the ability to control and to instil fear.

By the end of the Sixties, the school urgently required an injection of ideas into every area of its organization, community and curriculum. Unfortunately, conflicting politics and general apathy conspired to suppress reform. "We always got the impression that the local authority and the diocese couldn't come to an agreement," observed the head of English, "so St Marys was left as it was. It was certainly in decline and nobody seemed interested. Parents weren't consulted. We had parents' evenings, but they were perfunctory. Some of the staff, and Vin Morgan himself, were not particularly interested in parents and didn't want to involve them. The idea was, 'We know best'. Although good teachers were there, a lot moved on because they lost heart or didn't feel they were getting anywhere."

Vin Morgan had watched powerlessly as the heart of his school had been mercilessly torn asunder by faceless officialdom. It had left him a disillusioned figure, content to freewheel until his retirement. He had always been conservative by nature and in his autumnal years lacked the dynamism to introduce the necessary reforms that St Marys so badly needed. Former colleague, Graham Pink, was not unsympathetic. "He'd been served a rotten deal by the local authority and, most likely, the Church," he opined. "You had to keep in with them to get anywhere. Even if he'd wanted to do things, he could have been overruled. That didn't help. Vin just ran out of steam and lost interest. Looking back, he should have taken more of an interest in individual teachers and been more decisive, but he wasn't."

Morrissey knew none of the above as he blithely donned his first school uniform and trudged expectantly towards St Marys. Even as he entered Renton Road, his name was being taken in vain by a gaggle of youths in the playground. If he had eavesdropped on the conversation, Morrissey might well have turned back to 384 Kings Road and demanded an immediate transfer.

Noel Devaney had arrived early that morning and was immediately collared by several elder boys demanding to know who else had made the transition from St Wilfreds. "Michael Roe and Steven Morrissey," Devaney replied, unhesitatingly. "Morrissey!" cried one of the St Wilfreds old boys, "you ought to hear the voice!" Noel clearly understood the jibe. "It was a very effeminate voice and his mannerisms were effeminate," he recalls. "He was girlish, but not gay or anything. People were making comments, but not directly to him. He wasn't one of the lads and anyone who wasn't had the piss taken out of them."

The ominous jest about Morrissey's uncracked choir boy voice might have made him a potential object of intimidation, but he was soon forgotten as other more amusing specimens tentatively stepped through the school gates. A lad misfortunately clad in short trousers stood out from the rest and received an unreassuring jeer before being saved from further humiliation by the school bell. The raggedly poor and nearly affluent were equally liable to be targeted. It was easy to spot those innocent first year victims, naïvely unaware of St Marys' terrible reputation. Their parents were often the type who took the uniform policy too literally and liberally decked out their offspring in a superfluous school cap, unaware that this was akin to brandishing a badge of courage. At the first opportunity, grabbing hands would wrench the offending item free and pass it round the playground while the confused newcomer, caught between fear of parental retribution and peer group rejection, scampered furiously in pursuit. School caps were always at a premium after the first day of term.

As the bell clanged, the new intake was herded towards the assembly hall and addressed by the man already mysteriously immortalized as "Jet" Morgan. This was to be their first glimpse of the 'Headmaster Ritual'. Initially, the guardian of St Marys cut an impressive figure - tall, erect, soberly dressed in an old-fashioned way, and coldly confident in his military precision. After a brief welcoming speech, he crashingly laid down the law. The school rules were exhaustively explained and each child was allotted to one of four houses, appropriately named after the suffering martyrs, Thomas More, John Fisher, Margaret Clitherow and Edward Ambrose Barlow. Morrissey's house was Clitherow, a title which he sacrilegiously associated with the miniature kid of British radio comedy, rather than the sixteenth-century Martyr of York, who had been savagely crushed to death by the Protestant powers for harbouring outlaw priests.

The St Marys house system revolved around a series of rewards and punishments, known as credits and conduct marks. These were dispensed in the form of tickets, and pupils soon came to dread a blue receipt, the corner of which contained a figure from one to six, indicating the number of strap lashes a malefactor must endure. Conduct marks were subsequently added to house totals and if the culprit registered more than three in a month he would receive an additional flogging.

Impressions of the awesome Mr Morgan were instantly formed and long lasting. For Morrissey's class-mate Mike Moore, he seemed a "taller version of Mr Mainwaring in *Dad's Army*, a bit pompous and aware of his power; he kept aloof, even from the other teachers". The academically-inclined James Verrechia had met Jet outside the school and found him very affable, but behind the walls of St Marys he appeared "very regimented, always ferocious and certainly had a sadistic streak. The strap was used to excess and people had bad bruises because he'd occasionally miss you and hit your wrist". The prank-loving Patrick Quinn, who "got it many times for giving cheek", at least managed to overcome Morgan's inept strapping technique by dropping his hand at the last second to ride the approaching blow. Others like Tubby Patterson and Pat Smith used the more traditional method of "rushing to the bogs" and thrusting their burning hands under hot water taps for several seconds to draw out the sting.

Morgan's military conservatism was manifested most revealingly in his concern over correct dress. Although St Marys was a downtrodden secondary modern, he felt that pupils might take a greater pride in the place if they emulated the smartness of their grammar school neighbours. Every morning, the eagle-eyed Jet would stand at the back of the assembly hall, diligently checking the traditional uniform: blue and white tie, white shirt, blue V-neck jumper, grey or black trousers and dark shoes. As the parade of pupils trooped by, conduct marks would be distributed and persistent offenders hauled off and strapped. The fallacy of Mr Morgan's system, however, was that it was hopelessly arbitrary. Instead of a general check on uniform, he selected a specimen garment of the day. Consequently, a smartly-dressed boy with off-colour shoes could be reprimanded, while another clad in jeans or denim-shirt would escape unnoticed. For Morrissey and his class-mates, the daily Headmaster Ritual summed up the peculiar methodology of a ferociously fastidious, yet strangely distant presence. "Jet seemed oblivious to what was really going on," Mike Moore recollected. "As long as he whipped his quota in the morning and during the day, he felt he was running the school. He walked around very erect, like a bank manager, and sometimes wore a fisherman's hat as if he were a country gentleman."

All things considered, Morrissey fared reasonably well during his first few days at school. Electing to go home at dinner time proved a sagacious move, saving him from a barbaric initiation ceremony in which first years were chased across the playground, tossed into the air and deposited into a sand pit. He also successfully avoided the formidable whistle-blowing Mrs Casey, a dinner lady whose fearsome reputation occasionally rivalled that of the teachers themselves. "She'd have done well in the Gestapo!" deadpanned Mike Roe.

Another lucky advantage that Morrissey had was his imposing height. During the final days at St Wilfreds he had grown surprisingly tall, in striking contrast to his small parents. The extra inches granted a temporary reprieve from scaremongering bullies, but how long would that last? Noel Devaney felt that Morrissey was easy meat for any would-be assassin: "He was tall, but weedy and unaggressive. Steve was never a fighter. Even small kids weren't frightened of him. He just wasn't confrontational." Fortunately, elder bullies were wary of intimidating anyone in Morrissey's year. With such powerful characters as Tommy Killeen, Paul Whiting, Tubby Patterson and Patrick Smith standing in the wings and likely to protect the tough reputation of "their year", it simply wasn't worth the bother. The important consideration was to avoid the excessive wrath of certain teachers and tread carefully in the presence of the "rum lads" in your class.

Ironically, it was not Morrissey but the solid Michael Roe who came closest to a premature contretemps. While standing in a queue, he involved himself in a playful fracas with "friend of the powerful" Frank Kelly, who was then nursing a sporting injury. As they mauled each other, Roe inadvertently kicked his opponent on his vulnerable leg, opening some recent stitches. Kelly was duly removed to sick bay, while Roe was escorted to Jet's office to receive a stern warning and salutary whipping. Later that day, he faced an additionally blood curdling moment when the hellhound Paul Whiting casually enquired: "Did you kick Frank in his stitches? Do *you* want some stitches?"

There is an unwritten law of adolescent school dynamics that inexplicably throws together improbable partnerships, yoking the glamorous and the gauche, the weak and the rugged, the oppressed and the oppressor in a strange David and Goliath union. For the first couple of years at St Marys, Morrissey found his ideal *alter ego* in the shape of Mike Foley, a popular but troublesome boy, whose irresistible esprit and arty rebellion balanced precariously between mischief and anarchy. While Morrissey was perceived as the class loner, Foley ran with the pack and numbered Whiting, Patterson and Smith among his confederates and fellow sufferers at the weary hands of the headmaster. For all that, he was not a thug and Morrissey found him surprisingly approachable and a touch glamorous. He was also interested in fashion and pop music, and seemed very open to new ideas.

Foley's patronage provided Morrissey with a magic talisman that warded off the unwelcome attention of school psychopaths. The survival kit was completed by the realization, among both pupils and staff, that Morrissey was a promising athlete. However, it was his size and ability, rather than application or commitment, that brought him some minor fame over the next two years. Hopeless at most team sports, Morrissey was surprisingly gifted at track and field events. He had clearly inherited his father's speed and dexterity, even though he lacked his work rate, warmth and camaraderie. The importance of sport at St Marys cannot be over-estimated, for the teacher in charge of Physical Education, Paul Sweeney, was unquestionably the most powerful and feared man in the school.

"Sweeney was a little Irishman who thought he was Bobby Charlton," explained Mike Roe. "He had a fearsome reputation and used to bark a lot." Every week, the class was obliged to run to the sports field, nearly a mile away, and the last person there received a humiliating treat from Sweeney. Ordered to bend down, the unfortunate pupil would wait in grim anticipation while Sweeney "volleyed a ball up their arse". If the entire class misbehaved, they would be herded into the gym and made to run round in circles while Sweeney practised his shooting skills on selected offenders. Jim Verrechia still recalls his and Morrissey's very first PE lesson at St Marys. After an arduous workout, Verrechia confronted his new master and asked, in all innocence, "Do all PE teachers have to be this tough, Mr Sweeney?" Sweeney simply stared at him and laughed. He appeared to be flattered by the cheeky question and thereafter looked chari-tably on Verrechia. "If you were good at something he'd look after you," recalls Jim, "but if you showed you weren't bothered he didn't take to you. He had a very aggressive attitude towards getting you fit!"

After the first shock had passed, however, most of the kids adapted them-selves to Sweeney's grim regime. Some, like Roe, even had vaguely fond memories of him during an otherwise horrendous punishment session. After administering the strap one afternoon, he seemed uncharacteristically apologetic and said: "Keep a grip on yourself, Mike."

"It was the only time I ever got called by my Christian name," recalls Roe.

Mike Foley and several cronies were also treated with inexplicable clemency after being caught smoking and, on a later occasion, drinking ille-gally in a pub. As the guilty party acknowledged: "I shit myself. I thought I'd get four of the best, but all he said was, 'If I catch you smoking again...', and we watched as he whacked the belt on his own hands, pretending he was giving us the strap. There were six other poor bastards outside waiting to get it and we had to come out and pretend our hands were burning."

Sweeney clearly had a soft spot for tough lads who showed spirit, and a symmetrical dislike for idlers, schemers and softies. Noel Devaney, who was none of these, still speaks with bitterness and contempt about the pre-vailing macho mentality. "Sweeney was bullish, there's no two ways about it," he feels. "If you didn't like PE he put even more fear into you for not doing it. If we were playing football and it was getting towards home time and he was enjoying the game, everybody had to play on into their own time. If someone hadn't dried themselves properly or ducked having a shower, he'd make them strip off; have them punished. You knew no different at the time."

Morrissey was not in the firing line then, although he later made a cameo appearance on the wall bars, hanging like Christ alongside the idlers, loafers and recalcitrants. His reputation as the "fastest runner in the class" naturally elicited Sweeney's attention, but Morrissey failed to find the empathy with the PE department that other less talented kids enjoyed.

Two weeks after the start of term, Jimi Hendrix was found dead, the victim of a drug overdose. Soon afterwards, the single 'Voodoo Chile' was issued at the ludicrously cheap price of six shillings, a special offer that propelled the disc to number one. At school, guitar wizard Jim Verrechia was already playing the song on an acoustic guitar and was well on the way to constructing his own electric model, much to the amazement of his contemporaries. "He shouldn't have been in that school," observed class-mate Mike Moore. Morrissey was aware of the guitar mahatma but found the discussion of echo chambers and wah wah pedals too technical for his liking. It would be several years before he viewed Verrechia in a more appealing light.

Throughout his first year at school, one of Morrissey's abiding interests was collecting comics. But while his fellow class-mates chose familiar titles in the Marvel/DC range, such as *The Fantastic Four* and *Justice League Of America*, Steven was obsessed with garish, British monster magazines. Copies still exist with the carefully written "Steven Morrissey aged 11 years" scrawled across the cover. The titles, *Movie Monsters* and *Quasimado's Monster Magazine* were appealingly low budget affairs, full of bloody gore, but laced with potted biographies of actors Boris Karloff, Peter Lorre and Peter Cushing, as well as dramatic re-creations of the *Frankenstein* and *Dr Jekyll And Mr Hyde* tales. Morrissey's modest, second-hand collection dated back to the mid-Sixties when Hammer Horror films played to packed audiences eager to witness Christopher Lee's latest regeneration as Count Dracula. The Hammer formula was wearing thin by the early Seventies, with desperate scriptwriters resurrecting the Transylvanian vampire so frequently that he had been chronologically transplanted to swinging London before ending his "lives" as a Seventies property magnate. Morrissey remained fascinated by the wealth of Hammer Horror history and enjoyed the rare opportunity to sample a daring 'X' certificate film.

Outside of school, he found a neighbourhood friend in Edward Messenger, a blond lad whose father had known Peter Morrissey since the end of the Fifties when they played in the Northumberland pub's football team. The boys occasionally camped in each other's gardens and usually cycled over to Chorlton on Saturday afternoon to watch a film. Morrissey's tastes were not restricted to horror; he had a considerable affection for British comedies, especially the long-running *Carry On* series. While in Chorlton, they visited the house of a mutual friend who owned an electric guitar. Although the visitors enjoyed plucking on the instrument, neither was dedicated enough to take guitar lessons. Morrissey seemed more interested in listening to records, although Messenger does recall him messing around with impromptu lyrics, just as he had done years before with 'We Four Stevens'. His passion for pop music did extend to keeping a scrapbook full of cut-out photographs, charts and other ephemera, while his record collection was impressively eccentric. One of the first singles he played to Messenger was 'My Old Man's A Dustman', the 1960 Lonnie Donegan hit that had entered the *NME* chart at number one.

The fact that Morrissey could enjoy songs recorded in his infancy was an endearing trait that led him to discover other pre-Beatles artistes, most notably Billy Fury. The fascination for Fury later encouraged Morrissey to investigate other Fifties singers from the celebrated Larry Parnes' "stable of stars". Remarkably, one of these, the hitless and unheralded Vince Eager, provided what Morrissey subsequently claimed to be his all-time favourite single: 'The World's Loneliest Man'.

Despite his mediocre ability as a football player, Morrissey had not yet abandoned Manchester United. He still attended the odd home match with his father and was on greeting terms with some junior players who lodged at the house next door. There were always wild rumours that the landlady had taken in an aspiring star and even Messenger was wrongly convinced that George Best had once lived there. The kids in the street delighted in this speculation and when the subject was exhausted, they could always thrill to Morrissey espousing his theory that 384 Kings Road was haunted by an eccentric ghost. For all his charm as a potential raconteur, Morrissey remained a shy, low-key figure, who avoided the rough and tumble of street life. Messenger remembers him as a loner, who spent a lot of time at home. In comparison to the wide boys that patrolled the nearby quadrant, he seemed blatantly misplaced. As Messenger vaguely concluded: "Steve was quite effeminate in some ways, more an effeminate child than a masculine boy. He kept himself to himself." Even as a pre-teen, Morrissey was experiencing the insidious way in which such attributes as sensitivity, refinement and reserve tended to be bludgeoned into opaque, restrictive and occasionally pejorative pigeon-holes like 'effeminate' and 'masculine'.

As was often the case with Morrissey, if an outing met with his considered approval, then he would be happy to attend. Once, a group of university students organized a trip to an abbey near Leicester which required a couple of nights' stay. Annette Messenger remembers her brother Edward, Steven and Jackie taking in the atmosphere, walking in the abbey grounds at night. It was certainly a pleasant break from the drudgery of St Marys, which Morrissey has repeatedly recollected in appropriately nightmarish imagery. "I seem to remember it every night..." he explained. "The horror of it cannot be overemphasized. Every single day was a nightmare, in every single way you could possibly want to imagine. Worse - the total hatred. The fear and anguish of waking up, of having to get dressed, having to walk down the road, having to walk into assembly, having to do those lessons."

Steven's second term looked likely to be worse than his first. Britain was on the move. Old institutions were collapsing. The government had banned LSD (in the monetary sense) and introduced decimilization; the venerable *Daily Sketch* had closed down; *Opportunity Knocks* was the most popular television show with 6.6 million viewers. For Morrissey, however, all this was eclipsed by one crucial fact: T Rex were the most popular group in the country. The wily Marc Bolan, after years of near misses, had autumnally reinvented himself as a Seventies pop star and the progenitor of glam rock. This corkscrew-haired pixie, adorned in bright sequins and tastefully applied mascara, had the songs, looks and attitude that a generation of impressionable, musically undernourished, teenage pop fans found over-whelming. They cared not a jot for his contradictory past as the hippie messiah of Tyrannosaurus Rex; they were content to accept his new incar-nation on his terms. Bolan's quirky but striking nasal delivery and exotic, flowery imagery had already taken 'Ride A White Swan' to number two and, early in 1971, he enjoyed a massive chart topper with the chugging rhythm of 'Hot Love'. The follow-up, 'Get It On', with its galloping riff, sold even more, prompting an outbreak of T Rex-mania that was to con-tinue at an intense level for the next couple of years. The new pop star accepted his godhead greedily, while immodestly observing: "I've sort of become a rock 'n' roll James Dean."

Morrissey was entranced by Bolan and even bought a satin jacket as an emblem of glam solidarity. At school, instead of copying work from the blackboard, he spent entire lessons sketching a portrait of Bolan into an exercise book. The consequences of such dangerous defiance apparently never occurred to him. Mike Moore watched, transfixed and confused, as Morrissey re-sketched that same picture over and over again. "He used to spend the whole day doing it," Moore recalls, "but it was always the same - just his face. I kept thinking, 'why the same picture?'"

Rude reality was seldom far away at St Marys and Morrissey was fre-quently shocked out of his artistic reverie by some act of violence or vandalism. "In all my life, I've never seen anything as violent as my school," he remembers. In the woodwork lesson, the incorrigible Patrick Smith had decided to democratize the class standard by cheapening the quality of Morrissey's fine work. Seizing a model boat that Steven had been working on, Smith feverishly planed down the hull until, to use Moore's parlance, "It was a piece of shit, you could snap it". At the same time, Smith maximized his own feeble effort by switching models with Jim Verrechia. The guitar-playing good boy knew better than to issue a complaint so made the best of an inherited botch job.

During the summer term, Morrissey faced the indignity of posing as a cricket player. The PE department was highly amused by his inability to hold the bat and looked on in defeated bemusement as he attempted to score runs using one hand. Rounders, rather than cricket, was obviously his forté. Despite sarcastic comments, he stubbornly retained his fly-swotting style of play for the remainder of his inauspicious cricketing career. Morrissey soon took pyrrhic revenge on his detractors by excelling during the annual sports day. As well as his running and jumping skills, he was a fine javelin thrower and Sweeney remarked favourably on his gymnastic and basketballing abilities. Unfortunately, such attention backfired when Morrissey was called upon to represent his school in competition. "I had a terrible time and would have to go to places very far away," he remembers. "I never wanted to do it, but if you were athletically capable you had to, otherwise you'd get beaten to death." Along with class-mate Pete Green, he was encouraged to take additional lessons, but, after attending a couple of sessions, his enthusiasm evaporated. As Mike Foley recalled, "It was a complete cock-up. He was asked to stay behind in the dinner hour and there was *no* chance of that." As the school year ended, Morrissey took his place among the promising but reluctant athletes who regarded PE as just another lesson. "I don't like anything that's enforced," Morrissey confided. "I always adored games but, because it was blindly compulsory, I went off the whole idea of athletics and movement."

The summer recess saw an escalation of troubles in the strife-torn province of Northern Ireland. On 11 August, a priest was shot dead by British soldiers while giving the last rites to a dying man. The following week, a deaf mute, who innocently ignored an order to halt, suffered the same fate. While 5,000 Catholics had their homes razed during four days of sickening violence, the insouciant British Prime Minister Edward Heath led his country to victory in the Admirals' Cup aboard his treasured yacht *Morning Cloud*. In Dublin, the Irish PM, Jack Lynch, decried the "deplorable poverty of Ulster's politics" and demanded the immediate abolition of Stormont. Meanwhile, 300 IRA supporters faced the brutality of internment without trial, prompting threats from the Provisionals to bomb the British mainland. This was Ulster's worst crisis since 1921, the inevitable legacy of 50 years of British indifference.

Morrissey momentarily looked set to escape the bloody news thanks to an incredible stroke of luck. After entering a local newspaper competition, he was staggered to learn that he had won a free holiday to Morocco, travelling via Spain and France. The prospect of trekking across the world while his class-mates were stuck at St Marys was an alluring one but, sadly, the fantasy remained unrealized. His parents could hardly allow their 12-year-old boy to saunter off to Morocco unattended, so the dream ticket lay unclaimed. Regrettably, Morrissey could not cash in his prize, which must have proven one of the biggest frustrations of his life. Rather than exotic travel, he had to sit through tedious geography lessons, painfully listening to descriptions of all the places he might have visited. The teacher, Mr Barry, whose obvious hobby was woodwork, saw himself as the class entertainer and enjoyed ribbing his pupils. On one occasion, he casually quizzed Morrissey about a class absentee and was told. "He's gone home sir, he's got a bloody nose." Barry theatrically rose from his seat and announced: "We'll have no language like that in my class, Morrissey." Steven blushed quietly. As Mike Roe noted: "Morrissey would walk into it every time."

What passed as humour at St Marys usually tended towards the gross, rather than the subtle. One afternoon, several lads found themselves trapped in an empty classroom where they'd hidden for a sly smoke. Unable to emerge for some time due to a patrolling teacher, one of them defecated copiously into a desk. Another repeated the action and then attempted to set his shit alight using paper. Since the classroom doubled as a storeroom and was hardly used, the dirty deed lay undetected for many hours, and the stench inside grew overwhelming. One of Morrissey's occasional jobs was to distribute the bibles during religious lessons and it was on that defecating day that he was instructed to enter the stinking store-room. Seconds later, he reeled out in nauseous horror, simply uttering, "I can't!" The teacher, a former amateur boxer from Northern Ireland, became increasingly impatient with the delay and ordered Morrissey back into the breach. Understandably, Steven remained rooted to the spot. The fiasco ended with the shock-still Morrissey observing a torrent of blows whisk lightning-like around his head as his teacher provided the class with a play-ful exhibition of shadow boxing. Everybody laughed at Morrissey's humiliation but the giggles ceased when the pugilistic pedagogue hastily re-emerged, ashen-faced and furious. Jet Morgan, needless to say, was not amused.

Mid-week on the nearby playing fields the boys kept in shape. One cold winter, an unfortunate lad named Joe McGuire caught pneumonia after a games lesson and was placed on the critical list in hospital. As Patrick Quinn recalled: "We were asked to say prayers for him in assembly. He went into a coma and nearly died, but pulled through."

The competitive spirit, so lackadaisical in most subjects at St Marys, was intense on the sports field. The PE masters, Sweeney and Kijowsky, liked to "put on a tough show" and played football as though they were members of a rugged First Division side, desperately attempting to avoid relegation. Hard tackling and gamesmanship were par for the course, not to mention some shirt-pulling and a salutary warning for any flash Harry who dared upstage them. Anyone who argued the toss risked the additional likelihood of being sent off, which normally ensured that teacher's team would win.

In the competitive stakes, the generally easier-going Kijowsky was more than a match for his senior partner Sweeney. As Mike Roe observed: "Kijowsky didn't like being beaten when he participated in a sport. He couldn't bear one of his pupils getting the better of him." That attitude was manifested in PE lessons during which the kids were sometimes required to race around the school on a route past the bicycle sheds and through the playground. Kijowsky enjoyed stage-managing his entry to the race, usually appearing on the final lap so that he could gee up the lads and lead the team towards the finishing line like a gold medal-winning athlete. Although the leading pack of runners were already knackered, Morrissey occasionally spoiled Kijowsky's glorious finale with a devastating, heart-pounding victory sprint. "My *raison d'être* was the 100 metres" was a Morrissey boast not without justification.

In many respects, the PE department was a product of the all-male envi-ronment of the school which encouraged firmness and the constant need for order. Regimented role-playing was part of the process and the PE masters were victims as well as celebrants of the sergeant major syndrome.

Although Sweeney was the teacher that the kids feared most, Kijowsky also had a fierce temper which it was unwise to provoke. "Kijowsky was all smiles and everybody's pal," Mike Roe stresses, "but he could lose his rag over a comparatively little incident." Morrissey's class witnessed the darker side of Kijowsky during an otherwise uneventful English lesson. He was in the playground overseeing a fourth year five-a-side football match and clearly enjoying the game. One bright spark at a desk near Morrissey observed him from the window and wailed in a high-pitched soprano voice: "K-i-j-o-w-s-k-y". The PE teacher was stung to the quick by the impertinent but relatively innocuous jibe and wasted no time in reaching the pre-fabricated buildings where he confronted the now petrified class with a dramatic flourish. Mike Roe recalls the highlights: "He nearly smashed down the classroom door when he came thundering in. His face was purple with rage and he practically ordered this bloke out." As Roe and class-mate Chris Power remember, his wrath first fell on the innocent Ricky Zietek, who received a furious interrogation before being released. Eventually, the culprit was unmasked and duly led away, no doubt partly relieved that Kijowsky's indignant anger had now subsided. "The kid was a bit of an idiot," Roe concluded, "but all he did was shout out of a window. Compared to Sweeney, Kijowsky was supposed to be all smiles, but I'll never forget that one incident. The *rage* - you could feel the anger coming out of him. It was a particularly frightening moment." After that episode, Morrissey's year realized that it was not wise to ridicule Kijowsky, especially in front of other pupils. Like Sweeney, he could play the hard man when roused.

The St Marys blues were always alleviated by the release of a new T Rex record and at the end of January 1972, Morrissey was singing the praises of 'Telegram Sam'. Noel Devaney brushed past him in a science lesson and a page fell on the floor with the lyrics of the song carefully written out in that familiar, child-like printed style. T Rex were soon displaced at number one by Chicory Tip's 'Son Of My Father', complete with gimmicky synthesizer backing. Morrissey, to his surprise, rather enjoyed its ephemeral charm.

A more serious song to hit the charts that month was Wings' 'Give Ireland Back To The Irish', which cast Paul McCartney in the unusual role of a controversial political commentator. In the inflammatory climate of the period, his sentiments were deadly appropriate. The infamous Bloody Sunday killings, in which British paratroopers opened fire on civil rights' demonstrators killing 13 and injuring a further 17, had just caused a public outcry in Ireland. Even in peaceful Dublin, there were demonstrations and the British Embassy was burned down. Normally cautious politicians spoke with shame of "mass murder by the British Army" and demanded a full enquiry. The IRA announced its own solution in a chilling call to arms "to kill as many British soldiers as possible". The Prime Minister Edward Heath was crumbling under the weight of an impending national crisis and on 9 February declared a State of Emergency. After 20 days of power cuts and blackouts, England returned to a semblance of order and Heath turned his attention to the troubles in Northern Ireland. By the end of March, he felt obliged to intervene and imposed direct rule at Stormont, much to the disapprobation of hard-line Protestants.

Back at St Marys, the Ulster debate was less concerned with politics than a semantic point regarding 'Give Ireland Back To The Irish'. Morrissey was conducting a pop quiz at the back of the class with "the waifs and strays of the year" and kept suffering interruptions from Mike Moore who seemed intent on disrupting the proceedings by answering all the questions. Suddenly, an argument erupted when Moore insisted that Wings was not the name of McCartney's group but the new record label for whom he recorded. Morrissey rightly took the opposite point of view but the discussion raged for almost 30 minutes, with Steven becoming increasingly fractious at Moore's obdurate insistence that he was right. One can only imagine how long the verbal sparring would have lasted if the subject had been his beloved Marc Bolan.

Morrissey's adoration of T Rex reached its apogee at the Belle Vue, Kings Hall where he fulfilled his ambition of seeing them play in concert. Having already rejected school lessons in favour of Marc Bolan sketching and lyric transcription, it was not entirely surprising that Morrissey absconded on certain afternoons. Unlike the hard-core truants, however, his disappearances were not frequent and appeared to coincide with key concerts in the area. At this point, he still had a cordial relationship with his father who would often pick him up after a gig in his blue Ford Cortina. Morrissey's entire family appeared to be the envy of those class-mates who had seen them. For Mike Foley, they were "20 years ahead of their time" and seemed refreshingly willing to "let their kids get on with life and do what they wanted". There was a closeness and intimacy about the family which Foley observed and envied. On several occasions he met Morrissey's parents socially and found them stimulating company. "You'd have a great time with them, it was like going out with a mate and his girlfriend."

The youthfulness of Morrissey's parents was a constant refrain among his contemporaries. Although she was now 35, Betty Morrissey was still attractive, even to her son's school friends. As Foley reminisces: "The mother wasn't working then, and she always seemed like a bloody model!" Even her sister-in-law Patricia Corrigan noted: "Betty was very ladylike and quiet." Not surprisingly, some neighbours saw these traits as evidence of aloofness and privately dismissed the elegant blonde-tressed Irish woman as "hoity-toity". Morrissey always betrayed a strong filial affection for his mother, which even his class-mates noted. Mike Ellis still recalls the first time he saw Mrs Morrissey. "We were 13 and sitting out on the grass when she walked by," he remembers. "Steve walked right up to her and he gave her a kiss on the lips. That was really unusual. It was a sign of affection that kids of that age just don't do. The last person you want to kiss is your mother, especially in front of your mates. But she was more like an elder brother's girlfriend." After Elizabeth walked away, the lads gathered round Morrissey and asked in erotic amazement, "Who was *that*?"

If Morrissey's mother caused a minor sensation then that was nothing compared to the emotional flutterings unconsciously wrought by his sister. Since primary school days, she had been an unattainable object of desire for several boys in the area. Chris Lukes had secretly fancied her during the St Wilfreds period and there were many more admirers now that she was a developing teenager. Mike Roe was overflowing with leeringly lascivious eulogies and remembers watching her with his friends and commenting explicitly on her sexiness. The effect of all this on Morrissey is debatable, but he cannot have been unaware that his family were regarded as attractive. With a strikingly youthful mother, a beautiful sister and a universally popular father, who still played football at 37, there was more than a shade of reflected glamour to reassure the boy of his own worth. Yet, just as he had failed to emulate his father's cheerful personality, so he denied the evidence of any inherited good looks from either side of his family. As he advanced in his teenage years, the words "good-looking" were frequently applied to Morrissey by former friends and associates, yet he seemed oblivious or unconvinced by such sentiments. His self-image was that of an "awkward, ugly, gawky individual" and although there were moments of vanity and private grandeur, the shy, effacing persona remained his public face for many years.

It would be crass to speculate on his unconscious motivations, but one episode from this time is fruitfully symbolic. Morrissey briefly went through a period of sleep-walking and one night entered Jackie's bedroom clutching a pair of scissors. Moving across to her bed, he cut up some posters of George Best with which she had decorated the wall. It was an isolated incident, tantalizingly open to all sorts of interpretations. Was Morrissey subconsciously jealous of his sister's admiration for George Best? Was the laceration of the pictures an unconscious stab at his football-playing father, whom so many claim resembled Best at the time? Could Morrissey have been reacting against fan mania of all kinds by attacking Manchester's most celebrated idol? Or was he unwittingly striking out against Sweeney and Kijowsky by defacing a grand symbol of sporting achievement? All these theories can make plausible reading with the very important proviso that none or all of them may apply. An Albert Goldman would probably base an entire Oedipal history around this moment, dragging in Morrissey's unusual closeness to his mother and his subsequent conflict with his father, while later throwing in androgyny, celibacy and a Moors murder "fixation" to produce a harrowing portrait of a soul-tormented monster. However, such reductive psychology would do Morrissey as much a disservice as the pre-packaged portrayal of John Lennon as a murderous, mother-loving misogynist. Morrissey certainly did have a troubled adolescence which contributed significantly to the strange pop being he became, but there were many more influences, films, records and books, all of which helped create the myriad and occasionally contradictory figure that so brilliantly illuminated the music press of the Eighties.

Even while his Bolan obsession intensified, Morrissey found a space in his pop firmament for another aspiring star, David Bowie. The key date was 22 January 1972. On that day, *Melody Maker* ran an extraordinary interview, conducted by Michael Watts, in which Bowie announced: "I'm gay and always have been." The piece was full of innuendo, but brilliantly captured the sexual ambiguity that Bowie was deliberately nurturing. Glam rock was now increasingly synonymous with androgyny and thereby gained the power to shock. Morrissey felt immediate kinship with the new breed of pop star, whose outlandish costume, pancake make-up and dyed hair seemed as important a statement as the music they played. In a brave but outrageously premature display of solidarity he arrived in school one morning with his hair streaked blond. According to Morrissey, he was summarily sent home, though his class-mates have no recollection of this. However, Chris Power does recall Morrissey's amusing attempt to disguise the controversial gold streak by re-dyeing the offending locks black. The hair colouring episode may have had a secondary cause, as Mike Ellis speculates: "The day of the blond flash was also the first time I ever saw him wear spectacles. He was quite self-conscious about glasses then."*

Although hair-tinting seemed like a suicidally defiant gesture in the authoritarian context of St Marys, it was typical of Jet Morgan's rigidity that such an extreme action virtually transcended the rule book. Strict daily uniform checks continued, even while several of the more adventurous pupils experimented with confrontational hair styles. Mike Ellis sported highlights, another lad was bleached blond, and a couple of the tougher kids shaved their heads bald. In such colourful company, Morrissey's forays into glam rock usually went unchallenged. "Steve was still into Bolan and always looked as though he had some type of foundation on," recalled Ellis, who also remembers other kids occasionally wearing a smidgen of glitter and competing among themselves to discover who could wear the tallest platform shoes.

Sweeney's reaction to the glam rock explosion is unrecorded, but it did not interfere with his selections for the annual summer sports day. Morrissey and Foley were chosen to represent Clitherow and their long legs were enough to secure the second year honours. "We were more or less forced into it," recalls Foley. "It didn't seem to matter and it soon faded out for both of us."

Performances in the school examinations that year also betrayed an air of the lacklustre. Foley, Moore and others were already skipping school. Even Morrissey had taken afternoons off to prepare for evening gigs, and wasted many other lessons sketching Marc Bolan. Not surprisingly, his artwork improved considerably and he could still give Jim Verrechia a close run in the English examination. The history result, however, was a little disappointing despite Morrissey's extensive script. The teacher, Mr Scott, was sufficiently amused by Morrissey's paper to read a lengthy extract to the class detailing the mythical life of Oliver Cromwell. As Mike Moore remembers: "It was brilliant, but it had sod all to do with Cromwell."

As the school year ended, Alice Cooper was heading towards number one with the controversial 'School's Out'. Morrissey enjoyed the mock horror Cooper spectacle, with its cavalcade of dead babies, live snakes and gory decapitation. It was not difficult to support the sentiments of a visiting American whose subversive chart topper was implicitly inciting children to blow St Marys to pieces.

Over the summer, Morrissey unexpectedly discovered new heroes in the form of the recently resurrected Mott The Hoople. After years struggling around the college circuit, Mott had wearily concluded their career on an

* Morrissey later recalled the hair-dyeing incident in 'I Know Very Well How I Got My Name'.

anti-climactic note before fairy godfather David Bowie intervened with a much needed overhaul. He presented them with an irresistible chart single, assumed production duties and placed them in the hands of his forceful manager Tony De Fries. By the time Morrissey returned to school they were in the Top Three with 'All The Young Dudes', a tale about a boy who dresses like a queen and contemplates suicide while listening to T Rex. The theme of the song was dear to Morrissey's heart and the fact that Mott had name dropped his favourite group was taken as a personal compliment. He wasted no time in joining the Mott The Hoople fan club and remained a devoted adherent until their demise at the end of 1974.

"People who liked Bowie, Mott The Hoople and Lou Reed tended to be more passive and easily picked on," Morrissey recalled. There was certainly a degree of glam rivalry at school with the more aggressive contingent favouring the working-class stomp of Slade to the blatant androgyny of Bowie and his imitators. Fortunately, Mike Foley's emergence as a Ziggy Stardust enthusiast ensured that Morrissey was in good company and he neatly sidestepped the glam rock wars. During the autumn term, Morrissey and Foley attended several gigs and witnessed the latest pop sensation, Roxy Music. Heavily made-up, Steve and Mike haunted the backstage door and actually caught a glimpse of Brian Eno's garishly-coloured sequined cape. In the hope of seeing more, they made their way to the Midland Hotel but it was to prove a rash move. With their distinguishable make-up, and Foley's twin ear-rings, they soon attracted the attention of some boorish football supporters. Foley recalls the fracas on the steps of the Midland with a retrospective smile. "These geezers came up and one of them was having a go at me," he recalls. "I wouldn't take any shit. Steve just flew through the door of the Midland. He made sure he got away from those bloody queer bashers, or whatever they were." Fortunately, Foley escaped unscathed but the incident was a reminder to Morrissey that his glam friend could attract as well as repel danger.

Although Morrissey had subjugated school work in favour of pop music, he was still an avid reader with more than a passing interest in English Literature. The head of English at St Marys was Graham Pink, a former male nurse who had been at the school for nearly two decades. "He was an out and out eccentric," recalls Noel Devaney. "He used to try and teach people!". Pink cut a dashing figure with his cravat and refined voice, and the pupils liked to fabricate outrageous stories about his private life for their own amusement. Although he was the unwitting butt of class in-jokes, Pink nevertheless commanded respect. As Mike Roe explained: "He was well-spoken, but also a little street-wise and not a stuffed shirt. He knew how to handle the rough edge without being overtly threatening or violent." Devaney concurred: "Pink had fear. No one could mess about with him. That was his manner."

Like many teachers at St Marys, Pink was hampered by the prevailing conditions and lamented the lack of library facilities. "It was a sad state of affairs," he remembers. "We never had a librarian, and a school needs that." Pink had his own class library, but it was a poor substitute, in spite of his undoubted enthusiasm. Introducing his charges to literature was apparently Pink's priority. "He revelled in reading rather than setting compositions," Jim Verrechia noted. Like Morrissey, Pink had an abiding interest in the working-class literature of the Fifties and ensured that the standard syllabus-dominated reading list included a mix of familiar classics and modern works. Among the books covered during his lessons were *Lord Of The Flies, Cider With Rosie, The Old Man And The Sea, The Long And The Short And The Tall, Call Of The Wild, Billy Liar* and *A Kestrel For A Knave*. Pink also had a fondness for radio drama and occasionally used scripts from the police series *Z Cars*. Pupils were amused and amazed to read bracing texts in which such words as "bastard" and "bollocks" were liberally quoted in front of the class. Pink was equally permissive in allowing boys to express themselves saltily in their own writing. "I'd say, 'If you want to use obscenities it's all right as long as they're in inverted commas, but don't over-use them!'"

With his penchant for radio broadcasts, it was not entirely surprising that Pink included *Under Milk Wood* (a play for voices) in his catalogue of favoured texts. He even arranged a visit to the cinema so that the class could witness the cast of Richard Burton, Elizabeth Taylor and Peter O'Toole bringing the play to life. It proved a cultural eye-opener in more ways than one. Michael Roe vividly remembers the excursion, which was less memorable for the power of Dylan Thomas's poetry than the closing scene in which Mae Rose Cottage draws lipstick circles round her nipples. "It was the first pair of tits I ever saw on the screen," Roe boasted with philistine pride.

Apart from failing to derail Roe's lascivious fantasies, Pink feels that he may have missed the chance to inspire Morrissey's theatrical bent. "I spent a lot of time in scouting and helped produce gang shows written by Ralph Reader involving about 90 people. Morrissey might have been good at that". Alas, Steven's remote opportunity to star as a Boy Scout was suppressed by the steely hand of the headmaster, who would not hear of a Pink produced gang show. "It was sad really," remembers Pink, a view with which many Morrissey watchers would no doubt wholeheartedly concur.

Morrissey's frustrated thespian abilities, which had remained dormant since the 1969 St Wilfreds Nativity Play, found a new outlet in impromptu scriptwriting. "He was stone mad on *Coronation Street*," recalls Mike Moore, and this enthusiasm provoked a brief correspondence with the series' producer Lesley Duxbury. Although Duxbury has no recollection of Morrissey's missives, the dreamy dramatist claims to have concocted several unlikely scenarios for the series, including the installation of a juke-box at the Rovers Return. At school, the theatrical flirtation took on more concrete form when Morrissey somehow wheedled permission to rehearse a projected play. "It was like a Sixties kitchen-sink drama set in a terraced house similar to *Coronation Street*," recalls Mike Moore. For several days, bemused onlookers watched as Morrissey and the short-trousered Maurice Clarke pulled tables and chairs together and quietly rehearsed a scene. "I think Morrissey played the mother," suggests Moore. "It was top drawer." Like so many other projects in Morrissey's life, the play failed to progress beyond the early scriptwriting stage and was soon forgotten. In some respects, it was surprising that the idea reached even that far.

The possibility of cultural dilly-dallying was rendered redundant for a while due to another outbreak of unspeakable grossness. A teachers' strike had resulted in a curtailed timetable, with staff refusing to cover for absent colleagues as part of their industrial action. As a result, pupils in Morrissey's year found themselves with a number of free periods during which they were obliged to loiter aimlessly in the assembly hall. It was an obvious recipe for mischief. One wily wag suggested, in all seriousness, that it might be a good idea if they plotted the disruption of the following morning's assembly. The focus of attention soon switched to Mr Thomas and his piano. Thomas was the history teacher and the man Mike Foley ruefully regarded as the hardest strapper among the staff. His pride and joy was playing the piano and leading the assembly for the daily hymn. Eyes gleamed among the conspirators as a convoy of lads began to fill the precious piano with paper and bucketfuls of sand from the school sandpit. As Patrick Quinn recalled: "We were bored and decided to have a laugh in assembly, so we completely blocked up that piano." Foley punctuated the outrage by shitting into a fire bucket and afterwards adding his contemptuous rear outpourings to the unholy cause. Characteristically, Morrissey was not among the fray, as Quinn confirmed: "He wasn't one of the lads that took part but he sat there and watched them participate." Remarkably, the piano prank remained undetected for the entire day, while rumours of Foley's dirty protest spread like quicksilver contagion across the playground and through every classroom door.

The following morning, there was an eerie sense of expectancy at assembly as the school waited for the headmaster to commence the ritualistic song of praise. The tonal splutterings and rapid silence that left Thomas perplexed and embarrassed have since become key images in St Marys mythology. For Mike Moore, however, it was the reaction of Vin Morgan that proved more revealing. "Jet stood at the centre of the stage, swinging his arms to lead the piano in tempo," he recalls. "The piano went dum dum and then died. All the school was still singing because if Jet saw you stop he might take you out and whip you. Meanwhile, Mr Thomas was walking up behind Jet. As the 'music' was reaching a crescendo, Jet was in full swing and accidentally hit Mr Thomas in the face. When he looked round there was anger in Jet's face because Thomas wasn't in the position he should have been. Morgan was totally oblivious to the fact that there'd been no music coming from that piano. This man lived in his own world."

After the teachers investigated the sabotaged piano, dire consequences were promised for the vandals. Their identity did not remain secret for long. Foley still recalls with bitterness how he was "grassed-up" by another pupil and had to face the wrath of his mother, who was required to contribute to the cost of repairing and cleaning the instrument. "It was a lot of money," he reminisced, with the air of a reformed anarchist.

Foley's anti-heroic protest far from discouraged Morrissey's friendship and they continued to attend gigs together. Morrissey also met a girl named Angie, whom he accompanied to several shows and spent much time talking to on the telephone. "We were inseparable friends and shared a lot of secrets," Morrissey explained. Steven also befriended class-mate Mike Ellis, whom he converted to Bowie after lending him *The Rise And Fall Of Ziggy Stardust And The Spiders From Mars*. As an additional reward for his glam rock allegiance, Ellis was pleased to receive a cracked copy of the 1969 Philips pressing of 'Space Oddity'. Morrissey's fascination with pop music was now in its highest ascendant. "I listened to my records and had the impression of *knowing* the singer, of knowing everything about his feelings and every detail of his life," he explained.

The early summer of 1973 was a happy month for Morrissey's small pack of Bowie-fixated friends. On 7 June, four days after Gary Glitter's visit to Manchester's Hardrock, Bowie appeared at the Free Trade Hall. It was a momentous occasion for, one month later, the moonage daydreamer would announce his retirement from live performance to a stunned audience at London's Hammersmith Odeon. The preparations for seeing Ziggy Stardust were thorough, and both Morrissey and Foley decided, somewhat unwisely, to invest in an image change. Armed with a recent photograph of their mentor, they visited a local hairdresser who valiantly, but unsuccessfully, attempted to duplicate the elaborate Bowie cut. Mike Moore was especially critical of the results. "Whoever did it made a total balls-up," he recalled. "Mick Foley ended up looking like Frankenstein." It was many weeks before an approximation of the Ziggy style finally emerged. On the night of the Bowie gig, the St Marys concert-goers enacted the lyrics of 'Rebel Rebel' and "got their mothers in a whirl". "We got all painted-up and the old lady had a bloody fit," smirked Foley.

Morrissey maintained his sartorial individuality on the streets of Stretford. Edward Messenger recalls his neighbour wearing a voguish star jumper and flared trousers, with a blinding ankle star sewn on the hem. Morrissey's concern about attracting taunts from anti-glam fans was evidently minimal. One evening he accompanied a friend to the Quadrant pub dressed like a prospective candidate for Chicory Tip. The steely duo arrogantly withstood the intimidating stares of affronted beer-supping bikers. At school, Morrissey seemed equally unconcerned about the opinions of others and saw nothing untoward about sporting a Levi handbag, manufactured from the backside of a pair of jeans. "Steve had more bottle than a lot of the lads," explained Moore. "We could all look after ourselves, but even the hard lads wouldn't have had the nerve to do that. Morrissey seemed oblivious to school. He lived in a Walter Mitty world and wasn't with you." Even Mr Pink offered a similar viewpoint. "Steven was very retiring," he remembers. "If someone has a quiet nature and doesn't push himself forward, he can just get forgotten about. He could be there and you wouldn't know because you'd spent your time sitting on the loudmouths. We had some outgoing people grabbing the limelight and my feeling was that Steven was very happy to fade into the background."

Morrissey's selected friendships and deliberate distancing from the central activity of school life enabled him to transcend petty playground squabbles and inter-group rivalry. Moore interpreted his aloofness as both an expression of individuality and a means of survival. "He got kicked up the arse a few times because of that bag," he recalls, "but not a lot. He was never bullied. They said he spoke with a feminine voice, but maybe he just had less of an accent than the rest of us. He wasn't geared up for the atmosphere at St Marys, so he lived inside his shell. He existed and could walk about the school, but he wasn't with you. There were others who lived inside their heads, but nobody to touch him. We were first generation Irish, all from strong Catholic backgrounds, all in culture shock. We knew the macho world of Irish pubs. Most of our fathers worked in the building trade. You were told all the time that you were *men*. You've got this fellow wandering around with you and he seems feminine. It was a bit bewildering. When somebody didn't act the accepted norm, it set them apart. Steve Morrissey set himself apart from the word go."

In rejecting the stereotypical masculine mentality of St Marys, Morrissey was inevitably assuming the mantle of the outsider. "I was quite isolated... it was very aggressive," he confessed. "People say school days are the happiest time of your life but I never believed it." Even the few teachers who were culturally biased in favour of the artistic or aesthetic adolescent seemed subdued by the authoritarian zeal demanded by St Marys. The absence of drama and the limited outlet for any form of literary or cultural expression moulded the boys in a very streamlined fashion. "I thought school would be synonymous with education," Morrissey complained, "but, in fact, it was an education in reverse."

Graham Pink bemoaned the process which appeared to place heroism on the playing fields before less definable successes in personal or cultural development. "It was a macho atmosphere, especially with all boys," he remembers. "They felt they had to prove themselves. You had this masculine thing, which I didn't think was a good idea at all. There was a lot of crudity and roughness, and games were terribly important. Games and PE were always far too important and the people running them were hard characters. There was a lot of stress put on those areas and if you didn't play games you were, most likely, a cissy. That was sad because the most sensitive ones, whom I possibly felt more attracted towards (to help them in some way) were made to feel inadequate."

After all the glam rock shenanigans, scripts to *Coronation Street* and non-existent theatrical productions, the school year ended, as it always did, with a much-heralded sports day. As tradition dictated, Morrissey took his place on the imaginary rostrum for his customary gold medal, beating Ashley Henry and Pat Quinn in the finals of the long jump.

By his own admission, Morrissey seldom had holiday outings during his school breaks. He had not visited Dublin since his first year and thereafter vacations were at a premium. One notable exception, however, was a weekend camping holiday in Abersoch, North Wales, with Jim Verrechia and his parents. Despite his evident isolation at St Marys, Morrissey did have a sprinkling of friends whose company he would filter through when the whim took him. For Verrechia, he was "the person who impressed by talking about music". As a budding guitarist, Jim responded enthusiastically to Morrissey's pop rhetoric and even visited his house on several occasions. Their weekend camping jaunt, however, was not exactly fun-filled. "We stuck Steve in a tent," Verrechia recalls, "and the next morning when we fished him out he looked the worse for wear. He hadn't slept well. I think he enjoyed the break, but he was very quiet and a little morose. There were periods when he was very difficult to talk to and that weekend was one of those."

As the St Marys lads returned to school to begin their fourth year, the critic/writer JRR Tolkien passed away, poet WH Auden was close to death and Donny Osmond was number one in the charts with 'Young Love'. The latter said little to Morrissey about his life but held some nostalgic relevance to his parents - it had previously reached the top, in a version by Tab Hunter, on the day that they were married.

Young love in 1973 was usually to be discovered in the intimidating artifice of the Village discotheque, a venue that Morrissey pointedly spurned in favour of the solitude of his bedroom. Despite a reputation for shyness, he could still surprise colleagues by his remarkable and easy rapport with the opposite sex. One evening, he and the womanizing Mike Foley approached three girls and the entire troupe whizzed off to a house in Cheetham. Foley harboured ludicrous sexual dreams of saturnalian proportions, but was soon brought down to earth by Morrissey's homeliness. "All he wanted to do was talk, all I wanted to do was get their drawers off," he explained. "That was another thing I could never suss out about him. He could have had the pick of the women. He always had the chat." At the concerts they attended, Foley was often surprised to see Morrissey chatting-up a stunning girl, only to take the matter no further when the evening ended.

Although there are some who feel that Foley had a strong influence over Morrissey during this period, Mike feels that this was far from the truth. "Morrissey didn't hang on to me at all," he admitted. "If he didn't want to talk to somebody, then he didn't. He was very choosy about who he spoke to."

Foley and Moore discovered how private Morrissey could be when they turned up at his house one afternoon unannounced and he refused them entry. The door was kept nervously ajar as Morrissey intoned, "I'll see you back at school." Moore was amused by this unsociable welcome. "It was like he had a dead body behind the door," he recalled, "as if there was something he didn't want you to know about." Always his own person, Morrissey retained only superficial links with most of his school friends and by the fourth year he and Foley had drifted apart socially. Foley's wild escapades were becoming far too dangerous for anyone not blessed with a desire for violent self-destruction. At one stage, he was thrown from a speeding bus and ripped open his back; later, while riding a bike, he fell down a manhole and broke his collar bone.

Such excitement contrasted sharply with Morrissey's lifestyle which was increasingly veering towards the cerebral. Most of his leisure hours were spent listening to records or light reading, which is where the Oscar Wilde influence first surfaced. Morrissey remembers his mother introducing him to the Victorian wit's minor poetry, but it was not until his mid/late teens that the bard's aestheticism captured his imagination. School provided no outlet for such interests, besides which Morrissey seemed totally lacking in any motivation. Mike Ellis, who sat next to Morrissey in class, noted the lackadaisical quality of his work. "He always seemed to do enough to get through with the least amount of hassle," he observed. "He wasn't struggling, but his mind was somewhere else." Even in English lessons, Morrissey would only come up with an interesting piece once in a while and gave the impression that he was merely marking time. Mike Moore pinpointed the source of such defeated ennui in terms of St Marys' insidious grinding-down process. "When you talk about Steven Morrissey at that school he wasn't being educated," he claims. "He was being manipulated by a system that was streamlining him to work in industry. The whole principle of the system was that you didn't buck it, but accepted. If you showed any individuality, they tried to wipe it out. They preferred to ignore him at school and he ignored them because if you started to argue about the conditions you were whipped."

Although it was difficult to achieve a sense of ironic distance amid the daily conflict at St Marys, it was sometimes possible to appreciate the absurdity of school life as pure spectacle. "St Marys was a hotbed of eccentricity," enthused Mike Roe. His perspective was borne out by the former pupils' animated descriptions of their various masters. The mathematics teacher, Mr Chew, apparently saw himself as the unofficial health inspector at St Marys. He carefully scrutinized pupils' handkerchiefs to ensure that they were sufficiently clean for their purpose while uttering his familiar aphorism: "Coughs and sneezes spread diseases". Armed with an aerosol can, he would spray the classroom diligently whenever one of the kids ingenuously spluttered or wheezed. On one occasion, a lad loudly farted in the middle of a lesson and Chew made him sit with his arse dangling out of the window. "I'm not having you fouling up the atmosphere in my classroom," he announced indignantly. He then fumigated the room with a blast from his air freshener.

Chew's colleague in the Maths department was Billy Roberts, a tough but enthusiastic teacher who brought a touch of theatre to the classroom. A specialist in chalk and talk, his patience would sometimes snap if the lesson dragged or proved unproductive. "He was forever dashing up pieces of chalk against the wall in frustration," explained Mike Roe. "I'm too good for this place! I don't know what I'm doing here!" was his favourite litany. Jim Verrechia remembers his "remarkable ability to throw a blackboard duster and hit the wrong desk. He'd spend hours ranting about what you *should* be doing for yourself. Again, a very aggressive character". The idlers in the back row who ignored the crash of Roberts' flying duster could never feel too confident about their security. If the noise levels incurred his wrath he would spring from his chair and dramatically lurch towards the back of the class, pushing the intervening desks aside like a rampaging cowboy, before descending on his noisy recalcitrant foes.

The quiet and unassuming Morrissey avoided Roberts' theatrical surges and found, to his surprise, that his teacher was quite approachable. More revealingly, he had a vague interest in pop music. Amazingly, one of his friends was a session player who claimed to have worked with Mott The Hoople and one afternoon he rashly promised to procure backstage passes for their next Manchester gig. Frustratingly, the prized gratis tickets failed to emerge, but Morrissey still attended the performance.

While Roberts often upheld the hard line at St Marys, the mercurial Aileen Power brought a touch of unintended light relief and eccentric entertainment to the proceedings. If any teacher, Pink excepted, could claim to have captured Morrissey's interest during the drudgery days at St Marys, then it was this highly-strung, strangely kind-hearted, emotionally expressive and frequently misunderstood artist. Her sense of drama was often worthy of an actress, while her intense stare bored deep into the memory of any pupil who sat through her remarkable and eventful lessons. The mood of a Power afternoon was atmospherically set, even as you entered her room. Amid the commotion of crashing chairs and bustling conversation she would sit at the front of the class, head perched pointedly on hand, wistfully watching everybody with a distant, wide-eyed, discon-certingly melancholic stare. At times inspirational, but all too easily distracted, she expressed genuine concern about the future of her wayward pupils. A strong advocate of the importance of moral education, she was adept at discussing such adventurous topics as the meaning of relation-ships, the plight of the unmarried mother and the immorality of abortion. Her persuasive concern for the life of the unborn child and the barbaric way in which society treats its rights was graphically illustrated. The powerless embryo savagely slain was her theme. "She was showing pictures of babies in jars that had been aborted," Mike Moore remembers, "and kids were going green at the gills."

Moore and his cronies took cynical advantage of this scenario to engineer a truancy plot. Sneaking over to the art room water taps, they surrepti-tiously gulped a mouthful of water and watched while Moore proceeded to retch mockingly into the sink. "I've been sick, Miss Power," he lied, before receiving permission to leave the lesson, and sneak home. As he left, he heard Power requesting Morrissey and Verrechia to flush away the unpolluted sink, while others awaited their opportunity to repeat the water-spewing trick to convincing effect.

Power's touching concern about her pupils' welfare often manifested itself in an amusingly maternal affection. Mike Foley smilingly recollects seeing an embarrassed line of lads during the lunch hour, standing around in shirt-tails and underpants. The kindly Miss Power was locked away in a nearby room, carefully ironing their trousers. At St Marys, of course, such good intentions were often perceived by the hand-reared kids as evidence of weakness. Unsurprisingly, Power had discipline problems and her moody disposition merely exacerbated an already unruly atmosphere. "If somebody made her nervous it would make things very difficult," recalled Jim Verrechia. "She was very nice, but people used to torment her. It was the 'in' thing to upset her. When she was out of the room everyone would start slamming their desks and when she'd return she'd get hysterical. There'd be times when she tried her best not to lose her temper, but within 10 minutes of the lesson she'd be off. She would cry as well, and the knight in shining armour would appear to put things right."

The knight was otherwise known as Jimmy the Joiner or, more accurately, Mr Hawthorne. Volatile and fiercely protective of Miss Power, he took the boys for woodwork and was, according to Moore, unusually outspoken on the dangers of Communism. His colleague, Mr Chesworth, specialized in metalwork and had a particular fondness for a 3"x2" block of wood, which he nicknamed "Charlie". When the kids were fractious or misbehaving, he would pinch their side whiskers and elevate them to the tips of their toes until they begged for mercy and promised to mend their ways.

Amid such a Dickensian ambience, it was small wonder that Morrissey slumped deeper inside himself. "There's a perverse and bitter joy in feeling unique, but you pay dearly", Morrissey observed. "You miss a lot of things in life." The television news offered little respite from the prevailing sense of gloom, offering such unwelcome distractions as the chirpy marriage of Princess Anne to Captain Mark Phillips. Morrissey watched with incredulity at the masses thronging the Mall, many of whom had slept overnight to witness the happy event. The nuptials could not anaesthetize what Chancellor Anthony Barber described as "the gravest situation by far since the end of the War". Disputes in the coal industry, railways and power stations had forced Britain to go on a three-day week amid growing speculation that the government would fall. Suddenly, every home ensured that it was well stocked with candles as a new dark age threatened.

On the musical horizon, a gloomy barrenness was detectable. Bowie had gone into retreat, Mott The Hoople had lost ground and T Rex were in decline. Morrissey urgently needed new heroes. In November 1973, he found the perfect candidate while watching an otherwise unremarkable edition of *The Old Grey Whistle Test*. Enlivening the screen were the outrageous New York Dolls, dressed in high heels, tights and sluttish make-up. Already on the slide since the drug-related death of their drummer Billy Murcia in London the previous year, the group was presently promoting their critically acclaimed but commercially neglected début album. The same month that Morrissey first saw them, the Dolls wandered into Malcolm McLaren's London emporium Let It Rock to try on some drape jackets and listen to Eddie Cochran on the juke-box. McLaren was impressed by their audacity and enchanted by their sleazy tales of life on the Bowery, surrounded by drunks, junkies and prostitutes. Before long, he would follow them back to New York and briefly assume managerial responsibilities, an experience which would provide a valuable apprenticeship for his later exploits as the svengali behind the iconoclastic Sex Pistols.

Back in Manchester, Morrissey was equally enchanted by the Dolls' confrontational *élan* and proclaimed them "the official end of the Sixties".

Like Dean, Bolan and Bowie, the group brought a vivacious glamour to Morrissey's drab life which he grew to treasure. "The Dolls gave me a sense of uniqueness, as if they were my own personal discovery," he noted. "Back in 1973, the Dolls were total outcasts, and no one with any sense ever mentioned their name. As it was, I became the only visible proof that someone actually listened to them." Eager to unearth like-minded enthusiasts, Morrissey began placing advertisements in the music press and over the next few years corresponded with a number of bedroom-based glam rock fans. Significantly, Morrissey seldom met his pen pals. The epistolary relationship, with its reassuring anonymity and image-building potential, proved far too precious to be challenged by anti-climactic flesh-and-blood meetings with shy figures whose fictional personalities withered outside the pages of their effusive, life-enhancing scripts.

Within months of the Dolls' spectacle, there was another memorable musical event on British television when Sparks made their début on *Top Of The Pops*. The initial sight of Ron Mael's demented eyes, Hitler moustache and slicked-back hair was the most authentically disturbing yet novel anti-pop image seen in years. Morrissey was intrigued by the visuals and equally impressed by brother Russ Mael's falsetto vocal on the sparklingly-produced 'This Town Ain't Big Enough For The Both Of Us'. Young Steven immediately snapped up the single and seven weeks later purchased the attendant album, *Kimono My House*. During the first week of June 1974, he rushed off a letter to the *New Musical Express* and the following week was astonished to see himself immortalized in print. He took a copy of the *NME* to school that week and it was duly passed around the class. The letter captured Morrissey at his pernickety best, carefully cataloguing tracks with the precision of an egg-timer. He wrote, "Today I bought the album of the year. I feel I can say this without expecting several letters saying I'm talking rubbish. The album is *Kimono My House* by Sparks. I bought it on the strength of the single. Every track is brilliant - although I must name 'Equator', 'Complaints', 'Amateur Hour' and 'Here In Heaven' as the best tracks, and in that order. Steve Morrissey".

The letters' editor, Charles Shaar Murray, could not resist gently mocking Morrissey's enthusiasm with a reply of equal length. He concluded sarcastically: "The eyes of Mr Morrisey [sic] gleam with a missionary zeal that shames into submission the cringing doubts of those yet unconvinced". Morrissey was unconcerned about the ironic tone - this was fame. It was also the beginning of a long series of letters that would infrequently infiltrate the columns of the music press over the next few years.

With his new-found notoriety as a pop scribe, Morrissey concluded that the time was rife to consider the possibility of some sort of musical career. Unfortunately, he could neither sing nor play. He envied Jim Verrechia, the wizard guitarist in the class, who was playing in a makeshift group with Chris Power. The duo had made their début at a children's tea party at the Royal Ancient Order of the Buffs and subsequently appeared at local talent contests calling themselves the CJs. Before long, they had extended their set to feature an exhaustive nine songs, including faithful covers of Matthews'

Southern Comfort's chart-topping 'Woodstock', Steppenwolf's 'Born To Be Wild' and Badfinger's 'No Matter What'. By the fourth year, they had recruited James Twomey, a classically-trained pianist and a grammar school boy to boot. There was even talk of them putting on a school concert before Jet laughed the idea out of court. On a good night, they could nevertheless earn about £5 a gig. The big time beckoned.

Morrissey responded to the CJs' progress by requesting guitar lessons from Verrechia. The quiet surroundings of Morrissey's aunt's house provided an excellent rehearsal room but, sadly, there were no musical miracles. After several weeks, Verrechia despaired of his frustrated pupil and the experiment was suspended. "I tried to teach Steve to play," he now recalls, "but he was impatient and didn't get very far." Left alone, Morrissey dreamt on and unconvincingly plotted his fantasy route to superstardom. He duly purchased a saxophone for a fiver, only to discover, to his horror, that he could not even begin to master the instrument. It was the second of many such disappointments.

Morrissey returned to school in the autumn of 1974, thankful that he had only one more year left to serve. In the gymnasium, Sweeney was inducting a group of first years, among whom was a Kings Road lad named Gary Farrell. After his first gruelling PE session, Farrell watched in shocked amazement as a fat lad, who had performed predictably poorly, was pulled out and ordered to touch his toes. The volleyed ball-up-the-arse treatment followed. "It was grim, really grim," Farrell succinctly noted. "All the teachers were real bastards." Walking home along the Kings Road with Morrissey, he hissed: "That place is *hell*." Steven could only nod in resigned agreement.

During the first term of the fifth year, Morrissey struck up a renewed friendship with Mike Ellis, and the two spent much time discussing music, listening to records and reading comics. Surprisingly, Morrissey was still engrossed in monster magazines and Ellis seemed equally enthusiastic. They regularly scoured second-hand bookshops and regarded the Paper Chase poster shop as their mecca. Morrissey was fascinated with the selection of picture postcards, badges and US magazines, and Ellis recalls his particular passion for *Phantom Of The Opera* ephemera. The myth of the bitter, disfigured musician who lives in isolation, yearns hopelessly for love, yet still manages to control his subterranean world and accept his wretched existence, clearly struck a chord with the young misanthrope. The preoccupation with outsiders, criminals and so-called "monsters" would prove a recurring theme in Morrissey's written work.

Life in class A5 offered yet more pedagogic amusement thanks to the loquacious Mr Taylor. "Some of the adventures that he and his family were supposed to have had were totally unbelievable" was Mike Roe's bemused reaction. Commenting on the state of the British press, Taylor explained his daily ritual of scissoring topless models from the pages of *The Sun* to protect his children's sensibilities. Nobody bothered to ask the obvious question: why not just change papers? No doubt there would have been an equally lively and implausible explanation to cover that riposte. Taylor's blarney earned him the nickname "Billy Bullshit", though he remained innocently ignorant of the cheeky appellation. One afternoon, he arrived for a lesson and found the words "Billy Bull" scrawled on his classroom door. "If I find this Billy Bull," he thundered, "he will be severely punished". That was probably his finest moment.

The urgent need for a sex symbol at St Marys fell on the sensitive shoulders of the young Anne Judge. A Maths mistress by preference, she had found herself teaching English to the fifth years in the aftermath of Pink's departure to Australia. In spite of her owlish glasses and unattractive habit of wearing pop socks, irrespective of the length of her skirt, she was the sole source of sexiness that St Marys had to offer. Roe immediately proclaimed her the Deidre Barlow of Renton Road and relieved his fantasies about bespectacled women by watching her gliding across the tennis court in virginal white. On a school visit to Piccadilly Radio, he became irrationally jealous when a disc jockey presented her with a copy of John Denver's 'Annie's Song'. At one point, there were rampaging rumours that she was dating a millionaire building contractor and there was considerable excitement when she let slip about the possibility of attending a forthcoming Elton John concert. A far greater buzz ensued when she started going out with the dreaded Sweeney.

Young enough to communicate with the lads, Judge allowed Jim Verrechia to teach her to skate at the local ice rink. However, as a female teacher in an all-male environment, Judge could not afford to be overfamiliar, as Verrechia discovered. "She wasn't soft," he pointed out. "She could be hard, and quite a cow, actually. But she was attractive to us." Morrissey, a moth to any glamorous light, unsurprisingly regarded her with reserved favour and his appreciation increased after she commended one of his poems, which was read out in class. Such commendation failed to inspire any further literary flourishes from Morrissey, whose lackadaisical work rate was by now habitual. For some assignments, he would produce a mere handful of lines, as laziness and boredom increasingly took its toll. "I didn't need anybody except myself and my imagination", Morrissey noted defiantly. "They didn't like all that taking place in the intimacy of my brain."

1974 ended with IRA bombers attacking the home of Edward Heath, whose troubled reign as Conservative leader was swiftly reaching a close. It had been an eventful past few months with Princess Anne narrowly escaping a kidnap attempt from a gunman who had fired half-a-dozen shots at her royal personage in imaginative protest against the government's lack of mental care facilities. On 1 October, McDonalds had opened their first fast food restaurant in the UK at the very moment when Morrissey was seriously considering phasing out his regular consumption of bacon sandwiches. That same month, Harold Wilson's Labour Party had retained power by a frighteningly slim three seats. With the recent background of strikes and unprecedented inflation Wilson had coined a refreshingly frank political quip: "All I can say is my prayers". Prayers were increasingly concomitant with the news headlines, as the IRA intensified its terrorist attacks which spread from the streets of London to Manchester, and culminated in the Woolwich and Birmingham pub bombings in which 17 people were killed and 120 injured. On the anniversary of President Kennedy's assassination, police swooped on five bemused Irishmen and later arrested another. So commenced the first of at least two profound and tragic miscarriages of justice involving Irish immigrants.

The first school term of 1975 began with a geography field trip to White Coppice conducted by Mr Twist. Morrissey was not particularly taken with the village, which had once been a thriving mining town. His reluctance to participate in the world of Twist was petulantly demonstrated when the class was required to negotiate a rocky footpath over a weir. Steve stood there aghast and cried: "No way!" Interestingly, he was never afraid to reveal his timidity or risk the likely taunts of his fellow class-mates.

While The New York Dolls still held sway in Morrissey's pop pantheon, his other heroes were branching off into various offshoot groups. Sparks had spawned Milk'n'Cookies whom Morrissey felt sufficiently loyal towards to purchase their single, 'Little Lost And Innocent'. In a moment of largesse, he presented the disc to Mike Ellis. It still rests in the neat plastic cover that Steve carefully constructed for his favourite 45s.

The spring of 1975 brought Mott The Hoople descendants Hunter/Ronson to Manchester, and Morrissey, Ellis and Chris Power religiously attended the gig, sneaking in a camera to take some pictures. Morrissey was still in contact with his new friend Angie and there were now other girls on his horizon. Ellis recalls Steve escorting a petite, dark-haired Mott The Hoople fanatic to the gig, but suspects that the relationship was platonic. "Steve didn't talk much about girls," he recalls. "He wasn't heavily into them and seemed more interested in music." At school, however, Morrissey briefly achieved an undeserved Don Juan notoriety when it was learned that he had been entertaining girls in his bedroom. As Mike Moore recalled: "Some lads in the class thought he was getting their knickers off and plugging in, but we knew Steve wasn't into that." It later transpired that the girls in question regularly attended Morrissey's boudoir every Sunday evening in order to listen to the Radio 1 Top 20.

Visitors to Morrissey's house during this period could not help commenting on his latest acquisition, a piano. In an inspired moment, he painted the instrument white, as if in preparation for some imaginary pop star career. Unfortunately, his ambition and perseverance did not extend as far as actually learning to master the keyboards. Already, he was distracted by another idea and expressed interest in becoming a drummer. Heavily influenced by the Dolls, he concluded that attitude was far more important than musical competence. This meant that he could pour scorn on the views of Verrechia and company without bowing to their superior technical knowledge. Jim soon learned that there was little point in arguing pop aesthetics with his class rival. "Steve could be very catty. Towards the end, if you started criticizing his musical ideas he'd get quite bitchy. He'd go off on a tangent, or walk off". Armed with renewed confidence, Morrissey approached Ellis with the idea of forming a group. Typically, Steve casually dismissed their inchoate playing abilities as completely irrelevant. "We'll just turn the music up, give it hell and look good" was his simplistic prescription for pop success. Inevitably, the indecision caused by their inability to play meant that these grand ideas came to nothing. In the end, it was all empty talk. Yet, within two years, a new generation of school kids would follow Morrissey's dictum, forming groups from scratch, securing gigs and even inspiring devoted followings merely on the strength of a few chords and a suitably nihilistic attitude. Morrissey's dream was frustratingly ahead of time and fashion.

The final term at St Marys was predictably anti-climactic but at least the atmosphere was less oppressive. Even Sweeney had been charitably re-evaluated by many as a result of his matiness on recent school trips abroad. Jet Morgan, meanwhile had virtually faded into insignificance with the announcement of his imminent retirement at the end of the school year. After aeons of flouting school uniform regulations with irreverent aplomb, the pupils were now masters of sartorial rebellion. Mike Foley had taken to wearing a dress suit, dickie bow and top hat, while Ellis and his circle decorated their blazers with the Red Rose of Lancashire and embroidered a row of brass buttons on their sleeves. Morrissey, meanwhile, sported an illegal pink shirt, a long dark coat, a shoulder bag, some colourful badges and, when nobody was looking, some understated Dolls-influenced make-up. For the lads in the lower years, like Gary Curley, he seemed a remote, slightly weird figure who would stand alone during break-time, disinterestedly watching the animated playground games with scarcely a flicker of interest. Ellis also noted his friend's increasingly subdued nature. "Steve did change that last year and seemed more introverted. He took some time off sick and may have had problems with his nerves." Morrissey was more prosaic in his summation. "It was a dreadful time," he complained, "very isolated, very alienating, all the usual things that teenagers complain of."

Coincidentally, while Morrissey was looking inward, his sister Jackie had become more outgoing. "She never experienced the kind of isolation I went through," he reflected. "She always had quite a spirited life... never without the odd clump of friends. She felt alive at least." Always popular, Jackie had begun dating an ex-St Marys pupil and part-time disc jockey named John O'Brien. He was immediately struck by the affinity between Steve and Jackie. "I'd never been out with a girl who had as much time for her brother as she had. That's the truth. They were really close and I don't really know why." O'Brien was warmly received by Jackie's mother and regarded Peter Morrissey as "a great guy". Whenever the youngsters were stuck for a lift or missed a late bus, Peter would act as a surrogate taxi service. "The father reminded me of George Best, young, good-looking, black beard, very slim; he even had long hair, which was very unusual. Both parents were very modern." O'Brien, in common with Morrissey's class-mates, was particularly struck by the modernity of the parents and the freedom they allowed their children. Patrick Quinn recalled O'Brien obliquely complimenting Elizabeth Morrissey with the humorous aside: "I wouldn't mind trading Jackie for her mother!" With his Irish family background, O'Brien was an in-demand disc jockey for weddings in the area and knew several of Peter's friends. Like most people, he established an instant rapport with Morrissey senior, who was an engaging conversationalist. "He'd always talk about things that were of interest to young people, like music", recalled O'Brien. Indeed, Peter had a fondness for country music and nominated Don Williams' 'Gypsy Woman' as one of his favourite discs. Significantly, country music remained a genre that his son studiously avoided.

Morrissey's feelings about his sister's relationships were difficult to ascertain. "When Jackie was seeing John O'Brien, Steve always stayed in," recalled Mike Foley, who was then dating Jacqueline's best friend, Majella. Initially, O'Brien was even unaware that Steven liked records. "He seemed so introvert and never came out and socialized with us, whereas Jackie had loads of friends and was out every night". John finally broke the ice with Steve when he discovered that "he was madly into The Kinks". With an extensive collection of 45s, O'Brien was able to pass on some classic Ray Davies titles which opened new channels of communication. Although O'Brien was no glam rocker, he was impressed by Morrissey's determination to run a New York Dolls fan club and could not help noticing that the bedroom-loving loner was surprisingly stylish.

In July 1975, the St Marys era finally ended for both Morrissey and Jet Morgan. Steven would never forget those five-and-a-half years and the bitter memories would later inspire the classic, finger-pointing 'The Headmaster Ritual'. If Jet was Morrissey's nemesis, however, then it was doubly ironic that Mike Moore should perceive such strong comparisons between their personalities and behaviour. "Steve was like a younger version of Jet," he recalled. "They both wandered through the school and didn't seem to be aware of anybody around them. Jet was into his own ego and Steven was into his own life. They were the two people who were most apart in that school."

It would be another seven years before Morrissey took vinyl vengeance on St Marys but he was beaten to the punch by the Department of Education and Science. They undertook an inspection of the school in 1982, commenting extensively on its organization, curriculum and the quality of the school community. Parts of the report were quite sympathetic, particularly in light of St Marys' falling rolls. Not surprisingly, the lack of cultural activities, which had nevertheless improved significantly, were still frowned upon. The authoritative atmosphere in classrooms was said to inhibit learning, some exercises were described as stereotyped and the science laboratory was considered ill-equipped. What really damned St Marys, however, was a handful of sentences, far more damaging than any vitriol composed by Morrissey. After commenting on the apparently caring approach and interest in the pupils from many members of the staff, the Inspectorate concluded: "It is therefore surprising to note that there were 92 recorded instances of the use of corporal punishment during the first half term of the current year. Its use for some offences scarcely seemed warranted."

4

Half A Person

WHEN MORRISSEY LEFT SCHOOL, the unemployment figures stood at 1,036,000, the highest for 35 years. The dole queues had increased by almost 70 per cent since he'd started at St Marys five years before and the prospects for academically unqualified youths were abysmal. Postponing the gloom, Morrissey elected to enrol for a one-year O-level spree at Stretford Technical School. Characteristically, he did not extend himself, braving only a handful of subjects: English Literature, History, Sociology and the General Paper.

Almost immediately, Morrissey was cast as the class loner and remained virtually unnoticed in the opening weeks. During lessons, he seemed content to take notes and fade imperceptibly into the background, as if re-enacting his familiar outsider role at St Marys. One person he did talk to was Peter Slack, a pleasant enough lad who unfortunately left the college after just one term. Any chance Morrissey had of establishing further friendships seemed doomed by his decision to forego wearing spectacles. His myopia made it difficult to distinguish people beyond the radius of a couple of feet, and, by that time, any words of greeting would be strangled in the back of his throat. Dumbstruck, he would look away in shy embarrassment. "They must have felt I was a snob, but I really felt bad about the whole thing," he confessed.

Having unintentionally snubbed several boys in the class, Morrissey next approached a group of girls, who were clustered together protectively in intimidating insular groups. Resurrecting Mike Foley-period charm, Steven eventually struck up a tentative conversation with a nearby trio: Vickie, Julie and Karen. Initially, they too seemed cool and unimpressed. Morrissey would have been mortified to discover that they actually spent considerable time discussing the merits or otherwise of the lads in the class. No doubt his mortification would have switched to flattered amazement on learning that he was regarded as rather attractive. The major problem for the ever-discriminating girls was Morrissey's personality. As class-mate Julie Porter pondered: "A lot of people tried to get to know him but he was such hard work. He'd cut you short and appeared miserable and very reserved. Quite a lot of girls thought that he was ridiculous." Fortunately, Julie was not so willing to dismiss Morrissey on the grounds of unsociability and detected some favourable traits that her friends had ignored.

Terribly shy herself, she responded to Morrissey's taciturn behaviour with considerable understanding and waited patiently for him to feel at ease in her company. It looked like being an infinite wait. During break-time, this malcontent would stand alone, huddled in doorways, just as he had done in the closing years at St Marys. While most of the students chatted in the refectory at lunch time, Morrissey generally went home, which further alienated him from the group. It was only towards the end of the first term that his ironic humour overcame his self-consciousness. A major break-through occurred when he slipped a note to Julie during the history lesson, playfully caricaturing the teacher in typical St Marys fashion. On 3 December, she reciprocated by sketching some drawings in his history folder. Morrissey was overjoyed at discovering a kindred spirit, but still found conversation frustratingly difficult. "The sending of silly notes," as Morrissey called them, remained his favourite method of communication.

In early 1976, Morrissey learned that a new pop programme was scheduled for broadcast in the Manchester region. The proposed title was *So It Goes* and the presenter was Tony Wilson, an ebullient Cambridge graduate best known for reading the nightly news feature, *Granada Reports*. One morning, a package arrived on his desk, which included a battered sleeve of The New York Dolls' first album. Attached was a note, which read: "Dear Mr Wilson, I've heard about your show. It's wonderful news. Please could we have some music like this." It was signed "Steven Morrissey". Wilson admits that he had never even heard of the Dolls at that point, but he was suitably impressed by Morrissey's enthusiasm. Unfortunately, his busy schedule prevented him from replying to the strangely zealous kid from Stretford.

Back at college, Morrissey knew nobody with whom he could communicate seriously about music matters. Although the girls were proving pleasant company, their tastes were predictably mainstream by Steven's standards. Shyness was still a dominant factor in his relationship with Julie Porter and although they exchanged pleasantries before morning registration, they never met socially outside college. Notes and letters remained their favourite communicative currency and it was through this medium that they grew close. Paradoxically, this ensured that they found it even more difficult to speak intimately. Farcically, they were even embarrassed about accidentally bumping into each other in the street and so dreaded verbal communication that they went to considerable lengths not to meet. As Julie remembered, with nostalgic amusement: "We would avoid each other at all costs. I valued what we had and didn't want to spoil it. I would hide! There was such tension trying to converse face to face."

Another college girl whom Morrissey felt a strong kinship towards was Ann-Marie McVeigh. She appeared to take a special interest in Morrissey, and even suggested that he ask out Julie Porter. That, however, was proving an impossible match. Unconsciously paraphrasing one of Morrissey's own maudlin lines, Julie summed up what several women felt about the troubled youth: "Even though he was attractive, it was his mind I felt a passion for." Ann-Marie McVeigh was similarly disposed, and in

Morrissey's fantasies she became an unattainable object of desire. As Julie Porter concluded: "She was very beautiful, similar to the actress Jane Seymour. He was so obsessed with her, but any bloke would be because she was a stunner."

On Friday 4 June, The Sex Pistols played at Manchester's Lesser Free Trade Hall and unleashed their own brand of chaos. Morrissey remained a Doubting Thomas but was sufficiently intrigued to pen a letter to the *New Musical Express*. Duty bound to point out the extent to which the Pistols borrowed their influences from The New York Dolls and The Heartbreakers, he was charitable enough to conclude: "The Sex Pistols are *very* New York and it's nice to see that the British have produced a band capable of producing atmosphere created by The New York Dolls and their many imitators, even though it may be too late. I'd love to see The Sex Pistols make it. Maybe then they will be able to afford some new clothes which don't look as though they've been slept in." For the readers of the more staid *Melody Maker*, his prose was measured and his conclusions less optimistic: "I think that their audacious lyrics and discordant music will not hold their heads above water when their followers tire of torn jumpers and safety pins".

Despite Morrissey's ambivalence, there was no doubting that the Pistols had unwittingly inspired a significant number of individuals to form their own groups, thereby literally transforming the Manchester music scene. Among the audience that night besides Morrissey was the nucleus of what became Joy Division, and the entire line-up of the fledgling Buzzcocks. Howard Trafford (alias Devoto) was the key figure in the game at this point having brought the Pistols to Manchester and secured a deal with manager Malcolm McLaren whereby the Buzzcocks, and subsequently other punk-influenced groups, could appear at support gigs in London. Howard effectively acted as unpaid publicist to the Pistols and sent a demonstration tape containing three of their songs to Tony Wilson, who was duly invited to attend a follow-up gig at the Lesser Free Trade Hall on 20 July. That evening the group performed 'Anarchy In The UK' for the first time in public and would repeat the number on Wilson's new show *So It Goes* during the early autumn.

Amid the commotion, another important figure entered Manchester's new music community. Devoto's old school-friend Richard Boon had recently graduated from Reading University and, rather than pursuing a teaching career, decided to assist the recently formed Buzzcocks. Having already witnessed several Pistols shows with Devoto and Pete Shelley, he found himself innocently assuming the role of a pop manager almost by default. The Buzzcocks' birth was compellingly combustible and provided a blueprint for cliques of mutually-minded friends to follow suit. "The Seventies incarnation of the mythical Manchester scene developed from there," Boon now claims. "No one was equipped or experienced, so I drifted into independent artiste and label management." Within six months, the Buzzcocks would release their début EP, *Spiral Scratch* on Boon's newly-created label, New Hormones. Originally intended as merely a vehicle to issue Buzzcocks material, the label would later establish a small roster of artistes and attract the special interest of young Morrissey.

Having completed his O-levels during the early summer, Steven said goodbye to college and boarded a plane to New York. His final destination was his Aunt Mary's apartment in New Jersey on what was to be the first of several US visits. "Mary was always very close to him," recalls Peter Morrissey. The week Steven left, the exchange rate fell to a record low of $1.725 against the pound, a statistic that seriously threatened to curb his spending power. Upon arrival, the hot news on television and in the press was the Karen Quinlan affair. The "Girl In A Coma" had been unconscious for over a year and was finally taken to a nursing home to die in peace without further resuscitation. During the next few weeks, Morrissey assimilated all things American, spent much time sunbathing and learned to ride a motorcycle, just like his hero James Dean. He even enthused about flying for the first time, a novelty which would later wear off.

After escaping from Britain during its hottest summer in years, Morrissey was horrified to learn that he had been pursued by no less a personage than Her Majesty The Queen. Within days of his arrival, she appeared in Manhattan for the Bicentennial celebrations and received a stirring welcome from effusive New Yorkers. No fan of royalty himself, Morrissey had to endure the bland American response: "We just love your Queen". Such minor irritations were insufficient to spoil his trip, which left him remarkably stimulated and energized. Like many young people on their first vacation to America, he intended to return at the earliest opportunity and genuinely believed that he could finance another visit within a matter of months.

After returning to England, Morrissey received a brown envelope containing his long-awaited O-level results. He was immensely pleased to discover that he had passed English Literature, Sociology and the General Paper and only grimaced slightly at the "U" (unclassified) grading for History. Despite his obvious lack of empathy for "Social and Economic History since 1760", he decided to retrieve his history notes which he had conveniently lent to Ann-Marie McVeigh. After locating her address, he swiftly despatched a letter on 14 September and was crestfallen when she failed to reply. At least the misinterpreted rejection added to the romantic mystique. Morrissey would spent several more years intermittently on her trail in what was to become one of his more endearing little fantasies.

On the musical front, Morrissey was no longer extolling the virtues of David Bowie. A news article of the time remarked how scientists had at last concluded that there was definitely no life on Mars. It seemed a strangely appropriate valediction for the one true glam king. On Morrissey's musical throne, Bowie had lately been usurped by the New York punk poet Patti Smith. Steven was enthralled by her work and conscientiously typed the lyrics of 'Piss Factory', which he subsequently xeroxed and sent to friends as evidence of great confrontational punk poetry. He also wrote a fulsome letter to *Sounds*, which was printed under the byline "Steven" on 25 September 1976. It read: "*Horses* by Patti Smith has virtually no competition as the most exciting rock album of the year and it shows more potential than just about any other release in recent memory. There is no 'beat on the brat' nonsense, Patti is intriguing without being boring and every track is laced with her own brand of sardonic humour." Immediately above this eulogy was another letter, simply credited to a character from Manchester named "Morrissey". Substantially different in tone from "Steven's" missive, it took the form of a harangue against another correspondent who'd had the audacity to criticize the then faltering New York Dolls. Morrissey laid bare his feelings with a caustic sideswipe against the contemporaneous new wave of English and American punk rockers: "First and foremost, I consider it something of a joke that the Dolls should be compared to such notoriously no-talents as The Ramones and The Sex Pistols". After a further two paragraphs deifying his favourite group, he concluded: "The New York Dolls will be back. Period".

One of the major reasons for Morrissey's spree of letter writing to the music press was that he had considerable time on his hands. During early September he had placed himself on the unemployment register and was required to sign on every Wednesday at 10.15 am at the Civic Centre. Initially, he felt somewhat degraded by the experience but realized after the first week that he didn't give a damn. With preposterous optimism, he was already planning to save a portion of his dole money and book a cheap winter flight back to the States. His immodest ambition was to emigrate by the following February, a date which would continually be put back over the ensuing months.

What little chance Morrissey had of scraping together a few pounds from his meagre dole offerings was instantly thwarted by his insatiable love of music. He bought Patti Smith's *Radio Ethiopia* on the day of its release and the following week travelled to Birmingham to see her perform. It was a wondrous experience. He also witnessed Deaf School and Split Enz, whom he bestowed with guarded favour. On 6 November, he trudged across to Manchester University to catch the promising but ultimately unsuccessful Roogalator. It was his fourth gig in less than a fortnight.

Despite this wealth of incipient talent, Morrissey still clung perilously to his beloved Dolls and launched a vitriolic attack against *Sounds* scribe Jonh Ingham who had dared to criticize the group. After laboriously listing a catalogue of supposedly great Dolls' songs, Morrissey admonished: "If these rock classics don't give you thrills to the joy of living then I suggest you stick with The Sex Pistols whose infantile approach and nondescript music will no doubt match your intelligence." This was hard-hitting, bitchy stuff and indicative of the frustrated passion that Morrissey was experiencing during this particularly turbulent period. He was inflamed by the sexual politics of the time and regarded Jack Nichols' *Men's Liberation: A New Definition Of Masculinity* as his feminist bible. The fascination with masculine role play encouraged him to write reams of self-reassuring notes on the iniquities of "maleness". "Society is sick and the world is in a mess thanks to men," he pontificated. Male dress, male attitude, male etiquette, the denial of sensitivity and the suppression of emotion were all subjects that teased his imagination and instilled the desire to challenge outmoded social conventions. He hated the strangulating Mancunian macho environment that dictated how he must act and live his life. He railed endlessly at the fetters placed upon his grand ambition and longed not just to write for *Sounds* or *NME*, but to become a star. There was almost a suspicion of cosmic malevolence that this most desirous of events had not already occurred.

With the American dream postponed and his dole money squandered on Patti Smith excursions, Morrissey decided to seek a job. It was to prove one of his biggest mistakes to date. At the end of November, he secured a post with the Civil Service and was so appalled by the suffocating atmosphere and meniality of the tasks shoved before him that he quit within a fortnight. Upon returning to the Civic Centre, he became embroiled in an argument with a disgruntled DHSS official who concluded the diatribe with the biting rejoinder, "People like you make me feel sick." It was a humiliating moment and a woeful insight into the contempt often experienced by the unemployed. More salutary evidence of official disapprobation followed when Morrissey learned that his weekly benefit had been reduced to a paltry £5. His crime had been leaving the unsatisfactory Civil Service job for "no good reason". He was now in a worse position than if he hadn't taken the irksome job in the first place. It proved enough to put him off work for the best part of six years. "I've always been lazy, but now I'm *very* lazy," he gleefully told friends.

The continued submergence in feminist tomes inevitably led Morrissey to sharpen his perspectives on a number of issues. He grew to hate institutions. School and Church were frowned upon and he vowed to avoid marriage at all costs. The troubled state of his parents' relationship seemed to reinforce an already hardened antipathy. However, such cynicism did not blunt his sensitivity. He retained a special kinship towards orphans, as if perceiving in their loneliness a reflection of his own feelings of personal isolation. Catholicism had provided no spiritual salvation and his lapsed state extended towards near blasphemous boundaries, exacerbated by the rhetoric of radical feminist tracts. Morrissey severely questioned the Church's stance on homosexuality, while making some naïve and offensively inaccurate comments on the sexual psychology of the clergy. Increasingly supportive of gay rights, he announced categorically: "I am not prejudiced against homosexuals." His epistolary diary added, "... most of my closest friends are gay - especially girls." Such sentiments, although far from earth-shatteringly revealing, certainly differentiated him from the old hard-core St Marys clique. He even boasted of fraternizing with some convicted criminals who had served time for soliciting and drugs offences. "I'm the only sane one among them," he quipped. These shadily glamorous low-life accoutrements coupled with perpetual unemployment proved a potentially dangerous concoction, but Morrissey was never particularly impressionable. As ever, he preferred to remain the wild-hearted outsider.

Peter Morrissey had occasionally puzzled over and almost despaired of understanding a son whose demeanour, attitude and personality all too often appeared unfathomable. As one of his friends observed: "Steven was one of those hip kids who dressed funny and hung around with weirdos. Pete didn't like that and wanted him to be more of a man, as *he* thought." The differences between father and son were probably more nebulous than specific, and tended to manifest themselves in grand silences rather than bitter antagonism. Both father and son were placid personalities. As Peter himself told me: "He never seems to get upset or angry."

The easy-going father tried to lighten the tensions in the household with his customary good humour but, by late 1976, the situation was severely strained. Steven sided with his mother during the worst moments; it was a sad time. The underlying tensions are best exemplified by Steven's acknowledgement that he had not spoken to his father in over six months. A cataclysmic Christmas beckoned.

In spite of his championing of gay rights and fraternization with a coterie of lesbians, Morrissey was not about to join their number. He had what he termed an "inferiority complex" about relationships, feeling, despite evidence to the contrary, that he was unattractive. "People only like me for my mind" was a favourite dictum that later became a song lyric. Often, he joked about his reluctance to play the role of a Don Juan. "I have stopped the night with girls and *not* had sex and, believe me, it doesn't boost your reputation," was a typically arch response. For all that, he was no innocent and probably had more intimate encounters than several of the characters from St Marys. "I don't have sex much... I can almost count the number of times," he wearily noted in November 1976. Considering he was still 17, this was an admission of considerable experience. As in other areas of his life, Morrissey occasionally underestimated how innocent, inexperienced, deprived, lonely or downright miserable many of his seemingly confident contemporaries may have been.

Steven's insularity and sense of personal uniqueness clouded his vision at times, and many maintain it still does. It must be said, however, that Morrissey had an enormous generosity of spirit and displayed remarkable empathy when confronted with the personal problems of those he considered worthy. He dished out advice like a seasoned counsellor, yet never in a tone that was condescending or careless. Beneath his morale-boosting admonishments, there was always a brutal realism which addressed problems in an admirably unsentimental manner. Despite his customary introspection, he treated friends with a speciality value that invariably boosted their self-esteem. Few realized at the time that the agony uncle of Stretford was himself in sore need of a sympathetic listener.

December 1976 was to prove one of the most devastatingly memorable and emotionally disruptive months of Morrissey's life. Recently, he had heard some tragic news that threatened to shatter his cosseted world. Angie, the effervescent girl with whom he had attended concerts, confided in, written to, and frequently chatted with on the phone, was reportedly dying. After returning from Italy with her boyfriend at the end of the summer, she became ill and was taken to hospital. On the eve of her eighteenth birthday it was discovered that she had leukaemia. Morrissey visited her in hospital on 5 December and was shaken by the encounter. The breezy, vivacious girl he had remembered was now a pale, thin, vulnerable shadow of herself. She had lost nearly four stone in as many months and seemed close to death. In the wake of the visit, Morrissey was on the verge of tears. For a time, the experience made him dismiss his own meagre problems and be thankful for good health. In the long term, the experience contributed to a chilling antipathy towards hospitals and fuelled an already well-developed morbidity.

On 9 December, four days after visiting Angie, there was a distraction from darker thoughts when The Sex Pistols returned to Manchester. The atmosphere was highly charged, for the group had become a macabre *cause célèbre* over the previous months. Their name was synonymous with violence, and pubs and clubs throughout the country had banned "punk nights" and effectively pushed the movement underground. At the 100 Club's much touted Punk Music Festival, the acerbic Sid Vicious became involved in a glass smashing incident which ended in near tragedy when a girl was blinded by a flying splinter. Controversy was heaped upon controversy and only days before the Manchester concert the group had rocketed to national infamy following their use of obscene language on Thames Television's *Today* programme. The tabloids had a field day sensationalizing the event under such banner headlines as "The Filth And The Fury".

The price for such notoriety, however, was a crippling series of cancellations which decimated the December Anarchy tour. Manchester's then predominantly heavy-metal venue, the Electric Circus, was one of the few places in the country willing to risk the unholy consequences of a Pistols concert. Morrissey had bought an advance ticket for the show, purely on the strength of the support acts, which included former Doll Johnny Thunders with his new group, The Heartbreakers. The genuine excitement produced by the Pistols went some way towards mollifying his previously harsh view of the group and, by 1977, he would recant many of his earlier criticisms.

Two days after the Pistols' performance at the Electric Circus, an advertisement appeared in *Sounds* which read: "Dolls/Patti fans wanted for Manchester-based punk band." It was not too difficult to work out the identity of the youth behind the publication's box number. Unfortunately, reader response was decidedly cool and, in the meantime, Morrissey faced a family crisis which reached a head at Christmas.

On 23 December, Peter Morrissey, to use his son's sweet parlance, "took the plunge" and left 384 Kings Road. The decision was far from unexpected, but still momentous. Inevitably, there was some gossip, much of it directed against Steven's mother and unworthy of repetition. The crucial fact was that the marriage was over. Young Morrissey played the devoted son over the Christmas holidays and did not even venture from the house. While fending off criticisms of his bedraggled clothing from his grandmother (Bridget Dwyer), he found some Christmas cheer in a couple of Marx Brothers repeats on television and a small cache of presents, including a Parker pen, reams of notepaper, a box of chocolates and a book on his favourite idol, James Dean.

In January 1977, Myra Hindley was moved from Holloway to Durham Prison, much to her chagrin. "Society owes me a living!" she wrote frostily. She gave the impression that if anyone asked why, she would spit in their eye. Morrissey had similar feelings as he boarded the bus to New Brunswick Street to sign on. If the unemployment staff had learned of his latest plans, they would no doubt have raised their eyes to the ceiling in exasperation. For, as the New Year bells tolled, Morrissey was eagerly anticipating a new life as an Au Pair Boy. Striking a blow for male equality, he had actually applied for an au pair job and was ready to give his prospective employers a right royal mouthful if he was turned down at the interview on grounds of gender. "If women get equality, so can men," he told friends. The fantasy lasted several weeks more before ending with a written rejection.*

Having already extracted some of her savings to compensate for the loss of her husband, Betty herself decided to return to work. Inexperienced and unqualified academically, her previous employment had included stints at a blanket makers and a period working as a bingo caller. With her reasonably cultured voice and polite manner, she soon managed to secure an undemanding post as a librarian's assistant. Later, she would even attend an unrewarding course at the same college as her son. Meanwhile, daughter Jackie was haphazardly pursuing secretarial work, punctuated by long periods on the dole. It was far from the happiest of times and Morrissey was frequently miserable, and confessed to feeling foolish and unwanted. His sole panacea was the self-boosting litany: "Talk fast and keep smiling". All too often that was easier said than done.

In spite of his interest in the music scene, Morrissey had yet to ingratiate himself with any leading member of the Manchester punk or new wave fraternity. His shyness ensured that he was, at best, a fly on the wall at local revelries. Gradually, however, he would begin to establish a cluster of useful, like-minded enthusiasts and valuable contacts. Foremost among them was to be Buzzcocks manager and label overseer Richard Boon. He was first introduced to Morrissey by the legendary obscure Rick "Obi". While The Buzzcocks were still gigging locally, Rick had placed an effusive advertisement in *Sounds* requesting information from fellow fans. Frustratingly, the music paper misprinted the (061) Manchester dialling code as OBI, thereby providing a suitably punkish monicker in the process. Boon and his Buzzcocks were so flattered by "Obi's" devoted interest that they invited him out for a beer. When Obi turned up at a subsequent meeting with Boon, he introduced a fellow advertiser and punk enthusiast, Steven Morrissey. Both kids were decidedly low key, seemingly more interested in swapping information and tapes than founding fanzines or storming the new wave citadel with vitally radical ideas. However, while Obi came and

---

* Morrissey later immortalized this and the motorcycle-riding American trip on a promotional issue of 'Interesting Drug', which was credited to "Au Pair Motorcycle Boy". The title also recalled the central character in the film *Rumblefish*, who was nicknamed the Motorcycle Boy.

went, Morrissey was always there, sitting in the background, often barely noticed but increasingly cognizant of Manchester's musical undercurrents.

Having failed to discover Dolls' fixated youngsters eager to embrace his idea of forming a punk group, Morrissey turned his thoughts towards a more traditional ensemble. By 1977, the CJs had graduated from performing at the Royal Ancient Hall of Buffs to the more exciting and exacting surroundings of working men's clubs, hotels and pubs. Jim Verrechia's mother had proven an adept amateur agent and the boys were pleased with the pocket money that regular gigging provided. However, college commitments were already threatening to fragment the group and they suffered their first crisis when their classically-trained pianist and bass player Jim Twomey quit. Reduced to a trio, they urgently required a competent bassist to fill in the parts left silent by Twomey's untimely departure.

When Morrissey heard of the vacancy, he decided to reacquaint himself with his former St Marys class-mates. Jim Verrechia was surprised and somewhat sceptical when Morrissey nonchalantly turned up for an audition. During their school days, he had seen Steven successively attempt to master guitar, saxophone and piano and on each occasion the results had been calamitous. Now he was apparently a bass player too. Morrissey's technical deficiencies were rapidly exposed within minutes of the audition and, as Verrechia charitably observed: "We weren't too happy with him. I don't think he could play, basically. He had trouble with our rhythm, so we decided he wasn't the chap for us." Even if Morrissey had been a budding Chris Hillman, his induction would still have been a mismatch. The CJs' easy-going pub rock repertoire was far too conservative for Steven's hip tastes, although the experience gained would have proven most useful.

Undeterred, Morrissey next announced that he was intending to play drums. It was to prove a premature assertion. Once again, ambition and imagination outstretched aptitude and budget. The elusive drum-kit remained unpurchased. Instead, Morrissey contented himself with elliptical post-gig scribblings on the abilities and limitations of visiting rock drummers. Meanwhile, he pursued the more economical task of developing his creative writing skills. In an inspired moment, fuelled by dreams of authorial fame, he wrote a short story, grandly titled *Sic Transit Gloria Mundi*. The setting was a dilapidated tenement in Brooklyn, New York, which houses the major characters: Edward, Beatrice, Amelia and their manipulative, bed-ridden mother. Ostensibly crusty and middle-aged, the trapped offspring enjoy exotically secret lives: Edward is engaged in a homosexual affair, Amelia is an adulteress and Beatrice a prostitute. The climactic death of the matriarch threatens to break up the family, but rather than embrace freedom, the sibling trio continue their hypocritical double lives and remain uneasily together. The story provided a revealing insight into Morrissey's versatility. Although the plot was stylistically reminiscent of a Tennessee Williams psychodrama, it was interesting to observe Morrissey experimenting with settings outside his native Manchester.

"I didn't go to college to get a job running upstairs," Morrissey exploded during February 1977. Yet, within a month, he astonished colleagues, and even *himself*, by accepting a clerical post with the Inland Revenue. The wages were £22.50 for a 37-hour week and the working conditions seemed tolerable and untaxing. Despite breaking free of the dole, Morrissey was still uneasy about the prospect of starting work. "When I had no job I could pinpoint my depression," he mused, "but when I did get a job I was *still* depressed." It was that attitude that he later captured most vividly in the lyrics of 'Heaven Knows I'm Miserable Now'. The extent of Morrissey's ambivalence towards work was evinced during a chance meeting with former college acquaintance Gary Carroll, only days before starting at the Revenue. When Morrissey learned that several "old boys", including Malcolm Desmond, Andrew Riley and George Sutcliffe, were still studying, he felt genuinely nostalgic for student life. It was only when he recalled his difficulty in accepting the limitations of a set syllabus that he realized the futility of such thoughts. In his more altruistically enlightened moments, Steven mentioned the possibility of voluntary work for the RSPCA or the homeless, but such idealistic whims soon passed as he steeled himself for life at the Revenue.

As he approached his eighteenth birthday, Steven fell into one of those maudlin depressions that so often threatened to overwhelm him. After work, he would return home and spend solitary evenings in his bedroom wondering what was happening to his life. The shock of work, coupled with the fact that one of his few friends had moved to Devon, no doubt contributed to his malaise. "I am totally disillusioned with life, time passes and things get progressively worse," he noted; yet that affirmation of despair was undermined by the vibrancy of Morrissey's railing and the excitement he felt about his far from dormant creative energies. Alone in his room, he did not merely stare at the walls but composed two more short stories, *I Wanna See The Bright Lights Again* and *Diddy Wah Diddy*, both titles inspired by old blues songs. With his first month's wages, he hot-footed across to the Grass Roots shop in Newton Street and, full of the joys of April, purchased no less than six books: *The Facts Of Rape* by Barbara Toner, *Women And Madness* by Phyliss Chesler, *Dialogue With Mothers* by Bruno Bettelheim, *Diary Of A Harlem Schoolteacher* by Jim Haskins, *Sex And Racism* by Calvin C Hernton and *Against Our Will* by Susan Brownmiller. The titles were revealing, particularly *Women And Madness* which provided the provocative argument that women who reject or are ambivalent about their feminine roles may become ostracized by society and thereby pushed into self-destructive situations or tendencies. One section that seemed particularly pertinent to Morrissey's thinking was Chesler's discussion of the relationship between regimented sex roles and social behaviour: "What we consider 'madness', whether it appears in women or in men, is either the acting out of the devalued female role or the total or partial rejection of one's sex-role stereotype."

Morrissey's intense fascination with the blurred distinction between masculine and feminine roles was heightened by such reading. Looking back at his successive championing of Bolan, Bowie and The New York Dolls there is evidence enough of a youth celebrating celebrity androgyny. Not surprisingly, the stress on "demasculization" encouraged Steven to question his own sexuality. He had gone through a period during which he suspected that he might be homosexual but dismissed the notion completely upon realizing that he was no more attracted by boys than he was by girls. "I'm just not turned on by naked bodies," he concluded. "I could be gazing at a 900 page encyclopaedia on Greek mythology for all the thrills I get. I'm not really stimulated by male or female." This led Morrissey to conclude that he was most likely "a-sexual". Wary of marriage ("A newly wed is nearly dead" was a favourite aphorism) he became increasingly sceptical about ever having children. Despite his previous sexual fumblings, he found the mechanics of love-making awkward, uncomfortable and intimidating. Sexual arousal was frustratingly absent and the anti-climactic experience, at first greeted with concern, was eventually replaced by an enveloping disinterest in copulation. "I can't imagine my body feeling sexual excitement", Morrissey notes. "I don't reject sex. I don't accept it either. It simply doesn't exist, that's all." Already perceiving a future without sex, marriage or physical companionship, Morrissey's only concession to the possibility of "settling down" in adulthood involved an imaginary domestic scenario populated by deprived orphans. "Kids at orphanages have it bad," he sympathized. "They really are brought up to feel inferior."

Apart from devouring feminist titles, Morrissey had shown a noticeable interest in the plight of the negro in society. Both *Sex And Racism* and *Diary Of A Harlem Schoolteacher* provided important clues to Morrissey's liberal sensitivity. He had little patience for even the casual racism of everyday conversation and was not above correcting the bigoted with a smart rejoinder. One of his closest friends during 1977 was a black girl named Marcia, whose presence no doubt reinforced his egalitarian outlook. His sympathy towards the plight of the black community was sincerely voiced and deserves to be noted. In spite of all this, he could be characteristically inconsistent in his world view. Even while denouncing racial prejudice in stirring fashion, he was wont to admit that he disliked Pakistanis. "I don't hate Pakistanis, but I dislike them immensely," was his flippantly blunt adolescent observation. The basis of that aversion was crudely stereotypical, offensive and out of step with his general philosophy. But such is the irrational singularity and eccentricity of most prejudice. Morrissey was still 18 at this point - old enough, but perhaps not yet wise enough, to know better. Fundamentally, he accepted that ignorance was the father of prejudice and realized that he still had much to learn.

Years later, he revisited and, some would argue, reiterated those old prejudices in his controversial composition 'Bengali In Platforms'. What bothered many people about the song was its ambiguous tone and point of view. With such lines as "it's hard enough when you belong here" (thereby implicitly suggesting that Bengalis do *not* belong here) and the arrogant directive ("shelve your western plans"), it was hard to avoid accusations of condescension, at the very least. As a reviewer in *Q* perceptively noted: "In Morrissey's mind, this may be a profound statement about personal alienation but unfortunately it would still go down very well at a singalong after a National Front picnic. The noblest intentions - assuming that's what he has - are no protection from the consequences when you touch subjects like this."

Morrissey apologists would no doubt suggest that the song was intended as a condemnation of the Westernization of the Asian community rather than a defeated rejection of the idea of a multi-racial society. The differing views merely underline the essential ambiguity of the song. A greater understanding of Morrissey's point of view in 'Bengali In Platforms' arguably can be gleaned from placing the composition in the context of *Viva Hate*, an album that evokes several themes and images from the Seventies. With its precise descriptions of "platform shoes" and blinding ankle stars, the lyrics set the imagery of the song firmly in the past. It may be that the point of view promoted is similarly detached and dated. That is to say, the condescending connotations that prove so irksome are not intended to represent Morrissey's present attitude towards Bengalis, but document past prejudices, when his all-embracing adolescent liberalism eccentrically excluded certain aspects of the Asian community. By the time he came to write 'Asian Rut' on *Kill Uncle*, the old ambiguities were still there, but Morrissey's sympathies were far more noticeable. The drugged, gun-toting Asian is portrayed as a modern-day Promethean hero, outnumbered and ultimately consumed by his white adversaries. Morrissey's continued fascination with the plight of the Asian suggests a working through of his flippant teenage musings, when he speculated upon such dubious matters as their supposedly mysterious chewing habits and "aroma". Even then, he seemed to realize that it was a lack of understanding about their culture which provoked such stereotypical reactions. Now, he incorporates raga elements into his work, with violinist Nawazish Ali Khan adding spice to an otherwise conventional pop single like 'Our Frank'. More importantly, the liberal cycle appears to have long been completed, as Morrissey himself stresses in his catch-all conclusion: "I am incapable of racism."

Back in 1977, Morrissey testified to the depth of his artistic frustration in a most revealing note. "I'm sick of being the undiscovered genius, I want fame NOW not when I'm dead," he implored. Such flights of self-aggrandizing fantasy generally propelled him depressingly downwards or inspired a dramatic creative surge. On this occasion, the "undiscovered genius" decided to write himself out of the blues and into the annals of imagined fame. Less than two weeks after his eighteenth birthday, he proudly began work on his first book, tentatively titled, *When Will Ms Muffet Fight Back?* Ostensibly a distillation of his feminist readings, it seemed far too ambitious a work ever to reach completion, but Morrissey was enthusiastic enough to produce a detailed list of chapter headings while attending a dull Inland Revenue course. The preliminary contents read: Chapter One - 'The Beautiful Bride And The Intelligent Husband'; Chapter Two - 'Ladies First - But For How Long?'; Chapter Three - 'Women And Children First? Who Goes Second?'; Chapter Four - 'Men's Awakening

- Why Hasn't It Arrived?' It says much about Morrissey that he would linger admirably over the catchy chapter titles but never complete the work.

As well as musing over the great unwritten book, Morrissey increased his concert attendances as a battalion of springtime American invaders descended on Manchester. In successive weeks, he saw Talking Heads, The Ramones, Blondie and Television, and was only disappointed by the latter. The brief transposition of the East Coast élite to his hometown was particularly welcome as Morrissey had just received news that his relations were moving out of New Jersey. Their destination was Arvada, Colorado, a region that conjured up the winsome sentimentality of John Denver, rather than the hard urban edge of Patti Smith. Morrissey was mortified when he heard the news. For the past two months he had entered a peculiarly Anglophobic phase, bolstered by the realization that his £22.50 per week might yet be translated into an air fare. Having humorously denounced everything from the BBC and Angela Rippon to fish and chips and the M1, Morrissey was left with the uncomfortable knowledge that he would not be America bound after all. Suddenly, the need to escape from Stretford became all-consuming. In his most desperate moments, Morrissey even posited the possibility of emigrating to Australia. Clearly, he was a very confused young man.

Fortunately, England came to his rescue in June 1977. The Sex Pistols, whom he had once hated, had gladdened his heart with a subversive swipe at Her Majesty titled 'God Save The Queen'. Forgetting the apparent limitations of Angela Rippon and the lure of seedy New York, Morrissey concluded that Blighty deserved a second chance. As the summer grew hotter, he embraced the anti-establishment zeal espoused by the Pistols-championing music press. Tense excitement was in the air when 'God Save The Queen' climbed to number one in the *NME* chart during Jubilee Week. Sensing a commotion, Pistols' manager Malcolm McLaren had persuaded Virgin Records to mount a pointed publicity campaign pleading for liberality. The events of June 1977 were to prove the most significant in the Pistols' career as their macabre single and much publicized outrage tore into the heart of British Nationalism in a comic horror fashion that came close to an act of genuine situationism.

The inventive McLaren next organized a boat party on the Thames which enabled the Pistols to wax anarchic outside the Houses of Parliament. After disembarking from the appropriately named *Queen Elizabeth*, several of the anti-royal revellers found themselves under arrest. The assault upon Her Majesty presaged the ominous appearance of menacing mobs masquerading as the general public. The foolhardy wearing of a 'God Save The Queen' T-shirt, provocatively displaying Her Majesty's safety-pinned nose, encouraged McLaren's once revered Teddy Boys to break art director Jamie Reid's nose and leg. Johnny Rotten was the next victim, slashed with a razor while walking with producer Chris Thomas. Within two days of the attack, drummer Paul Cook received a good thrashing, topped off with the crunch of an iron bar across the head. When the Pistols subsequently went into hiding, the violence spilled on to the streets. The most prominent spot was London's Kings Road, which still housed McLaren's latest boutique, Seditionaries. Significantly, the warring factions consisted of Teds and Punks, the two youth sub-cultures which the red-haired haberdasher had so lovingly nurtured. Having ignited the passions of youth, The Sex Pistols were now in danger of being consumed by the conflagration.

Morrissey responded to the public disorder in an engagingly mischievous mood; he marched in a 'Ban The Jubilee' demonstration, promised to purchase some red drainpipe trousers and threatened to outrage the Inland Revenue by wearing a 'Now I Wanna Sniff Some Glue' T-shirt to work. He even suggested changing his name to Byron De Niro. For a time, his mood was positively jubilant but this spirit of enthusiasm was soon replaced by that familiar downward spiral. Within a month, Morrissey was to be found sitting in the X-Ray department of his local hospital. He was spotted by former class-mate Steve Wooley, who told friends: "He looks really ill." Wooley was not exaggerating. Morrissey had, in fact, been spitting blood frequently and his doctor was sufficiently concerned to prescribe a full medical. Fortunately, nothing serious was uncovered, although Morrissey reacted with embarrassed horror at the investigative diligence of the specialists. Their laudable search for a "Morrissey cure" merely left their patient ashen-faced and ungrateful. On leaving the dreaded hospital, he complained: "Castrated rats are treated with more affection!"

By a macabre coincidence, Morrissey's mystery illness occurred during the same week that one of his aunts was involved in a car crash. As part of his own convalescence, Steven was assigned the task of looking after his young cousins during the evening. The precocious pre-teens nicknamed him "Steve Austin - the Bionic Man", a singularly inappropriate title given his inability to find the energy to keep up with them.

The downward curve of the summer predictably reactivated Morrissey's emigrant dreams. His latest destination was the Alps, where he intended to work in an hotel. The idea proved as unrealistic as his attempt to become an Au Pair Boy earlier in the year. Instead, he visited London but, finding the metropolis disappointing, returned home in disillusionment. After a heart-to-heart with his sister Jackie, they both decided that a trip to America in 1978 was mandatory. That same night Steven fell asleep and dreamt that he was a character in the US television series *The Waltons*. "Shows how exciting my life is," he joked.

The next day, Morrissey trudged to work where reveries of a more familiar kind dominated his thoughts. Wandering through the office, he received a heart-pounding shock after spotting a girl who bore a striking resemblance to his "secret love", Ann-Marie McVeigh. As he approached her desk, he noticed a plaque on which her name was printed. It read: AM Ryan. The gods were clearly toying with his emotional life.

During the final months of 1977, Morrissey at last found some aspiring musicians seemingly willing to accept his services as a singer. For some time, he had been corresponding with a promising Wythenshawe guitarist and fellow New York Dolls devotee, Billy Duffy. As with many Morrissey connections their relationship was purely epistolary, but Duffy was impressed by the concert tapes and impromptu lyrics that infrequently arrived at his door. Often he would regale friends with Morrissey's correspondence, unveiling a small sheaf of lyrics with such titles as 'The Living Juke-box' and '(I Think) I'm Ready For The Electric Chair'. Despite his obvious empathy with the still-unseen Morrissey, Duffy seemed destined for far greater rock heights, having recently applied for the post of lead guitarist in Glen Matlock's Sex Pistols offshoot, The Rich Kids. After losing out to the more experienced and established Midge Ure (of the chart-topping Slik) Duffy returned to less elevated band matters. He tinkered undecidedly with a group tentatively titled Torpedo, whose ranks included another Wythenshawe hopeful Steve Pomfret. The twosome were frequent visitors to such bars as the Ranch, which had recently become a punk hostelry. By fortunate coincidence, the engaging Pomfret actually knew Morrissey and, aware of his postal relationship with Duffy, decided that a formal musical introduction was well overdue. Before long, this unlikely trio was busily undertaking rough rehearsals at Pomfret's house. Since he did not play guitar, Morrissey naturally slotted into the lead vocalist role. Duffy's school-mate and guitar protégé Robin Allman attended one of their get-togethers and recalls Morrissey's torturous vocal work, complemented by crude, incondite, Heartbreakers'-inspired musical backing. Duffy was eagerly incorporating Dolls riffs into the set, several of which he had adapted from live tapes supplied by Morrissey. The proceedings took a rather strange twist when Morrissey suggested, much to Pomfret's mystification, that they should attempt The Foundations' 'Build Me Up Buttercup'. Even at this early stage, Morrissey's love of undiluted, breezy pop clashed head-on with his tuneless new wave growl.

The casual rehearsals continued sporadically but it always seemed likely that the older Duffy might move on to more promising ventures. At one point, the aforementioned Allman received an invitation to join Duffy, Pomfret and Morrissey for a summit at the Milk Bar in Piccadilly, Manchester. The message indicated that Steven Patrick was eager to front a performing band. Over several cups of coffee, "Pommy" and Duffy laid out their plans for this new group and proposed Allman as rhythm guitarist. Unfortunately, the would-be recruit was unimpressed by the criminally vulgar shyness of the mysterious singer, whose passive role in the discussion was embarrassing. "I felt Morrissey was a fruitcake. He just sat there and said nothing all through this so-called meeting. It came to nothing."

As expected, the ever-resourceful Duffy soon found a more promising alternative when a couple of Wythenshawe musicians invited him to join what remained of the ailing Nosebleeds. Decimated by recent personnel changes, they also required a vocalist, so Duffy suggested the still untested Morrissey. A rehearsal was agreed. Although Billy committed the cardinal sin of keeping his faithful lyricist waiting in the November cold for a full hour, the thawing one was still eager to shine as lead vocalist. Had Morrissey known a little more about the candescent history of the group his enthusiasm might not have been so evident.

The Nosebleeds actually began life in the early Seventies under the name Wild Ram. By the dawn of punk, they had changed their monicker to the humorous Ed Banger And The Nosebleeds. Their leader, Eddie Garrity, was a singing milkman, just like his Sixties namesake Freddie Garrity, from Freddie And The Dreamers. Any other comparisons ended there. Whereas Freddie was known for his slight frame, high-pitched squeals and endearing comedy routines, Eddie was one of the toughest and vocally intimidating performers to emerge from the Olympus of Manchester punk. By contrast, the group's guitarist, a frail teenager from Didsbury named Vini Reilly, seemed incongruously out-of-place amid the laddish Wythenshawe clique. Reilly was particularly impressed by the power and presence of The Nosebleeds' manager Vini Faal, who swanned around tough clubs accompanied by a team of heavy friends. "Ed Banger used to confront and provoke the audience to such an extent that there was always a crowd waiting outside," recalls Reilly. "It was a very violent gig."

The music of The Nosebleeds was decidedly uncompromising and at one time they offered only two songs in a set which lasted a mere 20 minutes. An obscure single, 'Ain't Bin To No Music School'/'Fascist Pigs' (on Rabid Records) captured them at their unholy zenith. After the early fires of punk subsided, Reilly moved on, re-emerging in the perennial Durutti Column. He still recalls The Nosebleeds period with bemused affection. "They were very good to me and taught me a lot about life. They were all hard, and Vince the manager was the hardest of all. They were absolutely wild, completely out of the woods. Morrissey being involved blows my mind."

When Garrity grew weary of the Ed Banger persona the group fragmented, but bassist Pete Crookes and drummer Toby (Philip Tolman) soon resurfaced in a new version of The Nosebleeds. Following Billy Duffy's strong recommendation they agreed to the recruitment of the taciturn Steven Morrissey. The inexperienced new singer clearly lacked the powerful presence of the unforgettable Ed Banger, but his collaborations with Duffy suggested that they had the foundations of a promising songwriting team and the potential to pursue a new fruitful direction. For a second generation group, it wasn't a bad way to conclude the year.

Steven's grandparents, Peter and Ellen, on their wedding day. Note the family resemblance.
(Morrissey/Corrigan Family Archive).

Mary Bridget Morrissey, aged 17.
(Morrissey/Courtney Family Archive).

Christina Morrissey (1950). Aged 17.
(Morrissey/Courtney Family Archive).

1952. Crumlin, Dublin. Left to right: Mary, Ellen Snr, Patricia, Peter Snr.
(Morrissey/Corrigan Family Archive).

The Morrissey clan at Clonard Road in 1954. Left to right: Peter, Christina, Patricia, Peter Snr, Thomas, Ellen Snr and Ann. *(Morrissey/Corrigan Family Archive)*.

RIGHT:
Front row: Christina, Ellen Snr and Patricia Morrissey.
(Morrissey/Corrigan Family Archive).

LEFT:
1952. Left to right: family friend, Mary, Ellen Snr, Patricia, Peter Snr.
(Morrissey/Corrigan Family Archive).

Thomas and Peter Morrissey in O'Connell Street, Dublin, 1952.
(Morrissey/Courtney Family Archive).

Steven's father Peter Morrissey shortly after arriving in Manchester, 1955.
(Morrissey/Courtney Family Archive).

1953. Peter Morrissey aged 17, with his brother-in-law, Richard Corrigan.
(Morrissey/Courtney Family Archive).

1957. Steven's grandfather and uncle Richard drinking Guinness in a Manchester hostelry.
(Morrissey/Corrigan Family Archive).

Steven's mother and grandmother. *(Morrissey/Courtney Family Archive)*.

Steven's mother Betty in Manchester's Alexandra Park in the mid-50s.
(Morrissey/Courtney Family Archive).

Steven's sister Jacqueline and grandfather outside 20 Stockton Street, Moss Side, Manchester.
(Morrissey/Courtney Family Archive).

Jackie in 1972, shortly before her 16th birthday.
(Messenger Family Archive).

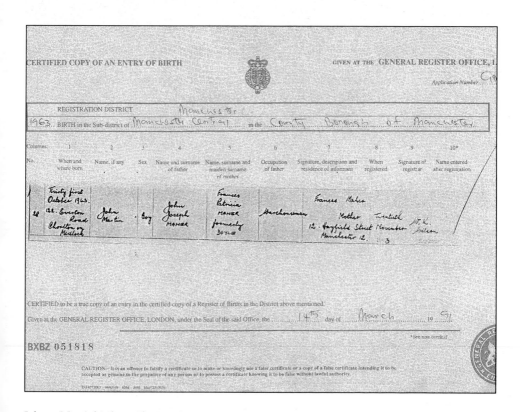

Steven Morrissey's birth certificate.

Johnny Marr's birth certificate.

1966. Fifty years after the Irish Easter Uprising, Morrissey celebrates his first Holy Communion. Middle back row: class-mates Chris Lukes and Steve Smythe. *(Morrissey Family Collection).*

Close-up of Morrissey in the above line-up. *(Morrissey Family Collection).*

Steven, aged 13, displays his over-sized heart. *(Messenger Family Collection).*

5

The Reluctant Rock Critic

MORRISSEY ENDED 1977 IN a discernibly impatient mood. His parents were reunited for Christmas but Steven showed little interest in the yule-tide festivities. He vowed to make a break from both home and work in the New Year, even though his wages had recently risen to £26.00 a week. On Friday 6 January, he became involved in a furious row with the Inspector of Taxes and felt angered and shaken by the regrettable confrontation. "Nobody understands me," was his frustrated reaction to the unhappy affair. Although he held hopes of finding a flat in Urmston with several of The Nosebleeds, that arrangement failed to materialize. Worse still, he was sceptical about the degree of their commitment to his future in the line-up. To complete his dilemma, there was the perpetually nagging lure of America.

Frustrated and desperate to achieve a fresh start, Morrissey rapidly slumped into inconsolable self-pity. "I can't stand it anymore... I want to run away from myself," he wrote. Instead of aimlessly running, he walked to the doctor's surgery and stated bluntly that he was depressed. After hearing the youth's mournful outpourings, the astute GP took Steven aside and advised, in all seriousness, that he should join a youth club. Stunned at the suggestion, Morrissey left the surgery and, after considering the advice, forlornly muttered: "Good grief!" Convinced that he was in a terrible rut, and inflamed with a great sense of urgency, Morrissey announced, with tongue-in-cheek melodrama: "If I'm still here by March, I'll kill myself!"

Remarkably, Morrissey survived his March deadline by the whisker of a leap day year. On 29 February, he was overjoyed to leave Manchester for a welcome and exciting visit to London. The occasion was nothing less grand than a Patti Smith press conference. Over recent months, Morrissey had been contributing to *Kids Stuff*, a Surrey-based fanzine in which he wrote effusively about the "Manchester scene". In the DIY climate of 1978 that was sufficient qualification to win an audience, albeit a distant one, with his favourite heroine. The uplifting effects that the invitation had on Morrissey's spirits immediately vanquished his previously negative musings. On the day prior to his departure, he popped into the Grass Roots shop in Newton Street and purchased a badge proclaiming: "Women's Liberation". The sales assistant was so impressed by his solidarity that she gleefully presented him with a gratis button advertising the more provocative "Lesbian Liberation". Morrissey was overjoyed when he received some quizzical looks on the way home to 384 Kings Road. Feeling suitably militant he placed 'Hard Nipples' on his turntable, read a chapter of Germaine Greer's *The Female Eunuch*, devoured several slices of cream cheesecake, packed his hold-all, and set off in search of Patti Smith.

After returning from London, Morrissey seemed charged with commitment. Revitalized by the sight of Smith, he made some bold decisions which included leaving the tedious Inland Revenue, agreeing to gig with The Nosebleeds and, least importantly, christening a kitten "Peppermint Patti". A sudden twinge of indecision saw him momentarily back at work in a dingy office in Old Trafford, but his stay lasted a mere 24 hours. Freedom beckoned in the form of another long spell on the dole.

During the spring of 1978, Steven Morrissey's life resembled nothing less than a rock'n'roll *Carry On* sketch. He careered back and forth to London, rehearsed with The Nosebleeds, learned that his public performing début was on Saturday 15 April, and then scuttled across to the doctor's surgery in search of solace. His problems had begun in earnest on the evening of 7 April. After rushing through his tea, he burped incredibly loudly and this set off a gaggle of galloping hiccups that lasted an entire week. "I couldn't leave the house due to these constant burps," he confessed. Mortified at the devastation this might cause his nascent singing career, Morrissey urged his doctor to provide a cure. The ever patient physician duly prescribed some submarine-shaped milk pills, which defeated the Morrissey indigestion in the nick of time.

On Saturday 15 April, the news of the day was the mysterious disappearance of Joyce McKinney, who had been accused of kidnapping and sexually abusing a Mormon missionary. Normally such a story would have intrigued Morrissey but he was rather more concerned with his evening performance at Manchester Polytechnic, where The Nosebleeds lined up alongside a package of Rabid Records artistes. At least this gig offered the opportunity of a celebratory gin and tonic, Steven's favourite tipple of the moment. The actual performance passed quickly and Morrissey was pleased enough with the reception. "We were monstrously good and went down very well," he recalled. The only negative aspect of the evening was seeing The Nosebleeds at the foot of the bill, beneath a roll-call of minor acts headed by Slaughter And The Dogs and John Cooper Clarke.

On 19 April, the following Wednesday, Steven was back in hospital, this time visiting his mother, who was lain low with a mystery ailment. Wearied by hospital hours, she slept through her son's dutiful visit. Steven compulsively chewed handfuls of grapes, practised "looking French" for the benefit of hovering nurses, and cradled a copy of Rita Mae Brown's *Rubyfruit Jungle*, a book that Myra Hindley had nominated as her own personal favourite.

The short-lived career of The Nosebleeds abruptly ended several weeks later with their second gig, a support slot to Magazine at the Ritz. By this stage, Duffy and Morrissey had written a sizeable chunk of The Nosebleeds' set, including such songs as 'I Get Nervous', '(I Think) I'm

Ready For The Electric Chair', 'The Living Juke-Box' and 'Peppermint Heaven'. On the evening of the gig, Billy's girlfriend Karen diligently applied make-up to the eye-lids of her beau in an attempt to transform the Wythenshawe youth into a New York Doll. Observing from the audience, Rob Allman noted: "Billy was doing his rock star bit and Morrissey was trying to look like the cover of David Johansen's first album. He had his hair all over his face". As the set began, Howard Devoto popped his head out of the dressing room and remembers Morrissey's "long hair that he kept chucking about". Half-way through The Nosebleeds' performance the lights failed and the club was thrust into darkness for several minutes. Recovering his poise after the delay, Morrissey continued with 'Peppermint Heaven', during which he distributed sweets to bemused members of the audience. The surprise song of the evening was a cover of The Shangri-Las' 'Give Him A Great Big Kiss', a New York Dolls' favourite in which Morrissey pointedly and predictably neglected to alter the gender of the title. Allman enjoyed the show and afterwards compared Morrissey to Japan's outrageously androgynous vocalist David Sylvian. *New Musical Express'* Manchester contributor Paul Morley was also on hand to see Magazine and perceptively noted the "charisma" of The Nosebleeds' lead singer. Given the positive response, it was a shame that the experiment was terminated after only two gigs. Stevie (as he was now calling himself) was back to square one.

Since re-signing on the dole on 20 April, Morrissey found that he had lots of time on his hands. The abrupt demise of The Nosebleeds had proven a major disappointment so Stevie returned to his bedroom and indulged himself in a Tamla Motown phase, with special emphasis on Martha And The Vandellas and The Marvelettes. Meanwhile, former Nosebleeds' compatriot Billy Duffy had teamed up with the remnants of Slaughter And The Dogs, who were still coming to terms with the departure of lead singer Wayne Barrett and the loss of a major record contract with Decca. Although Slaughter already seemed like historical casualties of the punk era, Duffy felt their original appeal could be invigorated and rechannelled. Guitarist Mike Rossi was tentatively handling lead vocals, and Duffy wondered whether another aspiring singer might enhance their chances. There were certainly strong reasons for considering Steven Morrissey, not least his musical tastes, which mirrored those of the group. As Rob Gretton (former Slaughter associate and later Joy Division/New Order manager) pointed out: "They were quite a strange group. They used punk fashion to a certain extent, but they were more like glam rock. Their heroes were The New York Dolls, Bowie and Roxy Music." As if to demonstrate their affinity with Morrissey, Slaughter's act included the Dolls' 'Who Are The Mystery Girls?'

Studio owner and TJM label boss Tony James Davidson claims that he witnessed Morrissey's audition, which took place in the autumn of 1978. "He had a certain charisma about him and seemed very much in another world; he did two to three songs and then went off to the park to think about it," Davidson claims. When Stevie returned, his most pertinent suggestion was that they should incorporate The Velvelettes 'Needle In A Haystack' into their varied set. Although Morrissey's induction was never ratified by any written agreement, he certainly considered himself a member of the group.

On 22 October, Steven accompanied Slaughter to London for a record company audition, which ended in rejection. In retrospect, that incident may have thwarted his chances of becoming their permanent lead singer. Within three months, Slaughter moved to London, changed their name to the Studio Sweethearts and secured a contract with DJM Records. What might have happened had Morrissey travelled with them and retained his partnership with Billy Duffy remains an intriguing speculation.

The week before Slaughter's unsuccessful London audition, Morrissey found his dole money under severe threat. "There's work for you if you want it," he was firmly told by the unemployment officer. Normally, such pressures and disappointments would have blighted his good spirits, but the Manchester blues were easily brushed aside. For on Wednesday 1 November, Steven was scheduled to fly to Colorado.

In the final days before his departure, Morrissey made another sterling attempt to contact the ever elusive Ann-Marie McVeigh. "I cannot deny my affection for this tempestuous creature," he noted judiciously. The trail ended unsuccessfully at Boots the chemist where she had last worked. Undeterred, Morrissey extended the search, sent a note to an old address, prayed for a reply, and was finally rewarded by a phone call from his fantasy femme fatale on the eve of his departure. It was a pleasant enough conversation, which prompted his theatrically arch observation: "I only wish there was something I could do to make her adore me, but there isn't... life is cruel, as is love." Stepping back from his imaginary drama, Morrissey summed up this frustrating relationship as "Another case of unrequited love in which I, as ever, take the leading part". At least the trip to the States offered the chance to forget.

Morrissey arrived in America on the evening of 1 November. After travelling through Georgia, he was driven to the rocky mountains of Arvada. On arrival, he christened the town Nirvana but, within a fortnight, he had renamed this haven "Aesthetes' Hell". Initially, he had been impressed by the breathtaking scenery but that was soon forgotten as boredom and illness robbed him of his optimism and vitality. The conservatism of Arvada niggled his punkish sensibilities and he rapidly grew weary of hearing country rock on the radio and reading bland American magazines. The final affront occurred when he wore a pink tie and felt as though he was being treated like a transvestite. His championing of new wave music and feminist politics provoked puzzlement rather than interest, and he soon despaired of playing the proselytizer. Instead, he adopted a new role: the modern day Oscar Wilde visiting America. Morrissey's waspish wit was seldom better exemplified than during the Arvada sojourn and a series of razor-sharp one-liners and amusing aphorisms survive this period. On being complimented as a genius, Morrissey retorted: "I know I am a genius, but you should know that one is never called a genius until one is dead." Questioned about the prospects of finding fame as a published poet, he quipped: "I will never make a successful poet because all of my poems make sense." The stately, Wildean tone oozed luxuriously from his lips and pen and was perhaps best summed up in his impertinent lament: "There is no sex in Colorado". Retiring to his sick bed, Morrissey found spiritual redemption in a battered copy of Agatha Christie's *Murder At The Vicarage*. Penniless and ready to borrow money for his return trip, he seemed content to abandon the scenic rocky mountains in favour of Manchester's monochrome streets.

After an eventful 1978, during which he had launched his performing career, Stevie seemed less certain about his direction in the New Year. The absence of a catalyst like Billy Duffy or Steve Pomfret meant that he was in danger of merely marking time. In an attempt to combine his musical interests with gainful employment, Morrissey briefly worked at Yanks Records in Chepstow Street. The opportunity to play records all day and meet people soon proved insufficient compensation for what he saw as long hours and low wages. By April, he found an escape route when some friends invited him to stay in London. For several weeks, Morrissey was a resident of Bermondsey, an area best remembered in rock 'n' roll history as the birthplace of Tommy Steele and Wee Willie Harris. In later years, Morrissey would pay homage to his brief Bermondsey sojourn in the video of 'The Last Of The Famous International Playboys'.

During the same May week that Stevie returned to Manchester, Margaret Thatcher swept to power in Downing Street with an inaugural speech spiced with borrowed words from St Francis of Assisi. Her promise to transform the economic and industrial climate of Britain would prove decidedly prophetic in the light of subsequent events. Morrissey barely lasted a month in Thatcherite Britain before whisking off to Paris for a week's holiday. Although he fantasized about living an artist's life abroad, his more immediate plan was to return to college in September. In the event, both ambitions were to remain unrealized. Instead, Morrissey drifted back to life on the dole and spent most of his time reading books, listening to records and watching films. During the first week of May alone he saw the disappointing remake of *Invasion Of The Bodysnatchers*, the comedy *California Suite* and the excellent black and white thriller *Double Indemnity*. His love of horror was sated with *The Hills Have Eyes* and *Halloween*, which he then regarded as the most compelling film he had ever seen. Light relief was offered by the "transvestite" comedy *Some Like It Hot* and *West Side Story* (the soundtrack to Morrissey's imaginary youth).

On the musical front, Stevie was downright appalled by the increased popularity of The Police's white reggae rhythms, especially when Sting and company had the audacity to headline over his beloved Cramps. A small barrage of letters to the music press exposed his wrath publicly. The *NME* missive was particularly effective in its metaphorically mixed contention that "The Cramps are worth their weight in gold for making The Police seem like a great big sloppy bowl of mush". Straining at the leash, Morrissey concluded: "The Cramps were enough to restore faith in the most spiritless. They have it all, and their drummer is the most compelling in rock history. Back to The Cramps or perish. It is written."

Morrissey's championing of fringe attractions was a familiar trait and he was already entranced by the musical experimentation of a young woman who became both a close friend and confidante. Liverpool-bred Linda Mulvey had moved with her family to Manchester and subsequently attended the Polytechnic where she studied Art. During the early days of punk, Mulvey was well known on the Manchester scene as the girlfriend of Howard Devoto. That relationship ended during the Christmas of 1977 but, by then, Linda had established herself as an aspiring sleeve designer. Her work appeared on several independent new wave singles and later reached the masses courtesy of an album cover from Magazine. Generally known by the nomenclature Linder, she decided to form a group after moving into 35 Mayfield Road, in the red-light district of Whalley Range. The house was a bohemian haven for a number of promising musicians including John McGeogh and Barry Adamson of Magazine. Adamson's schoolfriend and fellow bassist Willie Trotter next joined the household and was soon elevated to the attic flat, which he shared with Linder. After extracting the talented Arthur Cadmon (Peter Sadler) from tiresome rehearsals with Stockport's Manicured Noise, Trotter introduced his discovery to Linder and the experimental group Ludus rapidly evolved. The line-up was completed by Toby (Philip Tolman), who had previously drummed behind Morrissey in The Nosebleeds.

Ludus came under the friendly aegis of Richard Boon and rehearsed in the Buzzcocks' room at TJ Davidson's popular studio. A support tour brought them to some prestigious venues, including London's Hammersmith Odeon and Liverpool's Eric's. Their performances incorporated elements of jazz and be-bop, overladen by Linder's melodic yet piercing vocal. One of their most effective mood pieces was a musical adaptation of Sylvia Plath's poem 'Daddy'. Cadmon's improvisational arrangements and Linder's oblique feminist-inspired lyrics were an unusual mix, which did not fit easily into any rock genre classification. Trotter regarded himself as the anchor man who prevented Cadmon and Linder from falling victim to their own artistic ambition. "They would try and 'out-weird' each other," he observed laconically.

Linder's influence over the men in her circle was considerable. Richard Boon credits her with inspiring much of Howard Devoto's early work, while Trotter insists that Buzzcocks' Pete Shelley composed 'What Do I Get' as an unrequited plea in her honour. During the period he went out with her, Trotter was encouraged to dress expressively and soon began wearing nail varnish onstage. "She brought an awareness and a lot of confidence about being different," he reasoned. With her passion for feminist literature, art and music, she was clearly a rare kindred spirit to the teenage Morrissey. Their reading lists converged with remarkable precision, as did their strong feelings on a range of social issues. Unlike many of Morrissey's friendships, this one would survive the insulation and self-questioning that came with fame and money. Although there would be long periods when they were out of contact, the platonic kinship proved enduring. "I don't think he and Linder had a sexual relationship," stresses Trotter. "There were a lot of people around her, not just Morrissey. I'm not sure how much she realized it, but she was a very charismatic person; exciting and vibrant without being showy. It was all done in a collective mixture of street-wise sexuality and sensuality, a lot of make-up and a real strong look." According to Linder, she and Morrissey spent a considerable amount of time simply wandering the streets of Manchester, locked in their own worlds. One of their favourite haunts was the Southern Cemetery in West Didsbury where they would amble away hours contemplating the crumbling gravestones of the obscure and forgotten. "It wasn't done in any morbid sense", stresses Linder. "At the time, it seemed quite natural." Morrissey would later capture the wistful mood of those days in his mis-spelt composition, 'Cemetry Gates'.

Linder's conceptual ideas and artwork were equally as interesting as the music she recorded. The elaborately-produced *She She* was a prized supplement to her Ludus work, portraying the singer bejewelled and heavily made-up in a series of striking images apparently designed to instil an awareness of women as commodity. Elliptical lines such as "am I your death/behind my flesh/does my skull smile" were brutally enlivened by a fork and spoon tucking into her caked eyes, and a face ripped apart to reveal a second skin. The segmentation of bodily parts, arguably the most disturbing, degrading and dehumanizing aspects of pornography, was also hinted at in her work. In Linder's bedroom, there lurked a torso-shaped lamp, clad in a bodice, which to visitors seemed both attractive and disconcerting. Such unusual and powerful imagery was further exemplified in her manufacturing of "menstrual jewellery". Using broken coat hangers with absorbent lint dipped in translucent glue and painted red, she created beads and ear-rings that resembled blooded tampons. Initially, she had experimented with real dried, menstrual blood but was disappointed by the dark colour. Tony Wilson, a regular visitor to Mayfield Road, was fascinated by Linder's jewellery and encouraged her work on the menstrual abacus. A series of beads with different colours (red, white and purple) were devised to chronicle the feminine cycle from ovulation to period. The so-called "Menstrual Egg Timer" received a Factory catalogue number (FAC 8) but failed to emerge as a commercial entity.

The concept of the menstrual egg timer no doubt owed much to one of Linder's favourite books: *The Wise Wound*. The degree to which Penelope Shuttle and Peter Redgrove's seminal, indeed ovular, tome affected her writing and creative work was underlined by Richard Boon. "She was very influenced by *The Wise Wound*," he remembers, "and turned its contents into a neat rhythmical series of couplets." The aim of *The Wise Wound* was to destroy the negative myth of "Eve's curse" and present menstruation as a positive, celebratory function of womanhood. In a fascinating chapter titled "Does The Moon Menstruate?" the authors pre-empted Linder's menstrual jewellery concept in a discussion about 4,000 year-old lunar calendars and the existence of anthropological evidence indicating that early civilizations had carved notches on animal bones with red ochre. Later in the book, their thesis even extended to embrace the menstrual iconography of Hammer horror films. As well as championing the sexually alive "happy bleeding women" in *Dracula*, the authors provided a riveting interpretation of *The Exorcist* as a full blown menstrual allegory. Morrissey was no doubt intrigued to discover that his inveterate love of horror films had a fortuitously unexpected link with feminist argument.

Christmas 1979 again captured Steven in melancholic mood. His single expression of cheer occurred unexpectedly during a surprise screening of *Christmas In Connecticut*. "If not for *Christmas In Connecticut*, I would have hounded Stretford committing acts of gross indecency," he joked. For the remainder of the season, he was insufferably bored. On the night that the Seventies expired, he sat alone in his bedroom reading a copy of Jane Austen's *Pride And Prejudice* and marvelling at the fortitude of Elizabeth Bennett. The influence of the practically-minded Austen evidently left its imprint, for within days of the New Year Stevie shocked the world by securing a job. Even more remarkably, he appeared to be following in the footsteps of his father.

Since the break-up of his marriage, when he moved to the house of his sister Patricia, Peter Morrissey had been working as a hospital porter. Young Steven recklessly accepted a similar post but soon found himself with the more arduous task of cleaning surgeons' white coats. Revolted by the sight of dried blood and what appeared to be encrusted gobbets of flesh, Morrissey was doubly appalled by the philistinism of his four vulgar work colleagues. Within a fortnight, the vegetarian flesh remover had handed in his notice. "After two weeks' slaving over a cold corpse, I decided to throw in the towel," he confessed. Feeling suitably ghoulish, Steven returned to bed and ploughed his way through the chilling *Murderers' Who's Who*. Such topical reading coincided with the grisly murders of the Yorkshire Ripper, a leading candidate for inclusion in a future edition. The thematic link was continued on 3 February when Morrissey took to the streets for an anti-Abortion Act demonstration. One can only guess what Aileen Power would have had to say about such activity.

"Being lazy is a dreadful penance but it passes the time" was Morrissey's sardonic adage for the early months of the Eighties. Despite his apparent world weariness, he was still venturing forth to visit friends in London and occasionally experienced wondrous nights that even enlivened his cosmopolitan eye. On the evening of Sunday 9 March, he and a friend witnessed a fleet of flying saucers travelling across the sky in a hexagonal formation. The sighting lasted almost a full 10 minutes and rendered Stevie absolutely speechless. "The whole thing had an astonishing effect on me," he told friends. For days afterwards, he felt inexplicably strange whenever he recalled the incident. The eerie encounter left him firmly convinced that the government was covering up the truth about UFOs. His susceptibility to such ideas no doubt originated long before the London sighting. Two years earlier, he had twice visited the cinema to see *Close Encounters Of The Third Kind* and was so impressed by the movie's verisimilitude that he even purchased the lacklustre book of the same title. Now, he was the living proof that aliens scoured the Earth.

Returning to Manchester, the moonage daydreamer resumed his concert visitations, a pastime made more pleasing by the patronage of the *Record Mirror*. Although regarded as the most superficial and least prestigious of the inky weeklies, its regional review columns were commendably eclectic. Morrissey made his début in the 29 March edition with an appraisal of The Photos' appearance at Manchester Polytechnic. A scalding commentary was only partially healed by his characteristic charity towards promising percussionists: "Possibly their only remaining grace is their drummer Ollie, whose playing is excellent". The support act, Mark Andrew And The Gents, were received much more sympathetically and described as "musically and vocally faultless". Typically, Morrissey ended his report with a flourish of nostalgic mystery: "But no songs are suicide. I miss the old days."

The Polytechnic offered more substantial fare the following month when The Cramps arrived in town. Morrissey, a long time fan, could barely contain his quizzical excitement from the *Record Mirror* readership. "Who are The Cramps?" he wrote. "They are the most beautiful, yes, BEAUTIFUL group I've ever seen. The fact that they exist is enough. Meanwhile, Manchester will never be the same again (thank God)".

The weekend following his Cramps' review, Morrissey stayed at home to catch up on his reading. He spent at least part of the evening of Saturday 12 April watching the Granada Television detective series *Crib*, in which the hero foiled the plans of some anarchists. The title of the episode was 'The Hand That Rocks The Cradle', a phrase that Morrissey duly noted for future reference.

One week later, the horror-loving Stretford youth was visited by a strange and inexplicable presence. This time it was not the arrival of extraterrestrial aliens but an incorporeal guest - the ghost of 384 Kings Road! At 2.30 on the afternoon of Friday 18 April, Steven was standing by the sink in his kitchen when he swore he saw an apparition from the corner of his eye. When he swung round there was nobody there. Four-and-a-half hours later, he was reading in his room when the front door slammed and somebody walked upstairs to the landing, switched on a light and entered the bathroom. Assuming this was Jackie returning from work, Steve emerged from his bedroom for a chat. Bizarrely, the house was completely empty. Disturbed by these happenings, Morrissey confided in his mother later that evening and was amazed to learn that she too had noted a "presence" in the bathroom. They concluded that the culprit was probably a spectre of the previous tenant, a 50-year-old woman who had died suddenly on the premises. This latest otherworldly experience inflamed Morrissey's fleeting interest in all things supernatural. The following week, as a gesture of spiritual solidarity, he ventured out to see his favourite spooky film *Halloween*. Nine years later, he would document his love of the supernatural in the comical and oft-underrated 'Ouija Board, Ouija Board'.

The end of April offered Morrissey the chance to extol the brilliance of his local heroes when Ludus played a rare gig. The venue was the Beach Club, an establishment run by Tony Wilson and Richard Boon that offered a double feature of live music preceded by a film. The latest incarnation of Ludus saw Cadmon and Trotter replaced by Linder's new boyfriend Ian Pincombe (alias Ian Devine), a multi-instrumentalist of some talent. Morrissey ensured that the ensemble's lengthy three-song set was documented extensively in the pages of *Record Mirror* and praised "scene veteran" Linder for delivering "a wild mélange of ill-disciplined and extraneous vocal movements apparently without effort". New boy Devine was deemed "tragically anonymous, but probably prefers to be", while Toby, like many drummers in Morrissey's firmament of fame, simply "cannot be faulted".

The lionizing of Ludus temporarily concluded Morrissey's promising reviewing career. It was almost as if he found them an impossible act to follow. For the remainder of the year, he was absent from the review pages of *Record Mirror* and swiftly lost his standing as their Manchester correspondent. While many junior reviewers from that time were recruited as feature writers, A&R representatives and record company press officers, Morrissey remained static. He was not entirely happy about contributing to a paper whose readership elected The Police's 'Don't Stand So Close To Me' and *Zenyatta Mondatta* as their favourite records of the year. Unfortunately, the more prestigious *New Musical Express* ignored his plea for a contributor's job and the final indignity occurred when one of their employees callously put the telephone down on him in mid-sentence. With his *Record Mirror* output all but exhausted after only a couple of months, it was difficult to escape the feeling that he had lost his chance of infiltrating the music press.

One week after Morrissey's review of Ludus appeared in *Record Mirror*, the Manchester music community was shocked by the suicide of singer Ian Curtis on the eve of Joy Division's scheduled US tour. Although Morrissey was no great fan of the group, he had recognized their importance as an influential voice in the city's independent music scene. Indeed, Morrissey was one of the few people who had bothered to mention Joy Division's mother group, Warsaw, three years earlier. Writing in *Kids Stuff* number 7, he had predicted correctly that they would outgrow their limited parochial appeal: "Of the new bands, Warsaw, The Worst, The Drones, and The Fall look the most likely to make any headway. Most of them are clumsy, all are energetic and enthusiastic. Warsaw were formed some time ago by vocalist Ian Curtis and have performed alongside more prominent bands like The Heartbreakers. Although they offer little originality with Ian's offstage antics resembling one Iggy Pop, highliting [sic] their set is 'Another Kill' which is at least memorable, if slightly typical."

Joy Division had been the flagship of Tony Wilson's enterprising independent label Factory. The former Granada presenter had extended his entrepreneurial activities by opening the Factory Club and during 1980 was considering the possibility of forming a publishing outlet for promising young Manchester writers. Wilson felt an avuncular kinship towards the Stretford youth whom he occasionally saw during his visits to Linder's house in Whalley Range. Morrissey had already complimented Wilson in print for his "slimness" and the Factory supremo maintained an endearing image of his flatterer as "the specky kid in the corner of the playground who doesn't talk but is part of the scene as the rather peculiar intellectual". For a time, Wilson felt that he had the means to tap Morrissey's uncertain potential. The answer evidently lay in publishing.

In common with the legendary menstrual egg timer, Wilson's wild and whirling publishing programme would remain unrealized. Morrissey was never seriously approached, but Wilson has vague recollections of once seeing a handful of pages from a rough one-act play. "All I can remember is that it was about toast," he suggests hopefully. "The characters lived on toast. He had the dialogue and the feel just right." On the strength of this alone, Wilson makes the astounding claim that Morrissey missed a literary vocation. "He was fair set to be the Jeanette Winterson of the Eighties, the finest young novelist... he's a woman in a man's body, she's a man in a woman's body."

Such hyperbole needs to be placed in perspective. Morrissey was not known as a creative writer; his fiction had not appeared in any established literary journal or newspaper. Nor is there any evidence of some great novel gathering dust in an attic. Add to that the fact that Wilson never actually saw any of Morrissey's prose and the claim collapses under the weight of its own bombast. The idea of Morrissey as the budding teenage novelist says more about Wilson's idealistic view of young Manchester than the existence of a genuine creative writing talent. Morrissey had enthusiasm and imagination aplenty, backed by a remarkable ability to project an image of himself as a potential writer. The sober Richard Boon was another person who regarded the wunderkind as an exceptional figure "whom everybody liked and knew would do *something*". However, when pushed, Boon conceded that he had never actually seen any example of Morrissey's creative prose. "He wanted to write", Boon stresses, "but I never saw any. Rumours get around and people seem to know what others are doing without necessarily having any evidence. Someone must have seen his stuff, but I don't know anybody who did. I was aware of him in a corner doing something, but I wasn't sure what!"

In such an accommodating climate, the degree of Morrissey's talent almost seemed secondary to the intellectual image he nurtured. Wilson's grand talk of novels distracts from the reality of Morrissey's insecurities and laziness. He enjoyed writing short pieces, aphorisms, reviews, poems and lyrics, but the slog and concentration required of a lengthy work of fiction would surely have taxed his stamina. Nevertheless, the prospect of writing something more enduring than *Record Mirror* concert reviews appealed to Morrissey. A chance letter to a small local publisher, Babylon Books, attracted the attention of proprietor/editor John Muir. Babylon specialized in low budget pop pot boilers and might have been expected to ignore something as uncommercial as a New York Dolls' scrapbook. Muir, however, was rather taken by Steven's honest enthusiasm and quite surprised when the Stretford lad produced, not merely a bunch of clippings, but a short manuscript. Although the writing was none too spectacular, Morrissey betrayed a copywriter's talent in his inventive selection of chapter titles. One read: "And What's A Nice Girl Like Shadow Morton Doing With The New York Dolls". Muir was highly amused by this and admitted: "It was the first time I'd had a laugh in rock 'n' roll for years".

Muir was a free spirit of considerable flight but few retailers realized that Babylon Books was simply one man and his printing press. Consequently, the Dolls' project languished for several months, even though Muir felt committed to his young author. "I liked him from the start," Muir admits, "and had no reservations apart from the fact that I didn't have any money to publish him".

Muir's DIY approach to publishing, combined with a woeful ignorance of standard royalty procedures and copyright law, ensured that "there was no standard Babylon contract or Babylon book". The Society of Authors would no doubt have grimaced at Muir's eccentric dealings whereby he provided no detailed written agreement. Crazily, the whole laid-back venture depended on absolute trust and Muir's law of the publishing jungle. As he frankly observed: "Deals were based on nothing. It all depended on how much money I had."

The New York Dolls finally appeared in 1981, one week after a sensation-seeking youth had fired six blank shots at the Queen's open carriage in Pall Mall. It seemed an appropriate publication date for the anti-royal Morrissey and he was pleased to see a short review of his 24-page booklet in *Record Mirror*. Muir remembers presenting his author with a cheque and offering him handfuls of gratis copies. Surprisingly, the book proved a relative success and, assuming Muir's memory is not faulty, supposedly sold close to 3,000 copies after a second printing. At the retail price of £1.50, Morrissey could reasonably have expected a return of up to £450 had he been on a standard 10 per cent royalty rate. What he actually received remains uncertain.

Eager to submit further essays for possible publication, yet unwilling to attempt a substantial work, Morrissey next considered a brief appraisal of James Dean. "I don't think writing was his life's ambition," stresses Muir, "but a step towards that ambition." In case Morrissey harboured any fantasies about making a fortune as an author, his publisher offered the following valuable advice: "I think you'll make it, but writing isn't the way to do it. There are too many authors with a small audience."

While Morrissey was not averse to being marooned in his bedroom with a typewriter, he occasionally explored the Manchester night-life, venturing into various low-life clubs where glamour was measured in excitement and a hint of danger. He had discovered like-minded enthusiasts, one of whom won a flattering eulogy at the close of The New York Dolls tome: "This book is dedicated entirely to James Maker who lives it." In effect, the club-loving Maker offered the kind of vicarious glamour that Morrissey had previously associated with the long-forgotten Mike Foley.

Unfortunately, Maker's glam image and James Dean looks drew the same kind of confrontational attention that Foley had innocently attracted years before outside the Midland Hotel. In one of his later press interviews with *Melody Maker*, Morrissey provided a wonderfully sustained shaggy dog story about an evening in the company of Maker, complete with a nightmarishly topographical excursion through the heart of Manchester.

"I can remember the worst night of my life with... James Maker," he reminisced. "We began at the Thompson Arms, we left and walked around the corner where there was a car park, just past Chorlton Street bus station. Walking through the car park I turned around, and suddenly there was a gang of 30 beer monsters, all in their late 20s, all creeping round us. So we ran. Unfortunately, they caught James and kicked him to death, but somehow he managed to stand up and start running. So James and I met in the middle of Piccadilly bus station and tried to get a bus that would go back to Stretford. We jumped onto the bus and thought, 'Saved' and turned around - and saw that it was completely empty, no driver. We thought, 'My God. We're trapped on this bus'. They were standing at the door shouting, 'Get out! Get out!' We had all these coins and we just threw them in their faces and flew out of the bus. We ran across the road to a bus going God knows where outside the Milkmaid. We slammed our fares down and ran to the back seat. Suddenly, the emergency doors swing open and these tattooed arms fly in - it was like *A Clockwork Orange*. The bus is packed - nobody gives a damn. So we run upstairs and the bus begins to move and we end up in Lower Broughton. For some reason we get out and we're in the middle of nowhere - just hills. On top of this hill we could see a light from this manor house. We went up these dark lanes and knocked on the door. It was opened by this old, senile, decrepit Teddy Boy, no younger than 63, with blue suede shoes on. 'Do you have a telephone?' 'No!' We had to walk back to Manchester. It took us seven days. We came back home to my place, finally, at something like 5am, and listened to *Horses* by Patti Smith and wept on the bed. That's my youth for you in a nutshell."

Clearly, these youthful forays into club-land were not entirely joyous occasions. Linder confirms as much, recollecting: "Morrissey and I just sat there like we were at a funeral." At least live music retained its appeal, but even in that area there were signs of encroaching jaundice.

On 4 July, Morrissey celebrated American Independence Day by seeing his old favourite Iggy Pop at the Apollo. An impressive US flag was unfurled onstage, but Steven was unimpressed. "They didn't even bother to iron it," he recalled fussily. Two weeks later, he reappeared unexpectedly as a reviewer in *Record Mirror*, though not in a particularly positive mood. After denouncing support group Telephone as "intense mediocrity", he laid heavily into the erstwhile Godfather of Punk before concluding his criticisms with the stinging dismissal: "This year Iggy models the jaded gigolo look, a style for which the voice must always be out of tune, it seems. The new Iggy is really into crowd participation and insists that every song ends with a running 'la-la-la'. One would imagine that the next step for him would be the Golden Garter or, better still, retirement."

Morrissey's own predilection for impromptu retirement occurred the following month when he once more disappeared from the pages of *Record*

Mirror. As before, his finale coincided with a performance by Ludus, this time supporting Depeche Mode at Rafters. There was a discernible note of resignation in his championing of Linder and a weary epilogue on the artistic injustices of pop. "Linder was born singing," he chimed, "and has more imagination than Depeche Mode could ever hope for. Still Depeche Mode get the *Jackie* spread. No justice!"

Morrissey's prognosis was heartfelt but not entirely correct. Linder's limited appeal had less to do with a surfeit of imagination than a distinct lack of ambition. Since their intriguing EP *The Visit*, Ludus had garnered a sprinkling of critical acclaim, including a favourable review in the *NME* and a radio session for the prestigious *John Peel Show*. In his more effusive moments Richard Boon compared Linder's cool sexuality to that of Debbie Harry, but also observed a strong reluctance to extend that appeal. "There was something self-limiting about Linder," he now contends. "Any time she seemed to be on the brink of a breakthrough, even if that meant 50 extra people in the audience, or selling 50 more records, she would always retreat, just like the poet Stevie Smith. I don't know whether this was conscious or innate, but she stepped back. She seemed very hesitant about becoming some kind of pop monster for fear that it might consume her." Others noted Ludus' wilful artistic insularity with impatience. The irreverent John Muir had already disgraced himself by suggesting that Linder should "get a spread by showing off her tits", a comment which saw his office filing cabinet plastered with retributive anti-sexist stickers.

The break-up of Linder's relationship with Devine ended another promising episode in the group's convoluted history. However, Ludus achieved a notable moment of glory when one of their shows was filmed at the Haçienda. Two feminist colleagues, Liz Naylor and Cath Carroll, who then worked on the Manchester arts magazine *City Fun*, were heavily involved with the presentation. Boon remembers them on the Haçienda balcony, "showering the audience with chicken giblets wrapped in fragments of gay porn". Patrons were doubly amazed to discover that there were red-inked tampons placed in the men's urinals. The shock tactics were reinforced by Linder's performance, for she appeared onstage dressed in a frock festooned with giblets and raw meat. "It was extraordinarily strong and really pinned my eye-lids to the back of my head," recalled Howard Devoto. The show climaxed when Linder tore open her meat dress to reveal an enormous black leather dildo strapped round her waist. Facing the audience, she unleashed a final blood-curdling scream which brought the evening to an emphatic close. As Ludus' mentor Richard Boon pithily noted: "It was an interesting end to a very patchy career."

Although Factory's video outlet Ikon still own the rights to the filmed performance, it has remained deep in their vaults for many years. Like the menstrual egg timer, the long overdue video has become part of Factory folklore and its continued unavailability serves as an oblique comment on the entire Ludus saga.

Linder's importance to Morrissey as a soul mate in feminism was reflected in their similar traits as writers. They each favoured repetition as a stylistic device, doubling or trebling specific phrases or lines for emphasis. Morrissey also shared some of Linder's "artistic austerity" and, on occasion, would betray an ambivalent attitude towards the pressures and requirements of fatal fame. With his pop sensibilities, however, Morrissey had the instincts and potential to tap a more commercial market. Whether he had the personality or musical talent was initially more doubtful. As Tony Wilson cuttingly observed: "Anyone less likely to be a pop star from that scene was unimaginable." Passing time also told its own story. It was now five years since the dawn of punk and several of Morrissey's peers had already ascended the wheel of fortune and were back on the way down. Since the Slaughter debacle, Morrissey's prospects as a performer had been negligible. "The wild desire to make something of my life was the only thing that kept me alive", Morrissey noted melodramatically. Such desire now smacked of sad delusion. It was hard to avoid the suspicion that Morrissey's big chance had long since been and gone.

6

Someone Waved Goodbye

THE MAHERS OF KILDARE LED a life not dissimilar to that of the Morrisseys and Dwyers. John Joseph Maher left school in the early Fifties and faced the same bleak future as the rest of his generation. Emigration offered the only hope of financial advancement. The haemorrhage which had bled Eire of Peter Morrissey would soon include Maher among its victims, but he remained long enough to witness significant changes in the social and cultural fabric of the country. Youth was in the ascendant and, despite all the restrictions and repression, there was at least a shift away from the old-time dancing that had dominated parochial halls since time immemorial. While rock 'n' roll swamped the USA, and Britain fell victim to a nationwide skiffle boom, Ireland had its own mini-revolution in the burgeoning showband phenomenon.

It really began in Northern Ireland with the Clipper Carlton, a Strabane outfit that injected a variety routine into their act and actually dared to move across the stage. Their distinctly visual appeal provided an energetic alternative to the old-fashioned orchestra leaders like the evergreen Mick Delahunty and Gay McIntyre. Entrepreneurs and building contractors, most notably Jim and Albert Reynolds, saw potential in the showband game and rapidly constructed ballrooms throughout the province. Soon, other outfits were challenging the Clippers, spearheaded by Waterford's Royal Showband, who boasted their own chunkier version of Elvis Presley in the rugby-playing Brendan Bowyer. Under the canny management of TJ Byrne, the Royal performed six nights a week to average audiences of 2,000 plus, and took 60 per cent of the door receipts. Before long, they were rich beyond their dreams and spawned a plethora of rivals including the excellent Freshmen, The Miami, The Capitol, The Cadets, The Plattermen and The Dixies.

The showband explosion captured Eire at its most endearingly paradoxical. Although the role models for many groups were contemporaneous rock 'n' rollers from Elvis Presley to Cliff Richard and established Sixties performers like The Beach Boys, the shows retained the trappings and courtesies of the previous era. Sharp suits were obligatory for both artistes and male audience alike, while the girls spent hours teasing their hair, and starching their petticoats with sugar dissolved in water. The bands broke up their sets in tunes of three, punctuated by the familiar announcement:

"Your next dance, please". This would be followed by a flurry of activity during which the boys, segregated on one side of the floor, would enter no man's land and attempt to "claim" their dancing partner from the throng of females lined up invitingly or disinterestedly alongside the adjoining wall. The new ballrooms offered instant romance and the opportunities for youngsters to escape from the claustrophobic insularity of parochial halls to seek stimulating courting opportunities in towns and counties where they were unknown. Bicycles and buses transported youths across the country in a frenzy of dancing mania that culminated on St Stephen's and St Patrick's evenings, when an estimated 25 per cent of Eire's entire population crowded into the halls. Only during the 40 days and nights of Lent was the music silenced.

The showband cavalcade symbolized the affluence of a new Eire, wrenching itself free from the austerity and economic malaise of the Fifties. By 1959, Sean Lemass was in power and the de Valera era was passing into history. Tax-free incentives and foreign investments ushered in a long over-due period of economic prosperity and effectively ceased the exodus that had drained Eire of its unemployable youth. Although the emigration figures were at last declining, the lure of a better life abroad was a legacy not easily removed from the national consciousness. John Maher found himself part of the final wave of mass emigration at the beginning of the new decade. Had he been five years younger, he might well have remained in Kildare, but instead he took the crowded boat from Dun Laoghaire. Like Peter Morrissey, several years before, his destination was Manchester, where he sought work as a warehouseman and later entered the construction trade.

In 1962, Maher married an Irish girl from his hometown named Frances Patricia Doyle. They settled in a terraced house at 12 Hayfield Street, Manchester 12. After little over a year, on 31 October 1963, Frances gave birth to a son away from her Ardwick home at 122 Everton Road, Chorlton-on-Medlock. He was christened John Martin Maher. In order to distinguish the child from his father, the family called him Johnny and the name stuck. Two further children would follow in later years: Claire (1965) and Ian (1972).

The Mahers were a musical family with a strong interest in country 'n' western music. During the early Sixties, Jim Reeves was extremely popular in Eireann communities and there was a strong country 'n' Irish boom, headed by Big Tom And The Mainliners, Larry Cunningham And The Mighty Avons and numerous others. Carrick-on-Suir's Clancy Brothers, and their sinewy Armagh banjoist Tommy Makem, had returned triumphant from America, where even Bob Dylan had sat at their feet. The Clancys updated old folk ballads, rebel songs and drinking tunes, paving the way for the commercial acceptance of The Dubliners a few years later. Although many folk purists criticized the Clancys, the Aran-sweatered quartet undoubtedly popularized some of Ireland's great "lost" music and focused attention on the work of such important traditionalists as Zozimus, Patrick Joyce, Thomas Moore, PJ McCall, Ethna Carbury, Seosamh Oh

Eanaigh aka Seamus Ennis.

Johnny recalls several childhood summers in Kildare where the music flowed like Guinness and his guitar-playing uncle sang traditional ballads mixed with the pop hits of the day.

John Maher would often join in on the accordion and later taught his eldest son to master the harmonica. Back home in Manchester there were regular get-togethers at Hayfield Street and its adjoining roads, where Maher's extended family were clustered. "We had parties all the time," Johnny recalls, "and there always seemed to be a birth."

Housing conditions in Ardwick were far from luxurious. The Mahers lived amid rows of terraced houses, many damp and in urgent need of repair or demolition. By 1973, the council had moved the tenants *en masse* to an estate at Baguley in the notorious urban wasteland of Wythenshawe. Johnny was ensconced at the Sacred Heart Primary School and performed well enough to be allocated a place at the nearby St Augustines Grammar. This venerable institution was overseen by the awesome Monsignor Guinness, whose clerical rank alone seemed enough to instil fear into many of the pupils in his charge. The school was a conventional Catholic boys' grammar of the period, with a traditional syllabus that included compulsory Latin during the first two years. Maher's academic progress was initially promising but tailed off disappointingly in the third year when the élitist St Augustines amalgamated with two other schools and was reorganized along comprehensive lines as the newly-named St John Pleasington.

Johnny was considered a fairly confident youth, yet one of his closest associates was a remarkably quiet boy from Ashton-upon-Mersey named Andy Rourke. "He had long hair, kept himself to himself and wouldn't say boo to a goose," was the curt summation of a fellow school-mate, Steve Cassan. Rourke had good reason for his apparent introversion. His parents' marriage had recently dissolved and his mother relocated to Spain where she became romantically involved with the head of a footwear empire. Michael Rourke (who would later remarry) was left with the arduous task of governing a male-dominated household, which included Andy's musically-minded brothers, Chris, Phil, and the younger John. Although Andy appeared to live in the shadow of his two elder brothers and the lively Baguley class-mate whom he had befriended, he was never a depressive character. On the contrary, when teased from his shell, he revealed an engaging sense of humour and a near fatal love for practical jokes.

Andy was something of a "wild child" during his early school days, a trait he shared with the boisterous, truanting Maher. "There were five or six lads in the year who had longer hair or trendier clothes," Johnny recalls. "You spotted types. For the first two years there was a bit of rivalry between us because we were both bad lads." A crackdown by Monsignor Guinness resulted in several recalcitrant pupils switching classes and Rourke suddenly found himself placed in Maher's form. A sympathetic teacher, Mr Thorpe, recognized that Andy was having a troubled time and suggested that Johnny pal up with him. "We were already starting to be mates," Johnny explained, "but that was because Andy was openly taking drugs, as opposed to the way everybody else was doing it." Rourke's reck-lessness caught up with him following a trip abroad when his drug flirtation was uncovered and he was placed under the supervisory eye of a social worker. His indiscretion was not widely broadcast and, unlike many kids in similar situations, he managed to stay on the rails. Nevertheless, the temptation to experiment with drugs was not easily banished and would resurface in later years.

Maher's friendship with Rourke was reinforced by their mutual interest in pop music. Johnny had found his own personal heroes towards the end of primary school when T Rex ruled the airwaves. After purchasing his first single, 'Jeepster', he became interested in playing guitar and quickly learned to master Marc Bolan's Howlin' Wolf-influenced riffs. Before the end of his first year at school, the under-age Maher could be seen at Belle Vue, experiencing the live sound of The Faces. He soon became entranced by the leading guitar gods of the early Seventies: Ritchie Blackmore, Jimmy Page, Keith Richard and, most notably, Rory Gallagher. Buying records became a weekly ritual, but merely listening to music seemed a strangely mechanical pastime compared to the power and satisfaction that derived from assimilating the tunes, mastering the chords and transforming the vinyl sounds into live performance. Johnny had all the characteristics of a classic bedsit guitarist but he was spared many lonely nights of finger-bleeding introspection by the camaraderie and sheer wealth of aspiring musical talent in his Wythenshawe circle.

As a 12-year-old, one of the highlights of Johnny's week was Wednesday evening when he visited West Wythenshawe Youth Wing. Even the most anti-social youths were seduced from the streets by the club's irresistible combination of table tennis and regular discos. Teams of kids, clad in T-shirts, trainers and denim, thronged into the centre and Maher was pleased to discover a coterie of like-minded would-be musicians, including Steve and Pete Cassan, Bobby Durkin, Mark Johnson and Steve Lloyd. The youth club served as a focal point to discuss favourite albums, compare musical tastes and arrange to visit each other's houses for guitar practise. Dreams were fuelled by regular excursions to the city centre where the gang would wander into guitar shops and salivate over astronomically-priced Fenders and gleaming Gibsons. As Pete Cassan reminisced: "We couldn't afford anything like that but we'd pick one up, plug it in, sit there and play some-thing we knew, just to see how it sounded on electric." After overstaying their welcome, they would be ejected by an impatient sales assistant, only to appear in another shop further down the road. Virgin Records provided the hard rock soundtrack to their walkabouts and was also a prime source for the dazzling rock 'n' roll badges with which they emblazoned their den-ims. During one daring expedition, the fashion-conscious Maher risked parental disapproval by having his ear pierced. On Saturday afternoons and evenings, Mark Johnson's house in Churchstoke Walk was a regular meeting place for record-playing sessions, acoustic guitar workouts and pop star fantasies.

Johnson was a year older than Maher and Rourke, and attended the nearby Protestant Brookway High. He knew several budding musicians in the upper school, including Mike McCann, Billy Duffy, Robin Allman, Rob Maunder and Dave Clough, who were all playing in Four Way Street, a group christened after the best-selling Crosby, Stills, Nash & Young double live album. The name Four Way Street appealed to Andy Rourke, who was then playing acoustic guitar under the tutelage of his brother Phil, and attempting to master David Crosby's 'The Lee Shore'. One of Robin Allman's earliest recollections of Rourke is seeing the lad proudly carrying a copy of Graham Nash's *Wild Tales* under his arm. When Allman later visited the Rourkes' house in Ashton-upon-Mersey, he was amazed to see a wall covered in a mural of the *Wild Tales* back sleeve, painted by Andy's mother.

Despite their name, Four Way Street were not mere CSN&Y copyists, but featured a broad set of rock favourites, with a strong emphasis on Rolling Stones material. "It was everything from 'Jumpin' Jack Flash' to 'Woodstock'," Allman recollected. On Mark Johnson's invitation, the 12-year-old Johnny Maher turned up at an early Four Way Street session, fashionably armed with a can of Forest brown ale. The Brookway brigands were at first amused by Maher's apparently calculated cool, then charmed by his evident enthusiasm. "Even then, he wanted to be one of the big boys," laughed Allman.

Originally a drummer, Allman had become fascinated with the electric guitar ever since Billy Duffy acquired his first model in March 1974. Weary of being Dallas Taylor to Duffy's Stephen Stills, Rob found a more appropriate imaginary role model in his namesake - the late guitarist Duane Allman. By Christmas 1975, Rob had received a cherry red Hofner Veri and Four Way Street metamorphosed into Eye Routine, with Craig Mackay replacing lead vocalist Mike McCann, who became a butcher. With Joey McLoughlan recruited on drums, the group lasted a few months more before Duffy fell in with Wythenshawe hard man Vini Faal and joined The Nosebleeds. Allman, meanwhile, had mastered enough chords to attract the attention of the ever-inquisitive Maher. "One of my first memories of Johnny is seeing him sitting on a wall endlessly trying to learn the riff from Wishbone Ash's 'Blowing Free'. He was a cocky little school kid with a guitar who made me laugh. But he was very keen on learning. He paid attention and was very good to work with. You could tell he wanted to grab as much from you as possible."

Allman was impressed by Maher's enthusiasm and the speed with which he was capable of assimilating new material. Young Pete Cassan had already conceded any hope of keeping pace with Maher's learning rate. "He was one of those guys that had natural ability. When he played guitar, he'd just excel. While we'd be twanging away he'd come round our house and say, 'Listen to this'. In five minutes he'd play something that you'd been trying to master for the last year."

Maher was astute enough to seek the best players in his circle and even persuaded Billy Duffy to reveal some esoteric chord changes. Pete Cassan remembers a contentious piece of Wythenshawe folklore: "Billy Duffy used to teach Johnny tricks and licks and then I heard it later got to the stage where Johnny was teaching him. But I doubt if Billy would agree with that!"

Johnny partly confirms the teacher/pupil pub stories and credits Duffy for providing him with his first PA. "Maybe he did show me my first few chords, but I soon caught up and zoomed ahead. I was a bit more dedicated to playing. Billy was an inspiring character and had a lot of time for me. He was really helpful, which was quite unusual for lads when there's an age difference. I felt akin to Billy, and our lives followed similar paths."

Back in the shady lane of his estate, Johnny was still worshipping at the altar of Rory Gallagher, whose album sleeves and posters lined the walls of his bedroom. Significantly, his first electric guitar was a Rory Gallagher Stratocaster copy, and he followed the Ballyshannon bluesman's concerts with hawkish vigilance. Rob Allman was also fascinated by Gallagher's guitar pyrotechnics and, two years older than Johnny, he proved a useful source of information. Having digested Allman's favourite set of changes, Maher hungrily explored his large record collection. It was a pleasant change to escape from the ever-present Led Zeppelin brigade and discover a contrasting strain of early Seventies folk music, featuring such names as Fairport Convention, Pentangle, Martin Carthy, and Richard and Linda Thompson. Allman's tastes also extended towards the American singer/songwriter school and he was a devotee of Crosby, Stills, Nash & Young. Johnny was intrigued by the wayward career and sheer diversity of Neil Young's output. He particularly enjoyed *Everybody Knows This Is Nowhere* and swiftly added the riff of 'Cinnamon Girl' to his ever-expanding repertoire. He even bought a pair of elaborately-patched jeans from Allman, which had been modelled from the rear cover of Young's *After The Goldrush*. It was a doubly pleasant surprise when Rourke came to school wearing a badge proclaiming 'Tonight's The Night', in honour of Young's critically-acclaimed and harrowing 1975 album. Maher was mightily impressed.

The road from Neil Young led, not unexpectedly, to former Crazy Horse/Grin guitarist Nils Lofgren, whom Johnny revered. It was Lofgren who first inspired Maher to play with a thumbpick and whose slightly cocky, colourful stage presence, and intuitive feel for strong but subtle melody lines, left a lasting impression. The diminutive Lofgren shared another important characteristic with the barely-teenage Maher - he was a keen fan of Keith Richard. Nils had pointedly closed side one of his 1975 début solo album with 'Keith Don't Go (Ode To The Glimmer Twin)', a striking tribute to the perpetually-wasted Stones' guitarist. The track featured an amusing pastiche of Richard's fluid style, including a snatch of the famous riff from 'Satisfaction'. The song's appearance seemed perfectly timed, for Allman had recently lent Johnny a copy of Robert Greenfield's *STP: A Journey Through America With The Rolling Stones*. "We were fascinated by the mystique," Allman recalls. "That book was unbelievable. The sheer decadence appealed to teenage kids aspiring to become The Rolling Stones and Johnny was *very* into Keith Richard."

Given Maher's enthusiasm and insatiable appetite for music, it was inevitable that he would join a rock group some day. Presumptuously, he announced his burning ambition to become a pop star before even reaching his fourteenth birthday. "I was ridiculed for it for days after," he recollected. However, beneath the sarcastic gibes lay the realization that Maher had sufficient drive and ambition to exploit his fledgling talents to the full. His fraternization with the elder boys from Brookway had already been noted by his contemporaries at St John Pleasington. "If someone had an electric guitar and an amp, they were his best friend," Steve Cassan sarcastically observed. As Maher's guitar playing improved, Cassan and others detected an increasing confidence and occasionally overbearing sense of self-worth. "Johnny Maher's attitude was 'I'm Johnny Maher, I'm number one, I'm determined to get there and whoever gets in my way, I'll walk over them'. As a person he wasn't like that, but he was when it came to playing the guitar. He was very cocky, but only about something he was good at. He knew that he had talent and he was going to use it." Maher was acutely aware of his reputation and not entirely unsympathetic towards his critics: "Yes, I was an obstreperous, cocky little upstart, interested in playing in a group and nothing else."

By early 1977, Johnny was still attending Mark Johnson's house and fantasizing about forming a group. Part of the fun was choosing unlikely names like Adolf And The Tangerines. During the same period, Maher teamed up with two St Augustines compatriots: Bobby Durkin and Kevin Williams. According to Williams, the idea of forming a group was purely spontaneous. "We hung around the street playing football," he explained, "then one day we talked about music and it started from there." Amusingly, Williams unintentionally damned his former partner with faint praise. "I thought Johnny was probably one of the best guitarists on our street," he considered. "I still think he's excellent and I could see then that he was going to be good." During their first bedroom rehearsals, Maher converted Williams to the Rory Gallagher cause and the trio ran through a formidable array of cover songs from the work of Tom Petty And The Heartbreakers to Thin Lizzy. 'The Boys Are Back In Town' (voted single of the year by *NME*) was immediately incorporated into their repertoire and they later experimented with a slow version of 'Don't Believe A Word'. Rod Stewart's 'Maggie May', and several Stones covers, added spice to the set. The extent of their ambition was reached with a brave but uneasy attempt at Bruce Springsteen's 'Born To Run'.

With inspiration fuelled by cider, the new group named themselves The Paris Valentinos, an unusual nomenclature that provided a hint of the exotic. "There was a band out called Paris and we wanted something hip," explained Durkin. After turning electric, the group established a relatively stable line-up comprising Kevin Williams (vocals/bass), John Maher (vocals/lead guitar) and Bobby Durkin (drums).

The inimitable Durkin was already emerging as one of the great characters of Wythenshawe. A highly promising drummer, he had attended auditions for the Manchester Youth Orchestra and was subsequently awarded a scholarship. Characteristically, he failed to turn up at the next session and progressed no further. His dedication had evaporated after setting eyes on the voluptuous Julie Evans, who became his long-suffering girlfriend over the next few years. Durkin was happy-go-lucky to an almost self-destructive degree; the kind of person who could win a million on the pools on Monday and be broke again by Friday. With his garrulous charm, quirky humour and tireless capacity for partying, he seemed the perfect personality rock'n'roll drummer.

In order to bolster the line-up, Andy Rourke was added on rhythm guitar, an induction that would later prove crucial. Meanwhile, a girlfriend of Johnny offered them the chance to make their live début at a Jubilee Day street party in Greenwood Road, Benchill. Armed with a single tiny Vox amplifier, they assembled their gear atop four kitchen tables, while Durkin uneasily eyed a suspicious group of six-year-olds, whom he was convinced had designs on his drumkit. "We're playing to a load of tinkers!" he announced undiplomatically.

The Paris Valentinos were augmented by local guest vocalist Chris Milne, whose performance was rendered impotent by the disconcertingly rickety platform. Kevin Williams recollects the chaotic series of interruptions: "Every time Bobby hit the bass drum, the four tables would separate. We had to stop and push them back together. It was very odd." After completing their luckless début, the Valentinos tried to convince the Benchill girls that they were "rock stars". They then took full advantage of the free beer on offer before staggering home in a drunken daze.

Rhythm 'n' booze played an important role in the weekend life of the Valentinos. Unable to gain admittance to pubs, they congregated in the university precinct and toured the Friday discos. Along the way, they would take surreptitious swigs from a flagon of cheap cider. "Some laughs occurred," recalls Durkin. "We'd doss out in the park thinking we could drink and end up covered in damp." In spite of their exuberant behaviour, Durkin maintains that the group's only recreational vice throughout The Paris Valentinos era was cider, supplemented by the occasional crate of beer. The errant Rourke was apparently no exception. "Andy wasn't into barbiturates," Durkin notes. "He wasn't even into draw then. The Monsignor would've killed him! We didn't even know what drugs were. The only problem with Andy then was that he was quiet and there was no mother there."

In spite of their appearance at the Jubilee celebrations, the Valentinos were far removed from those other regal assailants, The Sex Pistols. Punk rock was regarded with disdain by Maher, who saw three-chord minimalism as no substitute for the rich pursuit of virtuosity. At a time when many of his contemporaries were glorifying the chaotic screechings of a disfranchised youth culture, Johnny was earnestly leafing through the back pages of rock 'n' roll history. He had recently alighted at the mid-Sixties and entered a Tamla Motown phase, spinning old hits in an over ambitious attempt to capture the melodies of Holland/Dozier/Holland on acoustic guitar. "I'd try to cover the strings, piano and anything else with my right hand," he recalled, "trying to play the whole record on six strings."

It was this irrepressible fascination for strong melody lines and strikingly original arrangements that separated Maher from his more pedestrian contemporaries. His rapacious appetite for knowledge ensured that he was neither blinkered by copycat revivalism nor unresponsive to contemporary musical trends. Despite his aversion to the cruder aspects of punk, he responded enthusiastically to the American new wave explosion. He was floored by the startling freshness of Patti Smith's *Horses* and respected the intelligence and inventiveness of Talking Heads and Television. Although too young to enjoy the club scene in Manchester, Maher accompanied Durkin to gigs by new wave artistes such as Blondie and introduced the drummer to the aggressive charm of The New York Dolls and Sylvain Sylvain. In many respects, Maher was travelling a similar musical route to Morrissey, as the Tamla Motown, Patti Smith and New York Dolls links testify. At this point, there was a musical osmosis between Wythenshawe and Stretford, with Billy Duffy playing the unlikely middleman. Although Maher and Morrissey had yet to meet, they shared certain influences and distant acquaintances, including Duffy, Allman, Toby, Steve Pomfret and Pete Crookes. For the present, the four-year age gap, geographical distance and the vagaries of chance were enough to ensure that their paths did not cross.

While Morrissey was performing at the Ritz and Manchester Polytechnic with the doomed Nosebleeds, Maher and the Valentinos were undertaking a more prosaic appointment at their local church. In return for rehearsal facilities at the Sacred Heart, the boys appeared regularly at the Sunday evening Folk Mass. Their mentor was a young ecclesiastic whom they privately dubbed "the groovy priest". Unlike some of the elder clergy, he saw no incongruity in allowing musical instruments to accompany 5.30 Mass. "It was just a couple of guitars and tambourines," recalls Durkin, "but as a result of that we played an open day at St Peters." In order to enliven proceedings, Johnny would throw in some fancy licks, while the sermon-reading Williams untuned a nearby guitar, causing the player acute embarrassment when he struck a discordant note. Such schoolboy pranks extended to the streets of Baguley whenever the group were obliged to transport their unwieldy equipment. The bespectacled Kevin Williams was often seen boarding buses and negotiating with the conductor about what constituted legitimate baggage. On another occasion, the Valentinos solved the perennial transportation problem by loading their equipment atop a supermarket trolley and leaving their wrist watches and other such valuables as a deposit. As Williams nostalgically noted: "These were the playground years. Instead of having a gang, we had a band. It wasn't that serious at the time. We didn't play our own material but just caused a racket and had a laugh."

By the age of 15, significant changes were occurring in Johnny Maher's life. At a local party, he met a girl from Brookway, two years his junior, whom he would later marry. Angela Brown had a profound effect on Maher and would prove a positive, stabilizing force during the turbulent years ahead. The sentimental Durkin still regards the relationship as the proverbial match made in heaven. "Angie was his best friend and she was there when he had nothing," he recalls. "She saw the hard times - all those gigs and sessions. Johnny was lucky to find her. When he met her he knew that he loved her. It was weird!" After school, Johnny would devotedly appear at the gates of Brookway High and escort Angie home. Over the next couple of years, she changed from a rather prim, conservatively-dressed girl to the more familiar pop chic of jeans, boots and jackets. Her casual wear was offset by striking black eye make-up, which many felt gave her a distinctly mid-Sixties look. As a Keith Richard fanatic, it cannot have escaped Maher's attention that 'Angie' was the only girl ever to have been immortalized by name on a Rolling Stones single. In spite of, or because of, her quiet disposition, Brown's presence was strong enough to elicit favourable reactions from Maher's contemporaries. At times, it seemed as if Johnny was dating a young teenager who resembled a cross between Sandie Shaw and Cathy McGowan - yet arguably more beautiful than both of those pop icons combined. If the match was heavenly, then it had to confront some decidedly corporeal obstacles during those early days. "The relationship was frowned upon at first," confirmed Rob Allman. "The Browns were a fairly middle-class family. I knew Angie's brother, Peter, and he did not approve of the relationship whatsoever." It took considerable charm and time before those initial reservations were thoroughly reversed.

The potent combination of music and romance was playing havoc with Maher's school life. Much to his parents' consternation, Johnny's termly reports chronicled an inexorable slide towards academic mediocrity. One teacher who held faith in Maher's ability was the head of music, Mr Jessett. He encouraged Johnny to enrol in a class for musical theory, but even that experience was greeted half-heartedly. "It was just something that would get me off doing maths," Johnny recalled. In conjunction with his declining academic progress, Maher's sporting prowess was wilfully atrophying. Earlier in his school career, he had shown promise as a soccer player, and Bobby Durkin felt he had the capabilities to go far. "He was a top footballer, played for Manchester Boys and had trials for City. He just ignored it. Rather than training, he'd be upstairs in his room playing. After he was 15, it was music, music, music... and Angela."

Maher's soccer career was not helped by his love of late nights and Friday evening cider drinking. "I'd never be in good shape on a Saturday morning," he laughs. "I played under persuasion from the teachers. There was one time I got into the house on a Sunday, after being at Andy's house all weekend. I walked in wearing leather trousers, a leather jacket and biker boots, and there was this scout asking me to play for Nottingham Forest. I just said: 'No way!' By that time, I was ready to leave school."

John Maher senior was none too pleased about the apparent decline of his son and counselled him to knuckle down to the approaching O-levels before it was too late. Johnny promised to rally, but he was already falling far behind; conversely, his songbook was expanding with each passing month. George Harrison's Rickenbacker sound had lately captured his imagination and he dutifully and arduously mastered the chords of 'I Feel Fine' and 'Ticket To Ride'. One of his favourite albums of 1978 was The Cars' invigorating début and he took considerable pleasure in teaching Steve Cassan the chord sequence to 'My Best Friend's Girl'. Increasingly, the 711 bus was playing host to Maher's musical interludes. "On the bus to school Johnny always had his guitar," Cassan recalls. "It was like a day trip for him. He'd be strumming away on an unamplified electric guitar and Durkin, who always seemed to have his drum-sticks with him, would tap on the windows and seats and provide musical accompaniment. It was like a Cliff Richard movie."

As Maher prepared for his final school year, however, changes were afoot. The Paris Valentinos had entered their final phase, having already seen a critical psychological shift in the musical power structure. On Johnny's recommendation, erstwhile bassist Kevin Williams switched instruments with the rhythm playing Rourke. Andy's brother Phil was a promising bass player so it was perhaps predictable that the younger sibling would display some proficiency on the instrument. "It was the turning point," claims Durkin. "Johnny pushed Andy and wanted him to go further. It was excellent to see how far he did progress. Andy was always quiet and always followed John; it was a good combination because John knew exactly which bass line he'd like from Andy. From thereon, it was second nature to them." Far from being aggrieved by the switch, Williams was all too willing to surrender his bass guitar spot. "Johnny was definitely the leader, especially with musical ideas," Williams confesses. "He had the brains and technique. We didn't have the skill on guitar. Then Andy came on in leaps and bounds, coupled with Johnny. They gelled together, whereas I was struggling. They were two race-horses and I was the donkey at the back."

Occasionally, the Valentinos dispensed with Williams' services altogether when they teamed up with another local group, featuring Steve Lloyd and the affluent Mark Edgington. In an imitation of The Glitter Band, both groups would combine their line-ups, using two drummers to thrash out a friendly, if ramshackle, jamming session. Williams, meanwhile, was drifting off into more productive ventures. Two years older than Johnny and Andy, he had left St Augustines and was slowly making his way in the theatrical world. Eventually, he changed his name to Kevin Kennedy and established himself in television's *Coronation Street* as the lugubrious and unloveable Curly Watts.

The break-up of The Paris Valentinos did little to dispel Maher's musical interests. His friendship with Paul Crookes, brother of The Nosebleeds' bassist Peter, ensured that he maintained reasonably close contact with Billy Duffy's former associates. While the resurrected Slaughter And The Dogs and their descendants The Studio Sweethearts were vainly seeking fame, Maher briefly joined a notorious local outfit named Sister Ray. Led by madcap vocalist Clive Robertson, the quartet had recently lost their guitar player and took on Johnny following a meeting at a pub. Before long, he found himself in a basement in the red-light district of Whalley Range, eagerly rehearsing their Velvet Underground-inspired set. A welcome booking at a festival in Manchester was publicized locally during early 1979, but the appearance was cancelled at the eleventh hour. However, they did play a gig supporting The Freshies at the Wythenshawe Forum, much to Maher's parochial pride. One former associate swears that it was at this gig that Sister Ray's excitable vocalist wielded a pig's head, which he thrashed liberally while screaming out some incoherent lyrics. Maher, of course, was still a carnivore at the time.

The stint as Sister Ray's ace guitarist lasted for only a handful of months. "They were a group of biker nasties, a lot older than me," Johnny remembers, "and it soon fizzled out." Sister Ray did manage an appearance on the TJM label's retrospective compilation *Identity Parade*, performing the self-penned 'Suicide', but by then their young guitarist had moved on.

Maher's musical adventures were greeted with increasing impatience by his father. During the final year at St John Pleasington, Maher allowed several O-levels to slip from his grasp and was now faced with the grim prospect of the dole and a troublesome period at home. In order to alleviate the disappointment of his concerned parents, he promised to enrol at a Further Education College and attempt to salvage some qualifications.

While summer days slowly passed, Maher stayed on the look-out for fresh opportunities. One area in which he displayed a discernibly unexpected talent was in his capacity as a salesman. His elders marvelled at the kid's capacity to sell unfashionable albums to unwilling buyers, simply by turning on a barrow boy's persuasive patter. "Johnny was always selling things," recalls Rob Allman. "He was the ultimate little spiv. He always reminded me of Private Walker, that character in *Dad's Army*. He was unbelievable at getting rid of things." It would not be long before Maher switched from selling albums to selling himself. Self-promotion, disguised by undiluted Mancunian-Irish charm, was to prove one of his major assets in later life.

A significant point in Maher's developing musical career occurred in late 1979 with the formation of White Dice. Brookway's Rob Allman had teamed up with Brookland's pianist Paul Whittall, a former pupil of Chetham's School of Music, who had previously played with The Freshies. The newly formed duo was experimenting with close harmony work and Maher was sufficiently interested to sit in on couple of sessions. Allman was pleased to discover that Johnny could pitch a harmony quite well and suggested that they should form a group. Maher was aware that Allman had already written a cache of songs, and with Whittall's solid musical background the team looked particularly promising. After a number of practise sessions on acoustic guitar and piano, the trio was ready to form a fully-fledged electric band. Characteristically, Maher wasted no time in recruiting his old rhythm section of Rourke and Durkin. Before long, the cider was flowing at Allman's house.

In order to facilitate his colleagues' work, Andy regularly stayed the weekend at Bobby Durkin's house in Baguley. When Mrs Durkin first saw

Rourke's long hair and cowboy boots, she took her son aside and chided: "I don't want him here, he's a druggie." Her resistance soon crumbled when the persuasive Bobby turned on his unctuous, rhetorical charm. "Once she knew her first impression of him was wrong, she grew to love the lad," Durkin recalls. "Too many people put problems on Andy's shoulders for no reason at all, simply because he was a dead quiet kid."

Within weeks of the formation of White Dice, the group unexpectedly found themselves competing for potential stardom. Allman had noticed an advertisement in the *New Musical Express* placed by Jake Riviera, who was seeking new talent for his F-Beat Records. Unknown artistes were requested to send in demos and the best would receive a free test session in London with the possibility of a recording contract to follow. As Riviera had required only one song, Allman hurriedly herded his newly-formed group into his front room, placed a C-60 cassette into a domestic portable recorder and, backed by acoustic guitars, encouraged the others to join in the chorus of his most accessible composition: 'Someone Waved Goodbye'.

"We sang really well," Johnny recalls. "It was killer harmonies with the four of us, and a good education." The group had long since forgotten about the tape when, a couple of months later, Maher returned home from school to be greeted by a telephone call from Jake Riviera. "I thought it was somebody winding me up," he confessed. The caller was emphatic, however. White Dice had reached the finals of tape hunt, alongside the wonderfully-named Harry And The Atoms. The reward was an F-Beat audition in London slated for April.

With such an important appointment before them, White Dice urgently required a rehearsal studio. Occasionally, they practised at the Sacred Heart Catholic social club, where Bobby's father Liam worked as a steward and the Mahers infrequently booked visiting country 'n' western acts. Although the club had a piano on the premises, rehearsal time could not always be guaranteed. Fortunately, an alternative rehearsal room was provided by Andy Rourke, whose sizeable home in Hawthorn Lane, Sharston, was available at all hours. Now that his children were older, Michael Rourke had more time to attend to his business and was frequently called upon to visit his base in Holland. The young, musically-minded Rourkes were therefore granted considerably more licence and the number of impromptu get-togethers at the house ensured that life was never dull. The return of Andy's wildcat brother Chris meant that Hawthorn Lane was a regular haunt for late night parties and rock 'n 'roll revelry. Allman was initially attracted by the freedom that the Rourke lifestyle offered and decided to move into their spare room. A bottle of champagne was opened to celebrate his arrival on 5 February 1980.

Over the next couple of months, White Dice completed a repertoire of songs, largely from the pen of Rob Allman. Maher contributed some sparkling riffs to Allman's lyrics and melodies, and was noticeably quick to claim a co-writing namecheck. Significantly, the classically-trained Whittall, whose keyboard skills and gift for arrangements might have been translated into composition, remained conspicuously absent from the songwriting credits. In spite of his fine harmony work, he featured as co-composer on only one song, 'Think Of Me'. Maher, by comparison, was dominant. From the outset, the prospect of an Allman/Maher songwriting team was very important to Johnny. "I like to work with people who are really good," he stressed, "and Rob Allman, for his age, was great. I was really into great lyricists - people whose lyrics were their art." In Johnny's imagination, Allman/Maher was no doubt inextricably linked with Lennon/McCartney or Jagger/Richard, and he was sharp enough to appreciate the importance of establishing his songwriting claims at the earliest opportunity. Clearly, Maher had learned the lessons of rock history well.

Although White Dice had begun as an acoustic CS&N-inspired harmony unit, their electric sound betrayed a greater debt to XTC and Squeeze. With Allman's folk leanings, Whittall's Supertramp keyboards and Maher's Gallagher/Petty riffs, it was a strange concoction. Johnny's latest love was sophisticated American FM-orientated rock: Steely Dan, The Cars and Heart. Twin lead guitar breaks and strong harmonies were the group's primary suit as they boarded the train from Manchester Piccadilly to London in search of imminent discovery.

After arriving at Euston, the group took a taxi to the Acton Park Hotel in West London, only minutes away from Nick Lowe's home studio where the session was booked. Inevitably, the boys had a late, restless evening, intoxicated by the prospect of working with a professional producer. Intoxication of a different kind occurred the following morning thanks to the incorrigible Bobby Durkin, who had mysteriously managed to acquire a crate of PILs lager which he deposited on Allman's wardrobe. Minutes before their departure for the studio, Durkin and Allman challenged each other to a drinking contest and speedily downed countless bottles of PILs, much to the mock exasperation of the assembled crew. Remarkably, the boozy duo managed to negotiate the short taxi journey to Lowe's house without throwing up, and their nervy excitement proved enough to offset any drunken stupors. Arriving at the studio, they were introduced to Paul Riley, a house producer who had worked with such luminaries as Graham Parker and The Rumour. The elusive Lowe was nowhere to be seen, but there was a beatific silence when his wife Carlene Carter descended the stairs from her bedroom. "Are you guys Harry And The Atoms?" she enquired, referring to the other finalists in the *NME* advertised competition. Rourke, unable to grasp her American intonation, assumed she'd said, "Are you hairy round the armpits?" and broke into unrestrained laughter. Durkin, transfixed by the sight of Carter's nightdress and bare legs, was uncharacteristically dumbfounded. Whatever the outcome of the audition, he would carry that vision in his head and enliven Wythenshawe pubs with lascivious descriptions of Carlene Carter's body for months ahead. Maher was equally agape that morning, although his stimulation came from his ego rather than his lower regions. While setting up the equipment, Riley had nonchalantly presented him with Elvis Costello's Rickenbacker to use during the session. It was a tremendous boost to Maher and proved the perfect instrument for his solo on Tom Petty's 'American Girl'. By the end of the day, White Dice had completed a further six songs (all self-penned): 'Someone Waved Goodbye', 'The Hold', 'Makes No Sense', 'On The Beach', 'It's Over' and 'You Made Me Cry'. Riley was most impressed by Allman/Maher's 'On The Beach' and spent considerable time beefing up the track and double-tracking the drums. Many hours later, the bulk of the recording session was completed, though a further day was required for additional technical work on the material.

Freed from the studio, Durkin conducted a celebratory surveillance of the local pubs, like Paul Newman's Hustler in search of a game of pool. Bobby still remembers that day as the first occasion on which he was introduced to the charm of soft drugs. Later that evening, the confrontationally-dressed Billy Duffy, and his girlfriend Karen, trudged across to the hotel to pay their respects and offer congratulations. Initially, they were barred entry until the smooth-talking Durkin and company allayed the fears of the fastidious hotel staff.

The following day, the mixdown was finished and the quintet eagerly stood listening to the playback of their first and only professional recording. They were soon joined by F-Beat's A&R person, Andrew Lauder. The over-excitable Durkin was circling him like a hungry, cajoling cat and enthusing: "It's really good, isn't it?" Allman was mortified by his colleague's uncool outburst, and rather crestfallen by Lauder's cold response. "His face said it all for me," Allman recalls wistfully.

Pessimism about the outcome of the audition was the last thing on their minds when they returned to Manchester. For days afterwards, they sashayed across Wythenshawe with the blindingly confident aura of newly canonized war heroes. "Johnny was walking around his patch signing autographs," Allman joked. In local pubs, the group was erroneously acclaimed as having worked with Nick Lowe or Elvis Costello, while Durkin was repeatedly called upon to tell his "Carlene Carter story" to the star-starved clientèle. The hopeful dreams were finally snuffed out by an all-too-brief telephone call from the F-Beat supremo Jake Riviera, who drily informed them: "It just wasn't what I expected."

The tantalizing audition ultimately proved a body blow to the group's morale. Within weeks, the increasingly unreliable Durkin found his pub life and perennial romantic entanglements more pressing and absented himself from rehearsals. Before long, he was replaced by Failsworth drummer Craig Mitchell. "It wasn't as if Bobby left or was fired," explained Allman. "He just stopped turning up." Party time at the Rourke house also proved more distracting than productive, and keyboardist Paul Whittall was reluctant to leave his equipment on the premises in case it was damaged or stolen by an intruder. "You never knew who might come into the house," Allman confirmed. "When the dad was away, the Rourkes was a madhouse!" With Whittall tiring of dragging his hefty Fender Rhodes keyboard back and forth in taxis, and new boy Mitchell filling the rehearsal room with his sprawling kit, all vestiges of organization had gone to pot. Even Maher was witnessing events through a drug-induced haze. "The scene with Andy was that we used to just get stoned out of our brains and smoke draw till it came out of our ears - *with pride."*

When the marijuana wore off, Maher realized that the White Dice needed motivating. Unexpectedly, it was Andy's mercurial brother Chris who provided the boys with a much-needed psychological shot in the arm. Donning the role of group publicist, he contacted the *Sale And Altrincham Messenger* and persuaded the paper to run a short piece on their recent exploits. Under the heading, "Chance For White Dice", the newspaper mentioned the *NME* tape, the F-Beat recording and Jake Riviera's favourable impression. In an inscrutable attempt by Chris to provide the group with respectability, a couple of fabrications were added by which John Maher was transformed into "an apprentice electrician" and Andy Rourke took on the unlikely occupation of "sign writer".

The small write-up was enough to galvanize the dispirited, at least for the present. Even bereft of a full line-up, Maher, Allman and Rourke were working on fresh material as the summer approached. At least that was one way of distracting themselves from the realization that their live performance could never match the quality of the treasured Paul Riley demo. Maher was nevertheless willing to persevere and take some chances. An impressive arrangement of 'Take Me To The River', paced somewhere between the Al Green original and Talking Heads cover, was remarkable for one important reason: it featured Johnny on lead vocal.

Allman always rated his colleague as a reasonable singer, yet Maher seemed uncharacteristically reluctant to pursue his vocal talents, despite flashes of confidence. "I used to sing early on," Johnny admits, "just because I looked better in front of a band than anybody else. I always had a comprehensive understanding of what it takes emotionally to be a really good lead singer. I always felt it was a lot more than intellect, gimmicks and stage presence, and that's an understanding I've kept up to now." Maher's ego, however, was not intrusive enough to demand vocal cameos and he displayed a similar reservation about songwriting. Initially, he had shown some interest in composing lyrics to accompany his occasionally-inspired guitar lines, and valiantly completed a song titled 'Don't Cry'. Allman showed enthusiasm for the Rodney Crowell-influenced arrangement, which featured a promising double-tracked vocal from Maher. The chorus alone suggested that Johnny was aspiring to membership of the psychoanalytical singer/songwriter school, complete with tightly-packed lines: "Don't cry if you're left alone/Maybe you'll feel better if you sit beside the phone/And you're glad that someone knows your name/But you're hoping that you'll never feel this loneliness again."

Interestingly, 'Don't Cry' was conceived as a Nashville lament and remains the sole example of Maher embracing the influence of his country 'n' western parents. "I wrote it in the bedroom of my folks' house for my mum," Johnny reminisced. "It was one afternoon in my life. I was on my own, did it, and thought, 'It can't be bad'." The track was subsequently re-recorded on cassette in Bristol as a duet with Allman, but Maher was ultimately displeased with the results and abandoned the composition. Instead, he concentrated on his increasingly imaginative guitar work and impressed Allman with the memorable riffs that he frequently conjured. One of the best was immediately slotted into 'Looking For Some Good News', a song that Allman had only just completed. "On 'Looking For Some Good News' he had this killer riff," Rob enthused. "It was one of his best, only matched later by 'This Charming Man' and 'Handsome Devil'."

The fact that Johnny declined to promote himself as a vocalist or lyricist was a telling aberration in itself. Often portrayed as pushy and cocky, his ambition was in fact circumscribed by the degree of his talent. As Steve Cassan had noted earlier, Maher saw himself as "number one", but only in those areas where such confidence was justified by genuine skill. He never deluded himself about his own importance and proved surprisingly willing to step down from the spotlight if he was outclassed. Allman realized very quickly that Maher had an unshakeable inner confidence in his developing musicianship. "To a lot of people Johnny exuded the personality of top dog. But he didn't ever have to *appear* top dog. It was enough that he knew it in himself." While acknowledging that Maher's intense ambition could result in ruthlessness, Allman felt his partner retained a fundamental humanity. "Johnny wanted to be somebody," Rob stressed. "He was a likeable rogue. There was a streak in Johnny that could tread on you, but he was not a backstabber. He wouldn't want to hurt you and was not a hurtful person."

With their new drummer Craig Mitchell, White Dice booked a room at the ubiquitous TJ Davidson's studio where they found themselves paired with a New Romantic outfit named The International Set. It was an unhappy relationship, punctuated by petty feuding. There was an air of despondency about the studio in the wake of the recent suicide of Ian Curtis, whose group Joy Division had once rehearsed there. Morale improved later that summer thanks to Allman's prize acquisition: a Telecaster and amplifier on hire purchase. A promising winter beckoned deceptively.

In October 1980, Johnny enrolled at Wythenshawe College of Further Education, much to the relief of his parents. Unfortunately, his lust for O-levels was subjugated by less strenuous pursuits. Fellow student Steve Cassan noted that Maher seldom attended lectures and spent most of his time in the refectory, often accompanied by Angie. His arrival at college coincided with one of his periodic shifts in musical taste. He raved over The Fall's single 'Totally Wired' and purchased several key albums, including The Cure's *17 Seconds*, The Comsat Angels' *Waiting For A Miracle* and, some weeks later, U2's *Boy*. There was also a noticeable change of image with black hair dyed blacker, an ostentatious beret, and leather trousers tucked into suede boots becoming *de rigueur*. Most significant, however, was Maher's willingness to use his experience at college to further his musical career. "If there was any limelight he'd hog it", was Cassan's piercingly cynical viewpoint.

Maher's ascendancy was emphasized by his rapid appointment as president of the college's Student Union. His latest cohort, fellow student Tony O'Connor, took an immediate interest in the White Dice and seemed "determined to manage them to fame and fortune". Before the end of

Michaelmas term, the group at last received a gigging opportunity when they were booked to play the Squat, an annexe of the University Theatre, situated in Devas Street. They were considered competent enough to be placed above the pyrotechnic rock 'n' roll outfit Scorched Earth, but the main attraction was reggae group Exodus. In order to fatten the White Dice sound, former Eye Routine drummer Joey McLoughlan was invited along as additional percussionist. Events took an ominous turn when Exodus failed to appear and were replaced at the last minute by the echo-laden Foreign Press. This proved an unhappy augury to a humiliating debacle.

The non-attendance of Exodus ensured that the audience was embarrassingly sparse as White Dice edgily took the stage. Their first number turned out to be nothing more than a belated soundcheck, bathed in the harsh glow of a solitary white spotlight. In the midst of a gaggle of apathetic spectators lurked the haunting spectre of the once exuberant Bobby Durkin, who watched disconsolately as his former group defiled their début with a shambolic performance. "Rob had been drinking Special Brew," Durkin lamented. "He could really drink. He was so paralytic that he couldn't play; absolutely out of his head. That was the evening when John made the break. He thought, 'Bollocks! I'm not messing about with this'. You could tell he didn't like what happened that night."

What Durkin had not considered were the technical hitches that conspired against Allman and the others. Frustratingly, the troubled lead guitarist had broken a string earlier that evening which rendered his brand new Telecaster temporarily unavailable. In his determination to salvage the show, Johnny had scoured the college desperately seeking a replacement model, which was finally provided by a student friend, Leo. Allman was dismayed to discover that the replacement instrument was virtually unplayable. "I don't know whether I was even heard," he confessed. White Dice struggled through a short set which included Johnny's cover of 'Take Me To The River' and "an XTC interpretation of The Rolling Stones' 'The Last Time', with jagged guitars sounding like The Gang Of Four".

Allman looks back at White Dice's live death with weary resignation. "It was a cock-up from start to finish," he candidly points out. "Drink was flowing freely and there was inebriation generally. I was centre stage and on the brink of glandular fever. We'd had no chance to rehearse, the main group hadn't appeared and we were fed-up. At one point, I felt like going home. From there on, it went downhill. It was a disaster."

The Squat gig represented the death knell for White Dice, though they occasionally reconvened for a desultory series of rehearsals. New boy Craig Mitchell soon lost interest and was replaced in the final stages by the returning Bobby Durkin. Recoiling from the Rourke residence, the group found alternative rehearsal space at a scout hut on Woodbourne Road in Sale. From there, they were reduced to practising in an archway beneath the railway tracks of Deansgate Station. After leaving their instruments there for several nights, they were dismayed to discover mildew forming on the kit. It seemed tauntingly symbolic of their corroding musical career.

The final White Dice rehearsal occurred on 13 January 1981. That same month, Allman left the Rourke household after a personality clash with Andy's eldest brother Chris. It had never been an easy relationship. Thereafter, nobody had the energy or enthusiasm to take the experiment any further. Maher was clearly thinking along new lines and had already begun working with Andy during Allman's convalescence from glandular fever. Strangely enough, the Maher/Rourke axis was veering in the entirely unexpected direction of funk. "Johnny was going nuts over The Brothers Johnson's *Stomp*," remembers Allman. Maher's record player was also blasting out albums by Chic and Sister Sledge as eclecticism reached new bounds of improbability. Through Chris Rourke's girlfriend Rickie Wright, Andy and Johnny were introduced to Jan, who worked at Decibel Studios in Ancoats. Over a beer, he agreed to allow them limited recording facilities. Several weeks later, they emerged with a finished tape titled 'Crak Therapy'. It left little doubt that their next project would be strongly funk-influenced.

Maher and Rourke informally put word about town that they were interested in acquiring a singer and percussionist. A schoolfriend, Dave Columb, suggested an Altrincham drummer, whose nickname, Funky Si, indicated that he might be a promising candidate. The 19-year-old Simon Wolstencroft had a limited but significant musical background. While attending South Sheffield College, he had played in a group called Patrol, which featured Ian Brown and John Squire (who would later form The Stone Roses). By early 1981, he was working in a fish shop, an occupation that made professional drumming seem a dream by comparison. Wolstencroft cautiously attended a session at Rourke's house and after listening to the material on offer agreed to become involved. "I was playing with them for well over a year, not gigging, just writing stuff," Simon explained. "When I think back now, what we were doing then was way ahead of its time. It was all dance stuff with wah-wah guitars and funk-style drumming. That was the tail-end of the Brit Funk movement and we were into Grandmaster Flash and all that, especially Andy and myself. We weren't playing smoochy soul songs, but hard, attacking funk like A Certain Ratio. No other bands of note were doing that stuff."

Like White Dice, Maher's new outfit seemed perpetually locked into elongated rehearsals. They tentatively named themselves Freaky Party but failed to enlist that all-important lead singer whose presence would magically complete the line-up. Over the next year, a handful of hopefuls auditioned, but all were deemed unsuitable. A good-looking Rourke discovery named Wade had the right image but could only sing PIL's 'Flowers Of Romance'. Rejected, he went on to become a male model. A small, blonde girl from Altrincham also turned up one evening, but although she could sing, her image was wrong.

The paramount importance attached to the singer's image meant that the dream candidate remained frustratingly elusive. "We didn't want someone with a good voice who didn't fit in with the clothes we wore," Wolstencroft bluntly noted. Maher was especially dress conscious after landing a job at X Clothes in Chapel Walks. The shop sold early designer fetish garb,

including leather jackets with the arms cut off and quarter-length coats purchased from Johnsons in London's King's Road. Coincidentally, Maher's
old mentor Billy Duffy was himself working in Johnsons at the time, having recently left the quartet Lonesome No More. It was typical of Johnny
to keep pace with Duffy, even though they were no longer living in the
same city.

Maher's period at X Clothes enabled him to meet a range of interesting
people, including several aspiring local disc jockeys. One such was Andrew
Berry, whom Maher had known since the West Wythenshawe Youth Club
days, although back then their paths seldom crossed. Berry had attended St
Gregorys Grammar School and was known as a keen fan of Bryan Ferry
and David Bowie. While Maher was practising guitar, idolizing Rory
Gallagher and dressing in standard rock denim, Berry was emulating the
sharp garb of Bowie, who had recently transformed from a space age
androgyne into a Philadelphia white soul boy. After leaving school, Berry
became a hairdresser and was noted for his outrageous silver leather
trousers and blowzy shirts in true New Romantic style. As one old friend
pithily observed: "Johnny and Bez were poles apart." What brought them
together in 1981 was a mutual interest in fashionable clothes and Maher's
new-found fascination for funk and soul. Andrew embellished his earnings
by working part time as a disc jockey, sometimes under the name Marc
Berry. Maher often joined him at clubs such as Exit, spinning James Brown
and Fatback Band records into the early hours. Johnny had recently gathered all his records in one place and was amazed by the number of dance
singles tucked away in his sprawling collection. At that point, the refrain
"Hang the DJ" would have seemed most inappropriate. Simon
Wolstencroft recalls Maher laden with disco singles, which briefly became
the inspirational soundtrack to their studio funk experiments. "Johnny was
always turning us on to these American soul singers. He had a vast
knowledge of the stuff, much more than Andy and I. Often, I didn't know
where he got all this knowledge from. He was one of those people that just
picked things up."

If X Clothes provided a touch of glamour, with its passing disc jockeys
and visiting musicians, there were also less desirable elements, including
several shady customers with tales of quick and easy money. Their arrival
coincided with a period of financial struggle for Johnny who was intent on
acquiring an expensive Les Paul guitar and Fender Twin Reverb. He was
temporarily buoyed by Angie, who was then fortuitously working at a
jeweller. The need for musical equipment, however, eventually led Maher
into a wide-boy association with some dubious characters. "I was pretty
'wide', but I was never into ripping people off," he stresses. "I was just so
obsessed with music. Ripping off people's houses wasn't my style. Never
anyone's house. I had to have money - I ended up with a Les Paul."

Maher also ended up with some stolen Lowry prints and fell victim to an
alarming and dramatic case of mistaken identity. The ensuing police swoop
was worthy of a television drama. One day, during rehearsals with
Wolstencroft and Rourke, Maher was distracted by some irritating

hammering on the studio door. After a few seconds, the door was literally kicked in and four burly policemen burst through. A discordant clash of notes reverberated through the room as Maher was pinned against a wall with his guitar still around his neck. "What's your name?" his animated assailants ordered. Maher was momentarily dumbfounded.

Further drama awaited the shaken guitarist when he learned the reasons behind the alarming investigation. "The police who kicked in the door were the Serious Crime Squad!" he recalls. "Two cases got mixed-up and they were checking out this crime where an old woman was killed in a house. They got this fence with a load of gear and they thought my gear was part of their crime, which it wasn't... That was the only time I was ever in trouble, really. It was important for me that I had a guitar and an amp and that's the only reason I ripped off!" Maher was greatly relieved when the confused matter was cleared up and the Serious Crime Squad, realizing their degree of error, set off in pursuit of the real villains.

Maher's speculative forays into the art market aptly commented on the times. It was unquestionably a disconcerting period to be contemplating leaving college and embarking on a musical career. Great Britain had found itself in the grip of a new conservatism, so grim and austere that there was talk of turning back the clock 100 years. The incumbent Prime Minister, Margaret Thatcher, resembled nothing less than a stern and inscrutably benevolent Dickensian mistress, encouraging thrift, orderliness, self-discipline and anti-permissiveness. Her dream of restoring dear old Blighty to the ideals of a hopelessly lost golden age apparently required an economic policy so stringent that it threatened to amputate the welfare state from the body politic and promote an increasing reliance on the Victorian vagaries of a few privileged philanthropists.

Across the Atlantic, an even fiercer conservatism gripped the continent; its national mood epitomized by a former Hollywood idol turned president. The 70-year-old Ronald Reagan had begun his administration with a surge of unprecedented nationalist fervour. By some Almighty providence, the day of his investiture coincided with the long-awaited release of US hostages following 444 days of incarceration in Iran. In the months that followed, it was hard to dispute the theory that Reagan had appointed some deific scriptwriter to transform his presidential office into a barely credible partisan B-movie. The villain of the piece was John Warnock Hinckley, a deranged obsessive suffering the pangs of an unrequited passion for actress Jody Foster. He duly demonstrated the depth of his infatuation by unloading his gun into the lungs of Ronald Reagan. Remarkably, the ageing president not only survived the assassination attempt but was back at work in the White House within 12 days. This was the stuff of Hollywood movies, in complete contrast to the real life tragedies of the Kennedys, Martin Luther King and, only a few months before, John Lennon. Reagan's survival and visibly indomitable spirit effectively rendered his political stratagems irrelevant. Overnight he had been transformed into an American hero.

Back in Britain, a new political party was forged from the disillusionment of four breakaway Labour Cabinet members: David Owen, Shirley Williams, William Rodgers and Roy Jenkins. The confusingly titled Social Democratic Party was launched with a firm promise to "depolarize society". The internal strife within the Labour Party allowed the Conservatives to continue the radical market-orientated policies that had yet to decrease unemployment, which rapidly soared to three million.

Economic concerns soon played an important part in forestalling Maher's first career move. During the summer of 1981, he had a happy encounter with a musician whose work he already admired. It was a record shop manager from Altrincham named Pete Hunt who first introduced Johnny to Matt Johnson. Hunt frequently travelled to London and one evening he met the singer on the way to a night-club. Like Mark E Smith and Kevin Rowland, Johnson was predominantly a soloist who enjoyed the security of a group name, but saw no sanctity in its particular membership. He was The The. Hunt invited Johnson to Manchester and introduced him to Maher, who treated the guest to a brief tour of the city's night spots. "We got on right away," Johnny enthuses. "It was one of those situations where you meet somebody and you're kindred spirits or soul mates. It was a pretty strong feeling, and we became close friends within a night. It was like we'd known each other a long time. Matt and I had similar backgrounds. He was the person I had most in common with."

Johnson was similarly invigorated by Maher's irrepressible enthusiasm. Characteristically, the Mancunian reappeared the following day, guitar in hand, and organized an impromptu jamming session. He listened with interest to Johnson's musical tastes, which ranged from The Beatles to Tim Buckley and Can. Matt even had a fondness for Lindisfarne's 'Lady Eleanor' and spoke about its flip-side with due reverence. Maher was happy to compare notes on the best singles of the Seventies and, as with every important person he met, conveniently found common musical ground. "He was very confident and seemed to know what he was doing," Johnson recalls. "Johnny's a friendly person and one of the things I liked about him was that he took a genuine interest in people. We hit it off straightaway. He was very sharp and deep thinking and I found we could talk about all sorts of things. There was a lot of empathy there and humour. A lot of people don't realize Johnny's a humorist. He's one of the funniest people I've ever known. If he hadn't been a guitarist he could have been a stand-up comedian."

After charming Johnson, Maher seemed on the brink of joining The The, but financial and geographical considerations rendered the idea unworkable. "It was a bit awkward," Matt remembers, "because I was based in London and neither of us had lots of money. On reflection, it was just as well. We were both pretty wild at that time, drugswise, and the pair of us would probably have ended up as fatalities. There was a link there and we later kept an eye on each other's careers. I knew we'd end up working together eventually and he felt the same."

Maher's musically eventful post-college summer coincided with the worst outbreak of home civil unrest this century. Panic on the streets of

London, Birmingham and Luton, supplemented by serious rioting in Liverpool, took place against the ironic backdrop of the multi-racial Specials' 'Ghost Town'. Even the distracting spectacle of a Royal Wedding could not assuage the feeling that England was in dreadful turmoil. While the Royal Family feasted themselves at a wedding banquet, a fifth hunger striker expired in the appallingly primitive Maze Prison in a vain attempt to win recognition as a political prisoner. Since the self-martyrdom of Bobby Sands, just two months earlier, the intransigence of the Prime Minister had been transformed into a startlingly effective weapon for the Bold Boys, as Sinn Fein celebrated an unprecedented number of electoral victories in Northern Ireland. The summer of violence ended with Ronald Reagan's grandly ominous plan to build a neutron bomb. It was a good time to leave home.

By the winter of 1981, Johnny had left the Baguley estate and moved into the luxuriously spacious Altrincham home of Granada television presenter and freelance journalist Shelley Rohde. It was a remarkable coincidence, for Rohde had recently written a major biography of Maher's recent nemesis, painter LS Lowry.* "She used to have a Lowry print in the house," Johnny remembers, "and every time I saw it my heart would sink. Shelley didn't know about that."

Another coincidence of the Rohde residence was that her son, Daniel Weaver, had been in the same school and year as Simon Wolstencroft. The drummer partially credits the family for inspiring him to take up the sticks. "Dan had a room in his house that he'd soundproofed and his brothers (Christian and Gavin) had guitar amps, and that made me want to play an instrument." Although Wolstencroft had lost contact with Weaver after their school days, he realized that the Rohde attic was a good base for any young musician. Clearly, Maher had fallen on his feet once again. The family had another lodger, a Swiss lad named Oliver May who had introduced Johnny to the household and would later emerge as part of The Smiths' road crew. The youngest member of the family was 15-year-old Michele Weaver, whom Johnny teasingly called his "Sixties flower child". She diligently summed up Maher's three consuming interests in life: "Angie, music and smoking spliffs."

The Rohde connection brought Johnny unexpected fame back in Wythenshawe, thanks to a couple of surprise television appearances. One of these was a youth programme, *The Devil's Advocate*, in which members of the studio audience were asked to throw questions at visiting politicians and local dignitaries. Never a shrinking violet, Maher made sure that his voice was heard. "If a camera was there, his face would be on it," noted his laconic contemporary Steve Cassan. "That's the kind of person he was."

By early 1982, Maher, Rourke and Wolstencroft were still rehearsing three nights a week at Decibel Studios. The French owner Philippe remained blithely unaware of their bargain-rate noctural progress. It was a pleasant, if undemanding, period for the once hungry musicians. Johnny was still at

---

*See Shelley Rohde, *A Private View Of LS Lowry* (Collins, London, 1979).

X Clothes; Simon was still in the fish shop; Andy was working in a timber yard. It was difficult to avoid the conclusion that they simply lacked motivation. The search for a singer had become something of a joke after a year, especially as the trio's only form of advertising was word of mouth. If history had taken a different course, and they had appointed a suitable vocalist, the group might have emerged as one of Manchester's dance music innovators. Instead, Maher finally lost interest and decided to pursue something new. "We fell out and Andy and I didn't see Johnny for over six months," Wolstencroft explained. "Johnny got bored hanging about and we still wanted to play stuff with funky bass lines." In the wake of Maher's departure, Wolstencroft was more than happy to continue his working relationship with Rourke. "At the time, I was more impressed with Andy, being a drummer. To this day, he's one of my favourite bass players. We weren't desperate to get into the Top 40 and just enjoyed doing it."

For Maher, however, the funk patterns had become increasingly restrictive after 13 months, and he was hungry for a new challenge. On reflection, Maher was clearly unable to limit himself to one style of music indefinitely. A questing spirit would remain his key characteristic. "Andy and I always knew what was good," he explained. "It was just a case of going our separate ways. The two of us had to find our feet."

7

The Formation Of The Smiths

JOE MOSS WAS A VERITABLE rag trade veteran by 1982. After stints as a welder and telephone engineer, he had started selling sandals in the late Sixties and was pleased to discover that he possessed a certain creative flair for transforming fashion into commodity. After building up a wholesale jeans business, he opened two satellite shops called Crazy Face in Manchester's Portland Street and Chapel Walks, plus a third in Tiviot Dale, Stockport. On Saturday mornings, Moss would have a wander around his emporia and pop into Chapel Walks, where he kept a guitar. In the backroom, he would wile away a lunch hour playing Little Walter riffs before returning to the grind of the warehouse. Joe had a large record collection and was particularly fond of blues and jazz. His favourite contemporary artiste was Van Morrison whose song 'Crazy Face' had inspired the title of Moss's mini-empire. Back in the Sixties, Moss had known a few local musicians, including Pete Flame And The Clan, one of many Manchester groups left stranded in the post-beat boom years. Moss was fascinated by the mechanics of pop, with its instant successes and dogged failures, and regarded this strange business as "80 per cent hype and 20 per cent talent". He often sympathized with the frustrations of struggling performers, whose dreams would inevitably remain unrealized.

It was during a Saturday visit to Crazy Face that Moss was first introduced to Johnny Maher. The teenager explained that he worked next door at X Clothes and let slip the news that he was intending to form a group. Since they both strummed a guitar, Joe suggested that Johnny should pop over whenever he had a free lunch hour. "Yes," Maher responded enthusiastically, "you could show me a few things." The perpetual learner, Johnny never missed a chance to feed his song catalogue and had the knack of making his listener feel important. In his conversations with Moss, there was no mention of his recent funk interludes. Instead, he emerged as a devotee of the blues, eager to master those Little Walter riffs and visibly pleased whenever Moss arrived with an old record he'd never heard. Joe was flattered to play the musical mentor before such a willing and obviously talented student. "He started to come over practically every dinner time," Moss recalls. "It was a welcome break and he was a nice lad whom you could relate to instantly. He was dead interested in the blues and the real roots music. I'd heard people play in company and most were boring, but when Johnny picked up a guitar he always had his own approach. I found him really innovative."

Like many others, Moss was charmed by Maher's lively and enthusiastic personality and won over by his skill. "Johnny was obviously looking for a first rung on the ladder", Joe reasoned. "He saw that I could offer security and stability and a base, and that's what I did, willingly." Maher spent many evenings at Moss's home watching videos, listening to blues records and discussing the merits of the great songwriters. "Joe was really great for me," Johnny enthuses. "He got me into loads of stuff and encouraged me as well as giving me jobs and letting me stay at his house. He was so good to me and taught me a lot." Maher liked to seek advice from his elder friend, who was an excellent sounding board for new ideas. It was evident that Maher was piecing together a group in his mind but, on this occasion, he was concentrating on songs rather than musicians. Instead of rehearsing with a rhythm section, as he had done for the previous year, he decided to seek a lyricist and singer.

Maher retained contact with most of his old musician friends, including the London-based Billy Duffy, who was then enjoying a modicum of success with Theatre Of Hate. Wisely, Johnny consulted with his sage elder about the difficulty of finding an accomplished songsmith. Inevitably, the name Morrissey entered the conversation. Four years before, Duffy had shown Maher some lyrics that Morrissey had written for The Nosebleeds. Johnny recalled that they were reasonably good, so decided to pursue the Morrissey tip. From both Duffy and Allman, he learned the need to proceed with caution. The Stretford bard was already generally regarded as eccentric, mercurial and difficult to approach. Allman himself had previously attended a Morrissey summit during which the singer had remained embarrassingly silent throughout the entire proceedings. What Maher needed was a favourable introduction. Eventually, he was given the address of the perfect mediator.

The man of the moment was the engaging Steve Pomfret, who had previously introduced Billy Duffy to Morrissey, thereby smoothing the latter's way into The Nosebleeds. In the initial discussions about Johnny's new group, it was intended that Pomfret would be incorporated as rhythm guitarist. "It was suggested out of fairness because Pommy knew Morrissey and he was the link," Maher confirmed, "but it didn't work out, and he was the first to admit he didn't have it." Allman painted a cruder picture of events: "What Johnny did was string Pommy along. He was never going to be part of the group in the long run. He was just another rung on the ladder, a way of getting to Morrissey. Pomfret wasn't a good guitarist and knew he would be ousted. I don't think there was any bitterness. Pommy certainly wasn't bitter." Indeed, it was stretching credulity to view the new project in terms of "ousting" for Maher was far from the stage of selecting a final membership. Pommy subsequently appeared for a few desultory rehearsals at Johnny's place and at a later stage keyboardist Paul Whittall was momentarily considered, then forgotten. The line-up of Maher's imaginary group would remain curiously unsettled until the end of 1982. As for the Pomfret/Morrissey connection, even Allman concurs that the proposed formal introduction was ultimately unnecessary. "Credit where it's due, Johnny worked pretty hard doing the leg work. He really sold himself to Morrissey."

Maher's decision to confront Morrissey directly came about partly thanks to Joe Moss. The jeans wholesaler had videotaped an interview with songwriters Leiber and Stoller which Johnny eagerly borrowed. Maher was intrigued by the career of the duo who, during their peak period in the Fifties, had written a wealth of strong, narrative hits for such artistes as Elvis Presley, The Drifters and The Coasters. One part of the tape that especially appealed to Johnny was the segment where Mike Stoller explained how Jerry Leiber had impertinently appeared at his front door and insisted they form a songwriting team. "My door-bell rang," Stoller later recalled, "and I opened the door and there I saw a young fellow with reddish hair, one blue eye and one brown eye. My jaw dropped and after I recovered, an hour or so later, I invited him in." From this single, impromptu meeting, a great songwriting partnership was born. It was a wonderfully romantic tale that immediately inspired Maher into action. Alighting at Pommy's house, he hastily took down Steven Morrissey's address. His next stop was Stretford.

By the time Maher arrived at 384 Kings Road, he was like an exhilarated, unleashed hound. A modicum of calm was required as he rang the doorbell. His secret fear was that his image and ideas might so severely clash with those of Morrissey that the dream partnership would prove untenable. When the door opened, Maher spoke in a rush, never managing to stay quite still, possessed of continual animation, the speed of his thoughts barely keeping pace with the consequential patter that was earnestly directed at his host. All the while he found himself wondering whether Morrissey would object to his confrontational X Clothes and Teddy Boy quiff. It was something of a relief to enter Steven's bedroom and be confronted by a large cardboard cut-out of James Dean and a photograph of Elvis Presley. Thankfully, Fifties imagery was more than acceptable. Maher's garrulous persuasion held him in good stead during the opening exchanges, and he even risked a touch of arrogance with the gambit, "This is how Leiber and Stoller met".

The grandiloquent gesture appealed to Morrissey, although he maintained his characteristic reserve. Maher was impressed by the silence. "I saw a lot of good things in him that I didn't see in myself," he explained. "He didn't say much and just let me tell him what I wanted to do." After the briefest period in Maher's company, Morrissey accepted his friendly compulsion to converse, not as an eccentricity, but as part of the essence of his person, as much a part of Johnny Maher as an arm and a leg and, without which, he would seem strangely incomplete. One question Steven did ask his chatty visitor was the pertinent: "What music do you like?" As with Joe Moss, Maher had the intuitive ability to tell Morrissey exactly what he wanted to hear. It was unconscious second nature for Johnny to accentuate those aspects of his musical taste that coincided with Morrissey's, while conveniently passing over such infatuations as Rory Gallagher, folk and funk. Maher's real power lay in the fact that he liked the best of everything and had the palette of a connoisseur attached to the tongue of a costermonger. His pitch was all the more effective because he believed genuinely and passionately in the quality of the artistes he extolled, while his breadth of knowledge hinted at boundless artistic possibilities. Morrissey quickly realized that he was not merely in the presence of an aggressively ambitious musician, but a keen and discerning student of pop history. "Immediately, it became apparent that we had a lot in common regarding our feelings towards pop culture and records generally," Maher explained. "If it hadn't worked out I would never have done it again with anyone else because I really opened up and he did the same. He just got this amazing vibe from me."

Morrissey was in fact completely invigorated by Maher's irrepressible enthusiasm and ambition. He handed his visitor a sheath of lyrics and was flattered by the awed response. Without even hearing Maher play, Morrissey was already convinced that their partnership would prove productive and save him from further frustrated years of unrealized potential. Maher was busy verbally stringing melodies together while reading Steven's words and the following day he reappeared with a guitar. One of the first lyrics that made an impact on Maher was the elegiac 'Suffer Little Children', in which Morrissey mourned the deaths of the innocents buried on the moors. "I was taken aback completely because the content was so serious, but at the same time very poignant and poetic," Maher recollected. What most impressed was the song's compact subtlety and the particularity of detail: the reference to Lesley Ann's "little white beads" from which her corpse was first identified; Hindley's awakening utterance, "Wherever he has gone, I have gone", so pungently echoing her first statement to the police, "Whatever Ian has done, I have done"; the ironic biblical connotations of the title 'Suffer Little Children'; the power of those three words to conjure up the actual suffering that the children experienced, reinforced and emphasized by the additional knowledge that the murderess's fellow prisoners voiced the full refrain ("suffer little children to come unto me") whenever she walked by. This was lyrical power without oration or sensation.*

Johnny was sufficiently impressed to produce a lustrous, reflective melody that entranced Morrissey. Already, they had a composition completed and ready for recording. Soon afterwards, Maher finished work on another song that still stands as one of Morrissey's most dense and oblique compositions.

'The Hand That Rocks The Cradle' not only evoked the innocence of childhood but also the genuine terror that childlike imaginings can

---

* Coincidentally, during the period they were working on 'Suffer Little Children', the *Sunday Times* featured a provocative insight into the life of Myra Hindley, titled 'The Woman Who Cannot Face The Truth'. The piece was co-written by Peter Gillman, who would later pen an equally controversial biography of another of Morrissey's touchstones, David Bowie.

inspire.+ The eerie mystery of the piano playing in an empty room, those wardrobes disguised as birds of prey, the tantalizing tricks of bogeymen and restless spirits, and the *Psycho*-like imagery of the "bloodied cleaver" brilliantly combine to create a sense of imminent, inexplicable danger, relieved solely by the obsessive protectiveness of the narrator who, like so many of Morrissey's characters, displays a strangely resolute desire for self-sacrifice ("my life down I shall lie"). Maher responded by adding a sparkling, insistent arrangement, so effective that it propelled them towards further intense collaborations over the succeeding weeks.

The impact that Maher had on Morrissey's life cannot be overestimated. Four years younger than Steven, Johnny had already realized many of the dreams that were such a crucial part of the Morrissey mythology. In one sense, he had lived out several of Morrissey's fantasies by the age of 18. Unlike Steven, Johnny did not merely tinker with instruments but learned to play with a precision and power that staggered his contemporaries; he did not hero-worship minor television personalities but appeared on screen himself, and even lived in the house of a name Granada presenter; while Morrissey wrote forgotten *Coronation Street* scripts in his bedroom, Maher was playing in a group with one of its future luminaries, the inimitable Curly Watts; rather than idolize the stylish Sandie Shaw, Johnny preferred a flesh and blood relationship with a girl whose looks, image and character meant more than any Sixties icon. Moreover, it cannot have escaped Morrissey's notice that Maher's immemorial love Angie shared the same name as the girlfriend he had watched withering away from leukaemia six years before. In so many respects, Maher was everything Morrissey *might* have been.

While the Pope visited England for the first time in 450 years and the war-mongering British press hailed the Falklands heroes, Morrissey and Maher continued writing and planning their futures. Pommy was already off the scene and the search for a group was forestalled as the duo concentrated on their songwriting. They had already agreed that if suitable musicians could not be found for a group, then they would continue writing songs for other artistes. Still inspired by the great American songwriting teams of the early Sixties, they spoke in terms of establishing a Brill Building in Manchester. Moss fantasized about employing a small school of young composers and Morrissey announced, "I'd like to write a song for Sandie Shaw". It was an incredibly exciting period with the anticipation of great work to follow.

By the summer, the duo decided to record some 8-track demos at Decibel Studios, where they were allowed free studio time after midnight by a friendly engineer named Dale. At that point, Maher realized that they

+ The title was not original to Morrissey. A birth control drama titled *The Hand That Rocks The Cradle* was released by Universal American Films back in 1917. Morrissey's source can be more accurately traced to Saturday 12 April 1981 when Granada Television broadcast a 40-minute episode of the detective series *Crib*, in which the Victorian hero "sets a trap for some anarchists". The episode was evocatively titled 'The Hand That Rocks The Cradle', and Morrissey probably wrote the composition during April 1981, a period when he was particularly productive.

needed a rhythm section so enlisted the assistance of drummer Simon Wolstencroft. Significantly, Rourke was not involved in the session, which featured 'Suffer Little Children' and 'The Hand That Rocks The Cradle'. The tracks were completed in two takes, with Maher and Dale adding the bass parts retrospectively. When it came time to listen to the playbacks, Johnny was a little apprehensive, but any lingering doubts vanished after hearing the first verse of 'Suffer Little Children'. Maher was overwhelmed by the sensitivity of Morrissey's vocal and realized for the first time that his partner was not only a composer, but an expressive singer. "The more we played it back, the more touched we were," Maher recalled. "All the time we'd been writing together we knew we had the conviction and the talent to put these gems together, but this was the confirmation of it all." The following day, Johnny and Angie paid a visit to Rob Allman's house, armed with a tape of 'The Hand That Rocks The Cradle'. "He was absolutely enthralled," Rob remembers, "and played it over and over."

An unexpected break came Maher's way when he learned that the Ritz was putting on a fashion show on 4 October featuring the much-hyped Blue Rondo A La Turk. With the assistance of hairdresser friend Andrew Berry and Wythenshawe style guru John Kennedy, Maher persuaded the promoters to allow his "new group" a brief support slot. The fact that Maher had not yet created a group, let alone a repertoire of songs, was merely a minor consideration in the circumstances. For the next few weeks, he urgently attempted to piece together the elusive rhythm section.

Johnny had already approached Simon Wolstencroft offering him a permanent place in the new group. "Throw everything in with me," Maher enthused, "we'll be making lots of money by next year." Johnny explained that Joe Moss was serious about helping the group but Wolstencroft cautiously dismissed this as blarney. He agreed to play on the Decibel demos without a fee, but otherwise proved surprisingly resistant to the famous Maher spiel. "There were no wages involved at that point," Wolstencroft confirmed, "and I didn't want to go in the direction they were taking. Morrissey, to me, was the grey overcoat brigade whereas I wanted to be in a modern funk outfit. I looked on Morrissey as being old school, miserable Manchester, and I wasn't impressed enough to jack in everything for that." In the event, Wolstencroft merely committed himself to recording the demo, with the proviso that he might be available for occasional gigs. He and Rourke were already jamming with a black singer in Stockport, intent on pursuing dance music. When Maher reported back to Moss that Wolstencroft could only play on an *ad hoc* basis, the haberdasher lost his patience. "You've got to get yourself a *proper* drummer," he told Maher emphatically. At that point, Wolstencroft was written out of the script. "If I'd known Joe Moss it might have been different," he mused, "but I couldn't see it happening."

It was Morrissey who produced the second candidate for the group. A promising demo tape had passed through his hands featuring Ivor and Andy Perry (later of Easterhouse), backed by bassist Pete Vanden and drummer Gary Farrell. The latter pair were former St Marys' pupils, albeit several years younger than Morrissey. Farrell had occasionally chatted with Steven while walking home from school and seemed a pleasant, easy-going kid. Johnny agreed that his drumming on the tape was competent enough and took his number. Several evenings later, he phoned Farrell to say that Morrissey wished to arrange a meeting. It seemed an odd request, not least because Farrell had never previously spoken to Maher, while Morrissey lived only a couple of hundred yards down the road. Sufficiently intrigued, he marched down to number 384 and received an inviting welcome. Morrissey explained about the group and expressed his favourable impression of Farrell's demo tape. Although Gary felt obliged to point out that he had sold his drum-kit, Steven seemed unperturbed and said: "Don't worry, we'll get you another one." The two had time to reminisce about the horrors of St Marys, and Morrissey was amused to discover that Farrell's venom often excelled his own. "All I ever learned there was hatred" was the youth's stark summation of the Renton Road years. Morrissey could not have put it better himself. He remembered the much-feared PE master, Paul Sweeney who, it transpired, had later married Morrissey's fifth form English teacher, Anne Judge. There lay a sweet irony. Farrell recalled how some bitter, troublesome pupils were wont to avenge themselves on the disciplinarian Sweeney via his fiancée. A friend of Farrell had taken a pot of red paint and daubed the school gates with the words, "Judge Is A **** ", adding the most offensive word in his limited vocabulary. Sweeney's reaction was devastatingly swift; the culprit was unmasked and duly punished with a severity that deterred similar pranksters. The saga was worthy of a Morrissey lyric.

Farrell left Steven's house clutching a cassette tape containing the Morrissey/Marr demos. He promised to let Morrissey know his decision within a week. In the meantime, he dyed his hair red, which caused a comedy of confusion when they next met. After reassuring Morrissey that he was indeed the *same* Gary Farrell, the two had another chat and Steven produced a postcard on which were scrawled three printed names: "Smiths", "Smithdom" and "Smiths' Family".

"Which do you like best?" Morrissey enquired. "Smiths," replied Farrell, without hesitation. Morrissey smiled. "I like that one too," he said. Johnny Maher was evidently of similar persuasion. In his mind, the name "Smiths" was an antidote to all those portentously grandiloquent group names such as Orchestral Manoeuvres In The Dark and Blue Rondo A La Turk. The Smiths implied a back-to-basics approach and an unexotic Englishness that promised songs about real people in real situations, rather than some fantasy island romance or techno-crazed incoherence. There were other Morrissey/Maher associations with the name Smiths, unconscious and coincidental, but nevertheless significant: their shared reverence for Patti Smith; the grudging respect for fellow Mancunian, Mark E Smith; the Moors murder tie-in with David Smith (who had turned in Hindley and Brady); and the famous Sixties Manchester club Mr Smiths in Brazil Street. There were also some minor reasons why Smiths wasn't such a great name. Its peculiarly English connotations gave the lie to its membership's full-blooded Irish extraction; its dour tone suggested an act of prosaic dullness, rather than the effervescent wit and musical sparkle that underlined the Morrissey/Maher partnership. But perhaps most damning of all were the words of Morrissey's literary hero Oscar Wilde, who had observed drily: "Surely everyone prefers Norfolk, Hamilton and Buckingham to Jones or *Smith...*"

Having chosen a name, The Smiths were no nearer to fielding a complete line-up. Farrell had listened to the Morrissey/Marr demos and was unimpressed by the material. Seeking a second opinion, he contacted Ivor Perry, another Kings Road resident and aspiring guitarist. "I knew Morrissey as a local weirdo, so I went round for a laugh to listen to it," Perry remembers. Like Farrell, Perry was bemused by the recording. "It had tape loops of dogs barking and what sounded like an atmospheric film mix overdubbed on one of the songs," he remembers. "Morrissey's vocal was flat and he couldn't really sing. I think one of the songs was 'The Hand That Rocks The Cradle', but it was really primitive. It sounded weird." Although Farrell felt the idea of joining Morrissey was tempting, he bluntly admitted: "I couldn't get anything out of it." Steven was not amused. "I never spoke to Morrissey again," Farrell smiled. "I think he felt I'd insulted him."

While the search for a drummer continued, those style kings Andrew Berry and John Kennedy promised to pass the demo tape on to any interested parties they met in London. One promising source was fellow clubland habitué Mark Dean, who was gaining something of a reputation as a music business whizz-kid. After leaving school, Dean had secured a post at And Son, a company that administered the publishing affairs of the chart-topping Jam. From there, he moved into A&R at Phonogram Records and immediately proved his worth by securing the rights to Stevo's celebrated Some Bizzare compilation. Stevo (Steven Pearse) was one of the more eccentric figures on the pop scene, specializing in electronic music and arcane talent. Most record company executives found his unpredictable behaviour and short temper difficult to handle, but Dean was young and enthusiastic enough to earn his trust. The success of the compilation album led to the signing of its principal participants, Soft Cell. That Dean could accommodate some of Stevo's rather odd demands, such as a regular supply of sweets for the entire duration of the contract, was deemed no small feat. The ability to communicate effectively with a new breed of temperamental artiste and McLarenesque management was tested further when Dean bagged Sheffield hopefuls, ABC. Within months, Phonogram was registering chart hits with two of the more critically-acclaimed and fashionable groups of the day and enjoying an unexpectedly hip credibility. Morrissey and Maher knew little about Mark Dean's background, but he sounded promising. That he shared the same surname as James Dean and had been vaguely involved with The Jam would have caught Morrissey's attention, while Maher could consider the fact that Stevo's compilation had introduced the world to the talents of Matt Johnson's The The.

The 21-year-old Dean was no mere record company scout, however, and had recently persuaded CBS to finance his own record label, Innervision.

Remarkably, CBS's managing director Maurice Oberstein sanctioned this wild idea and seemed convinced that the launching of satellite labels to seek out new talent could be commercially exploited by the financial power of the parent company. Accordingly, Innervision was set up for this purpose with a share capital of only £100. Dean's solicitor, Paul Henry Rodwell, was a minor shareholder and co-director, whose role in recommending the infant entrepreneur to Oberstein proved instrumental. In the circumstances, Oberstein's generosity was commensurate with Dean's inexperience and the deal negotiated between CBS and the newly-created Innervision erred on the side of financial caution. CBS agreed to pay the company a first year non-returnable advance of £150,000, rising by 25 per cent over five years. Dean admits that the contract was "extremely tough" and Innervision "wasn't that stable". What he was effectively doing was discovering and nurturing young talent on a relative shoe-string. The executives at CBS probably expected Dean to unearth a few oddball minor-league groups, a couple of whom might reasonably be expected to scrape a Top 40 hit, thereby turning over a small profit. It was a calculated corporate gamble.

Amazingly, Dean almost hit the jackpot twice in his first year. Shortly before receiving the Morrissey/Maher demo, he had signed a duo from his home town Bushey, who would soon crash into the Top 10 and subsequently drag him to the High Court. In order to protect the interests of Innervision, Dean had effectively translated the toughest terms and percentages offered by CBS into an even harsher long-term standard artistes contract. For the newly-signed Wham!, the deal became a contractual comedy of errors that rapidly soured their relationship with Innervision. The Smiths were saved from a similar mistake partly thanks to Morrissey's characteristic caution concerning the distribution of income. Although the Stretford youth was no expert on record contracts, he had a particular vision of how The Smiths should develop.

"It was almost like he was waiting for the group to form," Maher explained. "A lot had been decided years ago. He wanted to be involved with people like Richard Boon and knew how he wanted the group perceived. Morrissey had a very healthy outlook on how to run a group financially by not spending money on complete bullshit and not being extravagant." Morrissey's motto was: "What we make we put in our pocket and pay everybody from our pocket." The standard Innervision deal offered no such autonomy and Dean's small advances (the Wham! boys received £500 each) were hardly enticing. The Smiths always liked to be wooed but Dean's reaction to the demo tape was not enthusiastic enough to warrant hard chasing. The moment passed. Maher subsequently journeyed to the capital on a couple of occasions and stayed at Matt Johnson's flat while seeking record company investment. Nobody was yet biting. The Smiths were left to concentrate on the upcoming Ritz gig, for which they still required a drummer. Maher continued the search until a friend, Peter Hope, mentioned a promising candidate from Fallowfield. His name was Mike Joyce.

Born on 1 June 1963, Joyce was the youngest of five children. As his surname suggested, Joyce was of Irish descent. His father hailed from Galway, while his mother was reared in Portarlington, Kildare. Young Michael had begun playing the flute during his first couple of years at St Gregorys Grammar School, but switched instruments when his mother kindly purchased him a drum-kit. From that point onwards, the 14-year-old insisted that he would become a pop star. Inspired by punk, he fell under the spell of the influential Buzzcocks, whose records served as a "listen while you learn" manual. Joyce idolized their drummer John Maher, whose technique he adapted and perfected after months of hard practise. At school, Joyce played the punk and was known for his spiky hair, similar in style to Johnny Rotten. Whenever it rained, he was blinded by the eye-stinging lather, oozing from his soap-adhesive Sex Pistols' spikes.

Coincidentally, Johnny Maher's associates, Andrew Berry and John Kennedy, had both attended St Gregorys at the same time as Joyce. Occasionally, the fledgling punk would see these outrageous glam rockers hanging round the music room, but their orbits seldom met. "John was quite effeminate even then," Joyce remembers. "That was the start of his alternative trip as a 14-year-old."

While Berry and Kennedy emulated the Bowie look and developed their own garish dress style, Joyce sought attention through his drumming. At the age of 16 he received the unexpected opportunity to play with some older musicians in a punk-influenced quartet named The Hoax. After answering a newspaper advert, he was informally auditioned and immediately accepted. The group had originally formed in the spring of 1978 as a result of a chance meeting at the club Rafters. Fledgling bassist Steve Mardy was trying to flog an old speaker when his eyes chanced upon a dishevelled character slumped against a wall. The apparition resembled nothing less than a lurid reincarnation of Sid Vicious. "He just had to be in a band," Mardy convinced himself. The Vicious lookalike was Ian Chambers from Stalybridge and, in common with the former Pistol, he was neither a competent guitarist nor singer. However, he did have a friend, Andy Farley, who claimed to play rudimentary guitar and, equally importantly, wrote angry, confrontational lyrics. Farley had a keen sense of alienated outrage, in keeping with the punk spirit. He and his girlfriend, Jane, were known to cut up their faces and capture the bloody spectacle on passport-sized photographs. After a series of torturous rehearsals, the three-piece auditioned a succession of unsuitable drummers before finally settling on Joyce. "We were terrible," Farley confirms. "I'm only learning to play the bloody guitar now. Mike was still picking it up as he went along, that's what I liked about him. He was a developing drummer."

Initially, there was mild consternation when it was discovered that Joyce was still at school. However, fears that he might be barred from playing in licensed pubs and clubs fortunately proved unfounded. The group's prospects improved when they came under the wing of Dennis Matthews, who managed a record shop and occasionally booked gigs. Well known on the Oi scene, he kept faith with The Hoax through several tough years.

"Joyce was a bit distant," he remembers. "The first time I saw him he was wearing a white shirt and tie, like a Buzzcocks clone. That's what he wanted to be - a Buzzcock."

The Hoax began playing gigs at youth clubs in the Ashton/Denton area, though these sometimes proved more trouble than they were worth. "One gig we did was Flames in Ashton, which was for under 18s," Matthews remembers. "There were only about 40 people there. Joyce had to get a day off work and we got paid about £10. He didn't seem interested after that." Nevertheless, Joyce persevered with the group and, considering the number of similar units with ever-changing line-ups, The Hoax were surprisingly stable. With Matthews' assistance, they graduated to playing such venues as the Mayflower, the Band In The Wall, the Cypress Tavern and Manchester Polytechnic. "It was an adventure to Mike, a dream come true," recalls Steve Mardy. Although he lived a considerable distance away in Fallowfield, Joyce was reliable and even brought along his best mate John Fox (Foxy), who became the group's unofficial roadie and proved an excellent morale booster.

The Hoax benefited greatly from their involvement in the Manchester Musicians' Collective and, for a time, their career seemed promising. They regularly rubbed shoulders with The Manchester Mekons and The Passage, and enjoyed a spot of rivalry with the Hamsters, who boasted the patronage of a certain Mark E Smith. The Hamsters' singer Moey (Ian Moss) is still mischievously scathing about The Hoax's fancy backdrops and the printed lyrics that were distributed to the audience during their set. "We just thought they were a bunch of tossers," he declares. "They were out of date, they'd missed the boat." Another group in The Hoax's orbit was Mick Hucknall's The Frantic Elevators, which included Moey's brother Neil on guitar. Steve Mardy occasionally humped gear for the Frantics and noted that the group were busily cutting demos at Rochdale's Cargo Studios. He soon persuaded The Hoax to follow suit. In September 1979, they completed 'Only The Blind Can See In The Dark', which was issued some months later on their own label, Hologram Music. Two thousand copies were pressed in London and Matthews and Farley spent many hours attempting to off-load them at such outlets as Rough Trade and Small Wonder. The response was not promising enough to detain Ian Chambers, who sought work with another group. By the time he decided to return to The Hoax, Mardy and Farley had taken over vocals and elected to remain a three-piece.

A follow-up record 'So What?' received limited press coverage, which boosted their spirits. The West Coast bible turned punk monthly *Zig Zag* enthusiastically enquired: "I presume they're punks and if not they should be. This is insane, a mad delight. Eight interesting tracks (musically and lyrically) on beautiful blue vinyl that shines, regardless of a poxy cover..." Sadly, the record failed to sell. Several bulky cartons of vinyl found their way into Farley's house in Huddersfield Road and were eventually given away to friends and fans. "We had fancy ideas but never did anything," laughed Matthews.

A temporary uplift in the group's fortunes followed when Matthews secured them a support slot with Oi upstarts, The Exploited. The Scottish insurgents brought them their biggest audiences to date and in mid-1980 they made their one-and-only appearance on national radio. The ever-eclectic John Peel played the bombastically-titled 'World War III', which had been included on the promising Manchester compilation *Unzipping The Abstract*. Despite these sporadic breaks, The Hoax ultimately failed to rival the Oi élite. Perhaps it was just as well, for the Oi movement would soon be discredited in the music press, with most of its protagonists forced on to the fringe areas of rock. Gig cancellations, violence and bad publicity each took its toll on the scene.

Seeking fresh adventures abroad, they embarked on what became a politically conscious-raising mini-tour of Belgium, where their leather clothes and spiky hair provoked stern frowns from officialdom. After guesting on another Manchester-dominated compilation, *Ten From The Madhouse*, the group quietly folded. A final gig at Manchester's UMIST in June 1981 passed without mourning. "It was a hopeless case," Matthews laments. "It was never going to carry on with Joyce in it. He lived too far away - that was a big factor." Ironically, at the time of the group's demise, the drummer was about to receive substantial compensation for injuries sustained in a car accident some years before. By the time the money came through The Hoax was history.*

Like so many Manchester groups from the period, The Hoax had rehearsed at TJ Davidson's studio and it was there that Joyce teamed up with his next group, Victim. One of the great hopes of Davidson's TJM label, they had recorded two singles, 'Teenage', and the memorable 'Why Are Fire Engines Red' (with a sleeve designed by Linder). After concluding that Davidson was neither Malcolm McLaren nor Richard Branson, half the group returned to their native Belfast, leaving vocalist/guitarist Joe Moody and bassist Wes Graham to struggle on with a seemingly worthless name. Joyce stayed with them for two years and, although no vinyl was forthcoming, they played selected gigs, including a semi-residency at the Portland Bar in Manchester Piccadilly. "Victim was a step up for me," Joyce recalls. "The way I was playing in The Hoax was head down, no nonsense, mindless boogie. With Victim, I started looking from the outside."

By 1982, it was evident that Victim's prospects were lean and there seemed no easy way forward. When Joyce's flatmate Pete Hope mentioned The Smiths, the drummer was more than willing to check them out. After receiving a rough copy of their demo tape, he was starstruck enough to exclaim: "This is the most brilliant thing I've ever heard."

Joyce was mildly amused at the prospect of joining a group which featured the namesake of his Buzzcocks idol, John Maher. At the first Smiths

---

* Following the departure of Joyce and Mardy, Farley briefly struggled on with some younger musicians. The revamped Hoax released only one record, the EP *Blind Panic* in 1982. Farley then retired from music for eight years, but reappeared in the summer of 1990 in the extravagantly titled *Possible World Theory*.

meeting, Mike was surprised to discover that he recognized Johnny as a familiar face about town. Discussions were swiftly conducted at Shelley Rohde's house and the drummer was formally auditioned at Spirit Studios. Before he set out for the crucial audition, the happy-go-lucky Joyce consumed a hearty meal of magic mushrooms. In earlier days, Siberian tribesmen had enjoyed mushrooms as a recreational stimulus for their rhythmic drum- playing, while Scandinavian warriors had used the drug to acquire superhuman strength in battle. Joyce had no such grand schemes, but the results were not dissimilar. By the time he reached Spirit, he was feeling pleasantly spaced and the session passed in a semi-hallucinogenic haze. Upon arrival, he was told by Johnny that he would be playing a new composition, 'What Difference Does It Make?' Joyce was eager to put some muscle behind his performance and suddenly felt very psyched-up. As Dale ponderously ran through the bass line, the drummer felt an overwhelming surge of energy and decided "to put a load of bollocks into it". Opening his eyes, he expected to see Morrissey dancing enthusiastically to the beat, or else flailing maniacally in front of the microphone stand like the legendary Ian Curtis. Instead, the singer quietly removed the mike and prowled menacingly across the studio, like a leopard in search of prey. With his hunched shoulders and strangely furtive movements, Morrissey momentarily seemed a sinister presence. His almost Dickensian persona completely transfixed the stoned drummer. "You felt you had to watch what he was doing," Joyce recalls. "It was very intriguing. All I can remember is this dark figure in a long overcoat, walking stealthily around the room. He wasn't the archetypal singer with the microphone and it all seemed very grown-up to me. At that time, it wouldn't bother me to take a load of mushrooms and go out to meet somebody. But I wasn't a mess and I could converse. The fact that I could even play the drums was probably a plus."

Following his brief audition, Joyce turned to the earnest guitarist by his side and casually enquired: "What happens now? I'm out of it." Morrissey paid little attention to Joyce's mushroom-induced euphoria, but Maher was impressed by his cool. "Mike was tripping out of his head," he stresses. "I thought, 'Right, you're in. You've got balls'."

That same evening, Joyce was enthusing about The Smiths to Maher's mutual friend, Pete Hope. "They sound fantastic, I think they could be the next Psychedelic Furs," the drummer eagerly observed. After several years with the unfashionable Hoax and luckless Victim, Joyce found it difficult to imagine a level of fame beyond that of the spiky-haired Furs. Despite his enthusiasm, however, he felt embarrassed about leaving his former group in the lurch and hesitated before making the "big move" to The Smiths' camp. For several days he prevaricated while the impatient Maher goaded him with the words, "Come on! Don't be daft! Go for it!"

"The transitional stage was very difficult," Joyce confirms, "but I knew I would join The Smiths. At the time, I thought I'd be stupid not to." On the evening that The Church played at the Gallery in Manchester, Mike met up with Johnny and Angie and confirmed his willingness to become a Smith.

At the same time, he broke the news to Victim. He was greatly relieved when his compatriots responded sympathetically to his decision and wished him well. "They both said it was fine," Foxy remembers. "Mike really liked Joe and Wes and didn't want to do the dirty on them, which he didn't." Later that week, Joyce popped into A1 Music in Manchester and noticed, with some sadness, that Victim's equipment was for sale. It seemed the end of an era.

Within days, Joyce was busily rehearsing with The Smiths in preparation for their imminent début at the Ritz. He was particularly taken with one song, the teasingly-titled 'I Want A Boyfriend For My Birthday'. Unfortunately, the composition was soon dropped from their set and never returned. The old fixation with New York Dolls-influenced material was gradually thrust aside in favour of lyrics whose sexual ambiguity was more subtle and threatening.

On 4 October, The Smiths set out for the Ritz, with Dale still there on bass. During the soundcheck a friend of Johnny's from X Clothes accompanied the group on acoustic guitar. Morrissey then added a strange twist to the proceedings by recruiting his good friend James Maker as master of cere-monies and official go-go dancer. The Smiths were assured a reasonable turn-out and felt eager to make an impact. The much-hyped headliners, Blue Rondo A La Turk, were a multi-racial, London-based dectet whose salsa/jazz rhythms and showbiz posturings had won them considerable space in various style magazines. The Ritz fashion show was an ideal opportunity to promote their new album, *Chewing The Fat*, which was partly produced by Clive Langer and Alan Winstanley. In most respects, The Smiths were the complete antithesis of Blue Rondo, but the presence of Maker pandered to the fashion-conscious clientèle. He took the stage wear-ing a smart, Sixties-styled suit offset by high heels. After introducing The Smiths in French he proceeded to dance exotically while playing a tam-bourine and maracas. With merely a handful of songs to their credit, the group performed three numbers: 'The Hand That Rocks The Cradle', 'Suffer Little Children' and 'Handsome Devil'. During the first song, the skin of Joyce's snare drum split and he was forced to struggle on by playing the drum upside down. Not surprisingly, Blue Rondo refused to allow The Smiths access to their equipment, which merely exacerbated the problems. Maher attempted to compensate for The Smiths' troubled short set by play-ing as aggressively as possible in the hope that this might attract the attention of those who had retired to the bar. A pleasant, drunken Joe Moss watched proudly from the audience. "I was amazed at how good they were," he recalled, "and I have to confess I had a sneaking admiration for Blue Rondo because they manipulated the thing brilliantly." What puzzled Moss, however, was the presence of the James Dean lookalike dancer, whose visual antics seemed disconcertingly distracting. "James Maker was part of the band then, and he took me by surprise on that score. I just didn't know what he was there for."

The day after the Ritz gig (5 October), Maher wrote to Michele Weaver in France, expressing his feelings about The Smiths' début. "It was OK - about

300 people were there..." he noted. The remainder of the letter was full of good news: Angie had secured a job at Piccadilly Radio; flatmate Ollie May had agreed to become the group's van driver and "The Smiths have been offered a record contract with Morrison/Leahy Records". That last snippet was an endearing slip on Maher's part, for Morrison/Leahy were not a record company but a highly motivated and extremely hungry publisher.

Bryan Morrison had served his time in the mid-Sixties British beat boom, managing the controversial, long-haired Pretty Things. Along the way, he had moved into agency work and publishing, and during the Seventies administered The Jam's catalogue, And Son, where he gave the aforementioned Mark Dean his first break in the music business. Morrison's publishing partner, Dick Leahy, was another music business veteran from the Sixties. He had worked for Philips Records at a time when the company was enjoying a periodic upswing in its fortunes, with such hit artistes as Dusty Springfield, The Walker Brothers and Dave Dee, Dozy, Beaky, Mick and Tich. Leahy bathed in the reflective glory of those Sixties artistes and rapidly ascended the record business ladder until he was in a position of considerable power. As managing director of Bell Records, during the early Seventies, Leahy achieved the kind of success that many company men would willingly die for. Although lacking the financial clout of its rivals, Bell Records dominated the UK market with an incredible ratio of hit singles from such artistes as Dawn, David Cassidy, Gary Glitter, The Drifters, The Delfonics, Johnny Johnson And The Bandwagon, Barry Blue, Showaddywaddy and Slik. Leahy's eagle eye for chart potential focused mercilessly on dance floor hits and bedroom wall pubescent pin-up stars. In 1971, he signed the biggest UK teen phenomenon of the era, The Bay City Rollers, and as managing director of GTO Records he found further success with disco diva Donna Summer, as well as re-living the glory days of the Sixties with the re-formed Walker Brothers.

The tentacles that linked Morrisson/Leahy to The Smiths stretched from Innervision to yet another Sixties figure, Dee Fenton. A former member of Wimple Winch and Manchester's Just Four Men (aka Four Just Men), Fenton had received the Decibel demos and was sufficiently interested to arrange a meeting. Morrissey and Maher turned up at his house armed with a bottle of wine and discussed their writing plans and ambitions. Fenton was sympathetic and would later prove a valuable ally, but he was not entirely convinced by their 8-track demo. During the same period, Morrison/Leahy had received a tape from that other songwriting duo - Panos/Ridgeley. In contrast to The Smiths' rudimentary recording, their tape contained a song that was a potential evergreen: 'Careless Whisper'. And unlike The Smiths, they had already signed to a record label. So it was that Wham!, and not The Smiths, were taken under the wing of Morrison/Leahy and established themselves as the latest gods in the pantheon of New Pop.

In the wake of the Ritz gig, Maher had continued to badger Moss about managing The Smiths. Johnny was overjoyed when his mentor threw up his hands and finally agreed. Moss had noticed that every song his young friend played appeared to include the lines, "We need a place to rehearse." Taking the hint, Joe had offered them a room above his shop in Portland Street. Meanwhile, Maher was already looking back judiciously at the Ritz show as an incongruous but effective means of attracting local attention. "We only played three songs and we got paid," he joked. Maher was shrewdly aware that, even if The Smiths were denied mainstream success, they possessed enough original qualities to win a substantial cult following. According to Moss, "Johnny initially didn't think they'd have a mass audience, but thought it might appeal to the gay crowd - he knew it would get them known."

Originally, Maher had intended to form an entirely new group in the aftermath of the funk-influenced Freaky Party. Increasingly, however, he realized that Dale was an inadequate substitute for his former partner, Andy Rourke. Even Mike Joyce's ex-colleague, Steve Mardy, had commented unfavourably on Dale after watching The Smiths at an early rehearsal. "He shouldn't have been part of it," Mardy concluded. "You have a bass line, but he was taking up the lead and trying to follow Morrissey on the high notes. He looked at odds with them. I thought the whole thing was a farce."

After consulting Morrissey, Maher contacted Andy Rourke and persuaded him that the time was rife to throw in his lot with The Smiths. Rourke's sudden recruitment coincided with another lucky break for the group. Maher's former college associate and White Dice champion Tony O'Connor had landed a job with EMI Records and persuaded his superiors in A&R that The Smiths were worthy of an audition. An advance of several hundred pounds was forthcoming and the group assembled at Drone Studios in Chorlton to record a couple of tracks. "That was the first time I met Andy," explained Joyce, who was still under the impression that Dale was the bassist. The new line-up recorded demos of 'Miserable Lie' and 'Handsome Devil', which was most notable for including a guest session player on saxophone. Midway through the recording, the group peered through the control room window and saw Dale forlornly viewing their progress. Maher was ceremoniously despatched to tell him the bad news about his future in The Smiths. The timing was regrettable. Fortunately, however, the original bassist was already playing part time with another group so the blow was softened. "Dale got us the demo time, so we owed it to him to have him around," Johnny explained. "It was a matter of practicality. We had to have somebody to play bass and he had access to recording studios. He was used a little bit in that respect, but so's everyone."

After hearing the latest demo tapes EMI politely declined. It would be another four years before they received a second chance to sign the Mancunian quartet. By then, The Smiths would be the most critically acclaimed UK group of the decade.

8

A Rolling Stone Gathers Moss

THE SMITHS LAUNCHED THEIR CAREER in a year that had proven pivotal in the development of Britain's so-called "New Pop". Old-fashioned pop values had returned with a vengeance and a gallery of technicolour idols had effectively transformed the Top 40. Adam Ant, the punk turned pantomime pirate, had already demonstrated how a colourful image and catchy tune could produce a string of sizeable hits. While he topped the charts, a new generation of fashion-obsessed youths congregated in London clubs and celebrated the parochial triumph of peacock vanity over dreary post-punk ennui. The Blitz Kids, or New Romantics, or Futurists, as each movement was alternately dubbed, created instant media stars from inveterate poseurs, who hid musical impoverishment behind programmed synthe-sizer pop. The early recordings of Spandau Ballet, Visage, Ultravox and Duran Duran demonstrated the clever but limited charm of Eighties electronic experimentation. However, the most careerist of these new groups understood the need to move into mainstream pop if lasting success was to be assured. That point had been punctuated most forcibly by Sheffield's Human League who had split in half overnight, only to re-emerge as a surprisingly high gloss pop act. Their Christmas 1981 chart topper 'Don't You Want Me', and attendant million-selling album *Dare*, set the tone for the New Year. The message was singular and clear - the pop song, irrespective of fashionable trappings, was back in vogue.

When The Human League emulated their chart-topping success in the USA, all hell broke loose. Previously, it was generally accepted that since the entire UK punk movement had failed to make an impression in the adult-orientated Stateside rock market, these flashy new groups would fare little better. After all, even Britain's most consistently successful young chart acts of the late Seventies, The Jam, The Boomtown Rats and Madness, were virtually unknown across the Atlantic. Nor had the myriad of flash-in-the-pan revivals, from mod to rockabilly, fared much better. The conservatism of US rock radio had produced a cultural chasm between the US and UK youth markets which some pessimistic commentators felt might never be bridged again. What changed that unhealthy situation overnight was a miracle greater than any UK pop group could have achieved.

The launch of MTV, with its non-stop selection of pop videos, enabled UK record companies to overcome the puritanical programming of stuffy radio stations and reach young purchasers through a previously unexploited medium. The classic 'Don't You Want Me' video, along with several others, started a chain reaction which saw regional disc jockeys picking up on the video boom and actually playing UK pop songs that would normally have received little or no airtime. Before long, a select bunch of androgynous UK singers and groups took the US by storm.

Although the much-publicized gender benders stole the headlines, it was the music itself which was more important. Suddenly, the Blitz Kids and their contemporaries had become top tunesmiths. ABC successfully completed an album crammed with class pop songs titled *Lexicon Of Love*. Others would follow that trail with a sharpness and perspicacity scarcely evident in their earlier work. After two middling singles, Culture Club would virtually establish themselves as brand-leaders with a song that sounded like a standard: 'Do You Really Want To Hurt Me'. Spandau Ballet left synthesizers and Brit funk behind and attempted to push Tony Hadley as a junior Sinatra. They too would soon find chart-topping success with 'True'. Before long, even Doubting Thomases were forced to concede that the New Pop consisted of a lot more than frivolous fashion horses gallivanting around London clubs.

The Smiths were at once a part of this new wave of pop yet simultaneously divorced from its philosophy and repelled by its superficiality. They too supported the return of the well-crafted pop song, called themselves a group not a band, decried the hoary old spandex cock-rock imagery of the Seventies and the equally dated incoherent, non-melodic, three-chord crash of hard-core punk. What they offered and formulated was an intriguing fusion of old and new values. Formally, they resembled nothing less than an early Sixties beat group - the classic vocals, lead guitar, bass, drums line-up. Yet, they were not simply Beatles-copyists like, for example, The Knack, nor did they quite fit into the witty, light pop category of The Tourists, Orange Juice and Aztec Camera.

With Maher they boasted a genuine rock traditionalist whose compact, yet forcefully melodic guitar style would later invite comparison with such gods as Keith Richard and Roger McGuinn. Johnny's grounding threatened to take The Smiths to the student heartland and infiltrate the rock poll peaks dominated by Joy Division and Echo And The Bunnymen. Maher's simultaneous pop sensibility, that part of him that loved the naïve, epic grandeur of Leiber and Stoller, was embodied most forcibly in his paradoxical partner. Morrissey glorified in the ephemeral camp pop of the mid-sixties, but never in a way that was cheap, obvious or instantly nostalgic. It wasn't enough for Morrissey to cover easily recognizable hits such as 'I Only Want To Be With You' or 'You've Lost That Lovin' Feelin''. He eschewed the familiar and predictable, and revealed a pop scholar's fascination in championing obscure tracks by Cilla Black, Twinkle, Sandie Shaw, Rita Pavone and others. Even with a hit-making machine like Herman's Hermits, Morrissey eventually honed in on their least commercially successful Sixties single, 'East West'. Despite these singular reference points, he avoided obvious pastiche in his own writing, preferring to draw upon moods and imagery that recalled the provincial working-class writers of the early Sixties. His frame of reference seemed largely divorced from any of his New Pop rivals. His lyrics were too arch, too knowing, too Northern, and directly opposed to the escapist fantasies and youth-orientated yuppie consumerism promulgated through the work and lifestyles of his more facile contemporaries. For Morrissey, bedroom insularity offered a more realizable salvation than Club Tropicana frivolity. He was a strange amalgam of the old and the new.

In common with the New Pop school, Morrissey spoke about such topics as androgyny and the breakdown of conditioned male/female barriers, but in a more convincing and measured tone than his peacock rivals. He may have shared Boy George's views on celibacy ("I'd rather have a cup of tea") and sexual stereotyping, but could never be placed alongside the fashionable "gender benders" of the era. Morrissey's concept of "Men's Liberation" was eloquently expressed but never manifested in caked make-up, homosexual proselytizing or affected limp-wristed posturings. From the outset, The Smiths were reluctant to be part of any movement or too easily identifiable school of pop, just as they were unwilling to dispense with the familiar form or great tradition of rock. In effect, Maher and Morrissey were intent on pursuing a Holy Grail fusion of traditional rock elements and non-ephemeral pop: they sought intelligence and style, not simply through the album format, but the classic two-and-a-half minute single; they saw themselves as the missing link between The Rolling Stones and The Shangri-Las; they threatened to bridge the gap between the so-called rockist inky weeklies and the fortnightly pop-fixated glossies; they denounced the promotional video, yet still expected sizeable chart hits; they balanced miserabilism with wry humour, elegant melodies with strong riffs, self-absorption with social commentary and deep sensitivity with cavalierly violent and occasionally disturbing lyrical imagery.

The central paradox of The Smiths was that they remained a unity of opposites. Even Joe Moss had seen this from the start, and it was emphasized in his initial discussions with Maher. "A lot of people were mistakenly under the impression that The Smiths was Morrissey's baby," he argued, "but the exact opposite was true. Johnny created The Smiths and Morrissey as spokesman and frontman of the group was also Johnny's creation."

Maher had sufficient fast-talking Wythenshawe suss to carry himself off more than adequately in the music press, but cleverly resisted that temptation. Moss recalls various private discussions with Maher during which they concluded that the focus of attention on The Smiths would be heightened if Morrissey was left to take the media spotlight alone. Morrissey's articulacy and insouciant penchant for controversy was irresistible and the contrasting silence of the group effectively reinforced that power. It says much for Maher's innate confidence that he slipped so willingly into the background. His decision revealed the same clear-sightedness that had previously prevented him from pursuing work as a vocalist or lyricist. Johnny always recognized his limitations and could be relied upon to suppress his ego for the sake of the wider ambitions of the team. This, of course, left open the possibility that Maher's ultimate achievement might merely prove the establishing of Morrissey as a solo star at his own expense. Joe Moss maintains that his prodigy had this angle covered from the very beginning. "At the formation of the group, Johnny said to me that he would be the one to get out first," he reveals. "That tells you a lot about the calculation of the whole operation. It was obvious that they *would* break up. They were two disparate parts who had been put together for a purpose, and that purpose was to lift them from where they were... Johnny was aware of the dogfight between Lennon and McCartney as to who *really* left The Beatles first. He knew what that meant. Johnny couldn't stand the idea of picking up a music paper and reading, 'Morrissey Quits The Smiths', and finding himself holding the bag with Andy or Mike. He knew that if he left first there would be no Smiths because the other two had nothing in common with Morrissey."

With such reserves of confidence, Maher had nothing to fear from Morrissey's media persona, which was seldom perceived as a threat or distraction from his own musical worth. As in the Jagger/Richard axis, Maher was content to allow his partner to become the public face while he imperceptibly and effortlessly won the accolades for his virtuosity. It was a perfectly conceived musical partnership.

The role of the subsidiary Smiths was also of considerable importance in fashioning the group's sound. Musically, Rourke and Joyce were almost as antithetical as Morrissey and Marr. Although later acclaimed as one of rock's most effective rhythm sections, their styles and approach could hardly have been more contrasting. Joyce was still the thrashing punk, while Rourke craved the discipline instilled during two years of playing funk. Having also grown up with the music of Crosby, Stills, Nash & Young, Andy had a strong sense of melody and structured harmonies which the heavy-handed drummer found alien. While Rourke was intent on establishing a traditionally tight rhythm section, his partner's attitude was far more spontaneous. "Let's go with the flow and see what happens" was the familiar Joycean response to any orders.

The intense rehearsals that the quartet undertook prior to their second gig in the New Year emphasized these points. "I'd always be going against what Andy would be playing," Mike explains. "In 1982-83, the sounds that The Smiths were coming out with were never re-created. It's considered wrong to play *against* the bass player, but that was what people first latched on to. It made The Smiths sound different from other groups. We threw everything into the melting pot." What the group shared was a quest for the subliminal magic moment in pop. It was there in Morrissey's unearthly vocal yelping; in Marr's experimental open tunings; in Rourke's ability to create "a song within a song" through his imaginative bass lines; and in Joyce's tendency to alter the timing to unorthodox but spectacular effect. "When The Smiths' tracks slowed down or picked up, I thought that was good," the drummer noted. "I liked speeding things up in the choruses. I sped them up because I was excited and that's where everyone gets the goosebumps." The first recipients of those goosebumps were the fortunate few who witnessed Rourke's debut appearance with the group in 1983.

Manager Joe Moss often drank in the hip Manchester hostelry The Manhattan and soon persuaded the management to feature The Smiths as headliners. On 6 January, the group appeared fresh from Crazy Face's upstairs rehearsal room, looking radiantly confident. "Although we'd only done one gig before, we'd tightened up," Joyce recalls. "The idea of performing became such a natural thing." With a prestigious booking at Manchester's Haçienda slated for the following month, The Smiths were already drawing a small audience, which included a handful of local luminaries and old friends. Morrissey visibly rose to the occasion and at the end of the show slyly reached into his back pocket, then showered the stage and audience with confetti. Backstage, the group was besieged by a small band of well-wishers, including a camera man who had videoed the performance. Moss cursed his bad luck when the film proved faulty. Among the select circle of spectators were two of Morrissey's old friends, Tony Wilson and Richard Boon. As the pair left the building, Wilson remarked wryly, "Well, we always knew he'd do *something*." Boon was less surprised by Morrissey's development and felt "the style of music, the subject matter, the detail of presentation, all made perfect sense." One aspect of the show that he did find distracting, however, was the presence of the dancing James Maker.

"James was in stilettos," Boon recalls, "go-go dancing and banging a tambourine. He was dispensable. I thought it was spare parts, a nice joke but it didn't add anything and they didn't need it." The Smiths seemed equally vague about Maker's role in the scheme of things. "I never quite got that and neither did the rest of the band," Johnny explains. "It wasn't discussed. It was just a whim of Morrissey. Nothing personal against James, but it just looked silly. He was really a dancer. It's funny that he played onstage with us. It's wild." Joe Moss was concerned enough about Maker to take Morrissey aside after the show and chide: "James distracts from *you*." After that, Maker never again officially appeared as an auxiliary Smith.* Nevertheless, he played an important role in bolstering Morrissey's confidence onstage and, had The Smiths been the Happy Mondays, he would no doubt have been retained as a potential "Bez". Instead, he went on to pursue his own career, first with Raymonde and later as leader of RPLA.

The presence of Tony Wilson at The Manhattan encouraged some people to assume that The Smiths were likely to sign to Factory Records. Although Wilson was impressed by the group, however, he was over-cautious about adding new talent to his label. "Factory's once great low promotion had become a severe encumbrance," he argued. "It was only years later that I realized we'd become a dinosaur and our non-promotion was an albatross round our neck. I was depressed that I couldn't sell any Stockholm

---

* Later in The Smiths' career, Maker did join the group onstage briefly during a gig at St Austell, Cornwall.

Monsters' records. I believed deeply in them and still do to this day. So I was thinking, 'Hey, another great Manchester group but, wait a minute, why take on Steven if I can't sell records'. I just felt there was no point. I was down. That's my story."

Of course, Wilson was not the only voice at Factory. New Order manager Rob Gretton was the company's A&R head and had an important say in judging The Smiths' demo tape. His response was equally discouraging. "He thought the tape was shit," Wilson confirms. "This was the man who was walking round Manchester before and after the demo saying, 'Smiths are the new Beatles'. He kept saying it and yet he felt the demo wasn't up to it and that's what we go on. He thought they were the new Beatles but didn't like the demo. That was Gretton's attitude."

On 4 February, 1983, The Smiths played at Wilson's Haçienda club alongside Factory funk group 52nd Street and guest disc-jockey Marc Berry. It proved an interesting experience for Maher who noticed that the previous week's support was Foreign Press, who had headlined over White Dice at their one and only gig. Bad memories of that debacle were no doubt reinforced when Johnny broke a string just before The Smiths' appearance. Appropriately, he contacted former White Dicer, Rob Allman, who provided a replacement guitar. The performance got off to a blistering start with a raucous offering of 'These Things Take Time', after which Morrissey offered his humble thanks to the assembled gathering. Even as he spoke, the strident chords of 'What Difference Does It Make?' gathered pace, prompting him to unleash a ghoulish wail. Morrissey's vocal was much deeper during these early live performances and the arrangements were noticeably busier, with Joyce filling all the empty spaces. One of the earliest Smiths songs followed - the haunting 'The Hand That Rocks The Cradle'. Arguably the highlight of the set, the song featured an appealing variant of the standard riff during the 'Sonny Boy' coda. Suitably impressed by his own performance, Morrissey found time to throw in one of his Wildean epithets: "I repeat, the only thing to be in 1983 is *handsome*". The version of 'Handsome Devil' that followed would later grace the flip-side of The Smiths' first single, with Morrissey for once economizing on his engaging yelps. Two non-album Smiths tracks added variety to the proceedings: 'Jeane' and 'Wonderful Woman'. The latter was particularly noticeable for including lyrics that differed markedly from the later B-side recording. "She will plague you and I will be glad", the singer purred menacingly before the song gave way to 'Hand In Glove'. This striking performance demonstrated Rourke's mastery of the bass line, with some touches of funk clearly seeping through. Even the unintended feedback at the close of the number worked in the group's favour. Morrissey said little throughout the evening's performance and, as the set concluded, he restricted himself to a camp "Oh, you're very kind". A spectacular version of 'Miserable Lie' closed the show, with Morrissey stretching his larynx to breaking point, like a demented punk descendant of the yodelling Tiny Tim. An echo effect sent the words "I need advice" reverberating around the Haçienda, after which The Smiths took their leave to muted applause. They had to wait nearly two months before belatedly receiving their first live review, courtesy of the *NME*'s Jim Shelley. Comparing their sound to a cross between Magazine, Josef K and The Fire Engines, he concluded: "As commanding and restrained as this, The Smiths should soon be capable of reaching the greatest of heights."

The Haçienda gig was also notable for prompting Morrissey's introduction of flowers as a Smiths fashion accessory. When quizzed on their significance by *Sounds*, Morrissey explained: "They're symbolic for at least three reasons. We introduced them as an antidote to the Haçienda when we played there; it was so sterile and inhuman. We wanted some harmony with nature. Also, to show some kind of optimism in Manchester, which the flowers represent. Manchester is semi-paralyzed still, the paralysis just zips through the whole of Factory." Looking back, the singer later noted: "The flowers were a very human gesture... It had got to the point in music where people were really afraid to show how they felt. To show their emotions. I thought that was a shame and very boring. The flowers offered hope."

The floral spectacle owed much to Morrissey's mentor Oscar Wilde, who was notorious for decorating his Oxford rooms with lilies. As his fame increased, Wilde's love of flowers captured the public imagination and Morrissey clearly intended to achieve something of the same. In unguarded moments, he boasted that Smiths disciples would soon be laying gladioli at his feet. When The Smiths later returned to the Haçienda as single headliners, flowers were there in abundance. Proprietor Tony Wilson still speaks with grandeur about Morrissey's horticultural display: "It was one of the great moments in the Haçienda's history. I was proud. There have been certain great gigs in Manchester's history: The Eagles at the Palace, Lou Reed at the Free Trade Hall, Joy Division at the Derby Hall, in Bury. These are concerts you always remember, and The Smiths' at the Haçienda was one of the great gigs."

As well as their Haçienda appearances, The Smiths also played at Rafters, the club situated beneath Fagins in Manchester's Oxford Road. There, they supported the progenitor of punk, Richard Hell, whose torn, safety-pinned clothes and paeans to the blank generation had proven such an inspiration to Sex Pistols' svengali, Malcolm McLaren. Beneath his anarchic image and Bowery slur, Hell was an articulate writer and would-be publisher. It was appropriate therefore, that the Rafters performance should end with a surprise appearance from Morrissey's own friendly publisher John Muir. In his hand was a bound copy of Steven's latest book, fresh from the printers.

The original edition of *James Dean Is Not Dead* did not feature the author's name on the cover, but turned out to be a slightly more substantial work than *The New York Dolls*. Amid its brief 48 pages, Morrissey managed to namecheck Belloc, Wilde, Platus, and his beloved Ludus ("Touch-me-not, my mother's fixed me"). Unbelievably, Muir now estimates that the book sold an incredible 5,000 copies, a staggeringly high figure in relation to average UK sales of film/rock titles of the time, even by mainstream publishers' standards! Morrissey had meanwhile completed two more short scripts, a round-up of girl groups of the Sixties and a brief directory of Hollywood also-rans titled *Exit Smiling*. Muir completed preliminary work on the latter, collating old film posters for the heavily-illustrated tome. Morrissey's 53-page typewritten script remains an interesting artefact from his bedroom period. Although the prose is disarmingly plain and prone to spelling errors, Morrissey displays his frivolous love for wry chapter titles: 'The Meek Shall Inherit The Oscar'; 'Will Success Spoil Tab Hunter?'; 'Slush Be My Destiny'; 'All That Universal Allows'; 'Everything You Wanted To Know About Agnes Moorehead, But Were Afraid To Ask'.

Morrissey's reverence for James Dean was manifested in *Exit Smiling* by virtue of a veritable gallery of the actor's lesser co-stars, plus a section on supposed "New Deans", such as Michael Parks and Christopher Jones. Some of Morrissey's feminist preoccupations crept into the subtext, especially in his comments on the indomitable Eve Arden, whom he glorifies as a "hard-boiled dame who can hold her own in a man's world". His Sixties favourite Rita Tushingham, receives a back-handed compliment; her icy sexuality is unfavourably compared with that of Roy Rogers' dog, Trigger. In his summation of the unfortunate Sal Mineo, Morrissey obtusely noted: "His death was characterized as a 'homosexual murder', which doesn't make any sense". Not surprisingly, Morrissey's favourite minor screen stars invaded the text at various points and the references to Terence Stamp's performance in *The Collector* anticipated the lyrics of 'Reel Around The Fountain': "As a deranged butterfly collector, Stamp suddenly decides to collect women, and Samantha Eggar finds herself pinned and mounted".*

In spite of its brevity, *Exit Smiling* was probably the most appealing of Morrissey's minor forays into the bargain basement book world. Unfortunately, by the time that Muir was ready to schedule the work for production, The Smiths were in the ascendant and Morrissey was out of contact. After a fruitless request to publish the script, the book was shelved. Morrissey's other project, on girl groups, stubbornly remained on top of his wardrobe and was not submitted for consideration. When Muir later completed a celebratory compilation, *The Smiths In Quotes*, he received a letter from Morrissey's solicitor demanding that he desist both from selling further copies of the title and the *James Dean Is Not Dead* reprint. "I didn't reply to the letter and the books aren't being sold," Muir explained. "The distributors said they wouldn't sell any more copies until the matter was resolved." So ended Morrissey's 384 Kings Road writing career and on/off relationship with Babylon Books.

Having completed a handful of gigs, The Smiths' next task was the recording of their début single. The aforementioned talent spotter Dee Fenton had managed to secure them cheap recording time at Strawberry 2, the studio owned by 10cc's Eric Stewart. It was there that they cut the Moss-financed 'Hand In Glove' for the remarkably low cost of £213. "I

---

* This isn't to say that Morrissey necessarily deserves credit for the phrase "take and mount me like a butterfly". Long before *Exit Smiling* that line appeared in Molly Haskell's *From Reverence To Rape*, which Morrissey had read some time before.

remember listening back to it and thinking it sounded so different from anything I'd ever heard before," Joyce enthused. "Johnny tried to push the point home about a Phil Spector Wall of Sound. It sounded big, and Morrissey's vocal was so desperate." With the additional live version of 'Handsome Devil', taken from the mixing desk recording of the Haçienda gig, The Smiths were now in a position to seek recording company backing. It was at this point that Morrissey's mother appeared at a rehearsal session to check that the group's management was sound. She was sufficiently impressed by Joe Moss's obvious commitment to The Smiths to pen a note which said, "God will thank you for what you're doing for my son". Her words were to prove more ironic than she could ever have imagined.

The ghost of James Maker still haunted The Smiths prior to their London début at the Rock Garden on 23 March. The venue, hedging its bets, described the quartet as a "*five-piece* whose sound, though difficult to pigeon-hole, leans towards pop and the dance floor". The gig, though far from memorable, encouraged the group to capitalize on their recent demo recording. Morrissey contacted his old friend Richard Boon about a possible record deal but the New Hormones label was winding down its operation in the wake of financial constraints. Boon suggested that Steven contact Simon Edwards at Rough Trade Distribution. At that point, The Smiths were in a strong position as Moss had already agreed to have the record cut and pressed independently, irrespective of Rough Trade's decision. Significantly, it was the persuasive Johnny Maher who confronted Edwards on a Friday afternoon, excitedly extolling the virtues of 'Hand In Glove'. Edwards agreed that the disc had promise and felt that Rough Trade supremo Geoff Travis might be interested in arranging a record deal. That suggestion was enough for Maher and his quiet companion Andy Rourke to buttonhole Travis in the company's kitchen and demand, "Listen to this - we're *not* just another group." Travis was distracted by the sheer force of Maher's enthusiasm and invited them to his office where the tape was played. "I like it," Travis intoned cautiously. He then asked to borrow the cassette for the weekend.

The Smiths could hardly have found a more discerning supporter nor a more appropriate nemesis than Geoff Travis. Born in 1952, the son of an insurance broker, Travis was brought up in a middle-class Jewish family in the leafy glades of Finchley. Besotted with records since the early Sixties, he was fortunate to have an American cousin whose imported disc collection was both formidable and eclectic. After passing the 11-plus in 1963, Travis won a place at a direct grammar, Owens School, in Islington. As a youth, his tastes were already expanding beyond the confines of everyday chart music and after school he occasionally visited the Marquee, even catching one of The Who's earliest sets. The hippie era saw Travis metamorphose into a Noel Redding lookalike with dark, curly hair and a penchant for West Coast music. He frequently purchased expensive import albums at Musicland in Berwick Street and named Bob Dylan, Love, The Band and The Grateful Dead among his favourite artistes of the late Sixties. Like several of the Owens' fraternity, he also enjoyed soul music and has fond recollections of witnessing the Stax revue at Finsbury Park.

His favourite haunt, however, was that hippie haven, the Roundhouse, in Chalk Farm Road. Travis regularly attended Sunday afternoon concerts at the venue in the company of a younger pupil, Viv Berger, who would later gain considerable notoriety for his involvement in producing the *Schoolkids' Oz*. His phallic representation of Rupert The Bear was one of the key illustrations that the Vice Squad felt transgressed the Obscene Publications Act. Berger ended up giving evidence at the Old Bailey and met the civil wrath of Owens' deputy head, 'Goldy' Butler, who did not take kindly to an outrageous caricature of himself in *Oz*'s libellous pages. Despite his friendship with Berger, Travis was far from rebel material, and the extent of his delinquent humour was so slight that it could be measured in some inoffensive chalk marks. The sinewy socialist John Cotcher (son of the Conservative councillor, Alfred Lincoln Cotcher) recalls a school visit to Oxford to see *Othello*, after which he and Travis scrawled "Matriculation Makes You Go Blind" on their school wall. The recalcitrant sixth formers were rapidly apprehended and received a demeaning detention that proved risible rather than salutary.

Travis was generally regarded as a rather earnest young man, although he did once trick class-mate Norman Goldberg into smoking a cigarette laced with mixed herbs from the school kitchen. However, such behaviour seemed out of character and testified more to the incorrigibly childish joviality of another accomplice, Jonathan Pooley. When it came to music, Travis was considerably more knowledgeable than Cotcher, Pooley, Berger, Al Newman and the rest. The tankard Pooley noted the chasm from bitter experience: "I thought that just by listening to records by Family, The Nice and Tyrannosaurus Rex that I had some credibility, but compared to Travis I was mainstream. I bought the CBS sampler, *The Rock Machine Turns You On* and he rubbished it. He felt it was boys' stuff and for dickheads, basically. I should have been listening to 'proper' albums like *John Wesley Harding*." Two years later, Pooley was still hoping to impress Travis after purchasing Derek And The Dominoes' *Layla* from a junkie in Soho. The maestro's response was lukewarm. "Travis just said, 'I suppose it's all right if you like guitar albums'. He was a patronizing git! I never liked the geezer. I found him fairly acerbic. Then again, he probably thought I was a waste of space - and he may well have been vindicated."

The Owens' years were a reasonably happy period for Travis who, despite offending Pooley's sensibilities, was generally well-liked. By 1971, he was dating the popular Joy Fox and studying in the third year sixth in an attempt to pass the Oxbridge entrance examination and atone for paltry A-levels. That autumn, he was admitted to Churchill College, Cambridge, where for the next three years he studied English. An interest in drama encouraged Travis to pursue a teaching career and while studying for the PGCE he was assigned to a girls' school in Mill Hill. Disillusioned by staffroom cynicism, he found himself waiting forlornly for a bus one afternoon and thought, "If it doesn't arrive in five minutes, I'm giving up teaching." The bus failed to appear and, two days later, Travis was in America. He travelled extensively, hitching across the country and picking up caches of 25 cent albums along the route. By the time he reached San Francisco, the acquisitive graduate realized that he was ludicrously overburdened with vinyl. However, the buying spree did implant the germ of an idea, which he exploited upon his return to London. Before long, he opened a record shop in Kensington Park Road named Rough Trade, the title borrowed from the homosexual slang for low-life macho clients who are likely to provide their soliciting suitors with a sound thrashing.

It was to Travis's lasting benefit that the opening of his shop coincided with the arrival of punk. Within months, artistes such as The Desperate Bicycles and Scritti Politti were frequenting the premises and introducing Travis to their recordings. This, in turn, led to the setting up of an independent distribution system, the Cartel, of which Rough Trade was a crucial part. In the meantime, Travis was selling a considerable number of reggae records and gained immense experience visiting Jamaican households in Harlesden where he judiciously selected the best of the latest imports. Often, he would have to sift through a hundred pre-releases and make snap decisions on the quality of individual discs. This Jamaican *Juke-Box Jury* served him well and sharpened his talent-spotting abilities.

The birth of Rough Trade Records happened after the shop began importing obscure singles from abroad. French group, Metal Urbain, became the first artistes to release a record on the Rough Trade label with their frantic 'Paris Maquis'. They had first come to Travis's attention when his shop sold a couple of hundred copies of their French pressed début. Coincidentally, its translated title predated a more familiar song from The Smiths: 'Panic'.

With the marketing skills and business acumen of Third World manager Richard Scott, combined with the A&R nose of Travis, Rough Trade rapidly established itself with releases from a diverse series of artistes, including Stiff Little Fingers, Swell Maps, Subway Sect, The Residents, The Slits, Pere Ubu, The Fall, The Virgin Prunes and Scritti Politti. Travis's dream was to establish a record company whose electicism, innovation and quality would emulate the early catalogues of Elektra and Island Records. Nobody doubted Rough Trade's adventurousness, but its love of experimentation had so far precluded any mainstream success. It took 91 singles releases before the company finally registered a chart entry with Scritti Politti's 'The Sweetest Girl' in November 1981. Even then, the number 64 placing could hardly be deemed a massive breakthrough. However, by the time The Smiths reached London, both Scritti Politti and Aztec Camera had provided Rough Trade with rare hits and the label was at last in the ascendant commercially, as well as aesthetically. Morrissey, Maher and Moss weren't to know that both those artistes would leave Rough Trade before the year was out.

Over the weekend, Travis listened to the tape of 'Hand In Glove' and was smitten. "I didn't think this was going to be one of the most important groups there's ever been," he admitted, "but I thought it was a great record." The following Monday, he confirmed that Rough Trade would be pleased to release the single. With his recording career underway, Johnny decided that a subtle name change was required in order to distinguish himself from the venerable Buzzcocks' drummer John Maher. Inspired by the Irish pronunciation of "Maher", he retained the sound of his name but altered the spelling to Marr, which also echoed the first syllable of his middle name, Martin. Meanwhile, his partner was showing a distinct preference for the trisyllabic surname Morrissey, and henceforth banished Steven from public utterance, on record sleeves and promotional material. Coincidentally, his sister Jacqueline was also in the process of changing her name. During the spring, she married computers controller Peter Rayner, son of the uproarious Alf Rayner, a well-known character in the Stretford community. The couple subsequently moved to Prestwich.

In May, 'Hand In Glove' was released and soon scaled the independent charts, but failed to emulate the mainstream success of Rough Trade associates, Scritti Politti and Aztec Camera. Morrissey has always been reverently arrogant about the quality of the single, even calling it "the most important song in the world". Although not one of his greatest compositions, the track ably displayed his love of familiar speech. That vulgar directive to the vain ("You think the sun shines out of your backside") is neatly inverted to become a declaration of self-satisfied triumph ("the sun shines out of our behinds/this is NOT like any other love, this one's different because it's us"). Having opened the song with a double colloquial locution ("Hand in glove/The sun shines...) Morrissey includes some familiarly maternal, yet slightly dated, phrasing, such as "you little charmer" and "touch a hair on your head". In fact, there is not one word in the song to suggest that it was composed in the Eighties. To all intents and purposes, the words of 'Hand In Glove' could have been written 30 years ago. Morrissey's strained vocal argumentatively champions the unique quality of a love in the face of public derision and disapproval. However, the passionately defiant exhortations ("we can go wherever we please") are undermined to the point of impotence by the closing couplet in which the earlier shrill-voiced, arse-shining love is exposed as little more than a fantasy ("But I know my love too well/And I'll probably never see you again"). In Morrissey's fictional universe, arrogance and hopelessness are never far apart. Musically, the song proved most notable for Joyce's loud, upfront drumming and Marr's employment of harmonica. Indeed, the short harmonica breaks strongly recall the opening of The Beatles' 'Love Me Do' - significantly, the Liverpudlians' début single, and the only time they employed the instrument as the opening lead on a single. The Smiths always had a strong, self-conscious sense of pop history.

The lustful 'Handsome Devil', with its suggestive lyrics and playful gender-swapping (from "mammary glands" to "a boy in the bush" and that deliberately ambiguous word "handsome") anticipated the "paedophile" controversy that would threaten to swamp the group before the end of the summer.

Days before the release of their début single, The Smiths supported The Sisters Of Mercy at the University of London on 6 May. It was a significant performance, largely due to the presence of several future Smiths' acolytes, including Scott Piering. A sociology graduate from the University of California, Piering began promoting concerts in San Francisco and claims to have been the first person in the USA to book Bob Marley And The Wailers. This resulted in an introduction to reggae patron Chris Blackwell and the offer of a job with Island Records. From there, Piering hooked up with Rough Trade when the independent decided to establish a press and promotional department. Prior to his arrival, it had been Rough Trade policy to encourage people to pay for promotional records. Piering did a crash course on the British independent scene, listening to batches of singles every night and even sleeping on the firm's premises. When the entire promotions department was later shelved, Piering privatized his operation and was granted access to all Rough Trade's acts, as well as office space at the company's Blenheim Crescent headquarters.

Among the people Piering invited to the ULU gig was Grant Cunliffe, a former member of the sprawling Seventies anarcho-hippie ensemble, Here And Now. Glorifying in the name Grant Showbiz, Cunliffe previously worked as a sound engineer and co-producer for The Fall, and had been selected by Rough Trade as a prospective member of the road crew. Grant listened intently to The Smiths' performance and noted the peculiarly deep echo on Morrissey's voice, embellished by the cascading guitar sound that seemed to fill the hall. Midway through the performance, he turned to Piering and said: "They're the punk Hollies". By the close of the show, he confirmed his willingness to work with The Smiths and would emerge as one of the longest serving members of their crew.

Another key figure at the ULU gig was the gasbag John Walters, producer of the influential John Peel radio show. He too was impressed and, as the group left the stage, told Piering: "You've got a session". Scott was not particularly taken aback by the enthusiastic response from his guests. "It was so easy to see why The Smiths were special," he reasoned. "It was so clear. Everything you liked about music and attitude was right there - and they were still so young." Retreating backstage to meet The Smiths for the first time, Piering's intention was to conduct an impromptu interview for promotional purposes. After a short session with Morrissey, however, he turned off the tape recorder in bemused appreciation of the singer's engagingly eccentric responses. Like Moss and Marr, he immediately realized that Morrissey was a caption writer's dream.

Within two weeks of the ULU gig, The Smiths recorded four songs for the *John Peel Show*. The venerable disc jockey prefaced their appearance with a sage warning: "They've been touted slightly as the latest prophets of Northern doom. I should disregard that. At least you can judge for yourself on tonight's programme." What followed were thoroughly excellent versions of 'Handsome Devil', 'Reel Around The Fountain', 'Miserable Lie' and 'What Difference Does It Make?'. First broadcast on 31 May, the show was repeated an incredible five times over the next 18 months. The group returned to the BBC soon after to record further material ('Hand In Glove', 'These Things Take Time', 'You've Got Everything Now' and 'Wonderful Woman'), this time for the high-rating *David Jensen Show*. In the meantime, their spring tour continued with a support slot beneath fellow Mancunians, The Fall, followed by a visit to the Midlands which proved slightly intimidating.

On 2 June, the group set out for Cannock Chase where they were booked to play in a tent. Amusingly, they were the main musical attraction for a miners' gala at a fairground. An indication of what awaited them was provided during the afternoon when they visited several local pubs and were almost set upon. In the evening, the entourage entered the miners' "fun fair" and timidly made their way to the performers' tent. In what sounded like a scene from 'Rusholme Ruffians', Morrissey was forced to hold his own before an unsympathetic, macho audience. "The young miners weren't taken with Morrissey," roadie John Fox recalled, "or the band for that matter." Several bottles were thrown during the performance and a police escort was required to see them safely on their way.

It was something of a relief to return to the capital a couple of days later, where they played the Brixton Ace, supporting the notably obscure West London outfit, The Decorators. After the gig, Grant Showbiz finally met The Smiths backstage and was suitably taken by their strong image. Marr sat in a corner looking cool in his sun-glasses and elaborately quiffed hair, while Morrissey sported a floral shirt and bead necklace. The unshaven, casually-dressed Joe Moss was contentedly cradling a pint of beer and appeared both friendly and relaxed. He was quite unlike any manager Grant had ever seen. Taking the new soundman aside, Joe offered some pertinent advice: "Make Morrissey's voice as loud as the rest of the band put together." Cunliffe was mightily impressed by this suggestion and seemed surprised at the degree of understanding and appreciation that the middle-aged manager showed towards his charges. "What he said fitted in with the way I thought," Grant recalled. "He had this real empathy, love and care for the band. The vibes I got from Joe were of an immense fatherly protection. He seemed to be concerned and worried about Morrissey, whereas later he was painted as Johnny's buddy." The atmosphere in the dressing-room was insular but friendly, like a clubhouse that welcomed new members with considerable caution. "They were such a close-knit bunch," Grant observed. "Ollie May was the best mate and seemed fraught because he had to be the 'responsible' person. Joe was looking after Morrissey, and they were all chatting. They had these in-words and phrases and I wasn't entirely sure what they were talking about. I was impressed. I'd known Mancunian slang, but this was different. It was like watching The Monkees, or The Beatles at a press conference. They were very witty and all bounced off each other."

In spite of Grant's idyllic picture, The Smiths' family was not as unified as observers assumed. For a time, it seemed that Mike Joyce was on the verge of being replaced. Joyce's problems began when he sought to improve his rudimentary drum technique by engaging a tutor. He was recommended to a jazz player in Stretford whose past students had included Donald Johnson from A Certain Ratio and, significantly, The Buzzcocks' John Maher. Joyce was impressed by such credentials and even more overwhelmed when he heard the jazz player in action. Mike's requirements were engagingly modest. "All I know is straight, aggressive, uptempo rock played live," he explained. Joyce was invited to play some material but, even before he'd finished, his tutor was shaking his head with concern. "What on earth do you think you're doing?" he joked. "Firstly, you don't sit like that, you don't hold your hands like that and you don't use the drumsticks like that." Joyce was crestfallen. "Well, what do you want me to do?" he implored. The patient tutor took his pupil through some basics but, after a few weeks, Joyce realized he was getting nowhere. "It was such an arduous time," he remembers. "He was a fantastic player and I was eager to learn. I wanted to know what was best for me as a player and for my contribution to The Smiths. But it was the wrong thing to do. It didn't help at all."

Marr was the first to notice the negative effects of the well-intentioned lessons. "They put him back," he lamented. "They just ruined his confidence and where he was coming from." Although Joyce's emphatic drumming on 'Hand In Glove' had been applauded by the group, there was concern about his work on less uptempo material. Morrissey had already mentioned to Moss in passing that Joyce's abrasive style might be better suited to a hard-rock outfit. Joyce was not unsympathetic towards such a viewpoint. "Morrissey definitely found me a hard drummer," he agreed. "Especially with the little inflexions that needed to be put on The Smiths' quieter stuff. I was hammering it out and they had to turn the drums down. If they'd kept it at the one level, the drums would always have been at the front of the mix." While Joyce's aggressive playing style momentarily caused a rethink, there were other factors that threatened his future in the line-up. According to Marr, pressure was exerted from both record company and agency representatives. "I wasn't going to get involved with it," he stresses. "There was no way we were going to get rid of Mike. It wasn't a serious possibility. Myself and Morrissey got cornered by the record company, who said: 'Mike isn't good enough. You'll have to think about it'. We discussed it in the van (me, Morrissey and Joe) on the way back from a gig because they were *very* serious about it. But it never went any further... Mike was in and that was it. Then he got to be good very quickly... I didn't get Mike into the group lightly. I've never got anyone in any group lightly. He really had to cut it. There's no way we'd have gone back on that."

Joe Moss argues that the Joyce matter was considerably more serious than Johnny now suggests and recalls a proposed line-up change with Simon Wolstencroft named as the likely replacement. Although Joyce was blithely unaware of the backstage drama, he does remember seeing Wolstencroft's equipment set up at Crazy Face. When he mentioned this to Andy Rourke, the bassist sheepishly observed, "Oh, he just needs a place to rehearse." While Moss assumed that Wolstencroft was formally auditioned at this point, Simon confirms that this was not quite the case; "What happened was, they were doing fair-sized gigs in April/May 1983 and one night, whatever Mike did, they were really pissed off with him. Andy said: 'We'd like you back in the group'. I suppose I would have joined and they'd have given me a wage. But Joe Moss felt it was bad timing because the course of The Smiths' history had already started." So, for the second time in under a year, Wolstencroft missed the chance of becoming a Smith. Coincidentally, he subsequently teamed up with Johnny's best mate Andrew Berry in The Weeds, and the flip-side of their sole single, 'China Doll', was titled 'Crazy Face', an unintended allusion to the emporium where Marr first met Moss. Wolstencroft's fateful connection with the name "Smith" continued later in his career when he found himself in the employ of The Fall's quirky creator, Mark E Smith.

In the months following the Wolstencroft incident, Joyce steadily regained his confidence and re-established his importance in the line-up. "I improved mainly because I had to," he noted. "Andy was playing along with me and saying the bass drum should always go with the bass guitar. I took that on board, but only to the extent that I could. I had my own ideas about what I should be doing as drummer in The Smiths. I had to improve because Johnny was so proficient on guitar. It had to be done otherwise the Si scenario would have come to fruition."

The minor hiccup over Joyce was not the only challenge to The Smiths' stability during mid-1983. Even as they drove to their gig at the Brixton Ace, Joe Moss was questioning his continued involvement with the group. "There I was 40-years-old," he recalled. "I can still remember the frightened buzz jumping from the van in Brixton and thinking, 'You must be bloody mad at your age'." Marr was keen for Moss to grow with the group, as Wythenshawe manager Rob Gretton had done with Joy Division and New Order, but a long-term commitment was always unlikely. Moss regarded himself as "The Smiths' nursemaid" and claims he fully expected to surrender paternity once a certain level of fame had been achieved. He had no intention of travelling abroad or spending lengthy periods away from Stockport. A family man with a baby on the way, his greatest fear was missing the opportunity of seeing his children growing up. He also realized that the cut and thrust of business management was unsuited to his personality. "I'd get eaten alive!" was his favourite riposte to Johnny whenever the big time was discussed. Despite his retail background, Moss was the antithesis of the old style, entrepreneurially-minded huckster. "I wouldn't argue about 10 pence on the price of a T-shirt," he explained. "I had no interest in doing that. What interested me wasn't sitting at CBS but the grass roots, the sound men at the gigs... once you get on to the money side, it's pretty tasteless."

Ironically, Morrissey and Marr seemed far more money-conscious than their manager, who was not above criticizing their financial arrangements with the backing crew. "Some of the lads around The Smiths were treated pretty lousy," he observed candidly. "They'd put something in and didn't have lives to go back to. Some of them were treated pretty shabbily. I used to say to Johnny, 'These are the favours you'll have to swallow'. I tried to up their wages, even if it was by only £1 a week."

The Smiths' no-frills frugality was already part of their new group philosophy, however, and at a time when money was scarce, they ran an understandably tight ship. Many of their helpers were simply young kids and friends caught up in the fun and excitement. At the White Horse pub in Hulme, a list appeared on the bar-room wall requesting a coach load of supporters to travel down south with The Smiths on tour. Some helped with the equipment just to be part of the show and doubtless never expected to be rewarded with generous, unsolicited wages, which was just as well. The Smiths were fortunate to enjoy a steadfastly loyal crew throughout their career and there was seldom any serious dissension in the camp. An aura of privilege already surrounded the group. Grant Showbiz emphasized the morale of The Smiths' inviolable inner circle: "People like myself weren't talking about money. I did the first gig for £13-a-night. It was nice because I didn't do any of the carrying - just the sound. I felt I couldn't charge them that much. The inner core weren't worried about money because we were loving it... I never had any hassles with The Smiths about money."

The Smiths' early summer tour coincided with a flurry of interest from record companies and publishers. The prestigious Zomba group were eager to capture the signatures of Morrissey/Marr and felt indignant when Moss innocently explained that he had never heard of them. "But we're massive!" they retorted incredulously. Negotiations failed to progress after the boys discovered that Zomba's director, Ralph Simon, was a white South African, who had previously worked in that troubled country. Eventually, Morrissey/Marr signed to Warner Brothers Music. The selection of a suitable record company was more dramatic and entertaining. Several managers were sniffing at The Smiths' heels, with CBS A&R scout Gordon Chorlton leading the pack. This must have brought a pleasing grin to Morrissey's face as Chorlton had previously penned live reviews for *Record Mirror*. Now Morrissey's former rival was his suitor.

The once-fancied Factory had long since been dismissed by The Smiths as too parochial while its ethos was patronizingly described as "of a different time". Johnny eagerly told reporters, "What we're thinking of isn't even in terms of national success, it's more like worldwide." Given such statements, it was widely assumed that The Smiths would sign to a corporate record company. At the time, Marr gleefully noted how he and Morrissey were flirting with the majors and stoking up a tantalizing bidding war in the process. The truth was that none of the majors actually made a firm offer for The Smiths, but eagerly expressed their continued interest while reporting back to superiors and awaiting developments. In the meantime, Rough Trade continued to press their advantage and were relieved when the group confirmed their intention to remain independent. "Although nobody had yet offered a deal, it was a conscious intention to go the independent route," Moss stressed. "It was a credible and offbeat decision. We preferred to be the big fish in the small pond." Interestingly, there was no bartering session with Travis over the size of the advance. "We just decided how much we wanted, asked them, and they said, 'Yes'," Moss confirmed. The figure, approximately £22,000 according to Moss, was the largest advance in Rough Trade's history, yet still a mere fraction of what The Smiths could have commanded from a major label. "All we wanted was reasonable money," insisted Moss, "and we got a good deal."

The great advantage of Rough Trade was that they offered a profit-sharing agreement and, instead of setting all recording expenses against an artiste's royalties, split the costs 50:50. This meant that substantial monies could be accrued by the artiste if their records sold in large quantities. Both Factory and Mute offered similar deals and, as Geoff Travis argues: "There was never any question from New Order, Depeche Mode or The Smiths that the system was unfair. Nobody ever asked for a royalty." Of course, there were obvious disadvantages to the Rough Trade signing, most notably the label's lack of market penetration, low recording budgets, weak worldwide distribution and relatively poor promotion. The upshot was that if The Smiths could overcome such obstacles and achieve strong and consistent sales, they would likely emerge as very wealthy men.

With Morrissey and Moss in unison over the Rough Trade signing, Marr was more than willing to add his signature. "I trusted Morrissey's instincts on that," he recalls. "I knew he'd thought about it long and hard. Signing to Rough Trade was part of an overall philosophy that Morrissey had. Especially financially. The 50:50 deal was important, but what was more important was the Rough Trade aesthetic."

While the public perceived the group as a four-man unit, it was significant that only two signatures appeared on the Rough Trade recording contract. Contractually, The Smiths were Morrissey/Marr. Travis confirms that this arrangement was entirely at the suggestion of the songwriting duo. "It was Johnny and Morrissey's idea," he insists. "That was *always* their vision." Marr was bluntly unambiguous about the non-contractual arrangement with Rourke and Joyce. "The Smiths was me and Morrissey," he declared. "It was me and Morrissey at the start. When I brought in Mike and Andy that was made clear to them. It was unusual for the whole focus of the group to be around a songwriting duo for the first time in years. That was fundamental to The Smiths' ethic. When I went round to see Andy to ask him to join the group, I laid out terms. I wanted this to be a new group with a realistic outlook." Amazingly, the terms outlined by Morrissey/Marr consisted of a purely verbal agreement by which the junior members received fees and a percentage of earnings (obviously excluding songwriting). In return for this, the songwriting duo agreed to take aboard various administrative duties. The alarming lack of any written agreement between the parties would later lead to evident confusion over precisely what had been promised. Marr euphemistically confirmed that Rourke and Joyce had been offered "less than a quarter" for royalties. Yet, Joyce always assumed that he was receiving 25 per cent of all the group's earnings, bar songwriting. The naïvete of the subsidiary members was summed up on the day of the Rough Trade signing when they watched Geoff Travis present Morrissey/Marr with the all important recording contract.

"I felt that we were all signed to Rough Trade," Joyce innocently observed. "I assumed they just needed two signatures to cover all four of us. It didn't bother me until later when I realized what that entailed. Then, it frightened the life out of me!"

It is strange to consider that The Smiths was actually a far less democratic set-up than even such Sixties models as The Beatles and The Rolling Stones, which also revolved around songwriting duos. Morrissey/Marr required total autonomy and the implications of the recording contract could hardly have been more clear-cut. Realistically, from the record company's viewpoint, Rourke and Joyce were no more than powerless, hired hands who might be dispensed with at any time. Throughout the career of The Smiths, the drummer and bassist effectively remained at the mercy of Morrissey and Marr and, just as Joyce had seemed vulnerable to dismissal, so Rourke would later leave before being rapidly reinstated. Despite their insecure status, however, Rourke and Joyce proved remarkably unrebellious. The vague verbal agreement that bound the quartet would eventually provoke litigation, yet the group was always united. The camaraderie would remain bizarrely intact, even when administrative chaos later threatened to overwhelm them.

Within days of signing to Rough Trade, The Smiths appeared at Warwick University on 30 June. CBS A&R head and former Spencer Davis Group bassist Muff Winwood had travelled from London on a scouting mission but was dismayed to learn that he was too late. "We really wanted to sign you," he told Joe Moss. Virgin Records expressed similar disappointment shortly afterwards, but as Moss reminded them, "It was never on, we wanted to be independent." One week later, The Smiths played their first major bill-topping Manchester gig at the Haçienda. Tony Wilson had already learned of the Rough Trade deal and was surprisingly pleased about the news. A few days before, he had seen Morrissey crossing the road in Fountain Street and shouted his congratulations. Ever the plausible revisionist, Wilson now displays remarkable sophistry, not only in accepting Factory's failure to sign The Smiths, but in turning that missed chance into an unexpected triumph. Indeed, Wilson provides an extended thesis that credits The Smiths with singlehandedly saving the entire British independent record industry. Pinpointing his own label's reliance on Rough Trade Distribution, the loquacious Wilson prophesied a horrifying vision of complete capitulation to the corporates. "If The Smiths' record sales hadn't gone through their system, Rough Trade would have gone bankrupt. No question. Daniel Miller (of Mute), myself and Factory would have been forced to the majors. There would have been no choice. We know from Kitchenware, Postcard and the rest that once you go to the majors, within two years, you don't exist. You're finished. I can't imagine anything else that would have happened. Basically, Rough Trade would never have been able to put back the money that fell out in the Eighties. If they hadn't signed The Smiths the whole edifice of independent distribution and music would have crumbled."

Wilson's theory is characteristically provocative, but it should be noted that he had already covered himself after previous problems with Rough Trade Distribution. "It was Daniel who got caught holding the baby," he argues. "Daniel and his accountants were able to structure a repayment system with Rough Trade that they were able to meet because of The Smiths' record sales." What Wilson calls the "accident of history" obviously aided Rough Trade during a tough economic period but to suggest that without The Smiths their demise was inevitable demands some qualification. It seems quite possible that, under pressure, Travis might have maintained Rough Trade's low budget organization, found other backers, ferreted out some promising signings or chosen to play ball with the majors by developing more commercial acts. The subsequent formation of the Blanco Y Negro label, which included The Jesus And Mary Chain on its roster, was financed by Warner Brothers, a move that enabled Travis to utilize the resources of a corporation while sustaining the separate independence of Rough Trade. Nevertheless, the financial importance of The Smiths to Rough Trade would prove inestimible, a fact that Morrissey frequently emphasized. From the moment he was told that 'Hand In Glove' was not an appropriate disc for release as a 12 inch, he questioned the decisions of his record company with increasing astuteness, concern and alarm.

Viewing The Smiths' signing from a distance, Wilson, not untypically, convinced himself that he was well out of it. He still describes Morrissey with smiling ambivalence, his words laced with a waspishly vulgar impertinence. "I don't know if I'd have loved to work with him," he ponders. "From the beginning, I always thought I loved Steven, and that behaving like a cunt was intentional... He behaves like a stuck-up guy still, and it works a treat. If you behave like a sensitive, weird megastar, within months people think that's what you are. I think he is very difficult to work with as a manager and record company. Yet EMI now seem happy with him and he with them, which has always surprised me. So maybe I could have worked with him, but I wouldn't have wished that on myself."

August 1983 was to prove one of the most eventful months in The Smiths' history. Still regarded as a support act by many, they were placed third on a bill at the London Lyceum beneath Howard Devoto and the now forgotten experimental suitcase-banging "industrial" combo SPK. Despite their low-key placing, The Smiths served notice of their impending fame with a short but solid set. While flowers were distributed to the audience, Morrissey commenced with a rampaging version of 'You've Got Everything Now', complete with his famously exaggerated falsetto. As the song ended, he sneered, "So there!" before growling his way through a menacing 'Handsome Devil'. Although the response was tepid rather than scorching, the group expressed their growing confidence with a powerful trilogy of 'What Difference Does It Make?', 'Reel Around The Fountain' and 'I Don't Owe You Anything'.

Morrissey's increasing insistence that he had been robbed of a certain hit was emphasized in the introduction to 'Hand In Glove'. "If you bought this record, why don't you buy it again?" he demanded rather than implored. A strong, yelping affirmation of the song's worth was followed by the finale 'Miserable Lie', with Morrissey falsettoing into imminent immortality. It was an impressive performance by any standards, let alone that of a third act support. Sadly, it was not enough to impress the *Melody Maker*'s reviewer Adam Sweeting who swiftly retired to the bar complaining that The Smiths were acting "as though the indifferent crowd somehow *owed* them a living".

There was more to cheer about two days later at Dingwalls, Camden, where the group prompted a stage invasion during which Morrissey was temporarily relieved of his microphone. By the end of the evening, the exuberant talent scout Gordon Chorlton was dancing triumphantly on the boards. Several promoters in the capital told Moss that The Smiths were now ready for a headlining tour. Their live apprenticeship was over.

The Smiths spent many summer days ensconced in a basement studio in Wapping, working on their début album with Troy Tate. Morrissey was at first flattered to be working with the former Teardrop Explodes' guitarist and by the late summer 10 tracks were completed.* With the album, tentatively titled *The Hand That Rocks The Cradle*, set for winter release, everything was running smoothly. However, events took a strange and unexpected turn when doubts were raised about the quality of the recordings. "Troy was a really nice guy," stresses Marr, "but we just weren't happy with the way it sounded and had to put the mockers on it. That was it. Morrissey was more unhappy with it than I was - but he was right." The other members of The Smiths were also unconvinced by the power of the material. "I thought it was a bit too tame for what we were doing at the time," Joyce remarked. "That first LP was so important. Troy had a good go, but I don't think it was as precious sounding as it could have been. Then again, I'll hold my hands up and say that everything was rollercoasting along so quickly that I just wanted to get it done and released. We fell apart with Troy. We came back in and checked what he'd been doing. It sounded OK, but we needed somebody to tidy things up."

Although Johnny had an excellent working relationship with Troy Tate, the group eventually decided to postpone the project, delay the album's release and appoint a new producer. "We didn't fall out with Troy," Marr claims. "We were just sorry to hurt his feelings. It was a professional decision and he obviously took it very badly. He'd got himself really wrapped up in it, and understandably so." Joe Moss was disappointed by the decision, feeling that Tate had captured the vital spirit of The Smiths at a crucial time. In retrospect, he sees the change of producer as not merely musical but political, with Morrissey controlling events. "At first, Morrissey was over the moon about Troy Tate working with The Smiths," Moss stresses. "Then Troy became close to Johnny whom he had more in common with. That was it. It was that triangle. If you were close to Johnny or weren't

---

* The Troy Tate tapes comprised: 'The Hand That Rocks The Cradle', 'You've Got Everything Now', 'These Things Take Time', 'What Difference Does It Make?', 'Hand In Glove', 'Handsome Devil', 'Accept Yourself', 'I Don't Owe You Anything', 'Reel Around The Fountain' and 'Miserable Lie'. Three of the above titles, 'These Things Take Time', 'Handsome Devil' and 'Accept Yourself', were eventually excluded from the first album in favour of 'Pretty Girls Make Graves', 'Still Ill' and 'Suffer Little Children'.

Morrissey's friend, then you were out." Ironically, the man who replaced Troy Tate would eventually fall victim to that same deadly triangle.

John Porter had first become involved in the music scene while studying at Newcastle University during the late Sixties. Along with fellow Fine Art student Bryan Ferry, he formed the R&B-influenced Gas Board, which specialized in slick, soulful cover versions of songs by such artistes as Bobby Bland and Wilbert Harrison. During the Roxy Music years, Porter appeared as occasional guitarist and was also in bands with Ronnie Lane, Eric Clapton, Steve Winwood and Ginger Baker. After a spell in the States with the ill-fated Blood Poets, he returned to England with the intention of moving into production. Jobless, he wrote to the BBC and was soon pleasantly surprised to find himself working on a staggering 300 radio sessions between 1980-81.

Geoff Travis first contacted Porter with a view to remixing the Troy Tate tapes. After listening to a rough cassette version, Porter demanded to hear the original masters under studio conditions. He was decidedly unimpressed by the results. "I'm treading on dangerous ground here," he cautions, "but they weren't very good. The sound was rotten. It just wasn't worth bothering about... This was no reflection on Troy Tate. The Smiths just weren't a great recording band. They were good live and had done lots of gigs, but it's always different in the studio. They were pretty green." Porter concluded that it might be best to scrap the tapes and re-record the material. Travis agreed to a £500 fee and tentatively booked a short, two-week session at Manchester's Pluto Studios. Weeks later, Porter found himself working with The Smiths when they were booked to record a BBC session for the *David Jensen Show*. Four tracks were completed: 'Accept Yourself', 'I Don't Owe You Anything', 'Pretty Girls Make Graves' and 'Reel Around The Fountain'. It was the latter, already broadcast in an earlier John Peel session, that was to spark an unexpected furore.

One hundred years ago, Oscar Wilde had remarked, "The *sun* too, when used mechanically, is merely a reporter, and traduces instead of reproducing you". His apt words were to prove prophetic when applied parachronistically to the mechanical prose of Nick Ferrari in the 25 August edition of *The Sun* newspaper. Under the heading "Child Sex Song Puts Beeb In A Spin", the tabloid cobbled together a ludicrously inaccurate and garbled account, which claimed: "The Manchester band's controversial song is titled 'Handsome Devil'. It contains clear references to picking up kids for sexual kicks... As part of their live act, they also do a version of 'Climb Upon My Knee, Sonny Boy' about picking up a seven-year-old in a park." What was most amazing about the piece was not so much that it had magically created "a seven-year-old in a park" or confused 'Handsome Devil' with 'Reel Around The Fountain', or 'Sonny Boy' with the excerpt from 'The Hand That Rocks The Cradle', but that, in doing so, it had actually centred on three of Morrissey's most suggestive and ambiguous songs.

If there were three lyrics in The Smiths' canon that could be said to contain paedophiliac leitmotifs then 'The Hand That Rocks The Cradle', 'Reel Around The Fountain' and 'Handsome Devil' were definitely the correct candidates. In the circumstances, it was to The Smiths' fortuitous benefit that they had not incorporated 'Suffer Little Children' into their live set. If Morrissey's fascination for the loss of spiritual/sexual innocence or the lustful tone of 'Handsome Devil' had been juxtaposed indiscriminately alongside the subject of the Moors murders, then the tabloids would have crucified the celibate singer. As it was, the 'Suffer Little Children' controversy would not appear for another nine months and, fortunately, its theme was not retrospectively connected to the spurious "child sex song" of August 1983.

In retrospect, the absence of 'Suffer Little Children' from the first tabloid assault was a blessing, but Morrissey was aghast enough at what had already been alleged. The inaccuracy of the sensational, ill-informed *Sun* bulletin left him stunned and perplexed. Yet, it was easy to locate the origin and development of the "paedophile saga". Ironically, the matter had first been brought to the public's attention by one of The Smiths' leading supporters, Dave McCullough. Reviewing their University of London Union gig in the 14 May edition of *Sounds*, he championed Morrissey as a lyricist with a difference. "Most of his word-packed lyrics are about child molesting, and more mature sexual experimentation. He hates women with a vengeance, but is still the intellectual." Without the benefit of a lyric sheet, McCullough was straining to hear particular lines, which explained the following unfortunate slip in describing the coda to 'The Hand That Rocks The Cradle': "The refrain 'Climb Upon My Knee, Sonny Boy' in another song is used as a child-molesting come on to a seven-year-old in a park. This kind of ultra-violent, ultra-funny grime is just what is needed to pull rock 'n' roll out of its current sloth."

Significantly, McCullough saw nothing distasteful, disconcerting or immoral about Morrissey's lyrics and even the lines he misheard were applauded for their originality and humorous outrage. McCullough returned to that same theme in the 4 June issue of *Sounds*, noting: "The subject of child molesting crops up more than a few times in Smiths songs. They are hilarious lyrics, more so because they suddenly touch on the personal." What McCullough perceived as great hilarity was treated more sombrely by The Smiths' lyricist, who countered categorically: "We do not condone child molesting. We have never molested a child." Morrissey's viewpoint was volunteered to a journalist who was sympathetic to his lyrics at a time when there was no hint of any controversy. He could hardly have made his views on the subject much clearer. It was particularly frustrating, therefore, to read *The Sun*'s cavalier comments, not to mention a subsequent scathing sideswipe in *Sounds*, courtesy of tabloid pen-pusher Gary Bushell. When *The Sun* allegedly failed to represent Morrissey's ripostes accurately, Scott Piering pulled the familiar bluff of threatening legal action as "a damage limitation" exercise. "Obviously, you don't sue *The Sun*", he observed wearily.

Several weeks later, the troubled Morrissey was still pleading his angered case to the *NME*. "We're still in a wild state of shock," he exclaimed dramatically. "We were completely aghast at *The Sun* and even more by

Sounds. We really can't emphasize how much it upset us because obviously it was completely fabricated." Even Marr was displeased by the adverse publicity, partly because his younger brother Ian had been teased about the article at school.*

The storm in a teacup controversy unfortunately focused attention on Morrissey's intentions rather than the songs themselves. It was evident from Morrissey's media comments and indignation that he had not set out to compose songs about child molestation. Yet, the critics continued to chase the "intentional fallacy" by asking, "Did Morrissey mean to do it?" They would have been better advised to consider the more interesting question once levelled at Milton: "Was he of the Devil's party without knowing it?"

When misguidedly pushed for an explanation of his authorial intention in 'Handsome Devil', Morrissey explained: "... the message of the song is to forget the cultivation of the brain and to concentrate on the cultivation of the body. 'A boy in the bush...' is addressed to the scholar. There's *more* to life than books you know but not much more - that is the essence of the song. So you can take it and stick it in an article about child-molesting and it will make absolutely perfect sense. But you can do that with anybody. You can do that with Abba."

The point is, however, that you couldn't provide a serious or cogent argument about "child molesting" in relation to Abba or "anybody". Morrissey's pat explanation was at worst evasive and at best curiously obscure and dismissive. His tone indicated an impatient refusal to confront an important leitmotif conveyed through his writing. Of course, Morrissey could not justifiably be expected to articulate the nuances of his created work, let alone dictate its meaning. His accusations of misinterpretation were greeted sympathetically by the music weeklies, but the argument did not end with 'Handsome Devil', for both 'The Hand That Rocks The Cradle' and 'Reel Around The Fountain' contained similarly ambiguous allusions. Significantly, Dave McCullough at first took the paedophiliac connotations as given, and I assumed the same. The cult of the *Kinderschäder* certainly seemed an underlying theme in all three songs.

Despite Morrissey's strong disapproval of paedophilia (which I accept) there is nothing critically illegitimate about ignoring his statement of intent in approaching these compositions. Once a song has been written, its meaning is no longer the private property of the artist but has escaped into the public domain. In creating the work, the writer necessarily divorces himself from it. He may attempt to explain his intention in writing the piece, as Morrissey has vaguely done, but this tells us only the original idea behind the song. The conscious and unconscious processes of creation often alter the original intention beyond recognition. It would be fascinating to learn the authorial genesis of *every* Morrissey song and such exposition would no

* Marr actually claimed in *NME*: "I've got a younger brother who is 11, who on the day it was in *The Sun* went to school and was hassled by kids..." However, the piece was actually run on 25 August during the summer holidays.

doubt prove intriguing and revelatory. But, he could only tell us what he hoped to put into the work, not necessarily what is actually there. Morrissey's "subjective" intention may in fact differ markedly from the "enacted" intention in the finished song itself. Moreover, given Morrissey's love of borrowed lines, he is arguably less in control of the song's "enacted intention" and therefore more likely to produce unforeseen authorial ambiguities.*

In 'Handsome Devil', Morrissey appears in playful mood, deliberately creating gender confusion with the ambiguous use of the word "handsome" and the negating combination of "mammary glands" and "a boy in the bush". If the sex of the narrator's object of desire is intentionally unspecified, the strong sexual undercurrent is certainly not. From the opening lines, there are elements of erotic fantasy in the singer's perception of people as readily available sexual playthings ("All the streets are filled with *things*, eager to be held") and an aggressive air of sexual frustration ("I know what hands are for/And I'd like to help myself"). Fantasy rape is both hinted at through typical Morrissey innuendo and rationalized, as it so often is, by misrepresenting an innocuous gesture on the part of the victim ("You ask me the time, but I sense something more/And I would like to give you what I think you're looking for"). Fleshy lust ("Let me get your head on the conjugal bed") and sado-masochistic imagery ("I crack the whip and you skip, but you deserve it") culminate in the suggestion that the object of the narrator's lascivious attention may well be a school pupil ("A boy in the bush is worth two in the hand, I think I can help you get through your exams"). Morrissey claims that the closing couplet ("There's more to life than books you know, but not much more") contains the "essence" of the song's message. Yet, the rational tone of these lines contrasts markedly with the explicit innuendo and seething lust dramatized earlier in the song. If Morrissey's intention was to provide a mind versus body dichotomy, it is interesting to observe the extent to which the carnal obsessions of the narrator intrude and disturb. It seems remarkable that Morrissey failed to detect the paedophiliac connotations in 'Handsome Devil', the more so when you consider 'The Hand That Rocks The Cradle'.

In the latter, Morrissey details a love that is not merely fiercely protective but frighteningly all-consuming. The awe with which Morrissey perceives the child's innocence ("you're untouched unsoiled...") is juxtaposed alongside strong allusions of imminent danger. ("There'll be blood on the cleaver tonight"). In describing his relationship with the child, the singer employs images which suggest an obsessive allure that is irresistible, yet also harmful and destructive ("I just looked into his wondrous eyes and said 'never never never again'/All too soon I did return, just like a moth to a flame").

---

* In 'Reel Around The Fountain', for example, the lines "I dreamt about you last night and I fell out of bed twice" and "you're the bee's knees but so am I" were taken from Shelagh Delaney's *A Taste Of Honey*. The same play offered the theme of 'This Night Has Opened My Eyes' with such lines as "wrap her up in the *News Of The World*... " and "the dream is gone but the baby is real". As indicated earlier, the "butterfly" line previously occurred in Molly Haskell's *From Reverence To Rape*.

The Al Jolson-inspired coda features Morrissey singing, "Climb upon my knee, sonny boy, although you're only three, sonny boy - you're mine, your mother she just never knew - you're mine." The disturbingly proprietorial tone has a sinister edge which inclines the listener to feel that the three-year-old would be well advised to steer clear of the singer's knee. And what was it precisely that the mother never knew? The pervading sense of fear that permeates the song focuses alarmed attention on the foreboding relationship between the child and his intense, overbearing guardian.

Morrissey's tendency towards vague innuendo was even more evident on 'Reel Around The Fountain'. Here, the song opens with an eyebrow-raising reference to lost innocence ("It's time that the tale were told of how you took a child and you made him old"). A series of allusions to sexual submission follow ("Slap me on the patio, I'll take it now... Fifteen minutes with you, I wouldn't say no... you can pin and mount me"). Again, the erotic content is overwhelmingly potent. Morrissey dismisses the child molesting theorists by stating frostily, if rather vaguely, that the song's theme concerns "loss of innocence, that until one has a physical commitment with another person, there's something childlike about the soul." Within the context of the song, the word "child" provides a powerful paedophiliac link, though such an interpretation ultimately rests solely on that key word. Morrissey no doubt intended "child" to suggest aspects of adult innocence but, here again, authorial and enacted intention conflict. By categorically choosing the word "child", Morrissey creates ambiguity, intended or otherwise.

The paedophile connotations are just that. Morrissey is never explicit and, by his own admission, had no conscious awareness of their existence in his work. It would take a lengthy spell on a psychiatrist's or literary critic's couch to unravel subconscious or metaphorical motivations behind specific images in Morrissey's private mythology. What we are ultimately left with are the compositions themselves, their meaning conveyed through a complex series of constructions that the listener fits together in order to discover a coherent whole that is consistent and irreducible.

Throughout the short paedophile saga, both Morrissey and *Sounds* (and, not surprisingly, *The Sun*) failed to voice the crucial point that writing about child molestation (intentionally or not) is not the same as proselytizing or prompting such conduct. Nor was there any acknowledgement of the rich vein of paedophiliac themes in pop, some of which have provided much-loved chart toppers. Both The Union Gap's 'Young Girl' and The Police's 'Don't Stand So Close To Me' speak of older men grappling with the temptations of "going too far" with an under-age girl. Other songs, such as Nils Lofgren's 'Jailbait' and Van Morrison's 'Cyprus Avenue', feature female objects of desire, both aged 14. Significantly, none of these has ever caused controversy, let alone provoked outrage, or prompted a radio ban. It was ironic that Morrissey's far more oblique compositions should attract the interests of the national press. His archness and literary playfulness actually nettled his detractors far more than the explicit, hard-hitting sexual imagery of less talented contemporaries. The legitimacy of writing unambiguously about the temptations of sex with under-age girls was apparently more acceptable than the strangely menacing musings of the self-confessed celibate from Stretford. What still niggles is that Morrissey felt sufficiently intimidated to grace his tabloid tormentors with an earnest explanation that they, in any case, effectively ignored. He may as well have despatched copies of Nabokov's *Lolita* to his self-appointed censors and reopened a far more interesting debate on paedophilia in literature.

Fortunately, the paedophile drama ultimately proved advantageous to The Smiths, for not only did it provide them with national publicity but secured the unexpected bonus of a recording session. In the aftermath of *The Sun*'s allegations, BBC producer Mike Hawkes sagely contacted his superiors and decided to delete 'Reel Around The Fountain' from the *David Jensen Show* as a "precautionary measure". This was a bitter blow to the group as the song had already been chosen as their next single. White label copies were in preparation and an advertisement announcing the release was featured in the magazine *Jamming!* When fellow BBC producer John Walters learned of The Smiths' plight, and the circumstances surrounding the ban, he was outraged. Without hesitation, he offered them a second John Peel session as compensation. This retaliatory gesture ensured that the group was in the enviable position of enjoying two BBC promotional broadcasts in the space of three weeks. Moreover, the sessions were so popular that they were each repeated ahead of schedule. As Piering proudly noted: "Smiths fever was on. It wasn't just smouldering, it was aflame."

The second Peel session introduced four new Smiths songs: 'Back To The Old House', 'This Night Has Opened My Eyes', 'Still Ill' and 'This Charming Man'. Producer Roger Pusey had been instructed to monitor any controversial lyrics and interrupted 'This Night Has Opened My Eyes' to question Morrissey about the significance of immersing a baby's head in a lead-coloured river. The singer's brief explanation was deemed convincing. When Geoff Travis and Richard Boon arrived at the session, they were immediately struck by the infectious appeal of 'This Charming Man'. Seizing the moment, Travis persuaded Morrissey/Marr to record the song as a single in place of 'Reel Around The Fountain'. Given the recent minor furore over the song, it was probably a wise decision. "Geoff said 'This Charming Man' would be a hit," recalls producer John Porter. "He was very good like that. He had good ears and a knowledge of the market he was trying to sell to."

Originally, 'This Charming Man' was attempted at London's Matrix Studio in a mad 10-day rush. Marr and Porter had already agreed that Smiths singles should feature distinctive guitar introductions and 'This Charming Man' was a superb exercise in artistic précis. "It was incredibly linear at first," Porter recalls. "The introduction was about 28 bars and rambled. The Smiths were never a verse/chorus/middle eight band. Because there were no choruses, it was difficult and I couldn't get the hang of it. Then we knocked a few bars off and it all came together." Marr encouraged Porter's ruthless editing and, using the rigid restriction of the three-minute single format, The Smiths produced consistently excellent 45s.

The Matrix version of 'This Charming Man' was completed so hastily that the mix fell below par. The ever vigilant Geoff Travis immediately recognized its shortcomings and suggested they recut the song at Manchester's Strawberry Studios. Using the Matrix original as a demo, the group completed a more focused version, backed by a pre-programmed Linn drum. At the end of the session, Joyce's drums were overdubbed, and the Linn erased. The final product was one of the most refreshing pop singles of 1983 and, just as Travis predicted, secured The Smiths a deserved Top 30 hit. The Troy Tate produced flip-side 'Jeane', with its resigned acceptance of a staid domesticity and fragmenting relationship, had all the makings of a Morrissey kitchen sink drama. Although the song failed to appear on any Smiths compilation, it was later recorded by both Sandie Shaw and Billy Bragg. Rough Trade promoted the single cleverly by issuing an enticing, value for money, 12 inch that featured the Manchester and London versions of 'This Charming Man', the amusing 'Wonderful Woman' and self-analytical 'Accept Yourself'.* The latter became one of The Smiths' classic "outsider" songs, stressing the need for self-realization ("when will you accept your life"), while recognizing the unlikelihood of ever achieving happiness ("I once had a dream and it never came true/ And time is against me now"). Morrissey's pyrrhic glorification of his inability "to kick with the fray" was tantamount to a rallying cry for the self-righteously disaffected among his multiplying audience.

The Smiths' following strengthened substantially after their first appearance on *Top Of The Pops*. For Morrissey, the show represented a crucial epoch. Throughout his adolescence, *Top Of The Pops* had been a weekly ritual, its immutable format as permanent and reassuring as the weather forecast. The arbitress of chart fortune, *Top Of The Pops* championed and celebrated the true democracy of pop. What other show could house The Beatles alongside Ken Dodd and David Bowie beside Benny Hill without any sense of incongruity?

On 24 November, The Smiths entered the crowded Olympus of Morrissey's pop mythology to take their place alongside such deities as Herman's Hermits, Sandie Shaw, Twinkle, T Rex and Mott The Hoople. In a show which highlighted the chart-topping Billy Joel serenading his statuesque 'Uptown Girl' Christie Brinkley, The Smiths displayed a refreshingly urbane charm. Morrissey visibly uncoiled, flailing wildly across the stage, while Marr watched seemingly disinterestedly from behind his recently revived White Dice period fringe. On the studio floor, old friend Richard Boon witnessed Morrissey's dramatic acceptance of pop godhead. "It was intense," Boon recalls. "Morrissey was driven, almost glowing. It probably seemed tiny on television, but it was a big existential

---

* In an early appraisal of The Smiths, Nick Kent suggested that 'Jeane' and 'Wonderful Woman' might have been inspired by Morrissey's friend Linder, although there are no specific references or allusions to her in either song. A more likely source for 'Jeane' is Morrissey's aunt, Jeane Sheppard. Additionally, it might be worth noting that the bastard child of Oscar Wilde's friend (and possible lover) Lillie Langtry was named Jeane.

moment. This had to be done right and had to work. It was a pivotal moment in his life and he knew it would be." Joe Moss was also entranced by The Smiths' performance, but a flash of self-awareness prompted him to ponder some searching questions. "I always thought *Top Of The Pops* was diabolical and there I was jumping for joy because we were on it. What had happened to my standards? And what would happen later?"

Immediately after recording *Top Of The Pops*, The Smiths boarded a train to Manchester where, that same evening, they appeared before a capacity crowd at the Haçienda. Amid screaming and fainting fans, the group played four encores, much to the excited satisfaction of their manager. For Joe Moss, 24 November was also an epoch, but one in which he could no longer be a participant. Having promised to remain with The Smiths until they "made it", he realized that his bargain had been fulfilled. "When I left, I left on what was an absolute high," he recalls. "It was the only way to go. I ran down the street shouting, 'It's too late to stop now'."

Joe Moss's rush of exhilaration contrasted grimly with Johnny Marr's sense of desolation upon hearing the news. While aware of Moss's desire to concentrate on his family, he was completely unprepared for such a sudden departure. "I wasn't disappointed with Joe because it was obvious that he was feeling forced out," Marr claims. "He and Morrissey stopped seeing eye to eye." The unspoken *frisson* between Moss and Morrissey even caught the eye of the neutral Mike Joyce. "Joe had a greater bond with Johnny," he observed, "but he never used it to his advantage. He hung out with Johnny and smoked draw. I don't think it was to Morrissey's liking that they were so close. He felt that we were going to be taken down the same old rock 'n' roll avenue. Morrissey didn't feel it was right that he should be there managing the band. Ultimately, Joe had to go. Johnny was cut up *a lot*."

The shock resignation almost provoked a confrontation between Marr and Morrissey, until Moss diplomatically smoothed matters. "I was gutted," Johnny remembers. "Joe told me, 'I know what you'll do, you'll say you're leaving as well. *Don't*. You'll be making a massive mistake'. He knew me really well and said, 'Don't do anything about it. Keep your mouth shut and your mind shut'. I followed his advice and from then on I tried to forget about it." Nevertheless, Marr occasionally found himself wondering why it really had to end and, in the process, paid a flattering tribute to his former mentor. "Joe Moss was the unsung hero of The Smiths' story in more ways than one," he concluded. "To this day, I don't know why Joe wasn't our manager. Morrissey knows and Joe knows, but I don't know and I never did know. The only side I could understand is that if Joe realized Morrissey wasn't happy, then he wouldn't have stayed. It seemed like an involuntary resignation to me." Mike Joyce summoned enough courage to voice similar reservations. "We used to feed through Johnny and Joe," he admitted. "Joe had such a knowledge about the music industry and Johnny learned so much that it held him in good stead when we had to make decisions ourselves. That was the first obstacle The Smiths had to get over. Joe had paid for the recording and we were rehearsing there for free and, suddenly, it came to an abrupt stop. Ultimately, I think Morrissey was jealous. It was jealousy. I don't think there's anything wrong with that but, when you think of the situation we were in, it was very petty. But, he felt it was for the best."

In the wake of Moss's departure, life in Smithdom continued with a semblance of normality. The triumphant Haçienda performance was followed by a riotous gig at the Derby Assembly Halls, which was filmed for BBC's *Whistle Test*. A stage invasion ended The Smiths' set prematurely, forcing the programmers to reverse part of the song order in the film. That same month, Morrissey made a surprise appearance on Radio 1's *The Great Rock 'n' Roll Trivia Quiz* in the unlikely company of The The's Matt Johnson. The final British gig of 1983, and the group's biggest to date, took place at London's Electric Ballroom on 19 December. With a visit to America scheduled for New Year's Eve, The Smiths seemed on the brink of untold achievement. Few could have guessed the personal problems and background upheavals that were already threatening the very heart of the group.

9

Fun On The Road

THE CLOSING WEEKS OF 1983 were a turbulent time for The Smiths. Apart from the sad departure of Joe Moss, there were additional niggles following the appearance of a dance version of 'This Charming Man'. François Kervorkian's New York remix was intended originally as a limited edition 12-inch single for clubs and disc jockeys until Geoff Travis championed a full UK release. Unfortunately, the dance mix conflicted with the group's purist vision of pop and met a particularly cold response from their predominantly indie-based fan following. Morrissey blamed Rough Trade for needlessly milking The Smiths and implored, "It was entirely against our principles, the whole thing." The music press reiterated his objections, while failing to acknowledge his culpability. Travis brusquely countered: "It was my idea, but they agreed. They said, 'Go ahead', then they didn't like it, so it was withdrawn. That doesn't sound criminal to me. I didn't think it was that much of a mistake or big deal."

Travis was later nettled when he read a Smiths' retrospective in *Melody Maker*, which stated, "Rough Trade made their first blunder when they released a special dance mix." The company was subsequently censured in some quarters for supposedly cashing in with import releases and various reissues. This perverse perspective on what was undoubtedly sound economics baffled the Rough Trade supremo. "*Nothing* that ever happened in The Smiths occurred without Morrissey's guidance," he insisted. "There's not one Smiths record that went out that Morrissey didn't ask to do, so there's nothing on my conscience. Morrissey had to OK the records. If he said 10 seconds before the release date that he didn't want a single out, we'd pull it."

The Smiths' unlikely crossover on to the dance-floor was emphasized by their surprise booking at New York's Danceteria. The appearance was organized by Ruth Polski, who was well known for her patronage of independent UK groups. It was anticipated that The Smiths would greet the visit with jubilation, but morale was low in the wake of recent events. The sudden loss of Joe Moss had left a gap in the group, which proved far greater than expected. Even the characteristically manic Grant Showbiz felt a maudlin twinge of nostalgia as the New Year loomed. "When we first started, we were in a blue transit van - manager, roadies and the group," Grant reminisced. "Morrissey was definitely part of it. I'd be rolling joints in the back and he'd be well aware of it, and we'd be laughing. He was very funny and made us laugh a lot. He was really in there with the lads, but when we went to America, it started changing. Joe wasn't there. We were really miserable, whereas it was supposed to be exciting."

A far more alarming absentee from The Smiths' camp was Marr's girlfriend, Angie Brown. The road crew was shocked to hear that she and Johnny had split up just before Christmas. It was difficult to escape the feeling that an era of innocence had already passed.

Upon arrival in New York, The Smiths were met by the overbearingly vivacious Ruth Polski, who brought some razzmatazz to the occasion by arriving in a limousine. Her first action was to proffer some newly-rolled joints of marijuana to her guests. "We were all very cool and didn't actually smoke, but just watched her get very stoned," Grant recalled. The crew perked up as the limousine entered the city centre, but their spirits deflated again on arrival at the hotel. "It was their first time away from home and they were completely lost," Grant noted sympathetically.

Morrissey was already complaining about the food on offer and became inconsolable after discovering a cockroach in his room. Joyce was also dispirited and retired to his bed surprisingly early. Rourke, meanwhile, was conducting clandestine conversations with two residents who were evidently stoned. He briefly disappeared with them, but returned in happier mood. Inspired by Rourke, the faithful roadie, Ollie May, decided to conduct a lightning tour of the city. "He went to the park and came back with an ounce of strawberry leaves," Grant chuckled. "He was very upset." While the group was uneasily adjusting to New York life, Geoff Travis was busily concluding a deal on their behalf with Sire Records.

With Ollie and Grant left in control of entertainment, there was always the likelihood of a touch of excess. Grant decided that the Danceteria gig might be enlivened by the presence of Mark E Smith's former manager/lover Kay Carroll, who was living in New Jersey. Within minutes of arriving at the club, she started waving the British flag by discriminately goading every American in sight. While The Smiths sat shyly and politely in a corner, Grant made some diplomatic apologies on behalf of his exuberant guest. "I was embarrassed," he confessed. "Kay's not the type of person you introduce to vicars or persons of a nervous disposition. She had a right old time."

As the evening progressed, Showbiz fell victim to his name by teaming up backstage with recording star Lovebug Starski. Their collaboration was pharmaceutical rather than musical, as Grant explained. "Lovebug was huffing cocaine into my and Ollie's mouth, which I'd never done before. He'd put it on the palm of my hands and say, 'On the count of three, I blow and you suck'. We were completely demented. It was more of a hip-hop scene than a Smiths gig."

Morrissey has never been a lover of hip-hop, so perhaps there was a degree of self-fulfilling disaster in his edgy performance. New Year's Day was already in full swing when The Smiths took the stage, and Morrissey looked like he wanted to go home. After the first number, he fell off the back of the stage, causing himself public embarrassment rather than injury. Gamely, he carried on before belatedly returning to his hotel room in search of further furtive cockroaches.

That same night, Joyce felt strangely weak. The following morning he could barely drag himself from his bed, but managed to reach the bathroom where he was confronted with an horrific sight. Staring in the bathroom mirror, he was alarmed to discover that his eyes, scalp and tongue were covered in spots. Struggling back to bed, he called the other members of the group from his bedside phone. "I was looking for sympathy," Joyce joked, "but everybody screamed, 'Arrgh! Don't go near him'. That was just what I didn't need." A doctor arrived shortly afterwards and wasted no time in diagnosing Joyce's condition as chicken-pox - a serious contagion for a 20-year-old.

When Geoff Travis learned of the drama, he feared that the group's cameo East Coast dates would be cancelled. In desperation, he suggested that they should enlist the help of former Blondie drummer Clem Burke. Morrissey dismissed the idea, however, and the trip was curtailed. There was barely enough time for the crew to complete their New York shopping spree. "I don't look back at that period with relish," Joyce moaned. "I was in bed dying and the rest of the group were out sightseeing." Grant characterized the mood of the entourage more succinctly: "Everybody was tired and fed up, so we all went home." Just before they left, Morrissey and Marr completed preliminary work on a projected single which unintentionally summed up the first US trip. Its title was 'Heaven Knows I'm Miserable Now'.

The first month of 1984 was a time for putting lives back in order. Marr was still staying at Joe Moss's house with Andrew Berry, and he spent many evenings mulling over the "Angie" problem. Moss had considerable respect for Angie's strength of character and was categorical in his advice. "I told him the cool thing to do was to get married," he recalls. The pair were soon reunited but, meanwhile, there were Smiths related matters to sort out too.

Chief amongst these was the state of Andy Rourke, who had lapsed into his old ways. Since the latter days of White Dice, Andy and Johnny had enjoyed marijuana as a musical accompaniment, but Rourke always had the capacity for further experimentation. "I spotted him once on Brookway fields picking magic mushrooms," Rob Allman recalled. "He'd do anything." With pop star fame, Rourke had fallen victim to the insidious attraction of heroin. His habit extended to dragon chasing, and no needles were involved. Nevertheless, Marr was concerned enough to invite Rourke to stay at Moss's house and attempt to overcome his recent dependence. With an extensive UK tour on the horizon, it was all the more important that Rourke was clean. Johnny was wise enough not to draw the matter to Morrissey's attention, although Moss was amazed that he was unaware of the Rourke problem. During visits to Moss's home, Morrissey either failed to register the unusual condition of his bass player, or simply suppressed his worst suspicions.

In late January, The Smiths released their third single, 'What Difference Does It Make?', which became their most commercially successful yet, reaching number 12. Recorded late in the sessions for their début album, the track had a solid R&B feel, inspired by Jo Jo Gunne's 'Run Run Run'. The steady rhythm drove challengingly alongside Morrissey's twin tale of weary disillusionment and self-destructive romantic fantasy ("I'd leap in front of a flying bullet for you"). "The song was a breakthrough," confirms producer John Porter. "We explored overdubbing guitars and there's probably about 14 or 15 on there. I wanted to show Johnny what you could do and, by the end of the track, he realized it was fun. I doubt if there was less than 10 guitars on anything they did after that. Whenever I met Johnny it was guitar city." Morrissey was not entirely pleased with this new direction and even regretted the release of 'What Difference Does It Make?'. He felt the track did not "age gracefully" and criticized the elaborate production. The songwriting duo had long discussions about the recording, with Joyce and Rourke coming down firmly on Morrissey's side. "The Peel version is the way I wanted it to be," Mike recalls. "Johnny and John Porter felt it should be a more solid, laid-down track as opposed to a jumbled-up rhythm. Songs change in the studio, and sometimes not for the better." Marr won the argument in chart terms but within a few months, 'What Difference Does It Make?' was pointedly dropped from live performance and disappeared completely from The Smiths' set by the end of the year.

During the final week of January, arrangements for The Smiths' UK tour were hastily finalized by All Trade Booking. However, organization and communication were hampered by the group's worrying lack of management. Characteristically, Morrissey and Marr turned to the most sympathetic person on their horizon and requested John Porter to oversee their affairs. He promptly told them they must be out of their minds. The group's continued reluctance to appoint a professional adviser, or delegate any real authority, would continually prove their undoing over the next two years.

On 23 January, after several futile days chasing Morrissey, All Trade Booking's Mike Hinck formally introduced their prospective tour manager. Phil Cowie was the archetypal hard-living rock 'n' roll roadie, and a peculiarly inappropriate choice for the fastidious Morrissey. For his part, Cowie had certain reservations about The Smiths, not least because he was accepting a fee far below his usual standard. He contented himself with the expectation that a profitable tour would provide compensatory bonus payments. Without a written agreement, however, such hopes were to prove delusory.

Before embarking on their grand college tour, the group appeared on both *The Tube* and *Top Of The Pops*, where viewers were astonished to see the lanky singer shamelessly brandishing a hearing aid. Given Morrissey's love of pop history, it was widely assumed that the dangling hearing aid was an oblique tribute to Fifties singer Johnnie Ray. When pressed, however, Morrissey explained that the idea emanated from a fan letter he had received from a deaf girl. Ever the concerned counsellor, Morrissey empathized with her disability and wore the device as a gesture of support. It was a strange, though not uncharacteristic action, which always left the singer open to unfair accusations of mocking the afflicted. On later songs, such as 'November Spawned A Monster' and 'Mute Witness', there was a similarly ambiguous mixture of pathos and comedy.

Morrissey's strong association with his followers was reflected in a subliminal desire to be mobbed. Although both Rough Trade and All Trade Booking had optimistically insisted that there should be no stage invasions, The Smiths objected to the installation of clumsy metal barriers. Morrissey enjoyed audience participation and always believed that the chaos could be controlled. However, playing at colleges with low stages was always dangerous and, as early as the second date, Cowie was forced to play the security steward. Due to crowd excitement, one youth was injured and hospitalized. The night ended on a poignantly disconcerting note as road manager Ollie May poured out a long list of grievances. The following evening at Warwick University, he announced his decision to leave the crew.

The loss of May was initially a severe blow to The Smiths. He had been Johnny's mate since the Shelley Rohde days, but became more distanced and disillusioned as the group achieved success. His sudden exit was reminiscent of the undemonstrative departure of Joe Moss. As Grant Showbiz observed: "I'd seen Mark E Smith have fights and I'd once thumped The Fall's drummer Karl Burns, but that never happened with The Smiths. It was all very jolly, then, suddenly, somebody wasn't there... Ollie had been used to setting up the gear, having a spliff and watching the band... I don't think he knew the importance of a soundcheck. There was less time to have a chat with Morrissey or a laugh with the lads. I'm a big mouth and can take up a lot of space and I just felt Ollie was being squeezed out." Having started as The Smiths' close friend, road manager and chief confidant, May increasingly perceived himself reduced to the level of a mere functionary, so he avenged his hurt pride by abandoning the group. "As soon as it stopped being a crack, he left," concluded Cunliffe.

The abrupt departure of May meant that Cowie was forced to deal with the group on a personal level, which merely exacerbated existing tensions. That same evening, at Warwick University, Morrissey truncated his performance, complaining of a sore throat. When the equipment truck arrived the next day at Loughborough University, The Smiths were nowhere to be seen. After placating the promoter, the crew returned to Manchester themselves, uncertain about the future of the tour. In the meantime, Morrissey's doctor had advised the singer to rest his tonsils for several days, a decision which caused considerable concern at All Trade Booking. They duly despatched a specialist to Morrissey's home, who re-examined the sick one and declared that he required far more rest between concerts, but could continue.

After another appearance on *Top Of The Pops*, The Smiths were back on the road, performing at the *Oxford Road Show*. However, all was far from well. Gripes concerning Rough Trade and All Trade Booking were increasing, in what was undoubtedly a supreme example of poor communication, misunderstanding and conflicting ideals. The problem lay in Rough Trade's tendency to treat their artistes like hard-working musicians, rather than celebrity rock stars. Such a view was consistent with their budget, political views and unpretentious approach to the music business. Initially, Morrissey had appeared like a shy, unaffected young man, who decried the plastic excesses of the New Romantics by demanding a return to the honesty and idealism associated with the early days of punk. Certain parties at Rough Trade willingly took him at his word and, in doing so, severely underestimated his real wants and needs. "Morrissey liked to travel by train and at times they wouldn't even think of booking him first class," Scott Piering recalled. "Even then, Morrissey was a well-known figure and needed his space and privacy. We took his ordinariness too literally and didn't realize that he needed special treatment. He was too down-to-earth with us. We should have treated him in a high-class manner."

Piering nevertheless maintains that The Smiths brought on their own problems by displaying unclear signals. In effect, The Smiths required star treatment, relative austerity, independent status, sympathetic advice, total artistic freedom and the power to turn the record company round their little finger. At least Geoff Travis had read their conflicting personality correctly and realized that the road ahead would be steep and hazardous. "You've got to understand that the character of The Smiths was such that it was all or nothing with them," he argued. "They could never be satisfied with anyone's input into their affairs. It's either 24 hours a day and if it's 23 hours and 58 minutes, it's not enough. That's the way they were, and that was fair enough. It was part of their genius, but it didn't always make life easy."

Morrissey's need for preferential care was communicated to his friends and supporters who rallied on his behalf. His protective mother soon became a thorn in the side of Rough Trade employees by audaciously deflecting "urgent" telephone calls. Once, when Geoff Travis himself attempted to coax the off-colour star to a meeting, he received the sharp end of Betty Dwyer's tongue. Marr also fought for better conditions in keeping with his partner's needs. "Johnny didn't feel that precious about himself," Piering confirmed, "but he knew that Morrissey needed to be handled in a set way. Instead of sending a taxi, they should have had a proper chauffeur. These little touches mean a lot to people when they're under stress. I don't think any of us appreciated that." The gap between extravagance and necessity was to remain unresolved in Morrissey's mind for the duration of the Rough Trade years.

On 12 February, the stricken singer struggled through a performance at London's Lyceum, which barely lasted 40 minutes. Recriminations about poor organization and dragging the star from his sick bed abounded. Amid this cauldron of chaos, the irrepressible Ruth Polski emerged with the shock news that she had been appointed as The Smiths' manager. The attendant Scott Piering was unnerved by her presence and determined, there and then, to take serious counter measures. Ruth, meanwhile, monopolized Morrissey's attention and ingratiated herself to the wan one by casually berating the fall guy Cowie. Before long, she was telling anyone within hearing distance (which accounted for a considerable number) that if she gained complete control, radical changes would follow. Her litany of complaints embraced poor marketing, second-rate hotels, inadequate record deals, inept personnel, and much else. Ultimately, she seemed quite determined to dump both Rough Trade and All Trade Booking, and take The Smiths right back to square one.

For all her acerbity, Polski was actually a warm-hearted, enthusiastic and supportive figure, who had invested considerable faith in booking The Smiths at the Danceteria. "She really fell in love with them, almost literally," Piering observed. After hearing that they still had no management, Polski descended on the group like a crusading harridan. "It was time to make her move," Piering cynically noted. "She was making ridiculous offers, and had a good line in bullshit. She flattered. Morrissey was charmed. Ruth had the knack of ingratiating herself, but she didn't have a power base and was incapable of delivering. The guys weren't convinced, but Morrissey was quite taken with her." As Piering realized, Polski had the ability to exploit Morrissey's perennial indignation, while also appealing to his vanity. "Ruth made every effort to cater to those whims and basically point out how shabbily they were handled - which was, more or less, true! That psychology would attract Morrissey. His mother was constantly telling him the same. Nobody could do anything right for Morrissey, as far as his mother was concerned."

Polski's major error was not overestimating her power, but misinterpreting Morrissey's bland acquiescence as evidence of firm commitment and acceptance. "I've no doubt that at one point Morrissey said *something* to her," Piering admits, "but she went out and announced it to the world when it just wasn't real." Grant Showbiz observed the managerial machinations with a wry smile. "Someone would tell Morrissey or Johnny a plan and they'd nod their heads. They'd make their decisions after choosing their options, but they'd go along with everybody. People were taking two people's chatter in a day and using it as the basis to start a career. Ruth was simply larger than life, a super fan."

While the managerial grand gestures and political intrigue festered, The Smiths' long-awaited début album was released on 20 February. Morrissey had trumpeted its appearance with the effusive comment: "I think it's a signal post in music." The delay in the album's release, preceded by a wealth of radio sessions and several quality B-sides, convinced many that the first album would be a milestone. What emerged was a strong, accomplished work which, despite some classy compositions, failed to sparkle. The production seemed strangely leaden and the performances unpolished, as if the group found it impossible to transcend the strictures of a predetermined minimalist dogma. What the album offered was solidity and immense promise, rather than the sound of greatness achieved. Like many artistes after their first album, Marr was too excited to dwell on its relative limitations. "I was just happy to make a record," he recalls, "and the fact that it existed and the songs were there was enough for me. It wasn't until people started mentioning the production that I noticed. People make a lot of the production, but we weren't as good as we could have been. The only way to have nailed us down at that period would have been to record a gig because we were really good live. That's probably the best way those songs could have been presented."

Marr's view is open to debate, but probably correct. The majority of Smiths live tapes capture the excitement of a group with a well-rehearsed set and a vocalist caught between conflicting functions: singing, dancing and outmanoeuvring a constant invasion of adoring fans. In retrospect, the prevailing feeling of anti-climax surrounding the album was partly due to over-anticipation, heightened by the considerable time lapse between its conception and release. What remained undisclosed, however, were the circumstances surrounding its completion. Far from being a work carefully assembled and recorded over several months, *The Smiths* had actually come together in a matter of days.

Geoff Travis had instructed John Porter to book two weeks at Manchester's Pluto studios, where the group intended to regurgitate and embellish the work they had completed with Troy Tate. Their lack of studio experience, exacerbated by the woeful time restrictions, caused Porter considerable problems. On the Thursday evening of their second week, they played back the completed tapes and concluded that half the album was inadequate. Overnight, they re-recorded 'Reel Around The Fountain', 'Pretty Girls Make Graves', 'The Hand That Rocks The Cradle' and 'Miserable Lie'. It was a remarkable and bizarre conclusion to a hectic fortnight. The album was subsequently mixed at London's Eden Studios and some of the rough edges were smoothed over during an overdubbing session, partly financed by the proposed deal with Sire. "We were just bashing them out and trying them again," was Porter's judgement of the two-week sessions. "It was a race against time and I was constantly thinking, 'This is not good enough'. Even when it came out, I still wished we'd had more money."

Although the budget for *The Smiths* seemed ludicrously small at a paltry £20,000, the figure was not unusual by independent standards. Aztec Camera's début LP had cost a staggeringly low £6,000, while Rough Trade's aspiring hit act Scritti Politti commanded only £24,000. Even as late as 1988, the much-touted first album from Creation's House Of Love did not exceed the £8,000 mark.*

Travis still insists that his label was not guilty of skimping on costs: "After The Smiths' £20,000 album things escalated, but they were unusually prolific. Their recording methods were very 'un-muso'. They always wanted to retain the essence of doing things quickly and capturing the spirit, so they never spent huge sums of money. By the end of their career,

---

* These figures were provided by managers Alan McGee (House Of Love) and Bob Johnson (Aztec Camera). The latter was confirmed by Travis, who also volunteered the Scritti Politti and Smiths budgets.

they were spending £80-90,000, which is nothing in industry terms. It was always very cheap."

The minimalist feel to the album was additionally explained by Morrissey's reluctance to recut tracks or allow Porter to utilize backing vocalists. "At that point, Morrissey had a range of about eight notes," the producer recalled. "For somebody who was into Ray Charles and Aretha Franklin, it was quite a thing to listen to Morrissey. He wouldn't allow backing vocalists, so we used guitars instead of doing 'oohs' and 'aahs'. Johnny was very receptive to that. Later, people talked about Johnny's Rickenbacker sound, but most of the guitars used on the album were my old Fender Telecasters." Although the number of guitars employed appeared to be multiplying with each session, Morrissey was always sensitive to subtle changes in the arrangements. "Morrissey wrote his words around the original melody," Joyce explained, "and if Johnny was playing a slightly different chord progression he'd notice it because he'd have to change key for certain words."

In order to improve Morrissey's vocal technique, he was sent to a professional singing tutor for lessons. Although he was too embarrassed to provide an impromptu performance, he picked up some useful hints on breathing exercise. "Morrissey rapidly got better," Porter observed. "In the early days, I plugged his vocals. When we were mixing through a harmonizer I put notes in tune. He liked his voice completely flat, loud and dry. I introduced him to faders, pulled them down from where I'd had them and gradually pushed them up until he said, 'I can handle *that* amount'. He was very wary. If you could notice the effect on his voice, he didn't like it at all. The Smiths always knew what they wanted."

One concession Porter won from The Smiths was permission to use organist Mick Weaver and pianist Paul Carrack. Their work was evident on 'Reel Around The Fountain', the melody of which had been inspired by James Taylor's reading of the Jimmy Jones' hit 'Handy Man'. "I was trying to do a classic melodic pop tune, and it had the worst kind of surface prettiness to it," Marr recalled. "But, at the same time, Joy Division were influencing everything in England. That dark element. It wasn't that I wanted to be like them, but they brought out something of the darkness of the overall track." As the all-important opening cut of *The Smiths*, 'Reel Around The Fountain' demanded extra care but, despite its quality, Porter was not satisfied with the final results. "We didn't do anything like justice to the song," he lamented. "It was never as successful as it should have been. I put Paul Carrack on piano to add a bit of colour because it was a little lifeless on record. We needed more time. I subsequently wanted to do the song again, but nobody was into that."

The remainder of the album underlined the strength of the songwriting partnership, as well as providing retrospective glimpses into Morrissey's aching adolescence. 'Still Ill' and 'You've Got Everything Now' are positively contemptuous in their anti-work sloganeering ("England is mine and it owes me a living"). In the latter, Morrissey even has the audacity to accuse his materially-successful adversary of lacking humour. "I've seen you smile, but I've never really heard you laugh." Such an accusation could never be levelled justifiably against the singer, whose bitchy interjections ("Did I ever tell you, by the way, that I never did like your face?") brazenly steal the show. Morrissey's acerbic wit is constantly balanced by a self-deprecating humour, most notably on 'Miserable Lie', where he employs *Carry On*-style innuendo to describe sexual failure ("I look at yours, you laugh at mine/and 'love' is a miserable lie"). That same sense of the comic absurdity of sex was carried forward to 'Late Night, Maudlin Street', in which Morrissey observed: "You without clothes/Oh, I could not keep a straight face/*me without clothes?*/well a nation turns its back and gags".

The delicacy of the youth accosted by love in 'Miserable Lie' ("You have destroyed my flower-like life") is reiterated more physically in 'Pretty Girls Make Graves'. Here, the forward female proves so sexually voracious that her reluctant, and soon-to-be replaced, partner feels almost ravaged ("She wants it now/and she will not wait/but she's too rough/and I'm so delicate"). Losing the girl, along with his faith in womanhood, Morrissey ponders a more glamorous, macho image ("I could have been wild and I could have been free"). The fantasy is qualified by a line recalling the words of the homosexual barber in the film *Victim* ("nature played this trick on me"). The coy, "I'm not the man you think I am," is one of several coded references that give Morrissey's compositions a homoerotic impact, accentuated by the narrative gender games played out elsewhere in his work. Discussing the use of sex as a theme, Morrissey stressed his fascination with juxtaposing innocence alongside corruption. "It's quite playful for me to deal with it in unforgivably innocuous terms and then leap straight into the height of seediness," he mused. "There's a vast middle ground, a vast desert of romance that I would never set foot in." By avoiding the cock-rock clichés of heavy metal and the introspective romanticism of the mainstream singer/songwriter, Morrissey creates a new form of love song in which the lyrics are both provocative and strangely disconcerting. "They're not explicit in a hard-core sex way or in a sensual way," he stressed. "I tried to approach it from a different angle, from an angle that can seem wholly innocent, but dramatically known." That anti-romantic yet desperately yearning tone is equally present in the penultimate tracks, 'What Difference Does It Make?' and 'I Don't Owe You Anything'. Binding the whole together are some extraordinary vocal shifts, involving yelps, gruff exhortations and a screeching falsetto that reaches banshee decibels during the coda of 'Miserable Lie'. Finally, the Morrissey scream is silenced by the horror of 'Suffer Little Children', in which he reverts to an appropriately reverent vocal, reinforced by a beautiful and intensely moving arrangement from the deific Marr.

The Smiths came housed in a cover that featured a shot from Andy Warhol's underground movie, *Flesh*. Significantly, the director's name was Paul Morrissey. In the film, cover star, Joe Dallesandro, played a male prostitute and the original unclipped still displays him perched on a bed, alongside his homosexual client. While retaining its homoerotic ambience, the sleeve served to emphasize Morrissey's aversion to stereotyped sex roles. It was no coincidence that the male was displayed in a vulnerable, sensitive and decidedly introspective pose. The artwork was in marked contrast to rock's usual displays of cocksure male virility and breast-baring female glamour. It was at once a neat complement and cutting riposte to the self-consciously stylized pin-ups consistently employed by such artistes as The Cars and Roxy Music. Morrissey utilized album artwork as an advertising board to display his personal obsessions. Over a succession of albums and singles, he would build up a veritable iconographical hall of fame, filled with such heroes and influences as Terence Stamp, Viv Nicholson, Pat Phoenix, Billie Whitelaw, Shelagh Delaney, Joe Orton, James Dean, Truman Capote, Richard Bradford, Alain Delon, Yootha Joyce, Avril Angers, Elvis Presley, Billy Fury and Candy Darling.*

By 19 February, The Smiths were back in London, having traversed through East Anglia, Nottingham, Lancaster and Sussex. This gave tour manager Phil Cowie the opportunity to berate Rough Trade and All Trade Booking about the need for greater security at venues. Cowie's concern proved prophetic as, three days later, The Smiths faced a hostile, threatening crowd at Reading University. The next afternoon, Cowie again attempted to persuade Morrissey and Marr to sanction a profit-sharing scheme, by which the crew would get a 20 per cent cut. He received that same vague acquiescence with which the duo greeted every new suggestion. As the tour rolled on through Swansea and Bristol, however, Cowie encountered more pressing problems in trying to tame the ever outspoken Grant Cunliffe.

"I didn't respect Phil Cowie at all and wouldn't do what he wanted," Grant confirmed. "I refused to carry the gear. As far as I was concerned, if I had a good night's sleep, all I had to do was the soundcheck. I wasn't being a good team player. I'm sure there was resentment because at the end of the night, I'd be swanning around, rolling joints, getting beer, and talking to people at the front of the stage."

Cowie accused the soundman of causing dissension in the camp. "This seemingly wilful behaviour regularly upset the crew," he noted caustically. However, attempts to discipline Cunliffe proved pathetically ineffectual. Throughout the tour, he retained the ear of the almighty duo and answered only to them. Cowie had no power to fire his recalcitrant adversary and both Rough Trade and All Trade Booking showed scant interest in these personality clashes. Morrissey and Marr were equally unconcerned about such minor squabbles and instead found trivial complaints of their own. On the road from Bristol to Brighton, they demanded that their driver be replaced for the unforgivable sins of impertinence and over-familiarity. It was that kind of tour.

Following a sparkling show at Stoke's Hanley Victoria Hall, The Smiths again met trouble in student land. At Leeds University, an over-excitable

---

* The Terence Stamp sleeve was belatedly withdrawn after a complaint from the actor, and replaced with a shot of Morrissey standing in the same pose. The revamped cover anticipated the solo years when every record release featured Morrissey as the star of the sleeve.

youth was manhandled by bouncers during the opening number, 'Hand In Glove', and had to be rescued by members of the crew. Despite Marr's penchant for over-sleeping and Morrissey's dramatic last-minute arrivals, The Smiths successfully made their way across Scotland, while reports about their shows filtered back to Rough Trade's London office. "The complaints about Cowie from the band and Morrissey were loud and numerous," recalls Piering. "He had family problems that were playing on him and he was just scrambling to keep it together. He wasn't taking care of Morrissey in the way that they expected. He just underestimated what was needed." The extent of Cowie's disillusionment was chronicled during the Scottish leg of the tour in a diary entry that summed up the thankless thraldom of a harried road manager. The revealing entry read: "By now, I am getting very tired. My capacities extend to driving, dealing with all the finance, and being personally responsible for any loss up to approximately £10,000, which I could lose or be robbed of; frequently assisting with backline, being responsible for the physical and mental well-being of 14 people; dealing with whatever problem I notice, or is pointed out. In addition to this, there is the fending off of would-be, but wrong, prospective managers. The constant strain of simply being nice to people when often one has no respect, professional or otherwise; and perhaps, worst of all, the constant backbiting from all sources for grievances, real or imagined."

On the day that Cowie was penning his protests, further political intrigue was afoot. In the aftermath of Polski's power-play, Piering elected to play his trump card by aspiring to the vacant managerial throne. "At the time, I wasn't sure whether I wanted the responsibility," Piering confided, "but it seemed a good way of ensuring that Ruth would *not* become manager. I made that move to prevent Ruth from managing them, but she'd hung herself anyway by her premature announcements."*

Piering's ambitions were severely circumscribed by Morrissey, who seemed vehemently opposed to any form of managerial control. While Marr realized that The Smiths needed strong management, his partner predictably vacillated over the issue. Piering was euphemistically referred to as "caretaker manager", and "official representative", but failed to secure any form of written contract from Morrissey/Marr. Like Rourke and Joyce, Piering's ultimate role in the set-up was amorphous and ill-defined. As The Smiths' full-time record plugger, he eventually received a standard percentage on part of their royalties, but claims that his additional "managerial" services were poorly rewarded. "I never made anything out of management. The whole time I was working in that capacity, I was running things from my office. They gave me a total of £3,500 (minus VAT), which went towards general expenses which were, no doubt, five times that."

The appointment of Piering testified to The Smiths' naïvety and Morrissey's careful but, ultimately, short-sighted manipulation. Piering was a neophyte with no managerial experience or clout in the industry.

---

* Ruth Polski returned to New York and was subsequently killed in a road accident after being hit by a car.

Morrissey was no doubt deferring the appointment of a manager until the perfect candidate appeared, yet, throughout his career, he showed a woeful inability to surrender the reins of power, even in areas where his inexperience threatened the artistic and commercial development of The Smiths. Piering was not even a manager in name, and never received the trust to negotiate important deals on The Smiths' behalf. Morrissey was probably correct to limit the power of Piering, who should never have been appointed in the first place. What The Smiths urgently required was a heavyweight professional manager, who could be used as a buffer between themselves, Rough Trade and All Trade Booking. Instead, they took that mantle upon themselves and the results were predictably chaotic, time-consuming and frustrating.

On 3 March, The Smiths played Dundee University. It was a gig that quietly summed up the triumphs and tensions that they encountered during their tour of the college circuit. A long introduction to 'Hand In Glove' indicated the fluidity and confidence of the rhythm section, which was swiftly emerging as one of the best in the country. Morrissey appeared to recognize this fact and allowed the group full rein, interspersing his vocals carefully at key moments. The audience was less discriminating, however, and their boorish behaviour forced Morrissey to stop the show. Staring directly at the beer-swilling pack, he confronted these misguided revellers with a stately ultimatum. "Look, dear friends," he announced in a head-masterly voice, "you've got a very strange way of welcoming people. If anybody throws beer or spits or cans - we will *leave*. So you make your choice." The authoritarian tone of his voice suggested that Morrissey was deadly serious and the spectators duly took heed. An extraordinarily expressive version of 'Heaven Knows I'm Miserable Now' followed, with every chord and syllable testifying to the tension in the hall. Marr's exceptional sense of rhythm drove the group in a fashion reminiscent of the great Pete Townshend, with a flair and delicacy that simultaneously recalled Hank B Marvin. The introduction to 'Girl Afraid' was quite masterful, while Morrissey's feel for the song and ability to convey a sense of restrained emotion has seldom been bettered. Events again took a grim turn at the start of 'This Charming Man' when Morrissey abruptly left the stage. His colleagues played on, completing a full-length instrumental version of the song, in which Marr momentarily found his *métier* as an early Sixties instrumentalist. Although it seemed that The Smiths might suddenly transform into The Shadows and play a complete instrumental set, the greater likelihood was that the plugs would be pulled and the performance aborted. An angry student union official took the microphone and berated his flock with a much-needed lecture. "Listen," he demanded, "there's a lot of electrical equipment up here and the fuckin' assholes who are throwing water or beer, or whatever it is, should realize that it can kill people, so cut it out, otherwise there ain't gonna be a show... Are you gonna behave yourselves? OK!"

As the group waited to be recalled, calls of "Smiths, Smiths, Smiths" collided with the moronic football chant "Here we go! Here we go! Here we go!", laced with a barrage of offensive swear-words. Throughout the fracas, Morrissey had remained impressively calm and almost statesmanlike. Upon returning, he declared imperiously: "Remember the world is watching you, Dundee. Do you *really* care?" Before Dundee could answer, the chimes of 'This Charming Man' echoed round the hall and Morrissey ran through the song, mischievously altering the lyrics to "This man says it's gruesome that someone so *ugly* should care", as an oblique comment on the unruly pack. Remarkably, the disruptions had no effect on the quality of the playing, which was executed with metronome precision. Morrissey's continued bid to impose 'Hand In Glove' on the public's consciousness as revenge for not buying the single was evinced at the end of 'Pretty Girls Make Graves', where he added the lyrics, "the sun shines out of our behinds". Sound readings of 'Still Ill' and 'This Night Has Opened My Eyes' prefaced the startling six-minute wonder: 'Barbarism Begins At Home'. An extraordinary echo effect transformed Morrissey's voice into that of a deranged coyote. Here at last was the mature vindication for those strange dog yelps that Ivor Perry and Gary Farrell had laughed about after listening to Morrissey's cassette recording back in 1981.

Rourke's funk patterns seemed to quieten the audience, which had at last settled into a solid appreciative mass. After the poignant 'Back To The Old House', Morrissey concluded the set with a gargling version of 'What Difference Does It Make?' The exuberant spectators vociferously demanded an encore and The Smiths obliged with three "oldies": 'Reel Around The Fountain', 'You've Got Everything Now' and 'Handsome Devil'. It was a case of another night, another gig, another college amid an atmosphere that was fraught with unpredictability. Students, townies, beer monsters, flower-waving aficionados, lovers and detractors each contributed to a series of shows that captured The Smiths at a pivotal and arresting moment in their career. Despite the many disturbances, the group seemed resilient to disorder and, if anything, the occasional tensions added an engaging drama to their performances.

There was additional tension backstage as, earlier that day, Cowie had been locked in a serious discussion with Piering and Travis. The tour manager's demeanour had visibly darkened upon learning that his rival Piering had been made "official representative". Despite his troubled relationship with The Smiths, Cowie had half-convinced himself that he might yet aspire to managerial godhead. If The Smiths trusted no-one in power, then perhaps a humble road manager might organize their affairs with professional assistance from lawyers and accountants. It was a fatuous dream, which Cowie unintentionally pinpricked by presenting proposals for a European tour, backed by further discussion of the controversial profit-sharing agreement. Although Cowie believed that Piering attempted to scupper the European campaign, it was The Smiths' own ambivalent attitude towards the Continent that prompted indecision and eventual cancellation. The thorny question of crew bonuses also dragged on and, although Cowie assumed he had firm assurances from Morrissey, Piering was repeatedly called in to quell such discussions. "I diverted it so that we could deal with it in a logical manner," the caretaker recalled.

"They didn't see any reason at all why they should have bonuses. It was my job to diplomatically mediate. The crew worked hard. Don't get me wrong. Phil, and everybody else, busted their balls to get it right. They were under-equipped, underpaid, and were all doing it on the come, with the anticipation of getting better things ahead, if they were successful. The tour was organized on virtually a loss-making basis, then the big grosses came in and they sold out every show. But, frankly, the bottom line hadn't been counted. Towards the end, Phil had delusions of grandeur. He'd worked so hard at doing a mediocre job that he felt he deserved some extra reward. I felt he was lucky to have survived as long as he did."

After leaving Scotland, The Smiths played major gigs at city halls in Newcastle-Upon-Tyne and Liverpool. A minor road accident involving the group caused Morrissey sufficient concern to take Cowie aside and express a lack of confidence. There were further problems two days later at Coventry Polytechnic, where the normally reasonable Cowie was so appalled by the students' treatment that he had to be restrained by the entertainments committee from attacking the social secretary. At least he had succeeded in re-establishing good relations within the crew by appointing PA mainman Oz McCormick as first lieutenant. McCormick had previously taught the coltish Grant Showbiz a lot about sound during their time working with The Fall. The rapport Oz enjoyed as crew boss did much to improve morale as the UK tour reached its final phase.

10

Do They Know It's Christmas?

SINCE THE BEGINNING OF 1984, Morrissey had resided in fashionable Kensington, surrounded by such neighbours as actor Robert Powell and newscaster Alastair Burnett. Marr had also made the move and for several months lived in a flat in Earls Court. Despite a busy schedule and recording commitments, the London-based singer had found time to woo one of his former idols from semi-retirement.

Sandie Shaw was initially sceptical of Morrissey's enthusiasm and had responded coolly when he sent her a sycophantic letter and Smiths tape the previous August. It was only after the personal intervention of Geoff Travis that she reluctantly agreed to meet the Mancunian. Even then, there was a moment of further doubt following *The Sun*'s sensationalist attack on 'Reel Around The Fountain'. Shaw's self-admitted prejudice against "perverts" and paedophiles was so strong that she even objected to a composer writing explicit lyrics about child molestation. Fortunately, a recitation of Morrissey's lyrics from Travis reassured her that there was nothing remotely pornographic about the work. When the two pop icons finally met at Shaw's house, a budding friendship developed. Sandie cheekily described him as "more Quentin Crisp than Elvis Presley", while he sat transfixed at the sight of her late morning pyjamas.

Although flattered by Morrissey's devoted attention, Shaw was still sceptical of his music and motives. Having already partaken in BEF's pompous *Music Of Quality And Distinction, Vol I* with a weak, ironic version of Cilla Black's chart-topping 'Anyone Who Had A Heart', she seemed understandably resistant to the patronage of other fresh-faced young men. It was only after a second meeting that she softened and agreed to record some of her admirer's compositions. "Well at least it's going to be a giggle," she concluded with carefree Shavian wit. Morrissey anticipated the artistic union by penning an effusive and well-written reappraisal of her career in *Sounds*. Not long after, Shaw joined The Smiths at Matrix Studios for her latest comeback. Originally, 'I Don't Owe You Anything' had been proposed as the A-side until Morrissey decided to rewrite the wrongs of history by vicariously transforming 'Hand In Glove' into a hit. Shaw was on the brink of her first Top 30 entry in 15 years.

During the same period, Marr also undertook some extra-curricular activities and appeared on Quando Quango's 'Atom Rock'/'Triangle'. The decision puzzled commentators such as Mick Middles, who argued that Quando Quango's disco electro-funk "was totally alien to Marr". In fact, the opposite was true. Although Marr was popularly known as the "king of the indie guitarists", he had spent over a year experimenting with funk during the Rourke/Wolstencroft period and had a sizeable collection of dance records. The tendency to take Johnny at face value and assume that his present musical role defined his entire history was one of the pressures that would later hasten his departure from The Smiths. In 1984, there were no such frustrations, and Marr was content, indeed, proud of his public role as Smiths' lead guitarist. The Quando Quango project enabled him to play something different yet familiar, and anticipated other guest appearances with such artistes as Billy Bragg, Everything But The Girl, Kirsty MacColl, The Impossible Dreamers, Talking Heads and Bryan Ferry.

On 12 March, Shaw made a surprise appearance singing 'Hand In Glove' at the close of The Smiths' Hammersmith Palais gig. Nerves almost got the better of her when she disappeared moments before her scheduled emergence. Fortunately, the "live" experience proved worth the ordeal, and in the early hours of the following morning, she told Morrissey that she felt absolutely exhilarated. When 'Hand In Glove' climbed into the Top 30 the following month, Morrissey felt the pride of a composer whose neglected early work had finally reached the masses.

Prior to the Palais performance, Morrissey had spent the afternoon in conversation with a journalist from *Rolling Stone*. The article promised to be quite penetrating as Morrissey spoke intelligently about his role in the pop business, his musical and literary influences, and the deliberately gender-less point of view expressed in his lyrics. Warming to the subject of British politics, Morrissey lashed out at Margaret Thatcher, ending his tirade with the warning: "She's only one person and she can be destroyed. I just pray there is a Sirhan Sirhan somewhere. It's the only remedy for this country at the moment." His words would have an eerily resonant ring later in the year.

When the *Rolling Stone* piece was run on 7 June, the emphasis was less on Morrissey's political consciousness than his sexuality. In an extraordinary opening paragraph, reporter James Henke revealed: "He goes by a single name, Morrissey. He calls himself 'a prophet for the fourth gender', admits he's gay, but adds he's also celibate." This appallingly scurrilous, unfounded and highly irresponsible inference of homosexuality irked Morrissey, who had always promoted an a-sexual persona. It was inconceivable that his viewpoint could have been misinterpreted so perversely. The quoted material, printed later in the article, emphasized that Morrissey, far from admitting he was 'queer', was merely challenging the rigidity of sexual stereotyping. The outrageous, damning and gratuitous gay labelling prompted a stern rebuke from the celibate star. "I just think it's so untrue and so unfair," he stressed indignantly. "Obviously any kind of a tag, I'll dodge. I don't want to be shoved into a box and put into a category. That person said I was gay and he never asked me; he never approached the subject... I think it was just wishful thinking on his part. Ultimately, people will see what they want to see in the whole aspect of what I do and my motivations. I'm not embarrassed about the word "gay", but it's not in the *least* bit relevant. I'm beyond that, frankly." Fortunately, his followers were already aware of the nature of Morrissey's epicene persona and the strength of its appeal.

The singer's image combined aspects of male and female sexuality which appealed to both genders in a way that was neither macho nor unctuously effete. When Oscar Wilde had first visited America, Harvard students wore large lilies in their buttonholes and each male carried a sunflower as he limped facetiously along. Morrissey's audience also carried flowers, wore National Health spectacles, brandished rockabilly quiffs and imitated their idol's blowzy dress. Yet, this was a celebration of their empathy and admiration for the man, rather than a caustic caricature. It was Morrissey's achievement to transform prosaic aspects of his past into a potentially potent sexuality. The contrast between the riveting stage performer and the shy character locked away in a bedroom still seems frighteningly extreme. Morrissey once claimed that his "real" character only emerged in live performance. There, the maudlin misanthrope, who believed a nation would turn its back and gag at his nakedness, became a narcissist teasing at his clothes like a deranged stripper. In the later solo years, the exhibitionist in his character, starved of live performance, would turn inward and feed on its own image in the photographer's studio. In 1984, however, the image was animate and, thanks to The Smiths' gruelling itinerary, eminently available for public inspection or worship.

The final month of the UK Spring tour went noticeably smoothly and morale within The Smiths' camp was exemplary. A backstage souvenir video of those dates captures the camaraderie that unified the group at a crucial time. In spite of encroaching business problems, The Smiths never lost their sense of humour on the road. The video images tell their own story: Rourke, the affable humorist, ever ready with a comic routine for the camera; Morrissey, smiling broadly and betraying the air of a man who has found his perfect place; Marr, eagerly warming-up and even showing his inquisitive writing partner a simple chord sequence; Joyce, hovering in the background, grinning in satisfaction, and joining in the fun. The real strength of The Smiths emerged when they were together, role-playing the myth of four youthful Mancunian lads against the world. Morrissey always saw the group as a gang, true to themselves and wary of outside influences. It was partly for this reason that he seldom became close to Johnny's friends or creative colleagues. Within The Smiths' family, however, the characters betrayed a jovial spirit that belied their often serious media image. "We had our own sense of humour, which people don't realize," Marr recalled. "Morrissey used to have a good laugh with us. We were a really funny group - very funny and very witty. The two of us shared a unique sense of humour with clever word-play. It wasn't until the last year that it got really serious."

The road crew reflected The Smiths' good humour and also inherited a touch of their minor dramatics. What arguments there were seemed so petty that they bordered on the comic. The latest melodrama was provided by Cowie and Cunliffe, whose Laurel and Hardy rivalry provoked a long and heated argument over the hire of some monitors for an appearance on *The Tube*. Farcical recriminations abounded. "The band, owing to Grant's blunder, is set to have the largest single loss of the tour," Cowie crowed, adding that his subsequent "investigations" revealed "patterns of deceit". Showbiz was predictably unrepentant about squandering £300 and merely dubbed Cowie "the Raymond Chandler of Rock".

Back in London, The Smiths' tour accounts were prepared for the closing tax year and Cowie presented Piering with his grand plan for a European tour and merchandising deal. Mid-way through their meeting, he was alarmed to discover that Piering had been recording their conversation. When he pointed this out, the caretaker manager claimed he had not noticed. Today, Piering admits, "I might have been naughty enough to do that. At that stage, I could have been in the frame of mind that thought, 'People won't believe this unless they hear it'... I was fairly cavalier about dealing with Phil."

While Cowie's merchandising suggestions were curiously dismissed, the European dates proposed by ATB were accepted. On 19 April, The Smiths flew to Brussels, then onward to Amsterdam, where they played at a party for *Vinyl* magazine, with Nick Cave as support. The following day, they appeared at the Bree Festival in Belgium, supporting The Bollock Brothers. After days of frustration and lousy food, this proved an indignation too great to bear. The next afternoon, the bamboozled foursome found themselves in Zurich, where Ollie May's brother, Marcus, was promoting a gig at the Rote Fabrik. Although the group's spirits momentarily improved, Grant was concerned about Morrissey and Marr's vegetarian diet, which had been reduced to chips and chocolate. Johnny already looked wasted, his thinness accentuated by the nervous habit of throwing up before going onstage.

On 25 April, the group was scheduled to fly back home for the afternoon for a *Top Of The Pops* appearance. As they boarded their plane, Morrissey announced: "We're not going back". Later that day, they joined Sandie Shaw, whose version of 'Hand In Glove' had reached the Top 30. During the *Top Of The Pops* recording, she made a pleasing spectacle of herself by rolling around the floor in parodic imitation of Morrissey. The other Smiths, grinning broadly, mimicked her own Sixties gimmick by playing in their bare feet. It was good to be back home. Morrissey and Shaw remained in contact and she playfully composed her own tribute to the celibate vegetarian: 'Steven (You Don't Eat Meat)'. He reciprocated by later presenting her with the plaintive 'Please Help The Cause Of Loneliness'.

After taking his leave of Shaw, Morrissey returned to the sanctuary of his mother's house in Manchester. The scheduled gigs in Vienna, Munich, Frankfurt, Cologne and Bremen were now history, although Rough Trade made vain attempts to persuade their elusive star to change his mind. Piering had the onerous task of tracking down Morrissey but, in the event, failed to bypass his pugnaciously protective mother. The "official representative" was summarily informed that her son was his bread and butter and he'd better start treating him with greater consideration in the future. As Piering wearily explained: "When The Smiths had unruly audiences, or people stormed the stage or threw something, he'd report all this back to his mother and look for sympathy."

Fathoming the logic behind the cancellation of a Smiths European tour was never easy but, on this occasion, tiredness and unsuitable food played a key part. "They just found it boring and stupid," Piering observed. "It really boiled down to the fact that they couldn't find anything decent to eat. They didn't care about going out and seeing Paris. Hotel room service was important and if they couldn't get egg and chips 24 hours-a-day, it was a serious business." The Smiths' initially bad experiences of visiting Europe fuelled their xenophobia, causing doubts within Rough Trade about the prospect of a future American tour. Other markets, such as Australia and Japan, were completely ignored, even though the group would have been treated like princes by the fastidious promoters.

As a compromise, The Smiths agreed to return to Europe for two important televised dates, performing in front of a seated audience at Hamburg's Markthalle for *Rockpalast* and later appearing at Paris' El Dorado Theatre, where part of their show was broadcast on *Les Enfants Du Rock*. Towards the end of May, The Smiths' fourth single was issued. Given Sandie Shaw's recent success with a Morrissey/Marr composition, it was appropriate that they should follow her into the charts with 'Heaven Knows I'm Miserable Now', a song whose title was adapted from her Sixties single, 'Heaven Knows I'm Missing Him Now'. As with 'Hand In Glove', Morrissey seemed determined to rewrite history by breathing new life into a once-failed title. What began as a Shaw ballad of discontent inspired Morrissey to noticeably greater depths. In his composition, world weariness becomes endemic and the almost wistful melancholia is brilliantly complemented by Marr's Peter Green-like guitar work. More than any other song in The Smiths' canon, 'Heaven Knows I'm Miserable Now' launched Morrissey into the public's consciousness as the great malcontent of pop.

Morrissey's mercurial personality and ever-shifting demands were already eroding his once-promising working relationship with John Porter. During the sessions for the first album, Morrissey was very appreciative of his producer's solicitude and, on several occasions, sent cards and thank you notes. Thereafter, their interaction decreased in ratio to Porter's developing friendship with Marr. It was the Troy Tate syndrome all over again. Morrissey subsequently complained to Rough Trade that Porter was not paying enough attention to his vocals, which was a peculiar objection in light of the prevailing working methods. Marr and Porter often completed tracks overnight, delivered a cassette to Morrissey's house the following morning, and awaited his arrival to complete the vocal parts. Morrissey relied on a trusty notebook, which contained stores of phrases and odd lines, and invariably conjured up some startling lyrics to complement Marr's melodies.

"I don't think he'd labour over them," Porter remarked, "they would come together in a few hours." The recordings were completed extraordinarily speedily, not because of any lack of diligence on Porter's part, but due to Morrissey's apparent aversion to studio work. "I always wanted him to sing more," Porter countered. "I'd say 'One more take, Morrissey', and he'd say, 'No, that's it!' He'd do three takes and on a couple of occasions, it was just one. He didn't particularly like being in the studio. Unlike Johnny, I could never get Morrissey interested in the process of making records."

The bizarre circumstances surrounding the recording of 'Heaven Knows I'm Miserable Now' displayed Morrissey at his most capricious. After completing the first verse, he insisted upon travelling to Manchester to sing the remainder of the song. Porter duly booked a studio, packed the tapes and travelled north. After recording another verse, Morrissey announced that he was popping out to the chip shop. When 45 minutes passed, the concerned Porter organized a search party, but their efforts proved to no avail. Eventually, he telephoned Morrissey's mother only to be told: "He was here an hour ago, but he's gone back to London." The indignant producer cancelled the session, apologized to everybody, and returned to the capital in search of his elusive and frustratingly unpredictable, quarry. Porter was not especially confident about his future working relationship with Morrissey. Earlier, he had felt a little uneasy after noticing the singer judiciously jotting down house engineer Stephen Street's telephone number. The producer suddenly caught himself thinking: "This is how it's going to end." His gut feelings were to prove largely correct.

The Top 10 success of 'Heaven Knows I'm Miserable Now' was qualified by a minor news story that subsequently festered into a potential scandal. One evening in Manchester, a relative of the murdered John Kilbride happened to hear the flip-side of 'Heaven Knows I'm Miserable Now'. He was outraged by the song's provocative theme. 'Suffer Little Children' had escaped controversy as an album track, but the chance hearing of a B-side on a pub juke-box rapidly stirred up old grievances. *The Manchester Evening News* sided with the aggrieved relative and transformed his complaint into a lead story. As a result, the Boots and Woolworths chains withdrew the offending single from sale, and also banned The Smiths' début album.

The subsequent presence of Lesley Ann Downey's mother, Ann West, in the saga proved equally intimidating. By far the most vigorous and vociferous media campaigner among the victims' families, she had already seen off another "controversial" single - the unreleased Moors Murderers' 'Free Myra Hindley'. On that occasion, one of the outrage-seeking contributors was Chrissie Hynde, and West assumed that Morrissey's work was similarly insensitive. Matters were not helped by the presence of the bouffant-haired Viv Nicholson on the sleeve, as the press wrongly assumed that she was Myra Hindley.

The sudden, widespread banning of Smiths product caused severe ructions at Rough Trade, the more so because Morrissey was completely innocent of any sensationalist motives. Scott Piering, who had never heard of the Moors murderers, was stunned by the severity of the press backlash and wasted no time in preparing a heartfelt PR release, which proclaimed: "The Smiths stand behind 100 per cent of the lyrics to all of their songs and 'Suffer Little Children' is no exception. The song was written out of a profound emotion by Morrissey, a Mancunian who feels that the particularly horrendous crime it describes must be borne by the conscience of Manchester and that it must never happen again. It was written out of deep respect for the victims and their kin and The Smiths felt it was an important enough song to put on their last single, even though it had already been released on their last LP. In a word, it is a memorial to the children and all like them who have suffered such a fate. The Smiths are acknowledged as writing with sensitivity, depth and intelligence and the suggestion that they are cashing in on a tragedy at the expense of causing grief to the relatives of its victims is absolutely untrue."

In the meantime, Piering had contacted the Moors matriarch Ann West. Over the next few days, an extraordinary series of telephone conversations took place in which West detailed her years of suffering and even succeeded in reducing Piering to tears. After receiving various Smiths records, photographs, and even a personal letter from Morrissey, West was assured the The Smiths' intentions were honourable. "Mrs West sent us a letter," Piering explained, "saying that she believed Morrissey was a good boy and was serious about the song and she thought it was very touching. She was strongly on our side and really helped us."

The flames of controversy were virtually doused when West contacted the Kilbride family and spoke in favour of the beleaguered Smiths. Eventually, the relative who had first heard the song conceded that it was not offensive, but convinced Morrissey/Marr to donate some of the royalties to the NSPCC as a gesture of good faith. The only positive aspect of the controversy for Morrissey was that he met and befriended another character from his mythological past. He continued to correspond with Ann West, invited her and her husband to see the group, and even included their names on the credits to the next Smiths album.

The belated Moors' controversy coincided with The Smiths' latest chart entry, 'William, It Was Really Nothing'. Slight, yet irresistibly winsome, the single pinpricked old-fashioned, provincial values, with its jaundiced portrayal of a rain-swept town, whose population includes a downtrodden loser, remorselessly hen-pecked into surrendering his bachelorhood. The scene came straight out of Keith Waterhouse's *Billy Liar*, in which the eponymous William Fisher idly daydreams of leaving his humdrum town of Saturday afternoon "fat women" and marriage-minded girlfriends, in favour of either a fantasy life in Ambrosia or the gloriously fearful prospect of a move to London. The theme was close to Morrissey's heart, evoking memories of not so distant times when he scoured the streets of Manchester, filled with seemingly unrealizable dreams of achieving fame as a writer or pop star. In many respects, Morrissey was the William who escaped from the stifling northern town, only to discover that its insidious memories had been imprinted on his consciousness to such a degree that they had become the very fountainhead of his art, forcing him to re-chronicle past failures, yearnings and doomed imaginings like an obsessive necrologian.

The Smiths' busy recording schedule had not impeded their arduous performing commitments. Following the European cancellations, they played a handful of dates in Ireland and recruited a new tour manager, Stuart James. A former producer at Manchester's Piccadilly Radio, James had worked with Morrissey's favourite Ludus, and several other New Hormones acts. Highly respected as a sound engineer, he had branched out into tour management and was brought in by All Trade Booking's Mike Hinck as a replacement for the recently-departed Phil Cowie. Unfortunately, James' first date with The Smiths was abroad, an experience guaranteed to tax the endurance of any tour manager. An horrific plane journey prompted several Hail Marys and so unnerved Morrissey that he burst into tears. Luckily, this was a one-off date at a festival in Finland, and any further problems were rendered redundant when the show was rained-off after 35 minutes. During the first-class train-ride across country, James was struck by the xenophobic insularity of The Smiths, who expressed no interest in the Scandinavian scenery. Their attitude and priorities were summed up in the casual enquiry: "What chart position are we?" As James noted: "All the rest passed them by - the country they were in was irrelevant."

One week after the Finnish date, the group played at the Greater London Council's "Jobs For A Change" free festival. While Joyce and Rourke were distributing flowers to their followers back at the hotel, some over-excited fans dented a car owned by one of the catering staff at the forthcoming Glastonbury CND Festival. Undeterred by the caterer's indignation, the group took off for a short Scottish tour, then travelled down to Blackpool, where Morrissey met another of his Sixties heroines, Viv Nicholson. The tabloid press turned out in force to witness this strange meeting between a forgotten former football pools winner and her eccentric pop star admirer. Before the paparazzi closed in, Morrissey and Nicholson managed to enjoy a quiet walk along the Blackpool prom, while exchanging views on the merits and pitfalls of fatal fame.

Back at the Opera House, less cerebral activities were taking place as arrangements were made to celebrate Stuart James' birthday. As a special surprise, the crew had hired a kissogram girl who cornered the urbane tour manager in the dressing-room and displayed her breasts, much to the uproarious appreciation of the assembled gathering. An eventful evening concluded with several over-enthusiastic spectators plunging through the stage barriers and forming an untidy heap at the bottom of the orchestra pit. After these mid-week celebrations, the group and crew were in surprisingly good spirits for a much-publicized Saturday appearance at the Glastonbury Festival.

Morrissey was no great lover of festivals, but his increasingly frequent political outbursts in the music press ensured that The Smiths were head-hunted by worthy, left-wing organizations. Morrissey felt ambivalent about offering public support to specific causes but, having advocated the use of violence by CND campaigners, it seemed appropriate to attend the festival at Glastonbury. Unfortunately, The Smiths' performance was truncated by the late arrival of Amazulu and the backstage atmosphere was fraught. The aforementioned aggrieved caterer was standing outside the group's dressing-room haranguing James about car insurance, while her boyfriend from Glastonbury security looked on frostily. Meanwhile, the flamboyant Sire supremo Seymour Stein, dressed immaculately in all white, stood patiently awaiting an audience with Morrissey, who was feigning unavailability.

Stein had great hopes for a projected winter tour of America, but his intentions were dashed when Morrissey/Marr announced that the visit was cancelled. The decision was sound, rather than petulant, for Marr needed time to develop his newly-acquired production skills. After a mini-tour of Wales, supported by The Woodentops, The Smiths travelled to Liverpool's Amazon Studios, where they laid down tracks for their next LP, *Meat Is Murder*. In the meantime, Rough Trade rush-released an "interim album" bringing together the John Peel and David Jensen sessions, plus selected rare flip-sides. According to Morrissey, the album was prompted by a number of fans' letters and he felt the sessions and rarities deserved to be heard. *Hatful Of Hollow* proved an excellent compilation and superb value for money. Clocking in at just under an hour and retailing at mid-price, the album not only appealed to the hard-core fan but opened The Smiths' catalogue to casual, chance purchasers. There was nothing cheap or shoddy about the packaging, which compared favourably to their full-priced début album. This time around, the group was allowed a gatefold sleeve and a cardboard, rather than paper, insert sheet for their lyrics. Hearing the sessions provided a reminder of how excellent The Smiths were, even before they entered a London recording studio. What impressed most was the sheer number of quality songs they already had to their credit. Like an Eighties version of the prolific Lennon/McCartney, Morrissey/Marr instinctively soldered the great tradition of pop's golden age to a new vocabulary and questing spirit that created shivers of excitement at the sheer prospect of what might follow. For the collectors and old enthusiasts, there was the chance to possess a vinyl version of the previously unreleased title, 'This Night Has Opened My Eyes'. The song remains a remarkable track, both for its contemplative intensity and arresting subject matter. Against a plangent, melodic Marr backdrop, Morrissey narrates another understated urban drama, this time concerning the abandonment of a baby, and the emotional consequences for the pained mother. For the tragedians, the lyrics proved open enough to suggest the possibility of abortion, or even infanticide ("In the river, the colour of lead/emerse [sic] the baby's head").

The remaining radio sessions enabled listeners to appreciate the raw zest of The Smiths, captured in all their glorious technical naïvety, yet displaying a precocious awareness of their self-worth. The additional single cuts were a veritable treasure trove. The tendency of The Smiths to bury some of their most attractive work on 12-inch flip-sides indicated the enormity of their artistic wealth. The resurrected 'Girl Afraid' emerged as one of the highlights of the set. Marr's memorable opening riff, originally conceived as a piano part, was the perfect introduction to Morrissey's dialogue of mutual insecurity and disillusionment. Despite his feminist leanings, Morrissey was always willing to explore the dramatic possibilities offered by displaying women as money-grabbing or voracious, a perspective previously offered on 'William, It Was Really Nothing' and 'Pretty Girls Make Graves'.

Even more significant was 'How Soon Is Now?', perhaps the ultimate fusion of Marr's classical rock traditionalism and Morrissey's maudlin meanderings into the heart of darkness. In common with 'Still Ill' and 'These Things Take Time', the song documents a frighteningly resigned awareness of time slipping inexorably away. The tension, so brilliantly underpinned by Marr's brooding, amplifier-vibrating, open-tuning, is accentuated by Morrissey's sudden mood swings from bellicose self-assertiveness ("You shut your mouth/how can you say/I go about things the wrong way") towards moments of self-pitying despair ("see I've already waited too long/and all my hope is gone"). In order to add atmosphere to the recording, The Smiths bathed the studio in red light and responded to the dim, eerie glow with one of their most intense performances. As Marr concluded: "Musically, it was a perfect cross between a sweaty, swamp backing track and an intense, wired shock every few bars. I knew it was a good one."

Hatful Of Hollow concluded with the expressive 'Please Please Please Let Me Get What I Want', a potent distillation of Morrissey's yearning loneliness and another troubled acknowledgement of passing time. Remarkably, both 'Please Please Please Let Me Get What I Want' and 'How Soon Is Now?' had been composed from scratch and completed within the space of a few days. It was that session, in particular, which convinced Porter of Marr's abilities as an all-round musician and potential producer. "The main thing about The Smiths for me is that I really enjoyed working with Johnny," Porter acknowledged. "When we'd hire a studio I'd say, 'What do you feel like playing today? Have you got a riff? What's a good key?' About 90 per cent of it was made up in the studio. He'd come in with two riffs and I'd weld them together and say, 'Let's make that a chorus'. He was so quick on the uptake. I've worked with lots of musicians, but there's none that picked things up like him. He was so aware of what he wanted. Of all the people I worked with, he was the quickest learner. It was fantastic."

While *Hatful Of Hollow* began its ascent to the UK Top 5, Morrissey was in the press commenting on recent terrorist events. On 12 October, an IRA bomb had been planted in the Grand Hotel, Brighton, during the annual Conservative Party Conference. The explosion killed three people and 30 others were badly injured, maimed or crippled. Despite their failure to decimate the Tory Party, the IRA hailed the Brighton bombing as a major propaganda victory and despatched a chilling warning to Margaret Thatcher and her Cabinet: "Today, we were unlucky but, remember, we have only to be lucky once." Having already advocated the assassination of the Prime Minister earlier in the year, Morrissey saw no reason to back pedal and, disregarding the fact that several non-politicians had suffered horrendous injuries, spoke out strongly in favour of the Bold Boys' bombing. "The sorrow of the Brighton bombing is that Thatcher escaped unscathed," he reiterated. "The sorrow is that she's still alive. But I feel relatively happy about it. I think that, for once, the IRA were accurate in selecting their targets." This was to prove Morrissey's most provocative outburst to date... and more would soon follow.

Morrissey's controversial comments on the IRA aptly coincided with The Smiths' first major Irish tour to date. Tour manager Stuart James remembers a degree of excited apprehension in the wake of the Brighton bombing. "They'd offended a lot of people and when they went to Ireland they were worried," he recalls. Why there should have been more concern about danger in Eire rather than in England made no sense, although the visit to the North at the end of the tour gave some food for paranoia. If they were seeking ill omens, the journey to Eire provided augurs in abundance.

The group usually travelled in a notoriously unreliable but attractive white Mercedes but, on the eve of their departure, the vehicle chose to breathe its last. When Stuart James arrived at their doors in a hired minibus, there were immediate niggles about the loss of their one concession to low-budget flash. After arriving at the Holyhead ferry, the crew, and several members of the group, settled in the bar, but within 15 minutes of leaving the dock, chaos ensued. A visitor could be forgiven for assuming he had stumbled aboard the *Marie Celeste* as rows of Guinness glasses lay untouched on bar tables. Seasickness was rampant.

The Smiths' roadie Phil Powell had spewed up before reaching the door, while the green-gilled sound engineer, Diane Barton, spent most of the journey on deck struggling to settle her stomach. Marr, already weakened by heavy flu, felt worst of all, and his marble-coloured face told its own story. Incredibly, Morrissey was of the select few who was not sick on the crossing, and displayed his sea legs with casual aplomb. The state of Marr was causing so much concern that, against James' advice, a phone call was placed from the boat requesting an ambulance to be on hand when the party docked at Dun Laoghaire. The drama continued when Johnny was whisked off to Dublin's St Lawrence Hospital and dumped in the casualty department. While awaiting treatment, Marr witnessed some sobering sights. Blood-stained accident victims filtered through on stretchers, while aggrieved families battled for attention or sympathy. The spectacle convinced Johnny that he was "feeling a bit better", so he returned to the hotel, where the subject of Smiths security was under discussion.

Promoter Denis Desmond, who organized their two nights at Dublin's SFX, recommended his own security officer James Connolly as the perfect personal escort. It was amusingly appropriate that Morrissey should find himself protected by a man named after one of Ireland's most famous rebels. The SFX performances were well-received, with Peter Morrissey making a surprise appearance backstage. It was a strange experience for Steven, who found himself unexpectedly entertaining his father on the occasion of his mother's 47th birthday.

Prior to the Dublin dates, The Smiths had journeyed southwards to Waterford, where they were booked to play the Savoy, a once-thriving cinema, turned bingo hall. Travelling behind them were fellow Mancunians James, whose self-sufficiency extended to transporting their own organically-grown food. By contrast, Morrissey and Marr were perpetually scouring menus for vegetarian delicacies, an unrewarding exercise in Waterford where the top hotels, such as the Grand and the Tower, prided themselves on their copious offerings of superbly-cooked red and white meats.

One amusing feature of The Smiths' Irish concerts was the bemused reaction to the increasingly eccentric riders contained in their contracts. Earlier in the year, Morrissey had been asking for "flowers to the approximate value of £50 sterling, including gladioli; no roses or flowers with thorns." Soon, that demand was replaced by the more pressing and peculiar request for "a live tree with a minimum height of three foot and a maximum height of five foot." Stuart James soon took to carrying a saw in his briefcase and became adept at pruning branches. "Not all the promoters took the tree seriously," he recalls, "but they soon learned that it *had* to be taken seriously."

The organization responsible for bringing The Smiths to Waterford was Music Moves, a non-profit co-operative that had previously worked successfully with Denis Desmond's MCD Promotions. They guaranteed The Smiths £5,000 and arranged the gig on a break even/small loss basis. They even provided a second support group, The Village, whose lead singer, Paddy Jacobs, was on the co-operative executive. He recalls having to deal with Morrissey's unusual contract request for "a young sapling". "He wanted to flog himself onstage with it," Jacobs reminisces. "A young sapling! Being a co-operative, we didn't want to debase the public park, so we got the local florist to donate one." A remarkable concert ended with 660 musically-sated supporters spilling from the Savoy down to the quay, having left behind several mangled, but insured, radiators which had served as makeshift platforms throughout the evening.

From Waterford, then Dublin, The Smiths traversed through Limerick, Galway, Cork and Donegal. In Letterkenny, a doctor was called to examine Morrissey, but his mystery illness rapidly passed. "Johnny had been pretty ill and it seemed like Morrissey came out in sympathy," Stuart decided, "but maybe that's just cynicism!" Another feature of their final Eire gig was a sudden switch of hotel, which Stuart assumed was at the suggestion of security officer Jim Connolly. "Whether it was paranoia or not, we started changing hotels a lot," Stuart explained. "It became quite popular after that! We'd book in and check out five minutes later, much to my chagrin." At times, it was difficult to avoid the suspicion that The Smiths enjoyed causing their own little dramas for self-amusement.

The Irish adventure ended with gigs in Coleraine and Belfast and, despite the early transportation problems and sickness, the tour had gone much more smoothly than expected. All Trade Booking had hoped to re-open the European campaign during December and persuaded The Smiths to play

Paris. Their attitude, however, was less than enthusiastic. "It didn't really matter what happened in other countries," James noted, "the *NME* didn't come along. The group were pressurized heavily to move out of the British market and start expanding, but they didn't relish travelling and Morrissey wasn't a great flyer." Although the Paris performance proved surprisingly enjoyable, a visit to Copenhagen was blown out at the eleventh hour. All Trade Booking, by now accustomed to such sudden changes of heart, took the news stoically. Nobody could deny that The Smiths deserved a long Christmas break.

As the end of 1984 approached, public attention was focused on the appalling famine in Ethiopia. Over 3,000 people a day were dying of starvation and television pictures, movingly narrated by the BBC's Michael Buerk, captured the grotesque enormity of the catastrophe. Drought, coupled with the failure of a development programme in West and North East Africa, had caused the disaster, but the suffering was worsened by political inhumanity. Ethiopia was receiving a paltry $6 per head in overseas aid, while pro-Western areas, such as Somalia, were granted over three times that amount. The scale of the tragedy had a profound effect on public opinion, but it took the indignation of a nondescript pop star to transform that pity into hard cash.

The indomitable Bob Geldof implored, cajoled and herded a select group of English pop stars into a London recording studio where they rapidly completed the eleemosynary 'Do They Know It's Christmas?' The single went on to top the charts, selling a staggering three million in the UK along the way. Thanks to Geldof's foresight in gaining financial control of every aspect of the record's production, manufacture and distribution, famine relief received 96 pence of the £1.35 retail price. This sudden outbreak of pop star philanthropy even extended to the million-selling Wham! who donated a sizeable chunk of their own royalties to the appeal.

Morrissey was not impressed by pop's new-found high-mindedness and evidently disliked the catchy 'Do They Know It's Christmas?', which he dismissed curiously as "absolutely tuneless". Morrissey always felt uneasy about charity records, but his views on Band Aid provoked more bad feeling and wider comment than even the Brighton bombing whiplash. It was not Morrissey's political stance that caused offence, but rather the callously flippant tone of his remarks. "One can have a great concern for the people of Ethiopia," he observed, "but it's another thing to inflict daily torture on the people of England." For once, the Wildean tone was misplaced. The apparent insensitivity in placing the relief of famine, suffering, disease and death alongside his own petty gripes about a pop record displayed a woeful lack of perspective and humanity. As a result, he was destined to regurgitate his views in interview after interview. The best part of a decade on, Morrissey now articulates his criticisms no less forcibly, but less contumely. "The celebrity distracts from the message," he claims, "and I don't like that. I feel situations like Ethiopia could quite easily be solved and they're not for specific reasons, and I find concerts and benefit records quite pointless."

Back in the mid-Eighties, carefully measured tones were no longer in keeping with Morrissey's iconoclastic persona. In the space of a few months, he had refashioned his media image by revealing aspects of his character not in keeping with the shy, eccentric, horticultural, celibate caricature. Frequently portrayed as sensitive and wounded in his lyrics, Morrissey was now coming across as increasingly bitter and twisted, with an appetite for self-righteous retributive violence that seemed even more consuming than his raging loneliness. The fruits of his anger would be captured most forcibly on the new Smiths album.

11

Blood Thirsty Vegetarian

1984 HAD ELEVATED THE SMITHS to the premier spot amongst independent groups, an achievement underlined in various music press polls. While undisputed champions of the John Peel-listening student heartland, the group's impact in the pop mainstream was less easily gauged. Despite their talk of "classic pop", The Smiths' record sales and chart performances would never come near equalling those of their poll-winning predecessors, The Jam. Yet, The Smiths indisputably captured their time, albeit in spirit rather than record sales. Their combination of inspired musicianship and articulately oblique lyrics offset the frivolous approach of many of their poppish contemporaries and brought a new depth and dignity to a chart scene in a state of flux. Moreover, in Morrissey, The Smiths boasted a figure whose persona embodied the twin obsessions of the year: sex and politics.

For the children of the New Pop, 1984 was a period of intense competition, and the mixture of sex and politics determined status and dominated news space as perhaps never before. Morrissey's violent statements about Thatcher, Animal Rights and CND, backed by the continuing speculation concerning his celibacy and the sexual orientation described in his lyrics, should have made him pop's man of the year. Unfortunately, there were other hectoring and talented competitors with no less strong views and a string of hits that matched or excelled those of The Smiths in popularity.

Self-confessed homosexual Jimmy Somerville admitted indulging publicly in sexual practices which, 18 years before, would not only have destroyed his career but rendered him liable to a lengthy period of imprisonment under British law. His indiscretions did not prevent the rise of Bronski Beat, who enjoyed a succession of hits on the appropriately-named Forbidden Fruit label. At a more obviously commercial level, the gender-bending Boy George and his extravagantly effete media partner, Marilyn, provided a seemingly inexhaustible source of copy for tabloid gossip columnists. George unwittingly signed a Faustian pact with Fleet Street which would later prove his undoing but, back in 1984, he was still the press darling. Like everybody else that year, Culture Club had adopted a quasi-political stance with the protesting 'War Song', having previously topped the charts with the catch-all anthem, 'Karma Chameleon'. For a time, they were hailed as the leading lights of the New Pop.

The sexual/political mix was an irresistible pop attraction and The

Smiths had the perfect ingredients to prove themselves masters of the form. All too often, however, they were outmanoeuvred in the singles market by more canny rivals and never earned the chart-topping success or "all-time-classic" status that was bestowed upon other discs. The Smiths' devotion to the two-and-a-half minute single always threatened an anthem of the cultural longevity of 'My Generation' or '(I Can't Get No) Satisfaction', but left instead an understated succession of finely-crafted, memorable 45s. That capacity to capture the pop moment in chart terms as The Byrds had done with 'Mr Tambourine Man', Procol Harum with 'A Whiter Shade Of Pale' and The Sex Pistols with 'God Save The Queen', somehow evaded The Smiths during the early Eighties. With their vast knowledge of pop history, they seemed destined to fashion a single so immense in its power, originality and appeal that it would effortlessly elevate them to number one. Morrissey always insisted that The Smiths were never an 'albums' band but a singles group, yet they failed to demonstrate that point by transforming cult excellence into universally undisputed greatness. Consistent quality was rewarded with Top 20 hits, but the absolute number one that should have defined their moment, stamped their importance, and left an indelible mark on the pop charts of the Eighties somehow never happened. Instead, such honours went to another group, whose rise in 1984 paralleled that of The Smiths, despite their radically different approaches.

Frankie Goes To Hollywood, within the space of a single year, married sexual politicizing with media hype and completed the package with a staggering trilogy of chart-topping singles. More than any other group of the period, Frankie turned media manipulation into a fine art. The controversy provoked by the sexual playfulness of 'Relax', the anti-Reaganite sentiments of 'Two Tribes' and the irreverent video of 'The Power Of Love', ensured blanket rebukes from moral crusaders, politicians and the clergy. The attendant "shock" revelations concerning the sexuality of Holly Johnson and Paul Rutherford virtually guaranteed Frankie tabloid exposure of near-Beatles proportions. Although Johnson lacked the charisma or eloquence of Morrissey, Frankie ingeniously allied the product to the controversy, and ensured that each was potent enough to enhance their appeal. While The Smiths complained that limited radio airplay was affecting their chart fortunes, Frankie could provoke a complete ban on a song like 'Relax' and transform that handicap into a promotional plus that propelled them to number one.

Behind the Frankie image was the sharp marketing of their record label ZTT, with former *NME* journalist and Morrissey acolyte Paul Morley playing Andrew Oldham to Trevor Horn's Phil Spector. The slick promotion and epic production for Frankie was refreshingly original and delightfully daring. What made it all the more impressive was the quality of the recorded output. Their three chart-topping singles were masterful in their scope and audacity, and the rhythmic thrust, political punch and epical clout of 'Two Tribes' made it one of the most arresting and harrowing songs heard on daytime radio in years. Frankie's output ensured that they achieved one of The Smiths' ambitions by traversing that tricky route between pop and rock, thereby faring well in both the glossies and the inky weeklies, and scaling the peaks of the singles and albums charts. In a year when the *NME* poll results acclaimed The Smiths "best group", it was Frankie who dominated the best singles listing, with 'Relax' and 'Two Tribes' finishing at number one and three, respectively. The extent to which critical and commercial fortunes combined was emphasized by the fact that these acclaimed chart-toppers became two of the biggest-selling singles in British pop music history.

The Frankie flame burned with such intensity that the group foundered within a year. Sustaining the initial impact had proven impossible. Morrissey was largely unimpressed by the Frankie phenomenon and argued that "they've been peddled in much the same way as the groups in the Sixties were peddled". Given his affection for the Sixties, and his later correspondence with that archetypal pop svengali, Larry Parnes, the question of who controlled whom seemed largely irrelevant. The careers of such Morrissey icons as Billy Fury and Sandie Shaw were closer to the puppeteering of Frankie than the autonomy of The Smiths, but that had never affected his appreciation of their worth. Morrissey was correct in assuming that the steady progress of The Smiths would provide a more lasting impact than the frizzled Frankie, yet there was an engagingly Warholian charm to their gloriously brief reign and inherent obsolescence. One cannot help wondering how The Smiths would have fared on ZTT, a label whose innovative marketing and epic production contrasted so strongly with their minimalist ethos. Could ZTT have transformed Morrissey's controversy into commodity and Marr's insatiable hunger for technical knowledge into startlingly innovative production? Perhaps the individuality of The Smiths would have been lost in the search for a more realistic commercial level, but it is fascinating to consider what might have happened if The Smiths had enjoyed a massive number one in 1984, *à la* Frankie. For a group whose very life force was deemed to be the 7-inch single, it is sad to consider that The Smiths' best ever chart position was a lowly number 10.

The Frankie story emphasized the importance of a singular production, so it was not too surprising when Rough Trade exhumed The Smiths' catalogue in search of a less parochial, more substantial single. The obvious candidate was a track from *Hatful Of Hollow* that had previously appeared on the flip-side of a 12-inch single. The awesome 'How Soon Is Now?' displayed the power of The Smiths so effectively that it was amazing nobody had realized its potential earlier. John Porter had hoped the track might be issued as an A-side but claims there was initial resistance from Geoff Travis, who did not feel it represented The Smiths in the way he liked. However, Travis did concede that the song's traditional rock elements were perfect for the American market where the need for product was now paramount.

The Smiths' début album had barely reached the US Top 200, while such singles as 'Heaven Knows I'm Miserable Now' and 'William, It Was Really Nothing' were deemed unworthy of release. Promotions head, Scott Piering, also pushed hard for 'How Soon Is Now?' and was forced to present a case to Sire, backed by testimonials from influential disc jockeys. Seymour Stein was won over to the cause and proclaimed the song "the 'Stairway To Heaven' of the Eighties". Despite extensive airplay in Los Angeles and an unauthorized promotional video, culled from the 1984 UK tour, the single failed to sell in substantial quantities. "There was a real problem with the Warner Brothers' promotional department," Travis stressed. "I can't understand why 'How Soon Is Now?' wasn't a Top 10 single, though perhaps I'm being naïve. If it had broken them in the States, it would have made all the difference. I wasn't satisfied with the way Warners treated The Smiths. I don't think they recognized what they had. Having said that, there weren't many better places to go."

Back in the UK, the single stalled at number 24, a reflection of the song's prior availability on the mid-price *Hatful Of Hollow*, rather than an indication of its deficiencies as a chart contender. As Porter sadly attested: "They just threw it away." Notwithstanding its modest commercial success, 'How Soon Is Now?' became one of The Smiths' most famous tracks and its lasting appeal was emphasized by its reappearance as a sample on Soho's 1991 hit, 'Hippychick'.*

While 'How Soon Is Now?' was ascending the charts, Johnny Marr was at Virgin's Townhouse Studios, completing work on The Smiths' next single, 'Shakespeare's Sister'. He felt under immense pressure, not least because the future of The Smiths as a recording and performing unit was under severe threat. Less than two months before, Morrissey had assured the music press: "There's perfect harmony in the group". By January 1985, precisely the opposite was the case. Morrissey was aghast to learn that his bass player was addicted to heroin. He surely suspected Rourke of some drug abuse in the past, though his naïvety may have prevented him from grasping the truth. According to Marr, Morrissey suggested that Andy leave the group immediately and some valiant diplomacy was required before he would reconsider. Amazingly, the news was somehow shielded from the press, and even The Smiths' entourage and road crew were unaware of the drama in their midst. The worldly Grant Showbiz, who enjoyed recreational drugs, was also kept in the dark, and always assumed that Morrissey was completely undictatorial about other people's narcotic habits. "I didn't think he was puritanical," he pointed out. "He never expressed any disdain about anybody else taking drugs. I can remember sitting down with Morrissey and trying to explain to him what heroin felt like because I'd taken it about twice in my teenage years. He never imposed his viewpoint on anybody else, as far as I could see. It wasn't like Mark E Smith saying: 'Don't do *that!* Don't wear *that!*' We just went with the atmosphere of what was happening."

In early 1985, however, Morrissey had good reason to be sensitive about the implications of Rourke's habit on the reputation of the group. Towards the end of the previous year, he had taken up a lot of media space

* Morrissey/Marr received 25 per cent of Soho's royalties from the disc in settlement for the unauthorized sampling.

promoting the ethos of The Smiths as an extension of his own values. While Marr was, in many ways, the antithesis of Morrissey in terms of lifestyle, there was a certain aesthetic purity about The Smiths that the singer claimed could not be corrupted. In a revealing interview with *Jamming!*, he pinpointed a rigidity of outlook which suggested that neither he nor The Smiths would fall victim to the hedonistic high jinks associated with their great predecessors from the golden age of pop. "It's not tempting to break my own rules," he suggested. "Once you do that, it's very easy to lose sight of the reasons why you started in the first place. You can slip into the industry so easily. I could turn into an absolute social gadfly tomorrow and be seen everywhere with everybody. I could possibly handle it, but that wouldn't give me enough time to concentrate on the realities of writing. It's easy to get further and further away from the council estate, and you can forget how you felt for 24 years before it all happened. You can get quite bedazzled by the lights. Well, we never intend to do that."

Morrissey's public statements ensured that The Smiths were under even greater subliminal pressure to conform to the singer's ideal. Although Marr could risk stressing his Salford Perry Boy fashion influences, other matters were carefully deflected. Even Mike Joyce was surprised at the degree of eyebrow-raising that occurred among backstage visitors whenever he "skinned-up" after a gig. "We were terrified because we had an anti-drug philosophy," Marr confirmed. "All through that time what I wanted to talk about was clothes, football and smoking pot. I felt I had to keep that side away in a sense because it wasn't what the group was about." Marr and Rourke were also concerned not to embarrass their families, who were still adjusting to their siblings' new-found fame. "Their lives had been turned around as well," Johnny pointed out. "In mine and Andy's case, it was the first time the family had something to be proud of. Also, it's a really important point, we didn't want to screw it up for Morrissey. Genuinely, all of us would do anything for him. It wasn't just a professional thing, it was very personal."

Although Morrissey usually attempted to speak in general terms about the group, his own opinions inevitably focused attention on their conduct. His self-assertive honesty meant that few, if any, subjects were deemed taboo. When the discussion turned to heroin, he was both candid and cavalier in his interview comments. "I think people get into drugs simply because they want to," he countered. "I don't believe people who say, 'I'm trapped, I can't stop this'. It's a lot of bosh, really." Such words took on a particularly ironical light in view of Rourke's wayward behaviour. The bassist felt sufficiently despondent about his habit to accept a dismissal from The Smiths without protest. However, such a move would only have provoked press scrutiny and public attention, so a more pleasing solution was always welcomed. Once Morrissey was assured by Marr that Andy would remain straight while working with The Smiths, the crisis passed. As Johnny stresses, "Morrissey isn't judgemental. I can't give him enough credit for being a professional person. I know what it's like having to deal with people who turn up late because they have to score. It was better that he didn't get involved. I took care of Andy and that's the way our relationship worked. I was his best friend and he was my best friend, so that's what you do. I was more than willing to take it on. We thought we could beat it. I always felt, 'It's going to be over soon; it's just going to stop'." By the beginning of the next tour, Rourke's heroin habit was successfully curbed. It would be another year before the "Andy problem" once again reached danger point.

In February, the long-awaited new Smiths album *Meat Is Murder* was released and wasted no time in zooming to number one in the charts. It was an excellent package, with striking cover artwork, adapted from Emile de Antonio's 1969 anti-war Vietnam film, *In The Year Of The Pig*. Morrissey cleverly subverted the original image for his own propagandist purpose by altering the insignia on the GI's helmet from "Make War, Not Love" to the sloganeering album title, *Meat Is Murder.* In an era when rock and pop seemed swamped in causes The Smiths added their weight to Morrissey's vehement support for animal rights. This was a significant departure for the singer, who had previously been wary of using the group as an advertising board for anti-racism, homosexual proselytizing, drug addiction rehabilitation or famine relief. Although the CND and GLC had benefited from The Smiths' live patronage, Morrissey was acutely aware of the aesthetic dangers implicit in vinyl politicizing. "I think audiences get bored with groups introducing hard-core politics into every song," he informed the socialist-minded *NME*. "You don't have to be madly blunt in a political sense." The degree to which he was addressing political issues in his press interviews, however, suggested more and more that such matters would soon inevitably spill over into his art.

Throughout 1984, Morrissey had appeared as one of the great spokesmen and statesmen of pop, and his essays into speech increasingly leaned away from the personal towards the political. The Morrissey persona was now as much associated with Thatcher-baiting, the IRA, Greenham Common and animal rights militancy, as such old chestnuts as horticulture, celibacy, illness, misery, *Carry On* films and Sixties Northern culture. The intense humanity that had seemed strangely absent in Morrissey's flippant comments on Band Aid ironically found its full and righteous voice when applied to the plight of inferior life forms. Having already supported the lunatic fringe in the animal rights movement, Morrissey felt that the time was rife to provide his own thesis on the alleged ill treatment of animals. This meant abandoning the rich, lyrical ambiguity of The Smiths' début album in favour of a more direct and controversial assault on carefully-selected targets. The proselytizing title track revealed Morrissey at his most didactic, but the remainder of the album was similarly finger pointing. The dominant theme running through the work was violence - from the cradle to the slaughter house.

The progression from domestic child abuse ('Barbarism Begins At Home') to institutionalized brutality ('The Headmaster Ritual'), indiscriminate adolescent thuggery ('Rusholme Ruffians'), a 13-year-old's murder of a policeman ('I Want The One I Can't Have') and self-destructive urgings

('Nowhere Fast'/'That Joke Isn't Funny Anymore') complemented and reinforced the central climactic thrust of Morrissey's lament on civilized society's treatment of animals. The equation of meat-eating and animal slaughter with violence and war-mongering was emphasized by Morrissey while discussing the album. "I think as long as human beings are so violent towards animals, there will be war," he argued. "It might sound absurd, but if you really think about the situation it all makes sense. When there's this absolute lack of sensitivity where life is concerned, there will always be war." What is interesting here is Morrissey's unwillingness to differentiate between human and animal life. Consistently, his own humanitarianism seemed darkened by a perverse tendency to treat the loss of human life with suprisingly cavalier disregard. It was not only Band Aid that received short shrift. Ask Morrissey about the terrorist bombing of butcher shops and potential loss of life and he still replies coldly: "One dead butcher isn't such a great loss."

Back in 1985, Morrissey struggled to articulate a dualistic persona with a classic example of verbal doublethink: "Personally, I'm an *incurably* peaceable character. But where does that get you? Nowhere. You *have* to be violent." Clearly, Morrissey's "peaceable character" was not "incurable" if he *had* to be violent, yet the contradiction passed unchallenged. Writer Peter Singer, in his intelligently-argued *Animal Liberation*, warned of the dangers of such "justified" vengeance: "We may be convinced that a person who is abusing animals is entirely callous and insensitive; but we lower ourselves to that level if we physically harm or threaten physical harm to that person. Violence can only breed more violence... The strength of the case for Animal Liberation is its ethical commitment. We occupy the high moral ground and to abandon it is to play into the hands of those who oppose us."

Morrissey seemed unconvinced by such rationale and was more than willing to abandon ethical commitment and high moral ground by pledging support for terrorist factions within the animals' rights brigade. "It seems to me now that when you try to change things in a peaceable manner, you're actually wasting your time and you're laughed out of court," he argued. "As the image of the LP [*Meat Is Murder*] hopefully illustrates, the only way we can get rid of such things as the meat industry, and other things like nuclear weapons, is by giving people a taste of their own medicine."

Morrissey's retributive militancy severely undermined his previous glib equation of vegetarianism and pacifism. If anything it gave spurious credence to the opposing arguments of those equally self-righteous carnivores, who vaguely connected vegetarianism with social deviance. Of course, they already had the perfect villain to use as a propagandist riposte. The convenient example of Adolf Hitler as the ultimate animal-loving, vegetarian genocide emphasized a frightening perversion of values, as well as stressing the dangers of "selective humanity". Long before the Führer's arrival, radical carnivores had mockingly targeted vegetarians as society's true aggressors. The politics of ridicule were a handy weapon. One figure who led the attack was Morrissey's Victorian mentor Oscar Wilde. He wrote: "It is strange that the most violent republicans I know are all vegetarians. Brussels sprouts seem to make people blood thirsty and those who live on lentils and artichokes are always calling for the gore of the aristocracy and the severed heads of kings." Wilde's words took on an amusingly ironical ring in view of Morrissey's blood thirsty swipes at the Royal Family and demands for the guillotined head of Margaret Thatcher. If Morrissey's dictum was "Meat Is Murder", then Wilde's witty reply was "Violence Is Vegetarian".

While Morrissey succeeded in thrusting the vegetarian issue into numerous music press interviews, *Meat Is Murder* was rightly acclaimed as a major work. Its strengths were immediately apparent through the clarity of production, the improvement in Morrissey's vocal performance, the solidity of the rhythm section, the cutting edge of the lyrics and the brilliant diversity of Marr's musical menu, which somehow took in rockabilly, heavy metal, psychedelia, folk and even funk. The passionate performance owed much to Morrissey's feelings of intense righteousness while completing the work. "When we came to record that LP, we were quite angered," he recalled. "We were quite distraught about the way we had been treated by the music industry generally over the previous 12 months. We felt alone and in control... We produced it ourselves and that was a very important decision to make. For the first time we were on our own and devoid of any other influence." What emerged from such autonomy was an album of astonishing power and grandeur. Critics proclaimed the work a contender for album of the year; it now deserves praise as one of the finest of the Eighties.

'The Headmaster Ritual' was Marr's masterpiece. A richly-layered guitar concerto, it stands as one of rock's greatest album-opening tracks. It takes only seconds to realize that The Smiths have already reached a new plateau. Marr fills every chasm of sound with cross-current Rickenbacker rhythms and fascinating open tunings. Moreover, his colleagues have never sounded better. Joyce's drumming no longer betrays the cymbal-crashing, sibilant intrusiveness of the first album, but is perfectly integrated into the musical framework. The strength and precision of the production is a tribute to Marr's remarkable craftsmanship, hard work and imagination. "For my part, 'The Headmaster Ritual' came together over the longest period I've spent on a song," Johnny confirmed. "I first played the riff to Morrissey when we were working on the demos for our first album with Troy Tate. I nailed the rest of it when I moved to Earl's Court. That was around the time when we were being fabulous." A lyric of fire was needed for a backing track of such quality, so Morrissey chose to unleash his pent-up revenge, not only on St Marys, but against all Manchester schools and, by implication, every custodial educational institution. By the end of the song, his voice soars, stretching syllables into wailing cries of fathomless desperation. The track remains one of the sublime moments in The Smiths' songbook.

The inspiration for 'Rusholme Ruffians' came from an old 45 owned by

Marr's parents. '(Marie's The Name) His Latest Flame' was an Elvis Presley chart-topper the year before John Maher married Frances Doyle. Written by the great Doc Pomus/Mort Shuman partnership, the song contained a memorable riff which Marr liberally adapted and aligned to a rockabilly rhythm. "The real idea was to do something from the fairground," he explained. "I'd spent a lot of time at the fair in Wythenshawe Park and I worked at a speedway in a place down in Cheshire. I still maintain that the best place to hear music is at the fairground. If you get your records played at the fair you're a great pop group. I used to go there all the time, not necessarily to go on the rides, but to look at girls. I had this really romantic feeling when I was at the fair."

When Morrissey was presented with the tune, he responded to its Sixties ambience by composing a lyric whose theme delineated the threatening scenery and artificial stimuli provided by the Manchester fun fairs of his youth. "As a child I was literally educated at fairgrounds," he recalls. "It was the big event. It was why everybody was alive. On threadbare Manchester council estates once a year fairs would come around. It was a period of tremendous violence, hate, distress, high romance and all the truly vital things of life." While Morrissey was often horrified by the violence, he was also excited by the garish glamour and sense of imminent danger that the fair provided. "In Rusholme, it was the only thing people had," he lamented. "It was the only pleasurable distraction and they turned it into a total horror. You couldn't keep me away from them! I quite liked the idea of seeing people living on the emotional edge. Fascinating."

While Marr took his inspiration for 'Rusholme Ruffians' wholesale from Elvis Presley, so Morrissey borrowed freely from the work of his latest idol, Victoria Wood. He had already joked about the possibility of marrying the *comedienne*, and she had publicly responded with the witty announcement, "Morrissey and I have been married for 11 months, though due to touring commitments, we have yet to meet." He paid her the ultimate "compliment" by hijacking her song 'Fourteen Again' and transforming its sardonic nostalgia into a lacerating satire on mind-numbing proletariat leisure. In Morrissey's landscape, the fair becomes a carnival of violence tinged with bitter romance ("someone falls in love and someone's beaten up"); the scene is viewed through a jaundiced eye, dulled by the oppressive atmosphere and stimulated senseless by flashing lights and whirling sounds. Morrissey, as the detached and cynical observer, displays a prudish attitude towards female vanity ("Her skirt ascends for a watchful eye/it's a hideous trait on her mother's side") and a wariness of moneygrubbers ("an engagement ring doesn't mean a thing to a mind consumed by brass [money]"). These lines recall that "fat girl" in 'William, It Was Really Nothing', who asked: "Would you like to marry me and if you like you can buy the ring?" and whom, we were told, didn't care about "anything". By the end of 'Rusholme Ruffians', Morrissey's mock misogyny and pessimism about human relationships is not quite sufficient to destroy his devout faith in love, even if he has to walk home alone in dulled submission.

The images presented in 'Rusholme Ruffians' are sordid, aggressive and doom-laden, in striking contrast to Wood's more chirpy, undetached nostalgia. Morrissey significantly begins his song with a violent scene ("The last night of the fair/by the big wheel generator/a boy is stabbed/and his money is grabbed"), which undercuts the humorous innocence evoked by Wood ("The last night of the fair/French kisses as the kiosks shut/Behind the generator with your coconut"). Similarly, while Morrissey focuses on girlish guiles, Wood suggests a more transparent form of mutual exploitation ("Free rides on the waltzers off the fairground men/For the promise of a snog"). Wood reminisces fondly about French kissing exploits during which "The coloured lights reflected in the Brylcreem in his hair". Such requited passion has no place in Morrissey's fairground. Although he concedes that "the grease in the hair of a speedway operator is all a tremulous heart requires", sexual fulfilment is thwarted and a spurned schoolgirl ends up contemplating romantic suicide by leaping from "the top of the parachutes". At least Wood and Morrissey agree on the importance of self-mutilation (cf "I want to be 14 again/Tattoo myself with a fountain pen" and "scratch my name on your arm with a fountain pen/this means you really love me"), but otherwise their perspective and experiences of Manchester fairgrounds could hardly be more contrasting.

It is fascinating to observe Wood's characteristically self-effacing, but affectionate, adolescent recollections juxtaposed to Morrissey's almost cinematic melancholy. They both share an appealing laconic style and dour wit, but Morrissey's world view is more threatening, pessimistic and painful. Wood looks back with comfortable bemusement, whereas Morrissey engages totally and frighteningly with his own past. The extent of Morrissey's borrowings from the *comedienne* is noticeable, but less important than the subtle way in which he uses such material. This is "functional plagiarism" at its best - an art familiar to writers from Sterne and Wilde to Eliot. 'Rusholme Ruffians' remains the most extreme example of blatant adaptation from both Morrissey and Marr. Beneath the song's structure are the twin ghosts of '(Marie's The Name) His Latest Flame' and 'Fourteen Again', strangely united in a unique, and not entirely unmischievous, hybrid.*

'I Want The One I Can't Have' apparently came together in the studio extraordinarily quickly. While working on the backing tracks with Stephen Street, Marr took Rourke and Joyce aside and played them the basic chord sequence of the song. A brief jamming session followed before Marr's concept was hastily transformed into a finished take. Lyrically, 'I Want The One I Can't Have' seems more epigrammatic than dramatic and the opening line ("On the day that your mentality catches up with your biology") recalls the "Does the body rule the mind or the mind rule the body?" conundrum

---

* In later live sets, Marr playfully acknowledged his source by incorporating '(Marie's The Name) His Latest Flame' into the opening of 'Rusholme Ruffians'. "I loved 'His Latest Flame'," he recalls, "but from being a kid I noticed how many other songs had that chord change. When Morrissey sang it, it sounded really brilliant." The medley was captured for posterity on "*Rank*".

of 'Still Ill'. Marr's interweaving guitars add spice to Morrissey's musings, which end in cocky innuendo ("And if you ever need self-validation/just meet me in the alley by the railway station").

The often unsung Mike Joyce opens 'What She Said' with a deft display of percussive power, before Morrissey continues his mind versus body debate in which "heady books" lose out to a "tattooed boy from Birkenhead". Marr's decision to allow Joyce to let rip transforms the track into The Smiths' hardest rock item to date and serves as a neat antithesis to the side's closing classic.

'That Joke Isn't Funny Anymore' stands as one of the great moments in The Smiths' recording history. Explaining the origin of the song, Morrissey noted: "When I wrote the words for that, I was just so completely tired of all the same old journalistic questions and people trying this contest of wit, trying to drag me down and prove that I was a complete fake." What Morrissey did not add was the small debt he owed to the movie *Alice Adams*, which contained the lines: "I've watched this happen in other people's lives and now it's happened in ours". Morrissey's defiant lament against sneering cynics is beautifully framed by Marr's sublime acoustic and electric guitar interchanges. The incantatory vocal coda fits perfectly alongside Johnny's shimmering waltz-time arrangement, which is nothing short of majestic.

'Nowhere Fast' provides a reminder of how rapidly Morrissey's vocal improved from the tired, toneless sparsity of his earliest work. Marr's playful sound effects provide a suitable accompaniment to the singer's wittily outrageous anti-royal gibes, which would reach vehement fruition on the next Smiths album. "I wanted to make some anti-royalist statements," Morrissey recalled. "I wanted to say something that was very strong, yet with an undercurrent of absurdity about it. But, in a way, it's not absurd. The way I feel about royalty is that I don't even want to discuss it." The singer's contempt for the entire issue is effectively summed up in that arresting opening line: "I'd like to drop my trousers to the Queen".

The elliptical 'Well I Wonder' is another of Morrissey's despairing love songs, inserted at a key point in the album. Framed by two, harsher, bombastic songs, it serves as an excellent mood piece, as well as demonstrating the power of Morrissey's ever-improving falsetto. Marr still rates the song as one of The Smiths' more underrated offerings. "It's one of those things that a modern group could try and emulate, but would never get the spirit of. It's so simple."

'Barbarism Begins At Home' reveals Morrissey's determination to avoid ambiguity in the pursuit of axiomatic lines ("A crack on the head is what you get for not asking"). After accusations of writing songs about child abuse, the singer confounds his critics by tackling the subject head-on with a damning assessment of family life. As the song climaxes, Morrissey bays like a wounded hound, gargles enticingly and produces some of the most extraordinary vocal effects ever heard on a pop record. Marr and Rourke add a touch of overdue heresy to The Smiths' canon by riffing into the realms of Chic-influenced funk, thereby providing some clues as to what they were up to during the rehearsal/studio-bound months of 1981. "The bass line's a killer," Joyce enthuses. "It's interesting to see how Morrissey got his head around it. We'd be playing and when we'd stop Andy would often continue with a Stanley Clarke bass line. It's incredible the way he can shift into that. The beauty of Andy's playing is his adaptability. He could play with a heavy metal or a folk band. That shows up right through The Smiths' career. Andy could play his own song within a song. If you took out Andy's bass line from every Smiths track, it's a song in itself, not just a contribution."

The album's title track serves as a harrowing finale, laced with the death cries of cattle, trooping warily to the slaughter house against a background of sawing knives, whose aural menace is amplified by Marr's disturbingly funereal arrangement. Morrissey's vocal has seldom sounded so one-dimensionally sensitive, and he uses his lyrical thrust to maximum declamatory effect. The entire song draws its dramatic force from Morrissey's emotive misapplication of that single word, "murder". Abandoning the dictionary definition of "murder", which applies only to human beings, Morrissey employs the word as an accusative label, directed against all meat eaters. The song opens on a significantly anthropomorphic note - "heifers' whines could be human cries". Having elevated cattle to the level of human beings and transformed "slaughter" into "murder", the carnivore necessarily becomes a cannibal. The lyrics are riddled with propagandist sophistry and witty but transparent rhetoric. Such lines as "Death for no reason is murder" momentarily sound persuasive, until you realize that the statement is patently absurd. A death for no reason might be defined adequately as tragedy, but it is hardly murder.

Like the later 'Margaret On A Guillotine', 'Meat Is Murder' is pure agit-prop. Some commentators felt that the singer gilded the lily by overplaying the death throes for cheap emotional effect. However, subtle understatement was never one of Morrissey's characteristics. The touches of theatrical drama on 'Meat Is Murder' recall the "Hindley" laugh on 'Suffer Little Children' and the chop of decapitation at the close of 'Margaret On A Guillotine'. Those critics who complained that Morrissey lacked restraint in his employment of theatrical sound effects failed to appreciate the nature of propagandist art, which is less a search for some objective truth than a gut-wrenching assault, fuelled by simplistic rhetoric and unrestrained overstatement. 'Meat Is Murder' succeeds on its own terms which, of course, are the only terms it allows.

The critical acclaim that greeted *Meat Is Murder* was thoroughly deserved and even if The Smiths had broken up at that point, their future reputation would have been assured. The group had now entered a phase that most groups can only dream about - where excellence is effortless and greatness tangible. Like The Beatles after *Rubber Soul* and The Byrds after *Younger Than Yesterday*, a feeling of immense drama surrounded their artistic progression. It was time to ponder on what they might yet achieve, and shiver at the prospect. Pop at its epoch provides an almost frightening expectation and exhilarating sense of instant history in the making. The all-too-familiar alternative is a depressing anti-climax, akin to the disillusionment produced by a soured love affair. The Smiths were to suffer the crucial demand for brilliance and survive such scrutiny by providing another classic album the following year. During the interim, however, their standing in the scheme of things provoked some hard questions.

After releasing a milestone album, The Smiths expected a strong chart showing for their next single, 'Shakespeare's Sister'. With a title inspired by a Virginia Woolf essay and a theme recalling her own obsession with suicide, this tribute to the self-destructive lure of cliff tops was highly regarded by Morrissey, who called it, "the song of my life". Interestingly, in describing the song, Morrissey pays less attention to its suicidal theme than to the overwhelming desire for freedom hinted at in such lines as, "Oh, mama, let me go". As he diligently noted: "With 'Shakespeare's Sister' I tried to capture the voice of the downtrodden. In the history of literature, Shakespeare, of course, never had a sister, and in almost every aspect of art there's no female voice whatsoever... The song was really about shrugging off the shackles of depression and shedding the skins of one's parents and getting out and living and doing what one wants to do." Marr shared Morrissey's enthusiasm for the track and welcomed the opportunity to feature that distinctive riff on a single. "I just flipped all the while we were recording and really loved it," he remembered. For Marr, the single represented another important step in his role as producer. Unfortunately, in a fit of misplaced democracy, he chose to allow the entire group to "produce" the work, which meant that they were encouraged to determine the recording level on their particular instrument. Journalist Nick Kent, who heard Marr's original trial mix, damned the final version as "an abomination of the song's potential". It was a great shock to the group when 'Shakespeare's Sister' failed to chart higher than a disappointing number 26. Record plugger Scott Piering had feared the worst after receiving a lukewarm response from various daytime radio producers. One of them remarked: "But it's over so quickly, it just doesn't register in your mind". The lack of a discernible chorus and catchy hook-line ensured that the song received minimal airplay. "When other singles of equal or lesser value reached the charts, they'd get twice as many plays as The Smiths," Piering argued. "Morrissey was thumbing his nose at the Establishment in all sorts of little ways and it built up an atmosphere that The Smiths were renegades. They truly were subversive. I quit the plugging side very willingly because they were making more enemies than friends, and so was I!"

For Morrissey, the lack of radio airplay smacked of an evil conspiracy. "It's an absolute political slice of fascism to gag The Smiths," he complained. Piering was not convinced by this extravagant theory, but agreed that The Smiths were victims of ill-conceived prejudice. "There was no outright conspiracy *not* to play their records, people just didn't come to me for anything. They were always slagging off the radio and press, and the daytime radio people weren't comfortable with them. Their press legend preceded them. People should have been knocking on their door, but I really had to sell them. There were only a couple of things that they regarded as institutions; one was *Top Of The Pops* and the other was Radio 1. All they wanted was to have the radio play their records, and they didn't want to give anything back. They wanted to put out lots of singles but some were ill-considered, in retrospect. 'Shakespeare's Sister' was very intense, but it wasn't a radio record. Of course, *nobody* could tell them what singles were about."

A Smiths inquest followed the shock failure of 'Shakespeare's Sister' and their accusing finger pointed directly at Rough Trade's promotions department. When the superb follow-up, 'That Joke Isn't Funny Anymore', barely scraped to number 49, the rumblings of discontent increased. Morrissey was constantly complaining that the group's single releases were not fly-posted across the streets of London. Travis retorted that fly-posting was a waste of money and served the ego of the artiste, rather than the sales of the record. Quizzed on the relative failure of The Smiths' singles throughout 1985, Travis came out fighting. "They weren't good enough," he maintains. "That's my answer! It's no good complaining about 'Shakespeare's Sister' and 'That Joke Isn't Funny Anymore' - they weren't commercial records. There was a problem with Morrissey thinking he had a divine right to a higher chart position. We did as well as anyone in the world could have done with those records. No, I don't think EMI could have done any better. I think they'd have done far worse. Morrissey would have liked us to advertise every single on television, as though it was the event of the decade. But you can't do that. It's not logical. If you're selling 20 million records worldwide, you can afford to spend the kind of money you'd splash out on Michael Jackson, but The Smiths were not a major group internationally."

Despite Travis's hard reasoning and forceful apologia, Morrissey/Marr remained unconvinced. They always regarded themselves as consummate singles artistes and, having topped the albums charts, it seemed inconceivable that they could not crack the national Top 20. Nobody could convince Morrissey/Marr that in the modern market-place they were actually an albums group. Such a notion would have defiled their self-image as pop songsmiths. They wanted to be Sixties-styled singles specialists - that was their original *raison d'être*. Criticism of their singles policy would therefore be greeted coldly and a much more palatable explanation for commercial failure was the alleged inadequacies of Rough Trade. As the year progressed, relations between the parties would worsen.

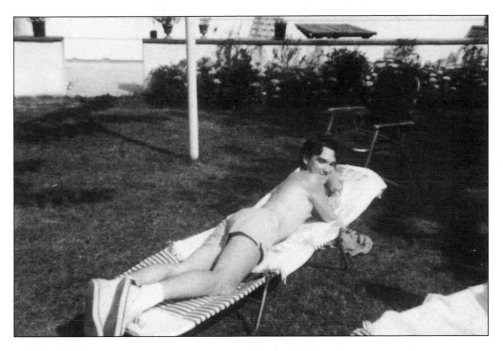

1976. Morrissey goes to America and spends the warm summer days out of doors.

January 1980. When this picture was taken Morrissey was working as a 'flesh remover' at a hospital.

Rob Allman and Johnny Maher, the first songwriting team, modelling the cover of Bruce Springsteen's *Born To Run*. Note Johnny's angelic visage and Tom Petty T-shirt. (*Allman Archives*).

Allman, Maher and keyboardist Paul Whittall drinking champagne at Andy Rourke's house on 5 February 1980. (*Allman Archives*).

The original line-up of White Dice. Left to right: Johnny Maher, Andy Rourke, Paul Whittall, Rob Allman and Bobby Durkin. *(Allman Archives).*

The second line-up of White Dice. Left to right: Rob Allman, Paul Whittall, Craig Mitchell, Johnny Maher and Andy Rourke. *(Allman Archives).*

Mike Joyce, Hadfield Road, Glossop. Winter 1981. *(Jane Whyle).*

The Hoax. Left to right: Mike Joyce, Steve Mardy and Andy Farley. *(Jane Whyle).*

(Paul Slattery).

(Paul Slattery).

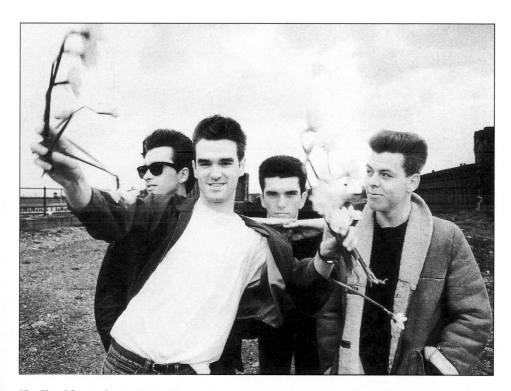

The Floral Spectacle. *(Paul Slattery/Retna).*

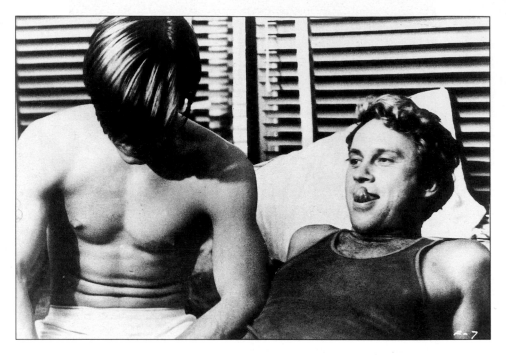

The original 'male prostitution scene' in Andy Warhol's *Flesh*, which was adapted for the cover of The Smiths' debut album.

Morrissey promoting *Meat Is Murder*.
(Howard Tyler/Retna).

The sweet and smiling alliance. *(LFI)*.

(Paul Slattery).

Marr. *(Andrew Catlin/Retna).*

Morrissey. *(LFI).*

Joyce. *(Todd).*

Rourke. *(LFI).*

12

I Don't Owe You Anything

THE *MEAT IS MURDER* TOUR commenced at the end of February and proved one of the live highlights of 1985. Prokofiev's 'March Of The Capulets' from *Romeo And Juliet* added an air of expectant tension to the evening before The Smiths appeared, resplendent and irradiant. After a solid year on the road, their power was devastating and as they spiralled across the country, appearing in town halls and theatres, they left behind an ever-increasing band of staunch devotees. Stage invasions were applauded by the group and always ensured that the shows ended on a climactic note. As Stuart James noted: "It got to the point where, if there wasn't a stage invasion, the group would think that the gig wasn't good, even if their playing had been excellent."

Inevitably, there were problems with venues that employed over-zealous bouncers, but a compromise was reached when The Smiths agreed to provide their own security. While two vigilant house attendants stood on the sidelines, the road crew took on the additional task of orchestrating the fan worship. Exuberant stage invaders were often waltzed into the wings, then deposited back into the audience. Persistent offenders usually received an official warning from crew boss Oz McCormick, while three-time transgressors were shown the back door. The group responded positively to the dancing hordes, although Marr would register annoyance if a gyrating assailant caused him to miss a chord. The musicianship remained important, even amid potential chaos, and high standards were demanded of the crew. As Oz remarked: "The band's attitude was critical - even of themselves. If they had a bad gig, they'd have a two-hour autopsy on it."

Morrissey revelled in the messianic adoration of his followers and cascaded across the stage with a presence that was electrifying to behold. Having spent years projecting his need for love, fame and acceptance on distant, untouchable idols, he fully understood, and encouraged, his followers' fanatical and unquestioning devotion. Morrissey's natural acceptance of star status did not always please past associates. Tony Wilson watched The Smiths/James home appearance and found himself critical of his old friend. "I remember a feeling of absolute revulsion watching Stuart James, who's a brilliant engineer, a good producer and a fine young man, scurrying across the stage with eight freshly-cleaned towels for Morrissey. That's the part of Steven I can't deal with - the way people are treated."

There is no question that Morrissey liked and demanded to be treated with respect. What seems more strange is the unwillingness of others to allow him the familiar privileges of stardom. Admittedly, rock star trappings of the kind enjoyed by "dinosaur" acts of the Seventies had been vilified in the music press since the emergence of punk in 1976, and The Smiths were seen by many to personify the "ideologically sound" independent ideal. Fortunately, those within The Smiths' inner circle accepted Morrissey's fastidiousness as part of his character and almost unconsciously found themselves pandering to his needs. Stuart James was aware of this subliminal process. "What Tony Wilson saw wasn't very important," he countered. "I didn't particularly feel used and abused. If anything, it was something I took on myself. It wasn't as if Morrissey was saying: 'I *must* have this!' Looking back, I regret doing that [with the towels] but it's something you get caught up in. I only resented it when I realized they'd come to expect it. The personal service element made them feel comfortable and was part of the job. But it did detract from the more serious aspects of the work, and became actually more important. After I'd picked up the money, I'd be saying: 'Now, have I got the butties, Johnny's tuna sandwiches and the Smarties?'"*

Morrissey's personality ensured that people consistently treated him with undue reverence. The fact that he did not socialize with the crew made him a distant, omnipotent presence, untainted by the contempt of familiarity. His interaction with visitors was often strained and strangely intimidating. As Stuart James observed: "He commanded a lot of respect and people would faff around him. Even when they didn't particularly respect him, they'd love to take something back from him. He was being treated like a star before he was anything." In one sense, Morrissey was receiving the treatment that people usually reserve for someone who is "not of their station". The overt politeness and irrational benignity with which some people treat nuns, negroes, priests, mental patients, royalty, foreigners, cripples and the deformed, were bestowed upon Morrissey with alarming regularity. Whether intentional or not, he had the power to make people extremely wary of causing offence. Such control was both extremely gratifying and completely exasperating, depending upon his moods and desires.

"I was wary of Morrissey at first, but not later," Stuart James confirmed. "Maybe that was his defence. But The Smiths were unified. Johnny and Morrissey were always scheming and vibing each other up. I felt like an outsider and Mike and Andy probably felt the same way at times. As it got closer to the centre, the whole thing became Marr and Morrissey."

Other crew members, such as Oz McCormick, also saw Morrissey as an isolated figure, who valued Marr not only as a friend and confidant, but a

---

* Students of the "Morrissey diet" or those fortunate enough to have the bard round for afternoon tea might be interested in his food rider, which comprised: plain crisps or salt and vinegar, bottle of red wine, bottle of Lucozade, corn flakes or cocoa pops or Special K, pint of milk, two green apples, a cup cake, a packet of cashews, cheese sandwiches with butter!

means of communicating and realizing specific goals. "Morrissey was very solemn and didn't speak much to the crew or the touring party," McCormick recalled. "He'd walk on, do the soundcheck, then go back to the hotel. He'd never hang around to pass the time of day. The Smiths was two extremes - a very inward person, Morrissey, and a couple of jack-the-lads who were just out for a good time. Johnny Marr was stuck perfectly in the middle. He'd be with Morrissey, putting on his glum face for a couple of days, then he'd hang out with the band and have a party. Johnny was the central foothold."

During 1985, Marr frequently referred to Morrissey as his "best mate", and the singer seemed to thrive on the friendship. He genuinely believed that The Smiths represented the old pop myth of "four young lads who shook the world", despite contractual, financial and creative evidence to the contrary. It was another exercise in doublethink: The Smiths projected a semblance of pop group solidarity and camaraderie, but all the power and influence lay with Morrissey/Marr. Beyond that dynamic was the increasingly incandescent spectacle of Morrissey the media star, burning up fame in blazes of publicity and rent-a-quote accessibility. During the spring alone, he graced the front pages of *New Musical Express, Melody Maker, Smash Hits, Time Out, Blitz, Jamming!, Sounds* and *Zig Zag*. As an interviewee, Morrissey was charming, witty, engaging, confident and eminently controversial. Music press pundits soon realized that the Mancunian was emerging as the most waspish orator in pop since John Lennon. It was as if the structured role play format of a one-to-one question/answer confrontation broke down the normal barriers of shyness that thwarted more prosaic everyday conversation. The *Zig Zag/Sounds* piece was conducted by Antonella Black, who had already committed a disgraceful, vindictive and thoroughly reprehensible libel against Cliff Richard, which was slowly winding its way to the High Court, following publication in the live review section of the *NME*. She engaged Morrissey in some playful, sexual banter and teased out his erotic fascination for cars and their cold "leather seats", an image already included on 'That Joke Isn't Funny Anymore'.

The wealth of interviews testified to Morrissey's availability during 1985. For a time, he even cultivated a couple of genuine "pop star" friendships and entertained both Lloyd Cole and Pete Burns. The flamboyant Dead Or Alive vocalist appeared at several of the *Meat Is Murder* shows and received the ultimate accolade of performing alongside Morrissey during the closing gig at the Royal Albert Hall. After admitting, "We probably picked the wrong venue, never mind", Morrissey reappeared for an encore and duetted with Burns on 'Barbarism Begins At Home'. Hearing the duo sing "unruly boys must be taken in hand" added an unintentionally comic air to an otherwise straightforwardly brutal sentiment. Burns' irrepressibly androgynous image, independent spirit and capacity to turn all to merriment, appealed to Morrissey. The pair were later interviewed together in *Smash Hits* in what emerged as a hilarious piece of camp innuendo. Although the article occasionally recalled a *Carry On* script, some serious issues were covered and the impression conveyed was of two pop subversives who, despite their different approaches, resembled kindred spirits.

Another friendship that emerged during this period was that of Morrissey and Howard Devoto. The former Buzzcocks/Magazine vocalist and ex-partner of Linder had already received some flattering comments from Morrissey in the press, but claims that although they appeared at the same venue in 1978, they did not meet until 1985. Despite the infrequency of their interaction, Morrissey has intermittently promoted the friendship, regaling journalists with tales of visits to cemeteries, where the pair studied gravestones in true Linder fashion. Devoto subsequently invited Morrissey to see his new group Luxuria at the close of their 1988 British tour. A surprised audience at London's Town and Country Club was bemused by the entertaining spectacle of Stretford's finest reading selections from Marcel Proust. In retrospect, 1985 displayed Morrissey at his most outgoing, but such bursts of accessibility were all too frequently countered by periods of withdrawal and unexplained lack of communication.

If Morrissey's social sphere was increasing, then Marr's seemed close to saturation point. Like his partner, Johnny had bought a large house in the *nouveau riche* suburb of Bowdon. He soon filled his domain with a vast collection of records and pre-recorded videos, purchased a Zodiac car and acquired two German shepherd dogs named Rufus and Carla. An inveterate night person, Marr was frequently invaded by party-chasing revellers, aspiring local musicians and a fair sprinkling of hangers-on and time wasters. Johnny enjoyed his status as king of the hill, but as his ever-expanding entourage crowded into the house, he realized that the non-stop socializing was insidiously sapping his creative energies. Attempted burglaries, drunken loiterers in the garden, ogling schoolkids and pressure of work eventually drove Johnny southwards for a much-needed sabbatical during which he stayed at Kirsty MacColl's West London flat. However, all things considered, he coped reasonably well with the trappings of fame.

Like Morrissey, Marr provided his mother with some new challenges by encouraging her to launch the FM (Frances Maher) School of Motoring. He also visited old friends in Wythenshawe, turning up unexpectedly at Bobby Durkin's door and checking out Rob Allman's latest group, French Without Tears. On the night they met, Marr convinced Allman that the time was right for him to team up with Stephen Fellows of The Comsat Angels. "I've been talking to him," Johnny enthused, "and I think you'll like him." It was a testament to Marr's matchmaking that he had completely forgotten about the proposal by the following evening. "You're up and down like a yo-yo," Allman remarked, with patient humour.

The former White Dice vocalist did receive a firm invitation to Bowdon for an "afternoon jam", but when he arrived at the appointed time, the house seemed deserted. After retiring to a nearby chip shop for an hour, Allman returned and rang the bell long enough to rouse the attendant Smiths' roadie Phil Powell. "Was that you ringing before?" Powell enquired. "I thought it was the pigs." Johnny, it transpired, had still not recovered from the previous evening's revelries. "The day started at 4pm and ended at 4am," Allman recalled. "Often I left there at 2am and people were still turning up. Johnny would disappear for half-an-hour on the phone, come back, then forget what I was doing there. It all seemed like pie in the sky and there were so many hangers-on, it was unbelievable." Despite his busy schedule however, Marr stresses that he genuinely wanted to assist Allman and even approached Warner Brothers Music about the possibility of signing his former singing partner. Allman was embarrassed at the prospect of being patronized by Marr and they parted following some heated, drunken words.

While Morrissey and Marr attempted to protect themselves from the pressures of the music business by consistently changing their phone numbers and prevaricating over difficult and unwanted decisions, a backlog of problems mounted. Former tour manager Phil Cowie was besieging Rough Trade with ominous letters demanding compensation following the cancellation of the 1984 European tour. Marr's reaction was caustically humorous: "He should have paid us damages!" The songwriting duo ignored Cowie's correspondence until the matter threatened to fester into an embarrassing legal wrangle. It was with considerable reluctance that Cowie was finally paid off, as the frustrated Piering recalls. "We weren't in control of the money. Both Johnny's and Morrissey's signatures were required on a cheque over a certain amount. Everything went through their bank accounts until we finally got a limited company. We could have paid off Phil Cowie a long time ago and saved so much grief. They just didn't want to deal with it. They didn't want to pay that money; that was the unrealistic part about it. They just felt it would all be handled and they should receive the gross monies and everybody else had to figure out what to do and find the money elsewhere. It was totally ludicrous. It wasn't even terminally naïve - just an impossible situation."

The unnecessarily long-running Cowie saga was overshadowed by a more serious and less savoury encounter with "the ghost of troubled Joe". The man whom Betty Dwyer had once told that God would bless for the wonderful support he had offered her son was now perceived as a fallen angel. After taking his leave of The Smiths, Joe Moss had attempted to settle his account by invoicing them with a bill for £6,000. "It was a piffling amount of money," Moss stresses. "I wasn't after a percentage, just my out-of-pocket expenses. I'd bought a PA and I could point physically to the amount of money I'd spent. It took over three years to get it!"

After several demeaning phone calls to bemused Rough Trade officials, Moss concluded that he was being fobbed off and responded by placing the matter in the hands of his solicitors. While the disagreement tortuously unwound, Marr regrettably found himself caught in the crossfire between his current partner and former mentor. "Joe felt he had something coming to him and Johnny did too," explained Piering. "But if Morrissey didn't go along with something, nothing happened. He would just baulk. You couldn't do anything without Morrissey's cooperation. Johnny was in an embarrassing position because Joe was his father figure and had helped to get it all together. But Morrissey was adamant." Indeed, Morrissey

appeared to regard Moss as fortunate for being allowed to work alongside
The Smiths in the first place.

The clumsy way in which Morrissey/Marr handled the "Moss problem"
was another example of their lack of managerial acumen, a feature worsened by the inability of their subordinates to assume responsibility.
Apparently, nobody bothered to point out the obvious: that Moss was letting them off very lightly. Despite the fact that he had never even bothered
to request any written form of agreement, Moss could easily have followed
pop management tradition by demanding a hefty settlement for all sorts of
imagined wrongs. Fortunately for The Smiths, he had no interest in chis-
elling away chunks of their earnings and, despite the intervention of
solicitors, stuck doggedly to his surprisingly modest claim. "I went away
with the 'It's Too Late To Stop Now' attitude," he rejoiced. "You can't have
both dreams. You can't then sit there and say, 'Let's go for *that*'. I'd have
considered it tainted money. When they look around and think about me
(and I'm not saying they do!), the psychology is that they should both get
slight tremors because they were wrong, whereas, in my treatment of them,
I wasn't. That's the only important part of it."

Within The Smiths' organization, the bland assumption was that Moss
felt aggrieved with Morrissey for dragging his heels on the issue. Ironically,
however, it was the politically-handcuffed Marr who bore the brunt of Joe's
initial disenchantment. "I wasn't disappointed with Morrissey because I
never expected anything from him," he explained. "I was treated badly by
Johnny, not Morrissey. If there was one person that the job was definitely
done for, that was Johnny... I thought to myself: 'Good Lord, the bloke can
sign a cheque for that amount, no problem, and get it out of the way'."
Matters were further complicated by the unfortunate collapse of Moss's
business and Marr's pained unwillingness to cross Morrissey by forcing the
issue. In retrospect, the swift solution that Moss expected could only have
occurred if Marr had independently footed the bill from his own account
but, at that point, such magnanimity was apparently asking too much. "On
principle, while I was in The Smiths, it wasn't fair that the rest of the band
let me pay for everybody else's expenses," Marr argued.

Despite his disappointment, Moss was philosophical about the
Morrissey/Marr financial dispute, which he put down to political points
scoring. "It was a game between Johnny and Morrissey," he concluded.
What was most unusual about the "game" was the lack of animosity
between the participants. Moss remained politely tolerant towards Marr's
dilemma, while the friendly guitarist continued to phone every few
months, often seeking moral support "when he found himself weakening."
At one point, Marr did succeed in bringing Morrissey and Moss to the
negotiating table and even retained vain hopes that the haberdasher might
return as manager. "He came back and asked me," Joe recalls wistfully. "He
was obviously very distraught about Morrissey. I didn't give any hint that
I'd go back. It was out of the question. Morrissey phoned me and asked me
to meet him. We spoke in general terms and he told me there'd be no problem about the money, and then there was again!" Regrettably, the matter

dragged on, and negotiations foundered. Marr admits, "Morrissey and me never got it sorted out. He felt Joe had got what he should have been given. But the first thing I did when I left was to pay him out of my own bank account because that was the only way he was ever going to get paid. It was really important to me... After The Smiths split, I paid him for the PA and I covered everybody else's costs. I went back and paid him a cheque out of my own money and I felt much better for doing that."

In retrospect, Morrissey remained remarkably calm and wonderfully aloof from the dispute, despite the fact that his reluctance to settle had perpetuated the unhappy correspondence. Moss bore him no ill will and even felt his inflexible viewpoint was "fair enough". It was part of Morrissey's quietly manipulative personality and overwhelming sense of self-justice that he could cross swords with adversaries without incurring their vindictiveness. The supreme example of this trait occurred in later years when he performed at Wolverhampton, backed by a group whose predominant membership was in the process of chasing him through the High Court. Morrissey's peculiar combination of artistic righteousness and painful vulnerability ensured that few opponents could dislike him and fewer still had the stomach for a battle.

Morrissey's stance on the Moss settlement emphasized his business naïvety and one-sided perspective concerning the merits of such a claim. He was so wary of losing control that he tended to take the hard line as a matter of course and surrendered power with great reluctance. Only Marr was regarded as an equal, while the status of Rourke and Joyce seemed like shifting sand, depending on their demands. "As a duo, Johnny and Morrissey had to present a united front," Piering reasoned. "The philosophy was always the band - meaning all four of them; everything could be messed up as long as that was solid. That solidarity was the only line of protection they had." Rourke and Joyce remained passive, undemonstrative and irrelevant in all the aforementioned business dealings. Swept along by the speed of events and seemingly transfixed by the vibrancy of Morrissey's imagination, their role was still unrecorded in any written agreement. The distribution of income was entirely in the hands of Morrissey/Marr, who signed the cheques and had their own bank accounts. "They dipped into the trough themselves and gave Mike and Andy amounts of money when they asked for it badly enough," was Piering's crude assessment of the financial set-up. "They just didn't want to relinquish their control."

The private arrangement with Rourke and Joyce, by which they received a percentage of The Smiths' non-songwriting earnings, had been acceptable to all four members and Morrissey/Marr felt they dealt with them honorably on that basis. Naturally, there was a growing chasm in the earnings of the various parties as most of The Smiths' revenue came through songwriting, from which Rourke and Joyce, of course, received nothing. Although such disparities in income have sundered other groups, Marr maintains that the non-equitable percentages were both carefully considered and reasonable. "From day one, Mike and Andy knew that they didn't have to do 25 per cent of the work," he stressed. "We were the ones who had to deal with shit from Joe, shit with Scott, shit with Rough Trade, and that suited Mike and Andy right down to the ground. It was me and Morrissey that ran the group... They could leave the studio whenever they finished and we couldn't. Everybody skedaddled when their bit of work was done whereas we were together every single day."

The question of money was always a sensitive issue, partly because there was no managerial mediator to deal with such matters. Those within The Smiths' orbit were extremely wary of appearing presumptuous or grasping, for fear of offending Morrissey. "The last thing he wanted you to be was clinging," Piering observed. "As soon as people were clinging, he'd shun them. He'd get you in this position where you'd try to say, 'What about *me*? What about *my* role?' And he'd make you feel embarrassed for doing it. It was a very clever psychological manoeuvre. There are people who can do that very easily. He knew very well that what you were asking for was your rightful due, but when it came down to getting that due, you always felt you were pushing. That's how he deals with people and those who knew him and wanted to stick around learned that."

Morrissey and Marr's remarkable control over the purse strings meant that they were always fending off the approaches of representatives from Rough Trade and All Trade Booking over a variety of financial matters. It was not unusual to see harried associates chasing Morrissey/Marr before a gig in the hope of obtaining their signatures on receipts or various other documents. "They'd make you feel ashamed about asking for money - it happened all the way down the line," Piering noted. "People didn't push until it got critical, then they'd pester and get a bit of money... They kept everybody in line on the great promise." For Marr, the financial strategies were brutally straightforward. "Morrissey and me wanted all four of us to get our hands on our money and get paid," he argued. "So that's what we did, much to the dismay of a million accountants and lawyers. And the struggle goes on to this day."

Rourke and Joyce's apparent contentment over the initial non-written agreements should not distract from the fact that these arrangements were noticeably clumsy for such an important group. Unfortunately, the subsidiary members had no advisers and betrayed a woeful lack of understanding about their contractual relationship with Rough Trade. The extent of their naïvete was summed up by their sheepish approach to Piering enquiring about their financial future. "Moves were made to clue them in as to how they stood," Scott recalled, "but they never did anything about it." Joyce confirms that he and Rourke were wide-eyed innocents. "I never thought about solicitors, accountants or managers," he admitted. "That side to me used to stink so I'd never let myself be open to it. It was just ignorance really. The most important thing to me was to put on a good show or play a good drum track on the record. That's as far as it went."

Meanwhile, The Smiths' contract, and the very name "Smiths", was strictly Morrissey/Marr as far as Rough Trade was concerned, which meant that any grievances from Rourke and Joyce could not be entertained by the company. "I was supposed to be representing all of them as a band but the fact was we were taking care of Johnny and Morrissey and making sure they were set up," was Piering's analysis of his own directive.

Amazingly, Joyce and Rourke were only just waking up to the full implications of their non-contractual relationship with either Morrissey/Marr *or* Rough Trade. "When The Smiths signed to Sire, I wasn't signed to them either," Joyce complained. "Any licensing anywhere was 'The Smiths'. I felt, 'I'm in the band, I play on the records, I receive gold discs in recognition'. But, legally, The Smiths were just Johnny and Morrissey. I found that tough to come to terms with."

It became increasingly desirable that some written form of agreement should be finalized to accommodate the needs of Rourke and Joyce, but this never occurred. Instead, a limited company, Smithdom, was formed with the intention of relieving some of the financial headaches and administrative chaos that the autonomous duo had brought upon themselves. Although Rourke and Joyce were partners in the company, Morrissey/Marr appointed themselves directors and retained control of the cheque book. In the meantime, there was never any suggestion that Rourke and Joyce should be elevated to the level of genuine "Smiths" on the all-important Rough Trade recording contract. The Smiths effectively remained Morrissey/Marr.

During mid-May, the group embarked on another ill-fated European tour, which commenced on a dramatic note at Heathrow Airport where a delegation from Rough Trade cornered Morrissey. The singer had already been voicing his reluctance to appear on Italian television, but the show was such a prestigious spot that the record company was reduced to pleading a case. Morrissey and Marr seemed convinced by the delegation and confirmed their commitment to the project, although that was no guarantee of actual capitulation. Minutes after their concerned pursuers had departed, tour manager Stuart James remembers the duo rebelliously exclaiming: "Well, we're not doing that!" Nevertheless, arrangements continued on schedule and it appeared that the capricious pair had recognized the importance of such promotional work to their standing in Europe. In a familiar game of unexplained fastidiousness, they checked into several hotels, before finally finding a suitable resting place near the television studio. They turned up punctually for rehearsals, went through the motions and waited patiently in the dressing room. Minutes before transmission time, news filtered through from Morrissey's mouth to the producer that The Smiths would not be appearing. They felt the show was appalling and wanted no part of it. Organizers Virgin Italy were told that none of their English acts would ever be invited to the studio again. It was a most unpleasant afternoon, and further recriminations were to follow.

At Tendetrisce, Rome, The Smiths played a stirring 18-song set and seemed in good spirits. Unfortunately, another mishap prompted the cancellation of a major appearance at San Sebastian. When the crew arrived for the soundcheck, they complained that the equipment was not up to scratch and word swiftly filtered through to The Smiths. The beleaguered

Stuart James investigated the matter and discovered that the innocent promoter had been sent a rider on behalf of New Order by mistake. "I felt the
show must go on, and didn't blame the promoter - but then he got stupid,"
James explained. As showtime approached, rumour reached the streets that
The Smiths would not be appearing and angry fans, many of whom had
travelled across Europe, began pelting bricks through the glass windows of
the sports hall. The crew was barricaded inside with an angry promoter
who insisted that they had brought such misery upon themselves. In the
midst of the fearful confusion, the telephone rang. On the end of the line
were Morrissey and Marr, safely back at the hotel and completely oblivious
to the plight of their entourage. "Come back *immediately*," they demanded,
indignantly.

Rough Trade had long ago learned to be philosophical about The Smiths'
unpredictable decisions, but were disturbed and upset by the cancellation
of the Italian television appearance. Having won over Morrissey at
Heathrow, they felt doubly betrayed. With a potential American tour in the
offing, Scott Piering decided to confront the group and boarded a plane to
Madrid. It was to be his final act as The Smiths' "caretaker manager".

Piering had precious few dealings with The Smiths' American record outlet, Warner Brothers, and they perceived him as little more than a flustered
incompetent. Whenever tour itineraries or singles releases were planned,
the company would enquire: "We must have an answer *now*." Such a
demand inevitably provoked an outbreak of prevarication from Morrissey
and Marr. "The Smiths were expecting us to control things because they
didn't want to deal with anybody," Piering complained. "Of course, they
withheld all the decisions, money and anything like that, making it impossible to keep your fingertips on things, much less control with an iron fist.
Warner Brothers must have been thinking: 'Get rid of these people!'"

From the outset, Piering had been in a subservient position to The Smiths,
whose reluctance to recruit strong management testified to a naïve belief in
their own ability to control such an important sphere. The ever-suspicious
Morrissey clearly preferred a neutered lackey to an autocratic svengali and,
against his better judgement, Piering was forced to play the management
game by his clients' rules. Piering was brutally frank about his job description: "I appreciated that it was my role to look after Morrissey and act as a
buffer between him and the world. We did the dirty work, basically. I had
to make excuses for whatever fucked-up thing he did. I would rationalize it
and try to sell it to whomever he offended and keep things sweet. After a
couple of episodes, especially with his mother, a lot of things were focused
towards giving Morrissey what he wanted."

In effect, the result of this policy was managerial impotence. Piering
signed his own death warrant the day he accepted such terms. As The
Smiths' reputation and expectations increased, his limitations became
embarrassingly apparent to everyone. "It was my own weakness," he confesses. "I really lost my stance as any kind of manager. A serious manager
has to tell the band what to do in certain instances and have enough input
to make a decision, otherwise you're a mere functionary... I was just

another evolution of Joe Moss after a certain point. I had no control over the money and couldn't make any creative or business decisions. Imagine trying to get crucial answers from The Smiths on every aspect of touring and record deals when you couldn't get them to say anything. It just made you feel and look incompetent... I lasted until things became so big that without any power or authority I could not handle it. I couldn't do business on their behalf because I was never authorized to make any decisions. It was impossible."

The frustration wrought by his own sense of powerlessness finally prompted Piering to act like a real manager. Sensing imminent doom, he decided to prove his worth by exposing All Trade Booking's alleged inadequacies and providing an alternative plan for the forthcoming US visit. His brave bid involved the recruitment of a high-powered American promoter named Hector Lazarides, who had worked with several major acts on extensive US tours. He put together a budget proposal that promised The Smiths a profit of between $60-80,000. When All Trade Booking's Mike Hinck was informed of Piering's meddling he was incensed and demanded: "What the hell do you think you're doing? Don't interfere!" In the meantime, Ian Copeland of FBI, who were organizing the tour, complained that Lazarides was demanding three sound systems when one was quite adequate. Piering, who had no love for the Copelands, rashly accused them of having sweetheart deals with promoters and insisted that Hector's budget was sound and would realize a substantial profit. Hinck threw up his hands and informed Rough Trade and The Smiths of Piering's interference. The most likely outcome of the disagreement seemed an abrupt cancellation, after which The Smiths would no doubt turn on Piering or Hinck, or both.

It was against this background of events that Piering, contrary to Hinck's wishes, flew to Madrid where the group was appearing at the Pasco De Camoens Festival. These were desperate times for Piering whose expendability had been rammed home by the concomitant success of his assistant Martha Defoe, who had supervised the formation of Smithdom and won Morrissey's confidence. "All the pressure was pointing to me losing the game," he lamented. "I figured, by God, this was my last shot. If the worst was to happen in Madrid, then at least I'd find out."

Morrissey and Marr proved surprisingly squeamish executioners and purposely avoided their victim as he scoured hotels seeking them out. "I knew they were hiding, and I was pursuing them," Piering admitted. "I was their conscience and they had to deal with it." When finally he tracked them down, the duo showed scant interest in his proposals, having clearly set their hearts against the condemned Hector Lazarides. "At that point, they just trashed me," Piering conceded. In his attempt to establish himself as a true manager, Piering had stumbled into his own coffin. It was left to his All Trade Booking adversary to complete the burial rites. "Mike Hinck made a powerplay for them and basically cut me out. I hated him for three to four years afterwards but, then again, he's such a pathetic figure that I feel I'm friends with him now. But he seriously torpedoed me."

The departure of Piering, who returned to the familiar world of record plugging, meant that The Smiths were again in need of strong management. Their tempestuous relationship with Rough Trade demanded the intervention of a seasoned music business taskmaster, but still they vacillated. In an attempt to salvage the American tour, All Trade Booking suggested the immediate recruitment of manager Matthew Sztumpf.

A former agent for several 2-Tone acts, Sztumpf had fortuitously inherited Madness's management in January 1982. He presided over the formation of their Zarjazz label and retained control during the tricky closing phase of their career. Although Madness's brand of exuberant ska failed to appeal to American tastes, Sztumpf had demonstrated his skills as an organizer of Stateside tours. During early 1985, he had been interviewed by Morrissey as a potential manager and although nothing concrete had emerged from the meeting, Sztumpf was content to proceed at The Smiths' tentative pace. "I had a lot of contacts and fancied the challenge of putting together an American tour in 10 days," he explained. "They had the dates booked, but nothing else. So I agreed to go, with no strings attached. They paid my expenses. I didn't know if I could work with them, so I said: 'Let's see how we get on and, if it works, we'll come to some formal arrangement'."

The American tour kicked off in Chicago with Morrissey insisting that the support act should be a drag queen. The transvestite performers were frowned upon by promoters and the miming sessions, backed by a solitary ghetto blaster, generally resulted in a barrage of flying cans. After the early gigs, the idea was abandoned. Morrissey, however, enjoyed the unorthodox support. The homosexual humour continued on the road where their coach driver communicated with gay truckers on CB Radio. He also carried a baseball bat aboard and glibly explained to customs officials and police that it was merely used for checking the air-level of his tyres.

The East Coast leg of the tour progressed smoothly with Billy Bragg's one-man-show providing a suitably English opening. There was even a sprinkling of media interest, including a feature in *People*, which humorously proclaimed Morrissey as "Pop's Latest Messiah". On a more human note, his sister Jackie suggested that the messiah's life would benefit from the love of an "independent, intelligent, mature and probably older woman". Clearly, she did not subscribe to her brother's view that he was doomed to remain "unloveable".

Despite the favourable publicity, relations with Sire Records were initially cool. Prior to The Smiths' Beacon Theater performance in New York, Stuart James had the unenviable task of informing Seymour Stein: "Morrissey doesn't want you to come to the show. You're *off* the guest list." The following day, 19 June, the group were set to fly to San Francisco, but James was already convinced that the tour was over. "Morrissey's fear of flying was at its height then," he recalled. "We were taxi-ing down the runway and he wanted to get off even then. How we got on the plane, I'll never know."

The West Coast extravaganza began with a double celebration on 20 June. Stuart James had a pleasant birthday, this time without the attentions of a stripogram girl, while Johnny married his long-time partner, Angie Brown. Grant Showbiz remembers that the wedding ceremony was "very new America, but touching." The following day, the group played in Oakland and then had a few days' rest before appearing at San Diego's State University Open Air Theatre. There, Morrissey belatedly paid a passing compliment to his supporting transvestite acts with the opening quip: "Yes, hello, it's just as you feared - *even more* drag queens." The festive atmosphere continued with several excellent shows at the outdoor Hollywood Palladium and Irving Meadows, where the group attracted sizeable crowds. Even the previously snubbed Seymour Stein was back in favour and demonstrated his dedication to the cause by spending an entire performance squashed against a crash barrier, surrounded by cheering Smiths fans. Morrissey was pleased by the touches of luxury that the Americans provided, including limousines and readily-available vegetarian food. Responding to Morrissey's affability, Stein invited the singer to LA's prestigious restaurant, the Ivy, and even burst into song in the middle of the meal. Later, he dragged Paul Simon across from an adjoining table to meet England's most critically-acclaimed singer/songwriter of recent times. Morrissey resisted the temptation to provide an impromptu rendition of 'Homeward Bound' or 'Bridge Over Troubled Water', much to the relief of the assembled company.

By the end of the tour, everybody agreed that the visit had proven extraordinarily successful. Without the benefit of strong promotion, healthy record sales or authorized videos, The Smiths had attracted audiences that excelled those of several major chart acts. This was a real revelation. Having virtually ignored America in the past, Morrissey/Marr were determined to improve their standing and return at the earliest opportunity.

The heroic welcome in the States was followed by an anti-climactic return to England where preparations were underway for the celebrated Live Aid concerts in London and Philadelphia on 13 July. The "global juke-box" inspired and organized by Bob Geldof, brought together many of the most commercially successful acts in the world in a combined effort to relieve famine-plagued Ethiopia. A television audience of 1.5 billion witnessed the event, which reaped over £50 million from telethon donations and television and ticket sales. Maintaining the critical attitude he had adopted towards Band Aid, Morrissey was unimpressed by the glowing statistics and seemed unmoved by the sense of history that the day evoked.

Marr was understandably cagey about expressing unambiguous enthusiasm for the event, especially in view of his partner's well-publicized criticisms. Nevertheless, he agreed that "the cause is admirable and Bob Geldof handled it admirably." Warming to his theme, the guitarist enlivened the pages of *Melody Maker* with some lacerating stabs at a couple of the Live Aid superstars. "It should be said that Bryan Ferry used the event for personal gain," Johnny accused, unjustifiably. "He disappears for a few years and then comes back with a new record and shamelessly plugs it at Live Aid. The decent thing would have been to play at least one old

song, but no. The other one who disappointed me greatly was Keith
Richard. He came on and played, what sounded to me, the completely
wrong tune. The man has paid a higher price for his hedonistic lifestyle
than any other artiste and it's just too big a price for any musician to pay.
What I'm saying is that Keith Richard cannot play the guitar anymore,
whereas someone like Eric Clapton, who has been through the same business, looked and sounded fine. But Keith really disappointed me. He was
my biggest influence in the early days, and now I have no respect for him
at all. How can anybody have respect for somebody who wants to spike
heroin for 10 years, and then regards that as a ticket for the whole event?
Nobody is impressed with that sort of thing anymore. And it showed,
because that was a big test having to play 'Blowin' In The Wind' on
acoustic guitar, and he couldn't do it. Can't play anymore."

What was most extraordinary about Marr's diatribe were not the sentiments, but the choice of performers. Within less than a year, Ferry and
Richard would be the two artistes with whom Marr was reportedly working and socializing, respectively. Their failure to read other people's
interviews in the music press saved Johnny from mild embarrassment and
precluded a display of vintage Marr charm. After meeting his tarnished
heroes, Marr found them thoroughly agreeable and has spoken highly of
them ever since.

Following the US tour, The Smiths momentarily found time to take stock
and, inevitably, further problems followed. Mike Joyce became concerned
about the unhealthy state of his bank balance and began to question the
group's financial management. Still starry-eyed from the recent Stateside
visit, he privately felt disappointment about the distribution of monies
from the tour. Accordingly, he telephoned the booking agent, Mike Hinck,
and requested a set of accounts to put his mind at rest. A few days later, he
received a call from Morrissey indignantly enquiring, "Why?" The singer
appeared to regard Joyce's action as a betrayal of trust and a personal
slight. "I explained that it wasn't that I didn't trust him," Joyce recalls. "I
just wanted to see for myself what was happening. Of course, the accounts
never came about so I started to get worried, really."

After consulting Andy Rourke, Joyce again decided to pursue the matter,
even though he was extremely wary of offending Morrissey. Both Rourke
and Joyce knew that they were in a very vulnerable position, and did not
want to be accused of biting the hand that fed them. Nevertheless, they
desired some protection beyond a vague verbal promise and felt it was
their right to be treated as fully-fledged group members. Ideally, they
should have been annexed to the Rough Trade contract, but were willing to
accept a lesser compromise. "We felt we should try and get some contract
between the four of us," Joyce explained, "never mind Rough Trade!" Their
efforts proved pathetic at best and wilted before the pained sophistry of
Morrissey, who felt that new agreements were unnecessary. "We tried to
sort it out," Joyce laments, "but all the time it was, 'Don't you trust us?'
which was something I'd never have thought about till they said it. I felt,
'Of course I trust you', because I had done. That was the great strength that

we'd had - we all believed and trusted each other." Increasingly, however, the question 'Why?' nagged away in the back of Joyce's mind whenever Morrissey voiced hurt indignation. Even Marr was unsympathetic towards the new proposals and felt that they should all stick to the original agreement. His formative vision of the Morrissey/Marr entity as a modern-day Leiber/Stoller overruled any suggestions of a new Smiths democracy.

What Rourke and Joyce urgently required at this point was a mediator to argue their case cogently, but an aversion to managers and solicitors precluded such a possibility. Morrissey and Marr were no better and, in any case, would probably have been appalled at the notion of a stranger prying into their affairs. Morrissey had enough problems fending off sympathetic managers, never mind re-opening negotiations with his own group. Rather than confronting the important points raised by their colleagues, Morrissey and Marr stood firm, then turned their attention to more pressing matters.

Temporarily free from recording commitments, the songwriting duo had time to mull over their relationship with Rough Trade. Communication between the parties had recently reached an all-time low and there were already unfounded rumours that the group was planning to jump ship and sign to WEA. On Friday 19 July, Morrissey added fuel to the troubled waters by pointedly failing to appear at a recording for the high-rating BBC Television show, *Wogan*. Matthew Sztumpf recalls that Friday afternoon as "the low point of my career". It was another of Morrissey's bizarre decisions and betrayed his familiar, selfish tendency to hide away, irrespective of the consequences. While his fellow members travelled down to London during the morning, the vocalist was already back at home in Manchester. "Morrissey decided that The Smiths should not be on *Wogan*," Sztumpf recollected. "The show was due on air at 7pm, and I was not a popular person. I made up some excuse that he was ill. It could have caused all sorts of repercussions. The embarrassment was having the members of the band and myself sitting in the studio waiting for him, and the lack of consideration Morrissey had for us. The least he could have done was tell his band!" Marr and the rest merely registered resigned acceptance of Morrissey's absence, as if anticipating worse problems to follow.

Although the clash with Rough Trade was still a matter of music press gossip, Morrissey's criticisms were alarmingly public. Having already complained about poor promotion and low chart entries, he was now pleading penury. When *Record Mirror* asked whether he was making lots of money, he retorted: "No - which is the crux of the present dilemma. I'm still too much acquainted with the whole aspect of poverty. I personally work 24 hours of every single day of the week - relentlessly - and the dividends in that area certainly don't pay off. In artistic ways they do because the records are successful, but I'm tired of being broke..."

Morrissey's self-image as a poverty-stricken workaholic was an extraordinary viewpoint, even by his eccentric standards. A relentless work rate had never suited Morrissey's lifestyle or personality and, whenever he pushed himself, illness or vacillation would undo his resolve. Those who had visited his homes in Chelsea or Halebarns would have been equally perplexed by his protestations of poverty. On the contrary, Morrissey/Marr enjoyed considerable financial security as a result of the profit-sharing agreement they had made with Rough Trade. Whatever reservations they felt about the label's promotion and performance in the rock marketplace, there could be no doubting the value of that deal. A major label probably would have offered an 11 per cent royalty, after deducting recording costs from the group's advance. The 50:50 agreement with Rough Trade, however, represented an equivalent royalty rate of approximately 23 per cent. Morrissey and Marr's impressive living standards indicated that they had become wealthy young men in a very short period of time.

Morrissey's disappointment with the financial rewards offered by Rough Trade no doubt stemmed partly from suspicion and misunderstanding concerning the nature of the profit-sharing. Fundamentally, the lesson that needed to be learned was that the "sharing" applied equally to losses as well as gains. All too often, the idea of recoupable expenses was anathema to Morrissey/Marr. "Nobody ever explained to them how a classic record deal worked," Scott Piering noted frustratingly. "They couldn't understand why they weren't making more money. To have the back-up systems and treatment they needed, somebody had to pay for it... They just expected it all to be laid on. They would always dispute how much things cost, whereas if they'd spent it themselves it would have turned out the same. A lot of the expenses that shocked them, they generated by hasty or impulsive actions - like cancelling a European tour. They would then insist that Rough Trade swallow that - but it was a 50:50 deal. No matter what it was, if they didn't like it, after the fact, they didn't want to pay half for it... It was a continual problem."

Responding to Piering's argument, Marr observed: "That's one way of looking at it! I think there's some truth in all that, but to take a specific example - tours. I'd say people should have asked for more money or made it realistic for us to play gigs. There's no reason that a group of our stature should not have been making money from gigs and that's pretty much why we cancelled those tours." Of course, Marr's explanation failed to take account of the sheer capriciousness that ruled so many of The Smiths' decisions.

By August, an uneasy truce was announced between Rough Trade and The Smiths, resulting in the autumn release of a new single. 'The Boy With The Thorn In His Side' reiterated Morrissey's customary themes of lovelorn loneliness, hatred and idealism, with a splendid and infectious acoustic backing from Marr. The song was extremely commercial, but failed to climb higher than number 23, despite Morrissey having reluctantly agreed to sanction a video for the first time. The lowly chart position reaffirmed recent concern about Rough Trade's promotional work.

Concern of a different kind accompanied discussion of the single's flipside. 'Asleep' presented a despair so languid and alluring that some felt it unintentionally glamorized suicide. Morrissey, whose gallery of heroes included several suicides, did not flinch from discussing the topic, invariably relating such tragic deaths to personal neuroses, unconnected to the power of his lyrics. He might have added that his championing of the outsider in society was more likely to prove therapeutic than destructive. On the bonus 12-inch track, 'Rubber Ring', Morrissey returned to another of his favourite themes: "the passing of time". The lyrics provided a reminder of earlier days when his record collection was regarded as his one true friend. Amid the additional sound effects, Morrissey included a favourite Oscar Wilde aphorism: "Everybody's clever nowadays".

The passing of time was also emphasized by a minor bereavement in the Morrissey household. Earlier in the year, he had been regaling journalists with tales of his extraordinary cat, Tibby, a veteran of the pre-Beatle era, still hobbling around the house at the ripe old age of 23. Morrissey proudly noted that the ageing animal was a full year older than any of his fellow Smiths. On 23 September, however, the geriatric feline said goodbye to its ninth life. After suffering a fit, it lay helplessly on the floor until its master carefully deposited its expiring remains into a basket. "The way he looked at me, it was like he knew he was going to die," Morrissey recalled with mawkish regret. The following day, the singer awoke early in the morning and found the creature dead in its basket. Hastening to bury the carcass in a garden, he was thwarted by a wretched downpour. Finding himself burdened with a wet, dead cat was not the ideal preparation for a Smiths tour of Scotland, which was due to commence later that day.

Despite the cat crisis, Morrissey appeared punctually at the opening dates, which proved very successful. As well as playing the major cities in Scotland, The Smiths underlined their love of medium-sized, impoverished pop venues by performing in such unlikely places as Irvine, the Shetland Isles and Inverness. Resolute, independent and as uncompromising as ever, the group's continued determination to eschew traditionally major rock venues suggested a willingness to remain small-time. This, however, was never the case. The Smiths were ambitious and overly-critical of their lowly commercial status, despite their unwillingness to travel the well-furrowed path of more careerist contemporaries. The belief that they had outgrown Rough Trade, coupled with the frustration that followed the middling success of recent singles, convinced Morrissey/Marr that a new direction was necessary. Given the degree of dissatisfaction that accompanied their relationship with the label, it was more surprising that they had remained independent for so long. Their suspicion and disillusionment was quietly summed up in a conversation between Johnny Marr and Easterhouse manager John Barratt. Prior to the performance at Glasgow Barrowlands, the sussed guitarist warned Barratt to be wary of Geoff Travis. No specific reason was given. Relations between The Smiths and their label rapidly reached crisis point after the tour. By November, the group had completed work on their next album but a release date was suspended. Amid increasing rumours of their intended departure from Rough Trade, and a collapse in communication, the record company took the first line of defence and secured a High Court injunction restraining the group from recording for another label.

13

The Queen Is Dead

THE SMITHS OPENED 1986 in a position of stalemate. Unable to record new material, they were doubly frustrated by the postponement of their new album, which Rough Trade was keeping on ice until the legal dispute was settled. Johnny Marr went through an uncharacteristically dark period at this point, as if realizing that the group's future was in severe jeopardy. He had worked extremely hard producing the album and felt exhilarated prior to its completion. "Johnny was so sick of it that he asked me, 'Could you finish it off?'" John Porter recalled. The producer duly engineered 'Frankly Mr Shankly' at the close of the sessions. "The album did him in," Porter revealed. "It was a lot of responsibility."

Marr's life might have been easier had he been allowed to concentrate solely on the music and production. All too often, however, he was plagued by the inevitable legacy of The Smiths' continued lack of management: wearying business and legal wrangles. At a crucial point during the sessions, a representative from Rough Trade telephoned the studio with the disturbing news that The Smiths' van hire company was pressing charges because the group had neglected to return a truck. It was at this point that Marr realized he was taking on too much. At earlier times, he had been known to socialize and party after a session, but *The Queen Is Dead* involved intense evenings working on overdubs and planning the following day's recordings. "Johnny became insular and detached from myself and Andy," Joyce recalls. "He was taking on a lot and wanted to do it himself. I remember him not wanting us around for awhile."

The isolation evidently took its toll. "It was really tough," Marr confirms. "I locked myself away for a couple of weeks after I finished that record. I sat in a chair, didn't move and got depressed, which was pretty unlike me. I lost loads of weight and was very skinny and unhealthy. I was ill quite a lot in The Smiths, being a hyper person. I've calmed down quite a lot. I used to throw up all the time. *The Queen Is Dead* was very difficult."

In the creative vacuum that followed the album, Marr and Rourke joined Billy Bragg on the Red Wedge tour. The full Smiths line-up played a four-song set at Newcastle City Hall, but their singer seemed bemused by it all. "I didn't really understand what was going on onstage," he recalls. "It all seemed a little limp to me, even though there were people involved that I do admire."

The following week, the group joined New Order and The Fall for "From Manchester With Love", a benefit concert in aid of 49 Liverpool councillors who were being taken to court by the government for refusing to set a legal rate. Predictably, Morrissey/Marr were absent from the preliminary meeting between councillor Derek Hatton, Mark E Smith and New Order. It was left to Stuart James to act as The Smiths' shoulder-shrugging representative. The concert at Liverpool's Royal Court was reasonably successful, but merely proved a deceptive prelude to what was arguably the biggest crisis in the group's career.

The "Irish tour" was, by now, a traditional part of The Smiths' gigging calendar and provided some of their most relaxed and convivial moments. The trip across the water coincided with the usual drinking session but, for Andy Rourke, stronger substances were required. The following evening at the National Stadium, Dublin, the group's set was marred by a lacklustre display from the troubled bassist. Given Rourke's integral importance to The Smiths' live performance, it was difficult to disguise his shortcomings. As Grant Showbiz remarked: "Andy had lost it. Out of 10 notes, he was playing three. He was completely gone and just stopped playing numbers... Everybody was deeply concerned about Andy."

Although the other two dates, at Dundalk's Fairways Hotel and Queen's University, Belfast, passed without incident, the state of Rourke became a biting issue. Precisely a year before, he had been warned of the need to stay straight while working with The Smiths, and this public relapse had broken that pact. "It was difficult with Andy because he was out of it all the time and it got to the point where you had to take a stance", Joyce remarked. "It not only affected his playing but when we were together. It was difficult to get through to him." Although the drummer had broached the subject with Rourke, the bassist knew that his partner had no experience of addiction. "You don't understand" was Andy's weary response whenever advice was dished out.

Marr was uncertain about what action to take against his friend, feeling that it was almost hypocritical to adopt a self-righteous attitude. "They had this friendship that was so strong that it was tearing Johnny to pieces," Grant explained. "I was one of the people who said we should get rid of Andy. I felt it would be for the best. The only way for him to sort himself out was to be kicked out of the band and told that he would have to stop taking drugs." Onstage with Rourke, Marr had realized the extent of his partner's troubles. "He just wasn't in a state to play," he observed. "That was the thing. It was more so when he was trying to come off heroin, and that's what happened on that Irish tour. He finally took too much methadone and wasn't fun to be around."

Morrissey and Marr informed Rourke of their decision and he accepted the news stoically. Far from arguing his case, he realized that he was in danger of letting the group down, which only made the dismissal more difficult. "It was really painful, but it had been on the cards for some time," Johnny recalls. "That was one of the low points of my life. Seeing Andy taking a couple of his basses from my house and getting in his car was really upsetting. But I knew he'd get over it."

After returning from Ireland, Marr urgently sought a replacement bassist. Drummer Simon Wolstencroft suggested Craig Gannon, whom he had played alongside in The Colourfield. Gannon was a talented journeyman guitarist, whose curriculum vitae included stints with Aztec Camera and The Bluebells. Marr initially offered Gannon the bassist spot, secure in the knowledge that, should Andy return, the new arrival could be retained as a second guitarist. Events took an unhappy turn the following week when Rourke was arrested for possession of heroin. On a purely expedient note, this might have prompted a complete ostracism, but, instead, his friends rallied around. "We were convinced that if we let him go, we'd find he was dead in six months," Grant confessed. "I was convinced of that and I think Johnny was too. The only thing that was seemingly holding Andy together was The Smiths. We were proved wrong, though, as you so often are with these things."

The double shock of being fired from The Smiths and arrested convinced Rourke that his heroin habit had to be banished permanently. Those who suspected that Morrissey's anti-drug stance would harden the singer against Rourke underestimated his humanity. "His leaving seemed more wrong than his staying," the vocalist confirmed. "It was too easy to turn like a pack and say, 'You're useless. Get out'." As a result, the group reconsidered their decision and invited the errant bassist to return. On this occasion, he kept his promise and stayed straight. "When he left he became even more depressed than when he was with the group," Morrissey recalls. "It was getting quite serious so he really had to come back... it seemed very unnatural and ridiculous to even consider such things as session musicians and people from other parts of the country." To Rourke's credit, he never fell out with his fellow Smiths, despite his bouts of drug dependence. "I've never come across a junkie who wasn't a bastard, except Andy," Johnny reasoned. "He never turned into a bastard in his life, and that's the first thing that usually happens. He came out of it and he's still not bitter, unbalanced or nasty, and he never was. The only person he ever took it out on was himself. There was great moral courage there, against the odds."

The rehabilitation of Rourke stabilized The Smiths at a time when they were under immense legal, creative and personal pressures. A further twist was added to the story when Craig Gannon was kept on as additional guitarist following Rourke's return. Marr realized that Gannon's adaptability would be beneficial to The Smiths in various ways. Johnny already had the considerable burden of approximating live the multi-track, wall-of-sound, guitar displays concocted in the studio, and this process would prove more challenging than ever with the release of their new album. It was intended that Gannon should beef up The Smiths' sound and prevent Marr from spreading himself too thinly. The restructuring of The Smiths also encouraged Johnny to explore new ideas and, over the next year, his influence on the musical direction of the group would be more profound than ever.

In the aftermath of the Rourke affair, The Smiths continued their renegotiation with Rough Trade. Marr had already introduced a buccaneering element to the proceedings by commandeering roadie Phil Powell in an attempt to liberate the mastertapes by cloak and dagger methods. One snowy evening, they set off from Manchester and drove to Guildford, intent on bluffing their way into the studios. The plan was foiled. With Travis maintaining his ground, the group found a more orthodox solution to their woes by re-enlisting Matthew Sztumpf as their manager. Working in tandem with solicitors, Sztumpf entered delicate negotiations with Travis. Neither party welcomed the prospect of proceeding to trial since, apart from the intimidating legal fees, the release of the lucrative new album could be postponed for a further year. Travis held firm, but agreed to increase Morrissey/Marr's advance and, more importantly, reduced their outstanding contractual commitment from two albums to one (excluding compilations and live recordings). The essential profit-sharing system remained intact and no attempt was made to append the names of the other Smiths to the revised agreement.

Within weeks of the renegotiation, Morrissey and Marr were discussing where they might record their next studio album. They planned to move to America, complete some sessions and concentrate on touring. In retrospect, it seems remarkable that the "travel-shy" Morrissey would countenance such a radical proposal but, for a time, he seemed taken with the idea. Accompanied by Sztumpf, the duo flew to Los Angeles and looked at a number of apartments, but none proved suitable. After promising to continue the search later in the year, they returned to the UK and promptly forgot all about the grand scheme. Their flightiness descended upon the perplexed Sztumpf, who soon discovered that his services were no longer required. "My mistake was not saying, 'I won't lift a finger until contracts are signed between us'," he reflects. "But that's not the way I work. The injunction had to be sorted out immediately... I wasn't there long enough for royalties to be commissioned, so I just billed them for my services. I'd fulfilled my purpose, but they paid me, and I enjoyed it while it lasted." Ironically, Sztumpf was in the process of setting up a European tour when the axe fell. Not surprisingly, the Continental jaunt was swiftly abandoned.

The convenient dismissal of Sztumpf reiterated The Smiths' determination to maintain control of their financial and artistic destinies; it also underlined a fundamental naïvety about the function of management. Marr gave the mistaken impression that he regarded Sztumpf as a potential hatchet man of Allen Klein proportions. In a discussion with Grant Showbiz, Johnny portrayed Sztumpf as the new broom who would prefer to bring in his own men and might even rid The Smiths of several key personnel. In fact, it was Sztumpf himself who felt pressurized into making changes. At one point, Morrissey cheekily suggested that he should forego managing Madness and concentrate entirely on The Smiths. Eventually, Sztumpf compromised by moving his office to a "neutral ground" away from the heart of the Madness empire. "The Smiths were always concerned that Madness would come first and I'd be playing second fiddle," he complained.

Morrissey's conviction that another act would distract Sztumpf from a total commitment to The Smiths betrayed a myopic perspective of the pop management role. With Madness and The Smiths on his roster, Sztumpf's clout and standing in the industry would have improved vastly and enabled him to negotiate from a stronger position. What Morrissey required was the subservient "neutered lackey" manager, a species that is not only entirely dependent on the artiste, but commands little respect from more powerful business rivals. Morrissey's possessive personality consistently prevented him from allowing anybody to "manage" The Smiths. After abandoning Sztumpf, he again fell back on non-managerial employees, who were nevertheless called upon to perform quasi-managerial tasks. Martha Defoe, an excellent organizer who had already proven her worth during the formation of Smithdom, fell in and out of favour, but lacked the music business experience to assume the traditional managerial role. As Scott Piering noted: "Martha wasn't a Jazz Summers who could really go in and kick ass with CBS, but she was someone they could trust." Defoe's strength was her directness and determined efficiency. She claims Morrissey once gave her the ultimate passing compliment: "Whatever you say you'll do, I'm always sure it will happen." Although sensitive to the personal dynamics within the group, Defoe remained closest to Morrissey, which may have proven a fault as well as a virtue. "Martha, in the end, figuratively fell in love with Morrissey and was totally besotted with him," Piering observed. "As soon as you start getting that way with Morrissey, your days are numbered. Many times, when things were fine, Morrissey was just keeping Martha at bay. Alternatively, he loved the attention he got from her. Intellectually, they were equals; she could relate to him, knew what books to buy him, and she was very good for Morrissey. But she clung to him."

Morrissey's love of feminine solicitude was emphasized by the number of women whom he relied upon as administrators. In addition to his mother and Martha Defoe, there was Pat Bellis, whose tasks stretched far beyond those of the normal record company press officer. Jo Slee, who enjoyed a separate sleeve artwork agreement with Morrissey, was another confidante who could always be relied upon to provide help whenever asked. Morrissey's band of female supporters was of considerable assistance during The Smiths' lengthy periods of self-management, but ultimately proved an inadequate substitute for a full-time, experienced, personal/business manager.

The upheavals of early 1986 were placed in a more pleasing perspective with the release of the long-awaited new Smiths single in May. The initial airing on BBC Radio 1's Janice Long evening show was a devastatingly dramatic moment and I still recall standing in my ascetically sparse, under-equipped kitchen, frozen in gleeful awe. 'Big Mouth Strikes Again' was a superbly structured single, which revealed Marr's absolute mastery of the form. The strident acoustic opening and pounding bass prefaces one of Morrissey's most sincerely sarcastic vocal pleadings. The soothing first line, "Sweetness, I was only joking... " is followed by a succession of typically violent images, with Morrissey comparing himself to a modern-day Joan of Arc. The references to being bound at the stake and ostracized from the human race for his "big-mouthed" outbursts were amusingly topical, particularly in view of his recent catalogue of controversial remarks. The single added a witty, satirical edge to The Smiths' ever-improving songbook. Marr regarded the song as his 'Jumpin' Jack Flash', with as dextrous a display of Keith Richard-styled rhythm-playing as one could reasonably demand. The song even contained a heart-stopping "moment in time". Joyce's fierce, speaker-splitting drum roll followed by Marr's gambolling rhythmic break was an object lesson in the brilliant use of economy. The entire effect was complemented by the unexpected appearance of a "female" vocalist, who sang in perfect syncopation to Morrissey. Identified as "Ann Coates" (a play on Ancoats), the mystery vocalist was actually Morrissey himself, recorded at a faster speed by the mischievous Marr.

Although 'Big Mouth Strikes Again' contained enough drama and commercial clout to threaten the Top Five, it slumped to an appalling number 26, faring no better than 'Shakespeare's Sister' and worse than 'The Boy With The Thorn In His Side'. It was a frightening injustice, no doubt made worse by Travis' insistence that the forthcoming 'There Is A Light That Never Goes Out' would have fared better. However, Marr had made a crucial point in establishing The Smiths as one of the few artistes of the Eighties that crafted singles of supreme worth. He now looks back at those chart disappointments with resignation. "I was happy to have certain songs on singles like 'Shakespeare's Sister', 'That Joke Isn't Funny Anymore' and 'Big Mouth Strikes Again' because they were radical rock singles, and that suited me. I was happy just owning them myself. The fact that we didn't get on *Top Of The Pops* with those records is neither here nor there. I preferred those to the ones that did get on television." Nevertheless, at the time of their release, the group were unforgiving in their condemnation of Rough Trade's promotion, and the threat of defection to a major label remained ever present.

For all their acclaimed "Britishness", The Smiths never exuded that most British of traits: "reserve". Instead, they trumpeted their achievements loudly and immodestly. The cockiness of Marr and the self-adulation of Morrissey were translated into a group motto that read: "We're the most important group of the Eighties". What might have sounded empty, self-satisfied arrogance in the mouths of lesser beings, served as an innocent statement of fact to Smiths aficionados. The Smiths used self-serving epithets as a form of party political broadcast and found that their boasts were rapidly transformed into critical cliché. The propaganda worked to spectacular effect encouraging insecure, fence-sitting journalists to trot out the "most important group of the Eighties" line without seriously considering its full implications. By the summer of 1986, however, the need to justify The Smiths was rendered irrelevant.

The Queen Is Dead is the ultimate proof, if one were needed, of the complete legitimacy of The Smiths' unironic self-aggrandizement. Arguably the most accomplished album of the Eighties, the work captures the

Morrissey/Marr partnership at its apotheosis. More than any other work in their canon, *The Queen Is Dead* crystallized the contradictory and complementary visions of its creators in a panoramic sweep of absolute grandeur. An album of strikingly different tones, the work begins with the drama of a fully-fledged concept album and closes with a comic lightness of touch that could not have come from any other pen but that of Morrissey. The range of mood, emotion and perspective is breathtakingly diverse: rage and laughter alternates, sometimes within the space of a single line; romantic idealism gives way to *Carry On* comedy; maudlin despair is alleviated by music hall frivolity; humanity and misanthropy coalesce uneasily, while world-weary resignation finds expression through a strange, yet glorious defiance.

On *The Queen Is Dead* Morrissey emerges as the most interesting pop songwriter of his generation, with a variety of personae: the scathing satirist, the introspective romantic, the gauche comedian and the playfully-ironic plagiarist. Marr's achievement is no less striking. The 19-year-old genius of yore is transformed into a mature wunderkind, whose work echoes the casually-cool rock classicism of Keith Richard, the brooding drama of mid-period Pete Townshend and the purist sensitivity of vintage Eric Clapton.

The Queen Is Dead borrowed its title from a section of Hubert Selby Jnr's notorious book *Last Exit To Brooklyn*. Within its new context, however, the homosexual angle is underplayed in favour of a mock-epic assault on Her Majesty The Queen. Significantly, the album was to be titled *Margaret On A Guillotine*, but Morrissey would not complete his anti-Thatcherite diatribe until 1987. Retaining the political theme, he focused attention on the state of contemporary Britain. The atmospheric Cicely Courtneidge singalong brilliantly captures the evanescent image of an ill-defined but lost verdant England that dissolves before Joyce's fierce drumming and Marr's epically-constructed soundscape of MC5/Stooges-influenced wah-wah guitar. "Morrissey said he wanted to include 'Take Me Back To Dear Old Blighty' on the track," Marr recalls. "But he wasn't to know that I was intending to lead into feedback and drum rolls. It was just magic. I got the drum riff going and Andy had the bass line, which was one of his best ever, and something that bass players still haven't matched. I went in there with all the lads watching, did the take and they just went, 'Wow'. I came out and I was shaking. When I suggested, 'I'll do it again', they just said, 'No way! No way!'"

What added to the song's tremendous power was Morrissey's startling vocal and fascinating lyrics. Scabrously satiric, he approaches the body politic armed with a scalpel that he will later turn unexpectedly on himself. No longer content merely to drop his trousers to the Queen, he now dreams of seeing her head in a sling. The fantasy execution, however, is superseded by a more convivial narrative. Unlike the agitprop 'Margaret On A Guillotine', 'The Queen Is Dead' is playful and irreverent, rather than vicious and vindictive. Morrissey does not enter the palace clutching a hangman's noose, but chooses a harmless sponge and a rusty spanner.

Moreover, it soon transpires that his intention is not regicide but pleasant banter.* The virulent social critique of royal decadence, church materialism, public house escapism and pre-teen drug-pedalling presents a nightmare vision of a country weakened by spiritual and moral decay. "You can get florid about politics and the state of the country," he declared, "but it comes down to the very basic arguments that they don't care, and they should!" Warming to his theme, Morrissey launched a familiar attack on the monarchy: "The royal family is an institution which is built entirely on murder and deceit and fraud and hate and we should never forget those things. We shouldn't feel that simply because it's an English tradition that it's good."

What is interesting about 'The Queen Is Dead', however, is that it transcends mere diatribe to focus on the personal. In what is undoubtedly his most serious, powerful and outward-looking Smiths song, Morrissey turns inward to relieve his rage and disillusionment with snatches of bathetic humour. The Queen's criticism of his singing prompts an amusingly self-deprecating reference to his non-musical abilities ("that's nothing, you should hear me play piano!'). The imaginary transvesticism of dear Charles displayed on the front page of the *Daily Mail* is mirrored by the singer's shock and shame at discovering skeletons in his own family tree ("I'm the 18th pale descendant of some old queen or other"). What begins as an epic is continually subverted into mock epic; the rant becomes a romp and, finally, a black fairy tale. In the final stanza, Morrissey emerges as a reassuring town crier, proclaiming the death of the Queen before returning to more familiar introspective musings that tell him "life is very long when you're lonely".

'Frankly Mr Shankly', which was mixed towards the end of *The Queen Is Dead* sessions, contrastingly evoked the uproarious spirit of George Formby. Morrissey reveals himself as a music-hall humorist with one of the most cutting voices in pop history. It is generally acknowledged in music business circles that such lyrics as "I want to leave/you will not miss me/I want to go down in musical history" are an oblique reference to the Rough Trade dispute, with Travis cast in the central role as "righteous", "holy" and "a pain in the arse". Absent from the lyric sheet was the spiteful coda "give us your money!" How did Travis feel about being labelled the butt of Morrissey's satiric wit? "Well, it's not a particularly charming thought, is it?" he responded. "There's a huge amount of humour in the song and I'm not really upset by it. Camp spite? I think there's a lot of that there, but I don't take it too seriously. Morrissey likes to have some fun and that's what rock 'n' roll is about."

The ordering of the album tracks was carefully constructed so that the canter of 'Frankly Mr Shankly' abruptly shifts to the desolate introspection of 'I Know It's Over'. A candidate for Morrissey's most bleak work, the

---

* This episode was inspired by the disturbed Michael Fagin, who not only broke into Buckingham Palace, but actually entered the Queen's boudoir and chatted with her over a cigarette, before being led away. Thereafter, the easy entrances to the palace grounds were reinforced by barbed wire, less scaleable walls and more vigilant surveillance.

song laments the loss of a happiness that was itself a fantasy ("I know it's over/and it never really began"). Against a funereal melody, Morrissey's central image of being buried alive gains poignant force. Marr felt overwhelmed by Morrissey's vocal reading of the song, which he regards as one of his finest. "I'll never forget when he did it," he remembers. "It's one of the highlights of my life. It was that good, that strong. Every line he was hinting at where he was going to go. I kept thinking, 'Is he going to go there. Yes, he is!' It was just brilliant."

The speculations on loneliness and uncertainty in 'I Know It's Over' continued on the elliptical 'Never Had No One Ever'. In recalling the lack of ease in patrolling Manchester's streets, Morrissey presents life as a nightmare that lasted "20 years, seven months and 27 days". Strictly speaking, that would date life's awakening for Steven as 18 January 1980. Predictably, there was nothing special about that particular day, which he spent at home, nursing a sore foot, reading a copy of *The Murderers' Who's Who* and recalling a recent horrific spell as a hospital porter. The central message of 'Never Had No One Ever' was repeated in the run-off grooves of the album, which read: "Fear of Manchester"/"Them Was Rotten Days".

The recollections of late Seventies/early Eighties Manchester culminate in the wonderfully witty 'Cemetry Gates'.* Marr's sprightly arrangement expertly evokes the *joie de vivre* among the gravestones. The melody was conceived in Marr's kitchen one afternoon when he was tuning his guitar. Morrissey was struck by a particular run of chords and announced authoritatively: "That's the song!" Marr was impressed. "When I sat down my idea was for it to be a Kinks song," he explains. "For some reason, it was speeded-up. It's strange." No less strange to source-hunting aficionados were those playful lyrics. Given Morrissey's insistence, "If you must write prose/poems/the words you use should be your own/don't plagiarize or take 'on loan'", it seems sneakingly appropriate that he would choose this moment to indulge some of his legendary "borrowings". The most moving stanza in the song is the cod Shakespearian soliloquy: "All those people, all those lives/where are they now?/with loves, and hates/and passions just like mine/they were born/and then they lived/and then they died/which seems so unfair/and I want to cry." The inspiration for these lines came from one of Morrissey's favourite films, *The Man Who Came To Dinner*. In the movie, Katharine Hepburn provides a similar philosophical lament: "All those people, all those lives, where are they now? Here was a woman who once lived and loved, full of the same passions, fears, jealousies, hates. And what remains of it now... I want to cry". The melancholic air that pervades the song is also the source of its exuberance. Literary oneupmanship is amusingly described in Morrissey's heretical placing of Wilde before such major poets as John Keats and WB Yeats. Other comic moments, such as the use of archaisms and crazy tense breakdowns (" 'ere long done do does did") provide an engaging self-mockery. The underlying nostalgic

---

* The misspelling of cemetery was not intentional. Morrissey always had problems with the word, which he spelt "cemetary" in the manuscript of *Exit Smiling*.

mood gains further force from the real life memories of sunny days at Manchester's Southern Cemetery, where Morrissey and Linder played out their own version of the graveyard scene in *Billy Liar*.

The sublime single, 'Big Mouth Strikes Again', opens side two on a suitably emphatic note, buoyed by the light touch of 'The Boy With The Thorn In His Side' and a further frolic of transvesticism in 'Vicar In A Tutu'. Marr's rockabilly rhythms forge an unlikely link between the mid-Fifties Memphis Sun sound and that quintessentially English phenomenon - the fabled, saucy vicar of Sunday tabloid infamy. The melody had emerged while Marr was riffing on some chords and Joyce casually joined in. Morrissey popped his head around the studio door and exclaimed: "Carry on! That's the song." As Joyce noted: "If we'd had a name producer I don't think 'Vicar In A Tutu' would have come about."

Comedy again gives way to melodrama with the anthemic 'There Is A Light That Never Goes Out', on which Marr displays his arranging abilities, courtesy of some subtly swirling strings. The song delicately describes the painful yearning for a sensual/sexual experience which seems doomed to remain tantalizingly ungraspable, even when the chance is offered. Morrissey's ultimate expression of adolescent wish-fulfilment, the composition dramatizes a seductive longing for a romantic death ("and if a double-decker bus/crashes into us/to die by your side/is such a heavenly way to die") whose pathetic futility might bring immortal meaning to a fantasy relationship.

After the high melodrama of 'There Is A Light That Never Goes Out', The Smiths close the album with the bathetic 'Some Girls Are Bigger Than Others'. On the previous two albums, the final tracks mourned murder and animal slaughter, but here Morrissey breaks with tradition to lighten the tone. In citing Antony And Cleopatra, Morrissey does not borrow from Shakespeare, but prefers the uproarious film *Carry On Cleo*, in which actor Sid James is shown cracking open a bottle of ale. As the song fades, Morrissey revisits the early sixties for a muted reprise of Johnny Tillotson's 'Send Me The Pillow You Dream On'. This purposely unportentous finale, with some excellent slide work from Marr, supplies a playful coda to an album of classic distinction. *The Queen Is Dead* was a magnificent achievement that would transcend its time to lodge at the summit of those deceptively mutable "Critics' All-Time Top 100 Albums".

The contribution of the rhythm section to the longevity of the work deserves special commendation, as Marr is quick to note. "There was perfect musical unity between myself, Mike and Andy," he stresses. "Mike really learned to play with me like no one else. I really felt I turned him on to the Charlie Watts ethic. It was a dream for me to play on. Mike was just behind me and Andy fitted in the middle. That's the way we worked. Mike learned to be a good drummer by playing in The Smiths. I had something playing with Mike and Andy that I won't have playing with any other people."

14

Death Stalks Johnny Marr

THE FIRST LEG OF *The Queen Is Dead* promotional tour took in a handful of dates at Glasgow, Newcastle and Manchester. The most noteworthy of these was the "Festival Of The Tenth Summer" at Manchester's G-Mex, where The Smiths again played on a bill alongside New Order and The Fall. Prior to their appearance, Marr copiously vomited, much to the concerned astonishment of visiting film director, Derek Jarman. Morrissey was largely unmoved by the G-Mex event and already had his mind on the more challenging prospect of conquering America. Even while The Smiths were packing their bags, yet another single was issued which, against the odds, provided the biggest hit of their career.

The genesis of 'Panic' can be traced back to 26 April, when Morrissey and Marr tuned into Radio 1, only to be greeted by a news flash about the Chernobyl disaster. The bulletin was allegedly followed by the upbeat vacuity of Wham's 'I'm Your Man'. Morrissey felt so indignant about this insensitive lapse in broadcasting that he decided to condemn the programmers by composing a single with the spiteful refrain: "Hang the DJ". The chorus simultaneously served as a vengeful riposte against the station's premier disc jockey Steve Wright, who had lampooned The Smiths consistently, and openly stated that they had no place on daytime radio. With Morrissey's pen already dripping in vitriol, Marr contacted John Porter in London and promised to send down a rough demo of preliminary ideas. The producer was amused to receive a copy of T Rex's 'Metal Guru' in the following morning's post. Inspired by his teenage affection for Marc Bolan, Marr emerged with a distinctive riff, which was neatly offset by Morrissey's underlying theme of urban unrest. On the 12-inch version of 'Panic', Marr introduced the shimmering 'The Draize Train'. Morrissey was unconvinced by the track and declined to add lyrics despite a personal entreaty from Geoff Travis, who felt the melody had hit potential. Guitar technician Alan Rogan subsequently lent Johnny two of Pete Townshend's Rickenbackers to enrich the instrumental, which compared reasonably well with its predecessors, 'Oscillate Wildly' and 'Money Changes Everything'. The enduring appeal of these mood pieces was later indicated by Bryan Ferry's decision to record a vocal version of 'Money Changes Everything', which reached the Top 40 under its new title, 'The Right Stuff'.

'Panic' duly climbed to number 10 in the UK charts, equalling their previous best showing with 'Heaven Knows I'm Miserable Now'. Fortunately, Radio 1 producers were not put off by the song's violent imagery, which they regarded as less graphic than that of the preceding 'Big Mouth Strikes Again'. The mainstream disc jockey, Steve Wright, who was then unaware of his role in inspiring 'Panic', magnanimously played the single on several afternoons. The irony was sweet.

Although The Smiths were not available to promote 'Panic', the controversial Derek Jarman provided his own visual interpretation in a commissioned 15-minute movie, which also included 'The Queen Is Dead' and 'There Is A Light That Never Goes Out'. Using fast cuts to suggest disorientation and imminent disorder, Jarman captured the *esprit* of the single to considerable effect, particularly in the strangely disturbing image of the children innocently chanting ("Hang the DJ, hang the DJ"). The nursery rhyme lilt was highly amusing in its taunting invective, especially amid Morrissey's tale of urban terror. For once, it seemed, the singer had unleashed his petulant fury without causing a media backlash. After all, who cared about a humorously reckless gibe against disc jockeys? The answer would be forthcoming in the autumn.

The Smiths' second major tour was preceded by another flurry of managerial solicitations. The latest candidate was Mark Fenwick, the mainman at EG Management, whose artistes roster included Roxy Music, Bryan Ferry and Emerson, Lake & Palmer. The public school educated Fenwick, who had the demeanour of an officer in the Household Cavalry, seemed an unlikely candidate, but he was certainly the most experienced professional manager ever to win The Smiths' brief approval. Although he commenced preliminary work on the US tour, the management deal did not reach fruition. After failing to agree terms with The Smiths' solicitor, Alexis Grower, Fenwick withdrew. Ironically, Morrissey and Marr would soon part company with their forceful solicitor in another of their perennial change arounds. An equally pressing consideration during this phase was the group line-up for the American tour. It was assumed that Andy's drug and legal problems would force him to remain at home, so a substitute bassist was recruited. The replacement was Guy Pratt, a talented guitarist, who would later tour with Pink Floyd and Madonna. Rourke showed a charitable willingness to coach his putative replacement and the pair studiously went through every bass line in The Smiths' canon. Pratt even displayed image consciousness and duly had his locks shorn in anticipation of the tour. His haircut ultimately proved unnecessary when officialdom granted Rourke permission to work in the States after all.

The Smiths' latest tour manager was Sophie Ridley, who had previously worked as wardrobe assistant for one of the group's least favourite artistes, The Thompson Twins. Ridley had her work cut out during the US visit and, even before the first gig, there was a threatened mutiny among concerned crew members, whose advance payments had yet to arrive. Marr was persuaded to telephone the record company and sort the matter out, much to his indignation. "There was always panic with people running round to my and Morrissey's hotel room," he recalls. "We just took on far too much."

During an exceedingly challenging six-week period, The Smiths played to more people than at any comparable period in their career. The itinerary took in 27 dates at theatres, ballrooms and stadiums scattered across Canada and a sizeable area of the United States. There were some mad moments along the way, including a remarkable gig in Orange County, where the stage was invaded by a gang of kids, high on angel dust. Temporarily granted super strength, they made mincemeat of the advancing bouncers but fortunately left The Smiths unharmed. Morrissey and Marr were intoxicated by the reception they received, and in more ways than one. "There was a lot of romanticism and Johnny was living to the hilt on that tour," Grant Showbiz recalls. Bottles of Remy Martin were par for the gig and Marr admitted that his excesses were worthy of a Hollywood alcoholic. For many dates, it was a case of Marr "being hungover, half drunk, sick on the airport floor and having to get on a plane to another soundcheck." Not surprisingly, the weeks passed in a woozy, nauseous blur. "I just remember really bad times," Marr confesses, "like laying on the end of a bed with Angie saying, 'Someone's got to do something about this'. I used to drink more than I could handle."

There were, of course, drunken snatches of light relief. At one performance, Johnny turned to Morrissey and noted, self-mockingly: "I'm so gone, I don't know what the next bit is!" Morrissey quizzically retorted, "But what song are you talking about?" Far from frowning on the party atmosphere, the normally reticent Morrissey welcomed the festivities and was often seen downing several glasses of wine.

For relative new boy Craig Gannon, the US tour was an eye-opener, but although he liked a drink and a laugh, his presence in the camp seemed strangely incongruous. "Craig was personable, but he never really connected," Grant Showbiz remembers. "The Smiths was a real family and he never honed in. He was this shy, slightly clumsy chap, who'd fall over things. The standard of his live work wasn't as brilliant as the rest of The Smiths and not quite right for them. He was looked after, but it never got beyond the introductory stage - he seemed to stay at one level. It was more like a mate coming along to play." As the dates unfolded, Morrissey began to wonder whether a "fifth Smith" was really necessary. For the present, he deferred the matter, but Gannon's future in the line-up was clearly precarious at best.

The hedonistic American tour ended abruptly at Tampa on 10 September and the four remaining concerts in Miami, Atlanta, Nashville and New York were cancelled. In spite of the excesses of the tour Morrissey/Marr had seen enough to convince themselves that the New World was at their feet. Unfortunately, the response from enthusiastic concert habitués was not reflected in record sales. Although perennial favourites on college radio, The Smiths failed to transform their campus credibility into mainstream FM fame. Geoff Travis was convinced that this jump had been frustratingly close in 1986. "There's no doubt in my mind that The Smiths would have been huge in America," he argues. "They felt angry that their singles weren't hits and I agreed with them. For a long time, they were neck and neck with REM. When REM hit with 'The One I Love', it changed their career. That's all it needed. The Smiths could have achieved what REM have done, if not more. If they'd continued that normal career trajectory of putting out great records and touring, they would have been massive. The Kinks were really loved more in America over the past 25 years than in England, and the same could have happened to The Smiths. They had that Englishness that appeals to Americans. They would never have been as big as Prince, or a stadium rock group like The Eurythmics, but Morrissey always put on a decent show and I think he'd have been fine."

Despite plans for another US invasion in the near future, the 1986 visit was to prove The Smiths' last. After returning to the UK, however, Morrissey was haunted by an interview he had conducted with a British journalist prior to a performance at the Music Hall, Cleveland, on 8 August. The reporter was Frank Owen (formerly Gavin Owen of Manicured Noise), who used his familiarity with the Manchester scene of the late Seventies to fashion a particularly graphic piece, which appeared in *Melody Maker* at the end of September.

Owen's inflammatory view was that 'Panic' represented "the most explicit denunciation yet of black pop." Rather than interpreting the single as a Swiftian assault on the inanity of pop radio presenters, Owen interpreted the work as an attack on disc-jockey dominated house music and hip-hop. In one sense, the writer had a point. Within the song, Morrissey steps far beyond Radio 1 banality in his general admonition to "burn down the disco". The conflagration of those subterranean nocturnal haunts where all forms of artifice are apparently regarded as worthy human endeavour was a fantasy that appealed to Morrissey's mischievously anarchic imagination. However, the *Melody Maker* piece went further than this by implying that The Smiths' music was "racist" in championing and reinforcing fundamental "indie" ideals that appeared to exclude black culture. It was an odd but provocative line of questioning that prompted Morrissey to launch a scathing attack on reggae as "the most racist music in the entire world" and "an absolute glorification of black supremacy".

Such intolerance was no great shock to Morrissey's followers, who had been alerted to the singer's detestation of reggae 19 months before. In replying to an *NME* poll in February 1985, he had caustically noted, "videos are vile" and "reggae is vile". His criticisms now extended to such black performers as Stevie Wonder, Diana Ross, Whitney Houston and Janet Jackson, whose contemporary work was dismissed as "vile in the extreme". Morrissey's emphatic conclusion was the blunt: "In essence, this music doesn't say anything whatsoever". The words effectively echoed the chorus of 'Panic', in which Morrissey had complained that "the music that they constantly play, it says nothing to me about my life". Lest the reader assume that his conclusions were based on the colour of the performer's skin, rather than the quality of the recorded output, Morrissey reiterated his love of the golden era of Tamla Motown. It was the emotionally sterile, homogenized sound of much modern black music that offended his sensibilities. His flippant comments on a supposed pro-black conspiracy at *Top*

Of The Pops were more puzzling than offensive, but there was already enough controversial grist in the article to prompt a major discussion in the music press. The weight of debate pronounced Morrissey guilty of "reggaeism" in the first degree. To the many lovers of contemporary "black music" in the radical music press that, in itself, was tantamount to racism. The tabloids, which would scarcely have understood the concept of racism in such bizarre circumstances, thankfully failed to address the issue. For Morrissey, the overblown "reggaeism versus racism" debate was far less damaging or irksome than Frank Owen's gratuitous references to numerous gay pubs and clubs in his article. The writer's dogged travelogue of the city's homosexual haunts continued for several paragraphs, despite Morrissey's repeated dismissal of such lurid, low-life establishments as being "too heavy for me". Owen's response to Morrissey's professed aversion was to call him "a big jessy" and "a big girl's blouse". A gratuitous reference to Whitworth Street toilets prompted the singer to close the distasteful discussion. A complaint over Owen's alleged misrepresentation was followed by the more amusing spectacle of Marr threatening to give the writer a right royal kick-in. "Violence is disgusting, but racism's worse and we don't deal with it," he informed the rival *NME*. The Smiths took a less strenuous revenge on their detractors when the disco-denouncing 'Panic', which had unexpectedly caused the "black" furore, was nominated as the year's best single and sixth best dance track by *NME* readers. Marr, as a funk merchant, was particularly pleased by this irony. The Smiths alleged anti-dance stance had proven mildly niggling to the guitarist, who was increasingly interested in the form. Although it was not obligatory for Morrissey and Marr to share musical tastes, their diverging interests would inevitably provoke some frustration and inner conflict over what constituted "The Smiths' sound".

While the success of 'Panic' and *The Queen Is Dead* suggested that Rough Trade's promotional work was exemplary, Morrissey/Marr had already decided to hasten their departure from the label. Marr explained that The Smiths were weary of financing Rough Trade's indulgences in signing demonstrably unviable talent and felt that The Smiths had long outgrown the company. The additional pressure of knowing that the budget for lesser recording acts depended on the delivery of Smiths' product was another vexing and unwanted responsibility. "We've grown to major status while the label is still stuck with the more negative aspects of the independent scene," Marr complained to *Hot Press*. Rather than awaiting the natural exhaustion of their contract, The Smiths elected to terminate matters forthwith and sign with EMI. Marr grandiloquently called this the "merging of two great institutions". The reaction from other quarters was somewhat less exuberant. A sizeable proportion of their hard-core fan following, and a smaller number of journalists, bemoaned the group's abdication as "king of the independents". As Morrissey pointed out, however, The Smiths were leaving the independent scene in order to achieve greater independence. Amid the myopic mutterings of "sell-out", few chose to stress the enormous contribution that The Smiths had made towards the indie scene and, in particular, Rough Trade. Monies accrued from Smiths product had enabled the company to expand and had forestalled financial troubles that might have proven overwhelming. Far from betraying their principles, it was arguably surprising that The Smiths had stayed with Rough Trade for as long as they did. "In all honesty, I've got nothing against Rough Trade", Marr now reflects. "I give them credit for taking a lot of stick from us but they weren't, by any stretch of the imagination, as professional a record company as they should have been - and they still aren't. They ran their business in a very offhand manner and made many mistakes with us. At best, it was six-of-one and half-a-dozen of the other between us." Initially, the group assumed that their next album would be released by EMI but Travis pointedly refused a lucrative settlement and insisted that The Smiths fulfil their contractual commitments. This was both a matter of principle and an indication of Travis's acumen in never underestimating the long-term potential of Smiths product.

While the ink was drying on the EMI contract, The Smiths commenced a UK tour and released a new single. 'Ask' was a return to the lighter pop of 'The Boy With The Thorn In His Side' and a tribute and rallying cry to the criminally shy. Memories of Morrissey's own youthful insularity were hinted at in the evocative and appealing lines, "Spending warm summer days indoors/writing frightening verse/to a buck-toothed girl from Luxembourg". As ever with Morrissey though, there was a harrowing sting-in-the-tail contained in the casually chilling refrain: "If it's not love, then it's the Bomb/that will keep us together". The singer's excursions into "nuclear power pop" would be reiterated more forcibly in later years with the John Betjeman-influenced, 'Everyday Is Like Sunday'.

During the recording of 'Ask', producer John Porter had the opportunity to work with new guitarist Craig Gannon, whose role seemed decidedly slight. "Craig was a good player but they used to tell him what to play," John recalls. "He was a very quiet chap in the studio and didn't come up with millions of ideas." At one point during the recording, Porter decided to use a guitar break from Craig only to discover that he had left the studio. The intense Marr was unimpressed by Gannon's carefree approach and felt that his commitment to The Smiths was less than a hundred per cent. "Craig really threw it away", Johnny noted scathingly. "We weren't closing doors, we were opening them for him and he just screwed it up for himself." Joyce was less critical, but understood Marr's frustration. "During recordings, Craig was a bit too quiet. When you've got Johnny Marr to bounce off, you couldn't ask for a better person to be with. Craig was pretty sweet but should have pushed himself a bit more. But you can't be somebody you're not."

Gannon, for his part, felt it was impertinent to force his presence on a group that had already established its reputation long before his arrival. Unassuming and trusting, he nevertheless became increasingly worried about the vague financial arrangement covering his tenure and was severely dismayed with the proposed distribution of monies accruing from the US tour. Once again, The Smiths' failure to clarify their arrangements on paper prompted suspicion and disillusionment as another unnecessary dispute began to fester.

Producer John Porter was initially pleased with his work on 'Ask', and particularly welcomed the decision to include Kirsty MacColl on backing vocals. He was less enamoured of Morrissey's decision to hand over the finished product to her husband Steve Lillywhite. Porter had suggested completing work on the tapes during a trip to Los Angeles, until Morrissey casually interjected, "Well, I don't like your mix!" Porter was nonplussed. "But, I haven't mixed it," he retorted, incredulously. It was only then that he learned of Lillywhite's involvement in mixing the finished tapes. "It was another one that didn't come off," Porter recalls ruefully. "There were a lot of guitars and only I knew how they fitted together." As well as the jigsaw puzzle of guitars, Porter had recorded a wave cascading across the beach, which was intended as dramatic relief in the middle of the song. "There was this great breakdown with the big wave splashing," he enthuses. "It was the most theatrical effect, with seagull noises done by Johnny on the guitar. It was fantastic but, on the record, you don't notice it. It's just gone. I was really pissed off because that was a spectacular track."

On the 12-inch version of 'Ask', Morrissey revived Twinkle's 'Golden Lights'. This quaint ballad was originally composed by the teenage songstress as a letter of disenchantment to her older boyfriend, Declan Cluskey, then a chart star in The Bachelors. Coincidentally, the Cluskey family lived one street away from Peter Morrissey's home in Crumlin. During his childhood visits to Dublin, young Steven was often driven past their house without realizing its pop star history. Now, with 'Golden Lights', he was unwittingly paying tribute not only to a Sixties girl singer, but to her Crumlin beau. After completing his tender cover version, Morrissey took the track away to be remixed, much to his producer's chagrin. Porter still laments the loss of the original mix. "I didn't hear it until it came out and I thought, 'Oh, no!'... Morrissey wanted to do a cover and kept saying, 'Can we record it with the guitars out of tune?' He didn't understand what that meant, but he wanted it to be weird somehow. We recorded it with these beautiful mandolins and it sounded fantastic. It had a Mexican feel. The stuff on the tape is beautiful, but the remix sounds appalling to me."

Morrissey's rejection of Porter's work indicated a lack of confidence in the producer's ear, even though Marr was usually impressed by the results. "We'd make plans and Morrissey would go ahead and ride roughshod over them," Porter stresses. "Johnny obviously had to keep his allegiance with Morrissey, which was fair enough. In a sense, Johnny was the go-between because, by this point, Morrissey almost never spoke to me. There was no animosity. I just think he'd already decided that he didn't want to work with me."

The Smiths' late autumn UK tour revealed the strength of the five-man line-up in a series of breathtaking gigs. Morrissey appeared in dark glasses and blazer, wielding a banner, which proclaimed: 'The Queen Is Dead'. For the second number, 'Panic', he produced a noose which he swung menacingly above his head. A T-shirt emblazoned with the words, "Hang The DJ" featured a photograph of his latest adversary, the disc jockey Steve Wright. In the background, Marr and company let rip with a more aggressive and arresting sound than ever, while the once standard 12-song set had been increased to 18 numbers and more. The Smiths rockier, flamboyant show unfortunately attracted a more raucous audience, untutored in the swaying, polite celebration of their predecessors. The Smiths' apostles were less and less identifiable amid a mass of essentially mainstream rock fans, who surged towards the front of the stage in a ritualistic show of strength. A handful of the machismo hordes even spat and jeered at Morrissey, as though he was Johnny Rotten incarnate. What remained from the old days was the passion and belief in The Smiths as the most important and significant artistes of the era.

The violent minority showed their disruptive strength a week into the tour when a show at the Newport Leisure Centre ended in chaos. Ten songs into the set, Morrissey was hauled offstage and fell face down on the floor. While he was taken backstage, the unfortunate Grant Showbiz announced that The Smiths would not be returning and received a bottle across the head. Bloody and bemused, he was taken to the local hospital and received treatment for cuts and concussion. Meanwhile, a handful of spectators took their revenge on the upholstery by slashing seats. By the time the police arrived, six stragglers were arrested.

The tabloids picked up the story and ludicrously suggested that Morrissey was reaping the wrath of a Royalist backlash. Eight days later, further violence erupted at the Preston Guild Hall when Morrissey was struck by a missile during the opening 'The Queen Is Dead'. The bleeding star was taken to Preston Royal Infirmary, but after waiting for an hour in casualty, he decided to return to Manchester to bathe his wounds. Despite the riotous behaviour of so-called "fans", The Smiths fulfilled their commitments and concluded the tour with three excellent shows in London and a grand finale at Manchester Free Trade Hall. Their performance at the Brixton Academy was particularly noteworthy for its Glitter Band-style employment of two drummers. Fred Hood, a former member of the Marr-produced Impossible Dreamers, was invited to take up sticks for 'The Draize Train' and was retained for the shimmering 'How Soon Is Now?'. "It was like scoring a goal at Wembley," Hood remarked of his cameo appearance.

A more prominent "auxiliary Smith" ended his days with the group at this point. The Craig Gannon experiment was turning sour and it had become obvious that his working relationship with Morrissey and Marr was no longer proving productive. "I knew they weren't happy with me personally," Craig confided. His friend Ivor Perry was a little more forthcoming. "They were saying that he was a piss-head", he joked, referring to Gannon's love of a good night out. Given Marr's recent excessive alcohol consumption on the US tour, it was hard to believe that Gannon's hedonism was anything other than a minor irritation. "It was pretty hypocritical," Perry complains. "He got done for missing a plane or smacking a

room, or something, a bit of rock 'n' roll lifestyle that wasn't in the image."
Of far more consequence, however, were the musical considerations. "I felt
Craig was lazy," Marr criticized. "Morrissey felt the same. We could have
picked a thousand people from our audience who would have made us feel
that they were pleased to be in the group. Trying to have a conversation
with Craig was just impossible after five minutes. He had nothing to say
and little to contribute. When he did come up with his own parts others
said it was like something I'd played on the last single. It wasn't exactly his
own style. Musically, he fitted in in that respect, but he was a lazy bastard
and that's all there is to it."

Although Marr previously admitted that he rated Gannon as a player and
appreciated the opportunity to utilize his skills on tour in order to embellish The Smiths' sound, he gradually realized that his own playing was
suffering as a result. Wary of becoming complacent, Marr agreed with
Morrissey that a four-piece Smiths would henceforth prove more practical,
both on a musical and personal level. Shortly after the performance at
Manchester Free Trade Hall, Gannon learned from his friend, and ex-
Morrissey associate, Gary Farrell, that his Smiths sojourn was over. The
news had already been relayed from Geoff Travis to Ivor Perry, who was
stunned by the decision. "We were on Rough Trade and Travis told us", he
remembers. "Craig was one of my best mates. I used to go out with him a
lot. To be told your own mate has been kicked out of The Smiths, and he
doesn't even know, was shocking. It was pretty callous." Gannon wondered why his colleagues could not have faced him at the death,
momentarily forgetting that Morrissey and Marr always felt squeamish
about wielding the axe in person. As Perry perceptively noted: "Morrissey
never does it himself, but always through somebody else. He hasn't the
bottle to do it. He doesn't like confrontation."

Like several other former employees, Gannon's departure was followed
by a serious wrangle over outstanding monies. Craig claimed that he had
been promised £1,000-a-night for playing on the recent US tour, and was
bitterly disappointed that he had not received this much-needed money.
Morrissey and Marr replied that they could not recollect having made such
an apparently generous offer. Once again, there was no written agreement
that could be produced to determine which account was truthful. All that
remained were verbal promises, which each party recalled differently, and
to their respective advantage. It was another example of the lackadaisical
way in which The Smiths ran their business and indicated the absolute
necessity to commit their private agreements to paper.

Although Gannon's primary claim was for touring fees, he also suggested
that he deserved some publishing credit for his work on 'Ask'. "If you mention that Craig stuck in a claim for songs, then I'll bring it up", Marr now
retorts. "That really hurt me. That's one of the things in The Smiths that
you *don't* do. We were always very careful from the very first day all the
way through the sessions to bring in our own songs. It was ridiculous. No
one ever had any inclination to write any songs, and that was fine."
Producer John Porter was equally astonished that Gannon was demanding

such credit. "I didn't ever imagine him having *any* input", he announced incredulously. For Porter, of course, the working relationship in the studio was clearly defined. Marr constantly experimented with a variety of chord sequences and arrangements, and was always open to ideas. Porter himself contributed significantly to the sessions, but had a clear-cut understanding with Marr that such guidance and experimental sketchwork certainly did not constitute composition. Gannon, however, was not a producer, and during the sessions felt that Marr had subliminally incorporated some of his own work into the song. It was a grey area that unfortunately said more about the dispute over monies than the integrity of composition.

On 14 November, The Smiths were due to play a concert at the Royal Albert Hall for the Anti-Apartheid Movement. That should have been enough to put the recent absurd accusations of racism in their true perspective. Intriguingly, the proposed warm-up act was Mancunian doyens The Fall, whom The Smiths themselves had once supported. Both acts had now left Rough Trade, but Geoff Travis knew that the departure of The Fall had been caused partly by the label's commitment to Morrissey and Marr. "When The Smiths were successful, that immediately alienated Mark E Smith," Travis contends. "I don't think Mark was thrilled to see these upstarts pass him by and I can understand why he felt like that... But it's not that straightforward either. At the same time that there was jealousy, there was also a great deal of pride that Manchester was doing something. Mark E Smith is not a simple character in that sense. You've got to understand the depth of his imagination. That's what is so interesting about him; he doesn't have a one-dimensional view."

The prospect of a double-bill featuring The Smiths and The Fall was a mouthwatering prospect and I still recall the rush of excitement upon reading the news in the *NME* and the frantic rush to the Royal Albert Hall fifteen minutes later to purchase tickets. In retrospect, the all-Manchester gig would have proven a wonderfully symbolic way to close The Smiths' live career. Sadly, events conspired against the union when, less than three days before the show, Johnny Marr unwittingly came close to emulating Morrissey's hero James Dean by ending his life on a tragic note.

Since the bacchanalian US tour, Marr had continued to drink heavily. "It was just something on tour that stuck with me," he explained. "When I wasn't behind a mixing desk I'd be either listening to records or watching videos and trying to get inspiration 24 hours a day, and drinking far too much. When you drink before you eat, it's not very good." Johnny's wife had already voiced concern about his physical state during the American visit and realized that he was far from happy. "Angie did a sterling job and often saw Johnny looking exhausted," Grant Showbiz remarked. "She must have wondered whether The Smiths was worth it. Angie was never pushy in that clichéd Yoko Ono/Linda Eastman way, just very quiet and supportive. Johnny and Angie had continual harassments and didn't have enough time to live their lives".

Marr required a macabre shock in order to take stock of his life and this was painfully provided after a late night out with Mike Joyce and his girlfriend, Tina. The party had been drinking tequila and wine and afterwards Marr offered to drive them home. After dropping them off, he sped back to Bowdon and stopped at a set of traffic lights, approximately 150 yards from his home. At that point, his cassette player automatically rewound a favourite tape, and Johnny decided to take a quick detour round the block in order to listen to one more track. It almost proved a fatal mistake. As the lights turned green, Marr inadvertently plunged his foot down on the accelerator and the vehicle took off at a frightening speed in the pouring rain. The next thing Marr knew he was careering round a bend and about to be sandwiched into oblivion. "The car went completely out of control," he explains, "then bounced off a couple of walls and ended up in the middle of the road. I jumped out and saw that the car was completely squashed. I couldn't believe that I was alive." Still in a state of shock, but painfully aware that he had been driving without a licence, Marr ran home, stumbling and falling several times along the way.

Relieved that no bones were broken, the injured one went to bed but, by the following afternoon, he was suffering shooting pains and stiffness in his neck, arms and fingers. After receiving hospital treatment, he was fitted with a neck brace and splints and ordered to rest. The Anti-Apartheid date was postponed and Rough Trade issued a press statement subtly covering up Marr's illegal driving by suggesting that Angie had been a passenger. Johnny knew all too well that, had his wife been in the car at the moment of impact, he would have become a widower after less than a year of marriage. Mike Joyce, who had acted coolly upon hearing the news, was astonished when he saw the remains of Marr's BMW. "It was like a concertina up to the windscreen," he observed. "One corner of the car had completely disappeared. I'm surprised the engine hadn't come through the front and removed his legs. Johnny was very lucky to keep his legs really."

The car crash warned Marr of the need to slow down, as well as underlining his mortality. On the evening of the Royal Albert Hall gig, a number of bemused ticket holders, including myself and some friends, stood outside the venue speculating about Marr's health. Apparently not everyone was as sympathetic. Marr was appalled after reading a letter from a disgruntled fan who not only complained about the cancellation but suggested that the guitarist was faking. Ironically, the unhappy missive helped place matters in a new perspective. "That was the first time I can remember feeling a separation between what the fans were believing and the truth," Johnny considered. "It taught me a lesson." Thereafter, Marr began looking at The Smiths in a more critical light and, reviewing recent events, reached the sad conclusion that they were increasingly losing touch with reality and in danger of believing their own publicity. "We were a mess," Marr concluded regretfully, "and had inflated senses of our own importance."

The postponed Artists Against Apartheid concert was rescheduled, without The Fall, for 12 December at London's Brixton Academy. By that time, Marr was fully recovered and the recent outbreaks of gig violence were a distant memory. Few in the audience that evening could have guessed that they were watching The Smiths' final performance on British soil. The set began with 'Ask', that strangely controversial single which, for different reasons, irked both John Porter and Craig Gannon. A healthy half-dozen tracks from *The Queen Is Dead* saw The Smiths caught in time, ready to step into a New Year which would actually prove their last. Appropriately, the pre-yuletide show conjured up the ghosts of Christmas past by ending with 'Hand In Glove', the song that had launched the group's superlative recording career.

15

Unhappy Birthday

By 1987, THE SMITHS WERE NO longer the bright young hopes of British pop, but seemed locked at a curious crossroads. Since their emergence, five years before, time and changing fashions had decimated many of their contemporaries. Triple chart toppers Frankie Goes To Hollywood had sought a new stage in the High Courts of Justice; pin-up pretenders Wham! had committed pop euthanasia; Spandau Ballet had long been exposed as more style than substance; Dexy's Midnight Runners had taken one sabbatical too many and their scintillating *Don't Stand Me Down* was criminally ignored; Duran Duran had outgrown their fans, or vice versa. Only The Pet Shop Boys maintained some of the glitz associated with early Eighties pop, while sustaining the interest of their audience with regular dashes of ironic wit. A large proportion of chart pop was about to fall into the hands of a relentless production team, whose run of successes would make previous plutocratic outfits like Chinn/Chapman seem impoverished by comparison. Stock, Aitken and Waterman sounded like a City firm of solicitors, but would soon become synonymous with instantly breezy, innocuously engaging, daytime radio pop. Ironically, their first major success had been with Morrissey's soulmate Pete Burns, whose group Dead Or Alive enjoyed a memorable number one with the production team's pulsating 'You Spin Me Round', back in 1984.

On the LP front, The Smiths looked on dispassionately at respected rivals Echo And The Bunnymen, whose support base and sales were insidiously dwindling. Other "long termers", such as New Order, Depeche Mode and The Cure, were all progressing in their various artistically-uncompromising ways, and steadily reaching new audiences. On a different level, there was U2, lately canonized as The Rolling Stones or Led Zeppelin of their generation. They had achieved wealth and international acclaim with an organizational efficiency that was exemplary in its simultaneous pursuit of commercial and creative autonomy. Beneath the Dublin quartet was a burgeoning band of stadia careerists, personified most plausibly in the bombastic vacuity of Simple Minds. The appeal of this deceptively alluring brand of pseudo-intelligent pop/rock was further demonstrated by the otherwise unremarkable Tears For Fears, who had twice reached number one in the USA.

There was good reason for predicting The Smiths' elevation to the rock super league. The music press polls testified to the passion of their following, which was demonstrably increasing. The impact of *The Queen Is Dead* and 'Panic' on the charts emphasized that the masses were ready to embrace The Smiths as both a rock band and a pop group. More importantly, the Mancunians appeared to have the artistic arsenal to produce regular, quality product. An annual album, quarterly single and well-paced touring programme would surely enable them to expand their market and transcend the self-imposed limitations that had accompanied the Rough Trade years. Of course, none of this could be achieved without a radical shift in policy and business organization. Once again, The Smiths urgently required an experienced manager who could represent them forcefully during this new phase of their career.

Ken Friedman hailed from San Francisco, where he had attended the University of Berkeley and later worked for the hard-nosed promoter Bill Graham. After switching to the management division of Graham's organization, he oversaw the affairs of various visiting UK acts, including Simple Minds. Personable and persuasive, Friedman decided that he had the talents to succeed as an independent agent and set up his own company. During the Bill Graham years, he had built up some good contacts but, despite his undoubted friendliness, affability and charm, Ken was not universally loved. Former Smiths' caretaker manager Scott Piering, who had crossed swords with Friedman as a promoter, was waspishly contemptuous of the man and responded with an unrepeatable stream of slanderous abuse at the mere mention of his name. By contrast, Piering's managerial successor, Matthew Sztumpf, found Friedman engaging and enthusiastic, but still spotted signs of over-reaching vulnerability. "Ken got a bit clever and set up on his own, at which point things started working out not so well," Sztumpf observed. "He lost Simple Minds. He was always good at attracting artistes, but less good at keeping them." The thistle-tongued Piering piercingly punctuated this point. "He was really quite a lightweight for all his talk," he sneered. "His place was littered with ex-bands."

The worst you could say about Friedman was that he was a fighter as well as a lover and had a tendency to overreach himself. In the music business, these were hardly demoniac traits, but commonplace virtues. Sztumpf had first introduced Friedman to The Smiths during their 1985 US tour of America. The San Franciscan immediately ingratiated himself with Morrissey, whom he took on a safari of book shops. After hanging out with the group and winning their guarded approval, he found himself unexpectedly championed by Sztumpf. Matthew's intention was to form a transatlantic management company, with Friedman representing all his acts in the USA, including Madness and The Smiths. The grand plan failed to materialize, however, and, before long, Sztumpf joined the ranks of jettisoned Smiths managers. Friedman stayed distantly in favour over the next year, a period in which he organized UB40's memorable trip to the USSR and generally enlivened their dour profile. For a time, he seemed a likely candidate to oversee Echo And The Bunnymen, but preferred the more challenging prospect of taking on The Smiths. After consulting

Sztumpf about his chances, he gently sought their hand. When Morrissey considered the moment to be right, he despatched Marr on a Friedman-finding mission and arranged a meeting. Friedman was excited about the prospect of working with a group of The Smiths' critical stature and was impressed by the apparent scale of their ambition. The enterprise was encouraging.

In January 1987, Friedman emphasized the degree of his commitment by transferring his operation to London. Against the odds, he even persuaded Morrissey to put his name to a two-page letter of agreement by which the American was officially appointed manager. Momentarily, it seemed that The Smiths had finally found a figure who had sufficient enthusiasm, belief and industry to convince them to tour the world. "Ken was younger and hipper than anyone else who tried to manage them," Grant Showbiz observed. "You could hang out with him. He'd been around and was pretty cool. I thought he was a groovy guy." Although Morrissey seemed similarly taken with the American, his true feelings were far more ambivalent. "Morrissey's relationships with people became far more private as time went on," Grant noted. "He would take you aside one day and make fun of somebody and the next day he'd be doing whatever they said. By that time I was spending a lot more time with Johnny."

The rise of Friedman coincided with the release of the group's twelfth single, 'Shoplifters Of The World Unite'. Although less commercial than their recent fare, the song climbed to number 12, a sure indicator of their popularity at the time. Many critics recognized the significance of the final lines of the song, in which Morrissey pinpointed the well of world weariness from where he drew so much artistic strength: "Tried living in the real world instead of a shell/But I was bored before I even began". The flipside, 'Half A Person', was equally revealing in its evocation of Morrissey's strangely obsessive youth, when figures like Ann-Marie McVeigh could secretly inspire irrational romantic devotion. Morrissey was a character who always required idols and the apotheosis of an ordinary but attractive acquaintance was as common as the idolization of a star. In keeping with its alluringly modest air, the song's melody was conceived in a moment of quiet inspiration. "We just locked ourselves away and did it," Marr recalls. "In the time it took to play, we wrote it." A third track, 'London', was featured on the 12-inch copies of the single. Built round a relentlessly driving riff, the song documented the ambiguous feelings of a youth fleeing Manchester for the bright lights of the capital. The scenario recalled the closing scene of *Billy Liar*, although in Morrissey's fictional universe the troubled protagonist takes the train to Euston.

On 7 February, The Smiths gave what was to be their last live performance, at Italy's San Remo Festival. They were scheduled to play before a large television audience who had gathered enthusiastically to witness the cream of Eighties British pop. The Smiths were placed on a revolving stage, alternating with a battalion of pop idols including Spandau Ballet, Paul Young, The Style Council and The Pet Shop Boys. It was one of those strange, but wistful moments in pop. Exactly 20 years and two weeks before, Mick Jagger had shocked the elders of British showbusiness by refusing to allow The Rolling Stones to mount the revolving stage at the close of *Sunday Night At The London Palladium*. Now, Morrissey was unwittingly about to repeat that memorable protest. A technical hitch in the sound meant that The Smiths had to reprise their act and, not surprisingly, the temperamental singer declined to perform. Friedman was forced to coax the star into reconsidering, with a laudable display of business logic. Much to the amazement of the assembled company, Morrissey relented. Upon boarding the revolving stage, The Smiths concentrated on recent material and played a sharp, five-song set, including 'Shoplifters Of The World Unite', 'There Is A Light That Never Goes Out', 'The Boy With The Thorn In His Side', 'Panic' and 'Ask'. It was amusing to consider that the group were closing their performing career as part of a good, old-fashioned pop package revue.

Surprisingly, the San Remo Festival saw The Smiths looking more relaxed and sociable than on any previous occasion abroad. Friedman encouraged them to appear less aloof and argued that it was healthy to "hang out, meet other musicians and have fun." Morrissey, who once claimed that he would never do anything as vulgar as having fun, said little but allowed the old and new pop aristocracy within his presence. He was even seen chatting to the animated Patsy Kensit. Marr, after years playing the role of a Smith, was even more amenable to the Friedman school of sociability and welcomed the opportunity to break down artistic barriers. Morrissey admits that he felt more bemused than offended by the pop bonhomie he encountered in Italy. "It was really intriguing to me," he explained, "because we'd never really mixed with pop stars before, and most of what they did, I didn't understand." One of the more memorable encounters during the visit was between Morrissey and Bob Geldof. Having traded media insults with the Band Aid organizer over the years, the Mancunian was visibly embarrassed when Geldof entered The Smiths' trailer, but Friedman's excited affability calmed hidden tensions. By the end of the evening, Morrissey's reserve had melted and he appeared to be thoroughly enjoying himself. "I don't know whether he got laid," Friedman mischievously suggested, "but he had a really good time". For Friedman, the San Remo Festival represented a major breakthrough in his relationship with Morrissey, but one that would not last.

One week later, The Smiths undertook some promotional appearances on Irish radio and television. During an interview with Radio Eireann, Morrissey damned pop videos and championed the cause of minor league, cult fame. "I don't want The Smiths to be a huge, untouchable mega-group," he declared. "I don't want that to happen, and it could happen. I'd rather just make the records and go home... I'm quite happy in my Smiths box... I don't want to venture outside the garden gate and be this multi-talented finger in every pie. I don't like multi-talented people." Given Marr's recent penchant for "multi-talented" session work and Friedman's hopes of reaching a wider audience, Morrissey's words seemed particularly pointed.

The vexed question of a worldwide tour remained on the agenda over the next few months, but Morrissey refused to commit himself unambiguously. Meanwhile, it was slowly becoming clear that Friedman was not the ideal manager for Morrissey, although, like many others, the San Franciscan was alternately fascinated, baffled and frustrated by the singer's mercurial temperament. "Morrissey was really indecisive," Friedman noted. "He'd make a decision, then just completely change it and not be able to deal with the consequences. So he'd go away and unplug the phone. The problem is, he can't very easily deal with the impact he has on people. He's afraid of success, like a lot of English people. I don't know what it is. To us, in America, it's what you achieve - everybody wants to be a millionaire or president or whatever. What I found baffling in England was that people didn't really want to make it; they were so embarrassed about it. Morrissey had that attitude more than anybody I'd ever known."

Friedman's quizzical attitude towards Morrissey's psychology indicated how divorced he was from the old values of Smithdom. Even at his most sympathetic, the manager represented a traditional business-orientated American outlook that was worlds removed from Morrissey's parochial insularity. Yet, it would be unfair to suggest that Friedman was unsympathetic towards The Smiths or crudely insensitive to their maverick ways. Clearly, one of the reasons he chose to manage them was because of their originality, a view expressed in his appreciative contention that they were "such a special group, such a phenomenon that it must be documented; there'll be a whole chapter on them in the history of British popular music, if not pop music." These were not the words of a philistine.

What Friedman had not bargained for, however, was Morrissey's indecision, amnesiacal caprice and rapid plunge into disillusionment over the question of mounting a serious challenge on the worldwide stage. For Marr, Friedman represented a logical way forward at a time when The Smiths sorely needed cogent direction and a new game plan. Such thinking was ultimately anathema to Morrissey who effectively rebelled by retreating. Old dogmas reasserted themselves with a vengeance.

With the imminent release of a double compilation album in America, Friedman had approached Morrissey about the possibility of filming a promotional video. The singer agreed that it was a good idea and duly committed himself to the project. On the day of shooting, however, he was nowhere to be seen. The crew reassembled, switching the operation from Bath to London, but Morrissey again failed to show. Like Sztumpf after the *Wogan* show, the American was experiencing the bitter aftertaste of Morrissey's legendary capriciousness. That evening, at the Portobello Hotel in Stanley Gardens, the exasperated manager confronted an unusually saturnine Johnny Marr. In a gesture of futility, they both looked at each other and raised their eyes to the ceiling, as if to say, "such are the ways of Morrissey". In that moment, Friedman realized that The Smiths' story had reached its final chapter. For him, it seemed only a matter of time before the songwriting duo would go their separate ways.

"Ken had organized that video at great expense and Morrissey didn't turn up," Johnny recalls. "That was the great breaking point between those two." Friedman's honeymoon period as Smiths manager had lasted barely two months and, thereafter, his relationship with Morrissey rapidly deteriorated. According to Friedman, they probably only spoke on one or two more occasions. The possibility of a world tour, which had seemed so hopeful at the beginning of the year, also receded as Morrissey voiced a variety of objections. Suddenly, Friedman realized he had two conflicting factions in the group that could not be reconciled. "When the smoke cleared," he points out, "Johnny wanted to go on tour, make videos and do everything he could to get the word up, and Morrissey didn't. Morrissey was quite content not to ever play Wembley Stadium; Johnny desperately wanted to play Wembley Stadium. Johnny felt 'We're a great group, we should play in front of people'. Also, he wanted to make money to build a bigger studio and buy more guitars. It was the typical rock 'n' roll dichotomy. Many groups have that duality."

In one of his last meetings with Morrissey, Friedman queried the singer's views on the role of a manager. He was firmly told that his job was to fulfil the artiste's behests. Although he could accept that, Friedman found Morrissey's complete reversal of instructions, often at a moment's notice, illogical and impossible to implement. His empathy with Morrissey was similarly circumscribed by his alienating American middle-class background. The character, as opposed to the music, of The Smiths owed much of its philosophy to the precepts of the English punk era, when DIY enthusiasm and anti-superstardom were regarded as the true antidotes to stagnation. In signing to Rough Trade, eschewing videos and championing the industry-plagued 45-rpm single, The Smiths had valiantly challenged the prevailing system, while retaining enough arrogance and self-belief to convince themselves that they were, in pop terms, major historical figures. The Smiths were never really shy of success, they just liked smashing through hurdles, and when they grew weary of self-imposed restraints, EMI beckoned. Morrissey, however, was remarkably ambivalent about success, not to mention life. He demanded, craved and expected recognition, and was constantly alert to the presence of imaginary financial predators. In certain cases, he even created them. Yet, the quality of fame was more important than the actual record sales or concert receipts, just as the paranoia about money and small-time exploitation was subservient to a greater fear of losing control. Compared to Ray Davies or Chuck Berry, Morrissey was largesse incarnate, but, in certain respects, he shared their self-destructive ways. The cancelled tours, abandoned appointments and sudden retreats testified to a character whose caprice ruled his nature, art and purse strings. He was, and probably still is, unmanageable in any long term sense. The reins of power and trust could never be reft from his suspicious hands.

Normally, Morrissey would have won the support of his partner in determining such a crucial issue as the group's managerial future but, on this occasion, Marr resisted. He felt that Friedman's strategy was sound and, more importantly, refused to surrender to the self-generated chaos that had so often threatened to engulf The Smiths. "Morrissey didn't want to continue with Ken," Marr remembers. "I think he was right to do that, but I didn't want everything to move back to my house as headquarters and for the two of us to sort out the band again. I'd just had enough of that. There was no way that I was going back to taking care of the group. By that time, there was an unhealthy situation with Rough Trade, and there was no way that I was going to take that on board again while making an LP." Friedman was in an unenviable position: he wanted the support of Marr and Morrissey, but effectively found himself managing half the partnership during their final phase. In this respect, he was at least more fortunate than his predecessors. For the first time, Marr was unwilling to sacrifice an employee in order to keep Morrissey sweet.

While Morrissey and Marr were busily disagreeing over the question of management, Mike Joyce briefly took time out to help some old friends and rivals. A new group, provisionally titled The Thin Men, were rehearsing in Denham, and Joyce was invited along to contribute to their demos. The miniature supergroup boasted a line-up consisting of ex-Hamsters vocalist Moey (Ian Moss), his guitarist brother Neil (from The Frantic Elevators) and Fall alumnus Marc Riley. It was a pleasant break for Joyce, who retained the capacity to chug along and avoid the higher politics that threatened the longevity of The Smiths.

The political differences over management and career direction were temporarily swept aside as the duo united to complete their outstanding commitment to Rough Trade by recording one last album. EMI had unsuccessfully attempted to buy up the rights to the forthcoming work, but Geoff Travis would not be swayed. Friedman privately felt sympathetic towards the independent king, who suddenly found himself left out in the cold. "I like Geoff a lot; I liked him a lot then," he stresses. "I thought he was treated very unfairly by the group. I always did. He knows that. Geoff could never relate to Johnny or, to put it the other way, Johnny couldn't relate to Geoff. I think they genuinely didn't like each other, whereas Morrissey and Geoff had a real love/hate relationship. Geoff was really enamoured of, and almost obsessed with, Morrissey." Even after signing to EMI, Morrissey naturally felt that Rough Trade should show the same old fawning appreciation of The Smiths. "He still expected Geoff to treat him like he'd treated him before, like royalty," Friedman concluded.

Surprisingly, Travis kept faith with Morrissey and, as the year progressed, he became more actively involved in the singer's complicated administrative affairs. Increasingly, his role resembled that of a quasi-manager. Mysteriously trusting to fate, or Morrissey caprice, the Rough Trade founder had not quite capitulated to the EMI signing. When questioned about The Smiths' impending departure by Craig Gannon's manager John Barratt, Travis pointedly refused to concede its inevitability. "Up until the end I think Travis still felt he could keep Morrissey on Rough Trade, or even The Smiths," Barratt argues. "It was common knowledge that they'd signed to EMI, but all he said was: 'We'll see'. I believe he still harboured hopes that somehow they would get out of it some bizarre way." Travis had seen enough of The Smiths to realize that nothing was ever certain until it happened. Morrissey had signed to EMI while still under contract to Rough Trade and who was to say that he wouldn't recklessly reverse that arrangement at a moment's notice?

Unfortunately for Travis, Morrissey gave no clues of any second thoughts about signing to a major label. On the contrary, The Smiths were eager to begin work on a new record and wave away their remaining commitments to Rough Trade at the earliest opportunity. The new era with EMI was now a kiss away, and the lucrative prospects awaiting them effectively thrust minor disagreements into the background. Technically, The Smiths could have hastened their departure from Rough Trade still further by presenting the company with a perversely uncommercial work, instrumental album or back-stabbing "experimental" piece in the vein of Lou Reed's *Metal Machine Music*. Instead, they took the project seriously. Marr's attitude as he set out for the studio was to try something different. As a keen music fan, he was growing weary of The Smiths' awesome legacy in influencing a whole new generation of indie label guitar groups. "It just became a bit of a pain," he complained. "I'd turn on night-time radio and hear this jingle-jangle four-piece guitar band from Scotland with their fringes and some girl squeaking about running through the flowers. I hated the musical climate. I thought there had to be a way forward." Increasingly, Marr convinced himself that The Smiths were in danger of being knocked off their perch by some yet-to-be-discovered assailants. After five years, their next challenge would be to avoid stagnation and stylization.

Appropriately, the forthcoming LP borrowed some of its inspiration and mood from The Beatles during their final phase. The hidden soundtrack to the album was *The Beatles* and *Let It Be*. Marr had been listening to the annoyingly-mistitled 'White Album', that strangely eclectic work in which the Lennon/McCartney writing credit could no longer disguise a resigned artistic neutrality. In recording the new album, he desired some of the taut, longing for discovery, that characterized The Beatles' latter work. Marr's view of The Smiths' concluding LP betrayed a hint of wonderment. "It was dark, stark, organic and held together by atmosphere with very few over-dubs," he remarked. "There was poignancy there. It might have been my imagination but, having seen the documentary *Let It Be*, I think there's an air of foreboding that's definitely there on some tracks. There's a lot of depth to that LP which came about because of our feelings at the time." Although Marr claims he had no reason to assume that this would be The Smiths' swansong, he could hardly have chosen a more suitable or inspiring valedictory than *Let It Be*.

While The Smiths were recording their new studio LP, Rough Trade released two compilation albums within the space of a couple of months. *The World Won't Listen* was the sequel to *Hatful Of Hollow*, and a welcome collection of the group's recent hit singles and flip-sides. The bargain-priced set included an alternate take of 'Stretch Out And Wait' and one previously unreleased song, the spiteful 'You Just Haven't Earned It Yet Baby', a title allegedly inspired by an innocent one-liner from Geoff Travis.

Hearing the songs in a new context was both an inexpensive delight and excellent marketing strategy.* The subsequent *Louder Than Bombs* was a more expansive collection, featuring 24 songs from every stage of the group's career. Although originally intended for American distribution only, Rough Trade elected to issue the set when highly priced import copies threatened to invade the home market.

The third Smiths release of the early spring was the single 'Sheila Take A Bow', which equalled their highest chart placing at number 10. The song had been written very quickly and, during the session, Morrissey recorded his declamatory vocal in one take. He was so impressed with the results that he refused the chance of a repeat performance. A splendid choice of single, 'Sheila Take A Bow' recalled the hammy, glitter sound of the early Seventies, complete with bombastic oompah drumming. With its mild plea for adolescent rebellion, the lyrics offered a temporary salvation from the headmaster ritual ("Throw your homework on to the fire/Come out and find the one you love"). There was even an arch example of gender confusion ("You're a girl and I'm a boy... I'm a girl and you're a boy") to add spice to the proceedings. The flip-side, 'Is It Really So Strange?', employed another of Morrissey's favourite allusions - the trip down south. Rather than the urban drama of 'William, It Was Really Nothing' or 'London', Morrissey creates a love song of comic confusion. Only Steven Patrick could wring meaning from one of pop music's most amusingly bathetic lines ("I lost my bag in Newport Pagnell"). And for once there was even a wilfully playful reference to, of all things, animal slaughter ("I got confused, I killed a horse"). On the 12-inch single, the sardonic 'Sweet And Tender Hooligan' took an unfashionable swipe at supposedly liberal juries or, more specifically, the wily ways of the wicked criminal. Morrissey would later return to this theme on 'The Last Of The Famous International Playboys'.

Both the B-side tracks had been recorded and broadcast the previous December on the *John Peel Show*. However, producer John Porter found little cheer in their release, which coincided with his final ostracism from The Smiths' camp. He had felt especially vulnerable since he and his wife Linda had accompanied Johnny and Angie on a trip to Paris. During the visit, the party received an effusive telephone call from Morrissey, which puzzled Marr. On the way home, Porter, whose communication with the singer was by now virtually non-existent, felt convinced that something was amiss. It was not until after the release of 'Sheila Take A Bow' that he discovered the worst.

Porter had originally been slated as the producer for the single and, when Marr completed the composition, he assisted with the editing and arrangement. As was often the case in his working relationship with Johnny, Porter was liberally allowed to add a slide guitar or puzzle over a middle-eight

---

* A number of white label copies of 'You Just Haven't Earned It Yet, Baby' had previously been released "mistakenly" in place of 'Shoplifters Of The World Unite'. Morrissey had originally nominated the former as an A-side but explained that "ultimately we felt it just wasn't good enough, so it went on the compilation LP".

while awaiting his young friend's arrival at the studio. Porter enjoyed editing Marr's chord sequences and, on this occasion, Johnny even left a slice of the producer's guitar work on the recording. Morrissey was unaware or unconcerned about such niceties and, as with 'Ask' and 'Golden Lights', he had a last minute change of heart about the merits of Porter's work. The producer still recalls his abject disbelief upon hearing what sounded like an alternate take of the single on the radio. "The first thing I knew it was out and it sounded slightly different," he recalls. "When I saw the record it said 'produced by Stephen Street'. Morrissey had gone in with Stephen Street, done the track again, but sampled guitars off the original and put them on this new one without mentioning it to me, asking me, giving me a credit, paying me, or doing anything. That was the last I ever had to do with The Smiths. I never said anything to anybody, but I thought, 'If that's what it's down to. You didn't even *ask* me!' In theory, I could have stopped the record and done a whole number. So that was the end of it. The original version of 'Sheila Take A Bow' was just as good as the one they put out. It was just Morrissey trying to prove a point - that they didn't need me."

Although Morrissey clearly had a preference for Stephen Street as the group's producer, Porter still believes that it was his developing friendship with Marr which most irked the singer. "I think going to Paris with Johnny was the end for Morrissey," Porter claims. "When I first worked with The Smiths, Morrissey was very appreciative, but subsequent to that he got jealous of my relationship with Johnny. We were good mates and used to hang out and party together. Morrissey, having always had Johnny as his close musical partner, began to resent my old fart influence and just my friendship with Johnny." For his part, Marr felt that the personal and professional relationship he had with Morrissey was invaluable and steered clear of emotional conflict. Nevertheless, the departure of various associates was sometimes regretted. "Everybody was just axed away from it," he remarked, "and it was a bit difficult for me."

One former associate whose decapitation was proving unnecessarily bloody was Craig Gannon. Since leaving The Smiths he had teamed up with two of Morrissey's former Kings Road associates, Gary Farrell and Ivor Perry, to form The Cradle. Their manager, John Barratt, took the guitarist to music business solicitors Russells, where, with the assistance of Legal Aid, he pursued his case against The Smiths. By now, Morrissey/Marr knew they had a fight on their hands so attempted to arrange a settlement. Friedman was despatched with an offer which Barratt dismissed as derisory. When Friedman countered that Gannon had merely been a session player during his period with The Smiths, the garrulous Barratt terminated the conversation. "See you in court" were his final uncompromising words. As it turned out, neither manager would still be around to see the end of the case which dragged on for nearly five years before Gannon belatedly emerged the victor with a pay-out of £42,000. Even Barratt conceded that the guitarist probably fared far better than if he had been given a formal contract with The Smiths in the first place. The

Gannon case ultimately underlined the fallibility of Morrissey/Marr in their administrative handling of the group's business affairs.

While Gannon was firing his first warning shots across The Smiths' bows, work on their new album was progressing surprisingly smoothly. Ensconced in Bath, away from the business pressures and external conflicts, the group found that they still had the spark and creative unity to overcome any personal differences. "The sessions were positive," Mike Joyce confirms. "I felt as though the pressure was off. Speaking first and foremost as a player, the relationship between the four of us at that time was the healthiest it ever was." Morrissey and Marr each echoed those sentiments, refuting later press reports that the group were at each others' throats. As the singer explained, "the wolves remained outside the studio door." Inside, any flagging spirits were revived by festive stimulants. "We were all getting well out of it with the ales," Joyce remembers. "Things were getting quite crazy at times, but that was the beauty of The Smiths - the craziness. A lot of people didn't realize how barmy it got."

Sober realities confronted the group when they returned to Manchester. After finishing work on the new LP, Marr went through a period of torturous reassessment over the future of The Smiths. The album had allowed him to explore some new ideas, but he still felt restricted musically, politically and personally. The Smiths had become like a club in which certain influences were deemed sound and others regarded as taboo. The fact that Marr was presently enjoying such old favourites as Sly And The Family Stone and The Fatback Band, as well as finding empathy with the latest developments in dance music, made him feel more divorced than ever from The Smiths' central fan base. Even before recording the LP, he had betrayed reservations about The Smiths being typecast as a "jingle jangle" group. Although the sessions had proven productive and indicated the possibility of a new direction, Marr felt boxed-in and overworked. Suddenly, The Smiths seemed like a tiring treadmill. "We're going to end up like The Beach Boys in the blue and white striped shirts," Marr warned Morrissey in frustration. With various legal and business problems on the horizon, disputed management interests, a forthcoming television documentary and a hungry EMI eagerly anticipating new product, Marr above all desired a long break. One evening, he confronted Morrissey in Chelsea and poured out his feelings. Before long, the subject of a complete break-up was broached. "If we went to a lawyer and dissolved our partnership I would see a great weight lifted off your shoulders, which would also be a weight lifted off mine," Marr told his partner. "That was the way I wanted it to go," the guitarist now explains. "It wasn't purely me, me, me. It really wasn't. I felt if the group were to split I'd see some massive physical improvement. The pressure was far too much. I wasn't fed up with the guys, it wasn't that at all. I just felt all of us were in an unhealthy situation and unless we made some moves towards thinking about our future direction, we'd become an anachronism."

Later that evening, Marr confronted Joyce at Geales Fish Restaurant in Farmer Street, Kensington, and repeated his comments. Joyce's response was incredulous. "What do you mean you don't want to go on anymore?" he demanded. In light of the recent album sessions, the drummer found Marr's attitude perplexing. "If we'd recorded another album and things had slowly ground to a halt it would have been easier to come to terms with," he explained. Looking back for motives that would explain Marr's disenchantment, Joyce could only find hints of strain and overwork. "Maybe I wasn't sympathetic enough to the way Johnny was feeling," he pondered. "He would express his dissatisfaction and anger about something more so than Morrissey. But I don't think he did on this occasion and because nobody saw the signs he got a bit upset. He wanted everyone to rally around him and say, 'Don't worry, have some time'. It was all a massive shock and I just remember it being surreal." Joyce did not take Marr's mood lightly. "I thought he really meant it," he admits. "That's why I wanted to sort it out there and then. I thought, 'If we leave this, then that's it, really'." In the circumstances, Joyce innocently uttered the kind of sentiments that Marr least wanted to hear. "I think we should do one more album," he suggested.

Morrissey felt equally deflated by Marr's attitude, especially with the EMI era looming. The Smiths seemed on the brink of even greater achievements and financial security and here was Marr threatening to throw it all aside. Despite the intensity of the conversation at Chelsea, Morrissey misread the signs and put Marr's disenchantment down to tiredness and overwork. That same week the group were filmed for *The South Bank Show* special and talk of a possible split was suspended. Marr then announced that he intended to take a vacation and advised everybody else to do the same. The reaction was negative and suspicious. "It was the ultimate sin to suggest that," Marr recalls. "The band made me feel that I was never going to come back, which wasn't the way I felt. Morrissey was acting so defensively. That annoyed me. They should have given me some time to sort it out and see a way forward." Marr continued his protest until Morrissey relented somewhat and suggested: "Maybe we should all take a holiday together." At that moment, Marr threw up his hands in exasperation and said, "No! You're missing the point."

What The Smiths urgently needed at this stage was a mediator. Instead, they ended up in opposing corners. Friedman was by now a distant presence, who was completely estranged from Morrissey and very sad about the conflicting attitudes that were tearing the group apart. Having returned to America, he took stock and planned a therapeutic holiday touring Thailand and Nepal. After all the recent Smiths problems, it would prove a welcome break. Morrissey, meanwhile, increasingly turned towards Geoff Travis for business advice and was now disputing the commission that Friedman had claimed for his managerial services. Marr stayed loyal to the American, mainly because the alternative seemed a return to chaos. "Morrissey had decided that he didn't want to work with Ken, which was OK," Marr explained. "That was a problem I could have dealt with. I just felt round the corner it was never ending."

Viewing events from the sidelines, Grant Showbiz lamented the absence of a single, authoritative voice. "If there'd been better management things would never have reached the crisis point," he remarked. "It was too intense towards the end. I felt it was like a furnace. Ken was manager. Writs were flying back and forth. Craig wanted his money for playing on the tour and there was a lot of emotional pulling going on. If they'd just had one person who could have said, 'I'll deal with it'. It was like The Beatles at the end." Friedman, who had long been consigned to Johnny's corner, noted the developing schism from a distance, with a degree of frustrated regret. "Everybody chose sides with The Smiths," he emphasized, "that's just what happened. Morrissey's mother was on Morrissey's side, Johnny's wife was on Johnny's side, Geoff Travis was on Morrissey's side. It just got to the point where it was high school."

Marr's attempt to play truant from The Smiths was again forestalled when Morrissey insisted that they complete a couple of B-sides for their next single, 'Girlfriend In A Coma'. "I fought against it," Marr remembers. "I felt I'd worked far too hard to be put in that position. I just felt it was complete insanity while we were under all this pressure." Despite Marr's objections, the sessions were scheduled to take place during May at the home studio run by Grant Showbiz and Fred Hood.

After the group arrived for the Streatham sessions, Grant rapidly realized that all was not well. "The divergence came at the time we were doing those last tracks," he recalls. "It was a very odd atmosphere all round. I'd never felt that with The Smiths and didn't really know what was going on. Johnny and Morrissey weren't really talking to each other which was weird. I'd say it was a communication breakdown caused by uncontrollable outside pressures reaching a peak. They were looking to each other for a solution that neither had." From the moment he entered the studio, Joyce realized that this latest get-together was a mistake. "It was total madness", he confessed. "Everybody was losing it. I was a bit flippant about it, really. A lot of things happened subconsciously and you couldn't put your finger on it. I just didn't feel my heart was in it. It was a strange atmosphere. I didn't feel there was any need for us to be there. I hadn't objected to Johnny taking a holiday at all. Why should I? If he'd said six months, it wouldn't have bothered me. I'd have gone off and done my own thing. Streatham was probably the last straw for him. Johnny was feeling the pressure from within."

Marr's memories of the Streatham sojourn were decidedly depressive. "It was utter misery," he recalls. "The group were really falling to pieces." Marr's grudging reluctance to even be there added a *frisson* that Grant Showbiz had never previously witnessed at any gig or recording session. "Having seen the harmony, I noticed this lack of communication. It wasn't as if the songs were properly formed. Morrissey was saying, 'Let's go and do the song!' and Johnny would say, 'What song, Morrissey?' He'd reply, 'Well that thing you were playing earlier on, I've got some words'. It was very weird. They had ideas for songs with different names. One was called 'You Don't Know Anything'. They were just sketches."

Morrissey seemed rather nervy throughout the fractious recordings, as if he realized that the entire future of The Smiths was inexplicably crumbling away. "There weren't a series of rows leading up to a break-up," Grant stresses, "just a sudden realization. It was lots of little things and hitting the bottom of a cycle and not having anybody to rationalize it and say, 'You're all knackered, go away and don't think about The Smiths'. Morrissey, for once, was desperate to do something and no one else was. The fact that he was willing to carry on suggested that at that time he wasn't thinking too rationally and was getting really obsessed with The Smiths. Morrissey was very unhappy in that period."

Perhaps as a subconscious attempt to rekindle the old camaraderie, Morrissey looked to the early/mid-Sixties for affectionate inspiration. At one point, he took Joyce aside and began raving about an obscure Sixties single that apparently contained some brilliant drumming. "It was insane," Mike remembers. "A quintessentially English, big band, orchestral arrangement - that's what he was into." Joyce's lack of appreciation for such a piece was not too surprising, but Morrissey expected a more enthusiastic response from his songwriting partner. The Morrissey/Marr duo had first found common ground in their love of girl groups and Johnny had always displayed a tolerant enthusiasm towards his partner's love of Sixties kitsch. At Streatham, however, even that creative link was fraying. Morrissey's whimsical idea of covering a Cilla Black B-side and film theme merely embarrassed Marr. "I hated 'Work Is A Four Letter Word'," the guitarist grimaced. "I didn't form a group to perform Cilla Black songs." When I reminded Marr that he had sanctioned a Twinkle cover eight months before, he swiftly added 'Golden Lights' to his black list. "That was another low point," he stresses. "Those are the two low points of our recording career, certainly, and don't deserve a place alongside our material." Joyce was not unsympathetic towards Marr's criticisms of the Streatham songs: "I didn't feel the vibe was there and Morrissey wasn't singing that well. He did a vocal and said, 'That's it!' I thought, 'Well, OK, if that's what you think'. Everybody seemed a bit flippant."

By 19 May, work was completed on the final Smiths recording 'I Keep Mine Hidden'. Morrissey whistled breezily through the track, sounding not unlike a modern-day George Formby. The song was to remain his favourite over the next few years and represented a treasured postscript to a partnership that had run its course. Three days later, Morrissey celebrated his 28th birthday. It was not a notably happy occasion. Morrissey wasn't to know that his unhappy birthday was effectively The Smiths' wake.

After taking his leave of The Smiths Marr soon boarded a flight to Los Angeles. "That was it really," he casually noted. "I made a decision that I was going to get away on holiday... LA was the only place I knew where there'd be sunshine, so off I went. I never saw Morrissey again."

The American vacation was the perfect opportunity for Marr to relax and discover what life was like outside The Smiths' cauldron. More and more, Marr realized that he had become too closely entwined with Morrissey's personal vision of The Smiths' godhead. After several years of subjugating aspects of his personality to fit the dictates of Smithdom, this was a happy release. "It was like when the love goes in a love affair," Grant sentimentally suggested. "You don't get angry with the other person but sad at the hopelessness of the world... Johnny just wanted to drop The Smiths for awhile but instead he dropped it forever." Through his friendship with Kirsty MacColl's producer husband, Steve Lillywhite, Marr met a number of new groups and session musicians. When Lillywhite was recruited by Talking Heads, Johnny gladly accepted an invitation to play on their new album, *Naked*.

More importantly, Marr was already laying the foundations for a new group and making tentative plans for a future without Morrissey. During the recording of the last Smiths album, he had specifically checked out bassist James Eller, who was then working for Julian Cope. While in Los Angeles, Marr encountered drummer David Palmer, a friend of "nearly" Smith, Guy Pratt. Palmer was currently completing a tour with Paul Young and had recently worked with Matt Johnson on the celebrated The The album *Infected*. Remarkably, Johnny found himself telling Palmer something that he could barely admit to himself. "It's interesting that the only person I told I was leaving The Smiths was David Palmer while I was in LA," he confessed.*

Back in England, the remaining Smiths were still uncertain about Marr's intentions. "I kept on trying to convince myself that it was OK," Joyce recalls, "and that once Johnny had a week or so off, we'd carry on. But obviously he'd given it a lot more thought than any of us had anticipated." During Marr's absence, Morrissey undertook some desultory promotion for the forthcoming Smiths album and wearily refuted rumours of an impending split. When confronted on the issue by Manchester journalist Steven Kingston, he seemed genuinely bemused and dismissed the split stories as silly gossip. "I'm not really sure where they came from," he pondered. "I find it very interesting. I'd be very interested to hear what the next rumour is, but I don't really have anything to say. The band's very happy - we all think the next LP is the best record we've ever made."

A more penetrating interview in *Q* magazine revealed Morrissey looking less certainly towards the future. He spoke optimistically about the forthcoming union with EMI but completely ruled out the possibility of a Smiths tour. When quizzed on his love of live performance, he sounded completely disillusioned. "It's totally, totally gone, which is something I thought I'd never say," he confessed. "And I don't really know what to do about it, to be honest... It's a situation where people can't really advise you because nobody really knows what it's like. Most people don't know what it's like to sing and front a group, so you can only trust your own instincts in this matter. I no longer feel it's something I want to continue doing. I wouldn't like to go on a stage if I just felt 55 per cent of an interest, and that really is the case. So I don't think I should do it." When pushed, Morrissey

---

* The Marr/Eller/Palmer triumvirate would maintain contact over the next few years, guesting on Kirsty MacColl's *Kite* and finally forming the backbone of Matt Johnson's latest incarnation of The The.

would not rule out the idea that The Smiths might never tour again. It was difficult to escape the conclusion that the group was in a serious state of flux. Even the spectre of Ken Friedman was gnawing away at Morrissey, who seemed to be psyching himself up for a war of attrition against his short-term manager. "It's very depressing to think that he is going to fight for 15 per cent of everything we earn for the next 12 months," he casually noted. "He's not going to get it but fighting him off is going to cost an enormous amount of money and physical hardship."

Marr's continued involvement with Friedman still irked Morrissey, the more so now that the guitarist was in America and beyond his influence. Morrissey understandably assumed that Marr was now taking serious advice about his future career from the San Franciscan, but Johnny denies that this was the case. "What Morrissey doesn't realize is that Ken wasn't even around," Marr argues. "He was half-way up the Himalayas. I didn't speak to him about leaving the band." When Friedman returned from his sojourn and belatedly learned of the guitarist's plans, he was the first to advise caution. "Ken said, 'whatever you do, don't say you're leaving the band'. That's the truth. He told me to do what The Police had done and just say we were having some time off. That was very sound advice. It was the soundest advice anyone had ever given us around the band. I wish Morrissey could have known that."

The Police had attempted, with some success, to cheat their fans and enemies of a funeral by suggesting that they were merely taking an extended sabbatical. When the music press suggested that this was merely clever subterfuge, manager Miles Copeland responded theatrically by threatening legal action for defamation of character. By the time the public fully realized that the group was no more, the split story had lost its sting. Marr hoped that The Smiths might be spared reams of melodramatic prose and speculation if they maintained a conspiracy of silence. However, the lack of communication between the parties always made this an unlikely outcome. Marr's much desired breathing space effectively ended during the first week of August. As already indicated, Manchester was buzzing with stories of trouble in Smithdom and before long the music press received the scent of a major scoop. The *NME*'s Danny Kelly was aware of the gossip and pub rumour but could not lay his hands on any firm evidence. Stonewalled by Rough Trade, he next phoned the *NME*'s Manchester correspondent (alias magazine editor and disc jockey, Dave Haslam) who reluctantly confirmed the story. He had known for many weeks that Marr and Morrissey were out of contact and had no firm plans to work together in the future. That, however, was the extent of his knowledge. Kelly was exasperated that Haslam had not voiced this fantastic news item weeks earlier, but was pleased enough to be one step ahead of the rival *Melody Maker*. He next confronted his editor, Alan Lewis, with a breakdown of the many rumours, backed by Haslam's testimony. Lewis was justifiably sceptical and demanded: "How sure are you?" Kelly replied: "I'm as sure as somebody who doesn't want it to happen can be." After some consideration Lewis told his colleague to write his piece. "I was very gratified that Alan

Lewis had the courage to run the story," Kelly recalls. "We had no way of knowing, we just went with it." Despite the fact that the issue was still clouded by hearsay and uncertainty, the NME cobbled together the corroborative "evidence" and in their inimitable style ran a major news story on 1 August under the provocative title, "SMITHS TO SPLIT". Readers familiar with headline code would have picked up the nuances immediately. The lack of a telling question mark after that word "SPLIT" suggested that there was substance to the story, but the reluctance to splash out with a glaring "SMITHS SPLIT!!" indicated that the paper lacked real evidence or confirmation. What they had gleaned was news of "a personality clash between Morrissey and Marr." This was padded out with a tissue of speculative gossip, much of which was fascinating, but veered heavily towards the fanciful and sensationally inaccurate. The NME's breakdown of break-up rumours was threefold:

1. "Marr has reportedly told friends in Manchester that he and Morrissey are no longer pals, and he is sick of the singer acting the self-centred star. He says the working relationship has also suffered considerably."

2. "Morrissey is not pleased with the company Marr is keeping, acting the guitar hero and playing on albums by Keith Richard, Bobby Womack and Bryan Ferry."

3. "The final straw was allegedly Marr interrupting Smiths recording sessions to fly to the States to record with Talking Heads, and using Rough Trade money to pay for the trip. Insiders say Morrissey blew his top and declared that it was the end of The Smiths, and he never wanted to work with Marr again."

All the above would later be strenuously denied, although the first paragraph spikily summed up some of Marr's private feelings. Beneath the gratuitously fanciful gossip lay one crucial point: the partnership was apparently on the rocks.

The NME's hopes of confirming the story were thwarted by Rough Trade's tight lips and a firm denial from Morrissey, who announced: "Whoever says The Smiths have split shall be severely spanked by me with a wet plimsoll." Clutching at straws, the paper next located Mike Joyce's home telephone number and rang to enquire about the "break-up". The call was intercepted by Mike's girlfriend Tina, who deflected: "He doesn't want to comment on that. He has nothing to say."

"No surprised reaction, no flat denial," the NME crowed hopefully, neglecting to consider that Joyce had already been alerted to the enquiries by Rough Trade. "I wasn't going to be the person to start stirring it," Joyce now explains. "If anybody was going to say anything, it wasn't going to be me."

Interestingly, the most telling comment in the piece came from a person identified as "a friend of Johnny Marr", who observed: "I'm surprised that the press hadn't got hold of this earlier. It's been brewing for months. Marr and Morrissey haven't spoken to each other for three-and-a-half months. There's a situation where they now see it as backing down to do so." That, at least, had a loud ring of authenticity, and the first sentence of the quote neatly paraphrased Haslam's words to Kelly during their curt conversation. Haslam maintains that the remainder of the quote could not possibly have come from his lips and suspects that it was invented. "That's not beyond the bounds of possibility," Kelly frankly admits. "I have been known to 'augment' my work." The fact that Kelly cannot even name one source for the quote, reputable or otherwise, indicates the degree to which he was relying on portentous rumour and exaggerated hunches to give spice to the news page. Despite the provocative tone and inaccurate speculation, the main thrust of the piece exposed the fragmenting relationship between Morrissey and Marr and had startling repercussions. "The *NME* ruined it", Morrissey reflects with bitter regret. "It bears a heavy responsibility in The Smiths' break-up. I was angry with them. They exhibited the coffin while the corpse wasn't yet cold. I was traumatized, and their attitude didn't help. They published a lot of lies about Johnny and me and, suddenly, we were overtaken by events. The rumour became reality. But if everybody had remained quiet, the problems could have been resolved in private."

When Johnny Marr read the *NME* story he was amazed and outraged. His first reaction was to phone the other members of the group, but instead he awaited a call himself. None was forthcoming. By then, Marr was convinced that a conspiracy was afoot. He still believes that the *NME* story was a set-up, perpetrated by Morrissey as an unsubtle means of forcing his hand on the issue of The Smiths' future. "What really hurt me was that none of the band phoned me," he explains. "I felt it was blackmail. How could they do that to me?" Today, Joyce admits, "I didn't phone. I didn't do anything at all", but he sees nothing sinister in such inaction. "I didn't know what was going on myself," he protests. "I was expecting Johnny or Morrissey to phone me. I didn't have the phone off the hook. We'd always keep in contact and somebody would phone and we'd get together, but the whole thing seemed to fall apart. When Johnny went off, it was obvious that was it."

Marr's suspicions about the *NME* news story were understandable. Previously, the group had used the music press as a means of embarrassing Rough Trade over promotion and pressurizing the company into renegotiation. Marr was convinced that he was now the victim of the same tactic. The other Smiths, however, had good reason to suspect the reverse. "The *NME* mole", as he was termed, had been identified as "a friend of Johnny Marr's", not theirs. Moreover, Morrissey had at least taken the time to issue a denial, albeit in his inimitably flippant style. Suspicion on both sides ensured that some face-saving response was inevitable and this made the silent "Police-like" severance impossible. Ironically, however, it now seems virtually certain that the story was cultivated by neither party. The anonymous Haslam had merely confirmed the split rumours surrounding The Smiths camp, leaving the *NME* to spice up the story with its own excited speculation. Danny Kelly stresses that he had received no whispers from anyone connected with Morrissey or Rough Trade. The story was simply the culmination of snippets of Mancunian "break-up" gossip which

Morrissey, far from fuelling, had already twice denied and even laughed off. Marr, however, could not rid himself of the suspicion that his partner had somehow used the *NME* as a propaganda vehicle. Sadly, the failure of either party to pick up a phone meant that the Machiavellian theory festered. In the end, Morrissey and Marr were victims of their own lack of communication. "Nothing would have happened if the *NME* hadn't heard certain rumours about Johnny's intentions", Morrissey now claims. "They immediately wrote that The Smiths had split up, that Johnny had left, whereas the group still existed." Morrissey's viewpoint, though technically correct, underestimated the extent to which his partner had already moved away from the group. Marr had previously elected to take a long break from The Smiths and pursue new ventures with other musicians. He was willing to remain silent regarding any long-term split, but was equally anxious to appear in control of matters. The *NME* story arguably hastened the inevitable by playing on Marr's increasingly suspicious and negative view of his partner's role as a media manipulator. The worst scenario in Marr's mind was a "Morrissey Quits Smiths" story, with the guitarist portrayed as the abandoned loser. With neither side aware of the other's plans, both attempted to protect their reputations.

One week later, both *Melody Maker* and *NME* received a face-saving press release via Rough Trade which stated: "The Smiths announce that Johnny Marr has left the group. However, they would like to confirm that other guitarists are being considered to replace him. It must be stressed that the concept of 'The Smiths' will remain the same and the group will continue to promote their forthcoming single and album releases and are eager to plan live dates once a new guitarist has been selected. The Smiths would like to state that although Johnny's departure is sad that they wish him every happiness and success with his future projects." The *Melody Maker* managed to secure a brief interview with Rough Trade's press officer Pat Bellis, who cut through the usual glib PR-speak with some piercing observations. "It's no secret that the pair's lifestyles differ and this has caused several arguments between them in the past", she explained. "It isn't over one argument. Johnny just wants to move in a completely different direction." Laughing off the rumours of Morrissey's disenchantment with Marr's outside friends and collaborators, she noted: "Half the time, he doesn't even know who Johnny's seeing. Johnny keeps these things very private."

While the *NME* were preparing to run the press release, they received an unexpected phone call which made Bellis's comments seem mere tittle tattle. Danny Kelly could hardly believe his luck when he picked up the receiver only to be greeted by a bemused and emotional Johnny Marr. Goaded by his partners' lack of contact, and clearly wary of being beaten to the punch, he issued his own "split story". The *NME* now had a second and, this time, very real scoop, which they portentously titled, "Marr Speaks". Still convinced that Morrissey was responsible for the previous week's revelations, he decided to set the record straight. "First of all," he said, "it's very important to me to clear up some of the inaccuracies that were in your story last week. There is nothing even approaching acrimony between myself and the other members of the band. I've known them all a long time and I love 'em. Nor was there any truth in the idea that Morrissey has any problem with the company I keep, personally or workwise; we're different people and lead different kinds of lives, but that stuff is just patently untrue. And lastly, the stuff about me using record company funds to pay for a trip to America is totally wrong. I'm not denying that there weren't certain problems involving the band, and it's also very true that a group like The Smiths can begin to take over your whole life and all your energy. That's certainly happened to me, but the major reason for me going was simply that there are things I want to do, musically, that there is just not scope for in The Smiths. I've got absolutely no problem with what The Smiths are doing. The stuff we've just done for the new album is great, the best we've ever done. I'm really proud of it. But there are things I want to do that can only happen outside The Smiths." His concluding comments on the split were pointedly straightforward: "In the final analysis, the thing that used to make me happy was making me miserable and so I just had to get out." As a postscript, Marr caustically refuted the cutting press gibes that had marked him down as Keith Richard, Mark II: "I never *ever* wanted The Smiths to turn into The Rolling Stones; that was just more lazy, journalistic bullshit."

At the time of his official announcement, Marr contacted Joe Moss and settled the outstanding debt that Morrissey had always contested. It was a relief to hear his old mentor's voice and be able to talk freely about his momentous decision. "He was the one person on this earth who I knew wouldn't have been surprised," Marr muses. "Everywhere I looked people thought I was crazy, but Joe knew what the score was behind the scenes." Indeed, Moss had never forgotten Johnny's words back in 1982, when he insisted that he would be the first to leave the group. The split came as no great shock and, if anything, Moss had expected the end to come sooner. For one character, however, the final act provoked an unfamiliar speechlessness.

Since his denial at the end of July, Morrissey had remained conspicuously silent on the split, leaving Rough Trade's press office to articulate his views in their brief statement. Contrary to Marr's suspicions, he was completely taken aback by the turn of events. "I was very, very shocked," he confirmed. "I couldn't believe it." For Morrissey the proceedings had a decidedly surreal air. The Smiths were breaking up before his eyes and he was reading about it in the press as though it were a road accident. " I felt completely betrayed", he recalls, "because, for me, The Smiths were a tremendous emotional investment. I'd given so much of myself to the group, and, suddenly, by a stupid whim, everything was spoilt. I found it so unfair." The person with whom he had shared five years' work and friendship was living only a few minutes away, but he may as well have been on the moon. Distinguishing fiction from fact was proving increasingly difficult. The absurdity of the situation was summed up in the following week's *NME* where it was rumoured that Morrissey had been approached to replace the departing Holly Johnson in Frankie Goes To Hollywood. The *NME* revelled in the tale, which was used as a form of light relief from the more serious aspects of the split. The chance to have a crack at Morrissey for not providing a full post-split confession was left to "a spokesman for Frankie" who spluttered: "We would never have Morrissey in the group, the band don't even like The Smiths. Anyone who says we have approached him to join us obviously has a very vivid imagination and no common sense at all. We want someone who can sing well and write good lyrics."

Throughout August, The Smiths vainly attempted to come to terms with Marr's departure by uneasily carrying on. "It's like when you have four quarters of something you adore and somebody takes a quarter, there's no reason to throw the rest away," Joyce noted. The feeling in The Smiths' camp was still one of disbelief. Grant Showbiz had spoken to Johnny about his decision and recalls the guitarist's sense of relief: "He said, 'I went to bed and told myself, "I'm no longer going to be a Smith" and I woke up the next morning feeling great. I knew then I had to do it'." In spite of Marr's firmness, Grant was not alone in convincing himself that the decision was far from final. As The Smiths announced their intention to seek a replacement guitarist, there was false optimism in the camp that Marr might reconsider and appear at the next recording session. Although it was an unrealistic analogy, the members reminded themselves that Rourke had been sacked, then swiftly reinstated. Maybe a similar reversal of events might occur if they remained united in Marr's absence.

By late August the situation in The Smiths' camp still remained unresolved and the music press were milking the story with news that Aztec Camera's Roddy Frame was on the shortlist to replace Marr. What actually happened was that Geoff Travis phoned Frame's management company in the hope of persuading the guitarist to tour with the streamlined Smiths and record a further couple of B-sides. When Aztec Camera manager Bob Johnson approached his charge, he received an emphatic, "No!"

"It didn't get any further than that," Johnson confirms. "It was just one call. Rod was busy at the time. From there, it got a bit out of control because of the media intensity around The Smiths. It was a non-story." Another name that the press squeezed from their unnamed source at Rough Trade was Ivor Perry, Morrissey's old friend from Easterhouse. "Ivor Perry didn't audition, but he was approached," an anonymous "mole" informed the *NME*. On this occasion, however, the *NME* missed a story that actually had some substance.

Perry was still playing alongside Craig Gannon and Gary Farrell in The Cradle when he received a call from Geoff Travis expressing interest. Despite his friendship with Gannon, Perry was still on good terms with Morrissey, whom he had known since his teens. The opportunity to collaborate with the singer provided the possibility of some lucrative publishing income and Perry welcomed the challenge. Sitting down in front of a cassette player, he laid down a series of riffs and posted a tape to Morrissey the following day. A couple of weeks later he was invited to a London studio. There, the remaining Smiths, aided by producer Stephen Street, were attempting to carry on without their premier musical director. Perry was impressed by Morrissey's working methods and praised his abilities as an arranger. "He'd say, 'Play that for 10 bars, now do this' and you didn't know what you were playing," Ivor remembers. "It sounded a bit weird but when he did the vocal, it made sense. The music didn't work until you heard the vocal."

Perry cut two tracks with the "new" Smiths, including a startlingly hard version of the controversial 'Bengali In Platforms'. The original melody and guitar work provided by Perry contrasted markedly with the Stephen Street version that Morrissey eventually used on his solo album *Viva Hate*. "It was completely different the way we did it," Ivor remembers. "More in the style of The Clash - quite aggressive." As the session progressed, Perry seemed unsure whether Morrissey merely wanted some B-sides or something more. "He was trying to keep The Smiths going," Perry argues. "I told him he was daft. I didn't want to be Johnny Marr, Mark II. I didn't even play like him. It would have been embarrassing trying to live up to somebody. I thought it was a bit weird because the other Smiths were there and he didn't have enough guts to break clear."

If Morrissey needed any confirmation that The Smiths without Marr was a hopeless cause, then the ill-fated session provided the answer. Although Perry had previously worked with Stephen Street during the Easterhouse period, they seemed strangely at loggerheads as the day progressed. "Part of the reason the session didn't go too well was that I didn't get on with him," Perry explains. "I don't like his production style and we were arguing about the way I should play guitar. He was telling me how to play and I was saying: 'You're wrong'."

Before the first day's work was completed, Morrissey took flight, amid feelings of frustration and exasperation. "We were supposed to do three days but he blew it out," Perry confirms. "He lost his bottle. I kicked off and said, 'You're wasting my time'. He later wrote to me saying he liked the music, but that it would only have been B-sides - and that was that." Meanwhile, Mike Joyce was rapidly realizing that the new look Smiths was a doomed venture. "The new songs sounded OK," he notes, "but we were clinging to and clutching at straws. The real beauty of The Smiths had gone." The drummer summed up the missing ingredient in two words: "Johnny Marr!"

Morrissey's sudden departure from the studio was followed by a grand silence. Joyce urgently attempted to call him over the next two weeks, but his messages remained unanswered. "In that short period of time I felt the pressure," he remembers. "I just forgot the power of Johnny in The Smiths and that, without him, it was futile carrying on. Everybody was so screwed up that there was no point continuing. I'd felt that Johnny might come back, but when I realized he wouldn't I thought it was ridiculous to try and cope with what was left. It wasn't gelling." Morrissey's non-communicative tactics were the last straw for Joyce, who made the brave decision to announce his departure and form a new group. For a couple of days he was not entirely sure whether Morrissey might continue The Smiths project with Andy, but felt this was unlikely. His suspicions were confirmed when Morrissey simultaneously announced that it was over.

It was not until the second week of September 1987 that The Smiths were officially pronounced dead by their singer. In the interim, Stephen Street had tentatively mailed Morrissey some cassettes for consideration and found himself appointed songwriting partner and producer for the singer's first solo album. Morrissey knew that even if Perry had proven suitable, it was never likely that the new line-up could have continued using the name Smiths without incurring legal objections from Marr, who was contractually 50 per cent of the group. In the event, the *final* split announcement came as a merciful release after all the wearying speculation.

Looking back at the tangled web of misinformation, intrigue and self-generating pressures, Morrissey chronicles The Smiths' fragmentation. "The Smiths broke down because of strain," he now suggests. "We didn't have management and it was quite hard. We took on everything on our shoulders and you can't really do that and operate terribly successfully. I think Johnny simply had enough of the intensified pressure and just wanted to play music and not have that. Also, every move The Smiths made was intensely over-observed by people who loved The Smiths, or by people who hated The Smiths, and I think he became bored with that. He just really wanted to play music and get on with it. That's why The Smiths ended." Searching for additional factors, Morrissey added: "In the studio, Johnny was the key to The Smiths and yet nobody talked about him. When he left, he wanted to make a name for himself, which he did. He wanted to be recognized as Johnny Marr. He was no longer satisfied with a secondary role of living in my shadow. He knew that if he stayed in the group he would always be the guitarist. That wasn't enough for him anymore."

Two weeks after Morrissey had consigned The Smiths to history Rough Trade released the final studio album, *Strangeways, Here We Come*. Morrissey had jokingly titled the work in honour of the Victorian gaol that was already notorious for its overcrowding and primitive conditions.* Reflecting on recent "Morrissey controversies", the singer wryly noted that "the way things are going I wouldn't be surprised if I was in prison 12 months from now." Prefacing the record's release, he immodestly observed: "*Strangeways* perfects every lyrical and musical notion The Smiths have ever had." Bereft of the hyperbole, *Strangeways, Here We Come* was a peculiar album, neither brilliant nor poor, but strangely self-questioning.

Much of their old enthusiasm had been revived during the creative process, which partly explains why Morrissey and Marr still regard the work so highly. Stripping down the songs, however, the most striking image is of

---

*Morrissey's title gained ironic force three years later when Strangeways became the subject of Britain's longest-running prison siege. The quip "Strangeways, here we come" was most likely adapted from the pages of *Billy Liar* where Arthur is heard to exclaim: "Borstal, here we come". I have also found a probable inspirational source for the album's rear artwork in an early issue of the fanzine *Kid's Stuff*, to which Morrissey contributed in 1976-77.

two talents travelling in completely different directions. There was always *frisson* in The Smiths' music but never before had it seemed so intensely oppositional. The mood of the album is remarkably elegiacal, with an oblique lyrical and instrumental edge that seemed darker than any Smiths recording since their first LP. The work is dominated by funereal imagery, with over half the album containing songs about the dead or dying. Indeed, two of the compositions even contain the word "death" in the title, as if to emphasize the bleaker aspects of Morrissey's vision.

Ironically, the opening words of this posthumous album are those of a Morrissey character already deceased and transformed into a ghostly apparition. 'A Rush And A Push And The Land Is Ours' signalled Marr's determination to subvert the old Smiths' sound by provocatively replacing the guitar with a piano introduction and xylophone-sounding accompaniment. Morrissey replied with one of his more strident vocal outpourings, in keeping with the militaristic title. The singer's captivating canine growl continues on 'I Started Something I Couldn't Finish', in which Marr concocts a Seventies-inspired hammy glitter sound. The lyrics, echoing the title, never quite manage to reach a conclusion, but take on a sardonic tone in view of The Smiths' sudden demise.

Morrissey's well known antipathy towards "sterile" dance music, already voiced in 'Panic', continues in a more melancholic vein on the lyrics of 'Death Of A Disco Dancer'. In passing comment on the irrational violence surrounding him, Morrissey sarcastically notes, "Love, peace and harmony? Oh very nice... but maybe in the next world". The song proved an eerily prophetic comment on the Manchester drug wars, Moss Side slayings and closure of the Hacienda club three years hence. Marr recalls that The Beatles' 'I'm So Tired' was a favourite track during the sessions, and there is much of Lennon's world-weariness in the doleful disco diatribe. The intriguing coda, complete with Morrissey's untutored piano accompaniment, is very reminiscent of the chaotic mid-section of The Beatles' 'I Am The Walrus', while Marr's acid-influenced arrangement prefigures the psychedelia-tinged style of Mancunian successors, The Stone Roses.

The contrastingly light 'Girlfriend In A Coma', with its subtly dark humour, had appeared somewhat appropriately during the week of the split announcement. Morrissey regarded the track as an excellent pop song. Its doom-laden theme is lightened by the plush orchestration and subverted by the neurotic narrator's playful admission, "there were times when I could have strangled her". The contrasting "No I don't want to see her... would you please let me see her" amusingly captures the emotional confusion amid the bedside drama. Despite all the posthumous press, The Smiths last serious chart assault failed to crack the Top 10, stalling at an unlucky number 13.

The first side of the album ended on another high point: 'Stop Me If You Think You've Heard This One Before'. Marr's riveting knife-edge opening dramatically prefaces a rock workout of considerable power, with Morrissey dissecting the scrap ends of a weary relationship. The title was universally interpreted as an arch acknowledgement of encroaching self-parody, with the singer driving the old themes into a grave of frustrated repetition. The track would have made an excellently mischievous last single and was intended as such until the BBC took exception to the reference to "mass murder", which they regarded as insensitive in view of the recent massacre in Hungerford during which the deranged Michael Ryan shot 17 people dead and injured 14 more.

The musical schism between Morrissey and Marr was never better exemplified than on the startling 'Last Night I Dreamt Somebody Loved Me'. Ironically, at the point of increasing separation, their contrasting visions collided, then coalesced in a work of unforced poignancy. Marr's opening dirge of screaming hordes sounds like a musical evocation of Dante's *Inferno*. The funereal piano evokes the death march, before the pullulating vocal of Morrissey belatedly emerges with another tale of defeat and despair. The tragedy of passing time leading to nothing echoes Morrissey's favourite theme and the lyrics are a virtual rewrite of 'How Soon Is Now?' five years on. With his fondness for strings and inventive arrangements, Marr betrays the hungry experimentation of a Boy Beethoven, longing for tomorrow. By contrast, Morrissey looks back, wearily, regretfully and despairingly towards an immutable and unexorcizable past that he seems doomed to recycle endlessly.

'Unhappy Birthday', Morrissey's spiteful letter of retribution, couched in pleasant singalong form, was one of several songs on the album that won Marr's unanimous approval. "'Unhappy Birthday' is fantastic," he enthuses. "Only Morrissey could do that to my music and only I could give him that music to sing." The guitarist was less enamoured of 'Death At One's Elbow', in which Morrissey returned to the old *Psycho* imagery and grimly warned of "splattered remains". Marr also echoed the past by reintroducing the harmonica, albeit wildly mutated by his contemporary arrangement. The closing track, 'I Won't Share You', was another of Morrissey's more maudlin essays and ended matters on a quietly bathetic note. The sentiments proved moving enough to reduce Mike Joyce to tears.

The most discussed and widely quoted lyric, however, was the longest track on the album, 'Paint A Vulgar Picture'. With a title borrowed from Oscar Wilde, Morrissey launched a scathing attack on the rapacious marketing tactics of the record industry, while also bemoaning the self-alienating aspects of the star system and pondering the peculiar relationship between the fan and the idol. By the end of the song, death and rock star hagiography seem a strangely satisfactory outcome. Although Morrissey denies that the composition was intended as an attack on Rough Trade, it was widely interpreted as such by both the music press and the hard-core Smiths fraternity. It was doubly unfortunate that lines such as "Re-issue! Re-issue! Re-package! Re-package!... Extra Track" coincided with the recent release of *The World Won't Listen* (with one previously unreleased song) and *Louder Than Bombs*. The defection to EMI and its attendant acrimony was still the subject of passing comment in the pages of *NME*. Any satiric thrust that 'Paint A Vulgar Picture' might have offered was somewhat undermined by the fact that Morrissey had fully approved of Rough

The Smiths at Liverpool Royal Court, 8 February 1986. *(Steve Double/S.I.N.)*.

The Smiths on *The Tube*, 5 July 1986, with schoolboy on guest vocals. *(LFI)*.

Twinkle, whose 'Golden Lights' was unwittingly written about a near neighbour of Morrissey's father in Dublin. *(Pictorial)*.

Cilla Black provided the last non-Smiths original, 'Love Is A Four Letter Word'. *(LFI)*.

Sandie Shaw briefly replaces Morrissey in The Smiths for the hit version of 'Hand In Glove'. *(Pictorial)*.

Johnny and Angie on their wedding day. San Francisco, 20 June 1985. *(Marr Family Collection).*

Marr, minus the angelic looks of yore. *(Steve Double).*

Early publicity shots.

December 1985. Arndale
Shopping Centre, Manchester.
(Stephen Wright).

The Cradle, whose unique membership included ex-Smith Craig Gannon (centre), 'pre-Smith'
Gary Farrell (far right) and 'post-Smith' Ivor Perry (far left). *(Stephen Wright).*

Feeding the ducks in Bath, 1987. *(Vini Reilly)*.

Morrissey,
the profile.
Winter of 1987.
(Vini Reilly).

Morrissey besieged by fans at
Wolverhampton, Civic Hall, 22 December
1988. *(Steve Double)*.

1991. The *Kill Uncle* tour.
(Jane Huntington/S.I.N.).

1991. Morrissey, Springtime in Paris. *(Renaud Moufourny)*.

Johnny Marr joins The Pretenders, with Chrissie Hynde. Back row: drummer Fred Hood and bassist James Eller. *(Pennie Smith)*.

Electronic 1991, Bernard Sumner and Johnny Marr. *(LFI, Andrew Catlin)*.

The The in 1989. Left to right: James Eller, Matt Johnson, Dave Palmer and Johnny Marr. *(Steve Double)*.

Trade's retrospective compilation. Travis was predictably puzzled by the sentiments of Morrissey's "vulgar picture". "I thought the song was about someone else, but perhaps I'm being naïve," he reflects. "I know we never did anything except to his absolute sanction. Perhaps he was trying to expunge his conscience in some way and give himself a good reason to sign to EMI. I know some people read it as being about us... I think that's Morrissey being a coward and taking the line of least resistance and trying to set up a situation that gives himself some justification. That's how I read it. I don't think we're guilty of anything. It's quite unfathomable. So, in a sense, I don't really mind. But I do worry why the *NME* seems so spiteful." It is interesting that Travis, like Morrissey, should conclude matters with a weary criticism of the music press.

Predictably, *Strangeways, Here We Come* was lionized upon its release, then mauled in subsequent Smiths' retrospectives. Like Shakespeare's "problem plays" it forced critics to question their generic prejudices, but provided no easy answers. The album still sounds like a good, old-fashioned transitional work - neither wholly experimental nor quintessentially Smiths-sounding. With Marr restlessly pushing forward into new territory, irrespective of its fertility, and Morrissey constantly returning to the well of his old inspiration for security, the work was remarkably taut and inevitably flawed. Its beauty rested in its tension and languid melancholia, which was given an even darker edge as a result of Marr's experimental arrangements. The overall effect was that of a great story left uncompleted. After listening to the album you looked forward to an entirely new phase, only to realize that the players had left the stage.

In the wake of *Strangeways*, there was the valedictory *South Bank Show*, which originally had been intended to celebrate The Smiths' elevation to the level of highbrow culture. Hastily rewritten to feature their demise, it suffered from a lack of perspective on the split from any of the interviewees. The most memorable part of the programme occurred when former *NME* writer Nick Kent audaciously commented: "In 10 years' time The Smiths will be viewed in the same way that The Beatles are now viewed". The comparison was extravagantly inappropriate, even by Kent's passionate standards. The Beatles' cultural significance was inextricably linked with their immense international, across-the-board appeal, a luxury which The Smiths never enjoyed. In any case, The Smiths' godhead was ultimately tainted in Kent's mind by signs of human fallibility. "I'll have to live with that comment," he now remarks. "But when I made that Beatles comparison *Strangeways* hadn't yet been released. Up until then, The Smiths' career was like a carefully ascending trajectory." Kent was correct, however, in suggesting that the group's critical reputation would increase rather than fade after their death.

The failure to complete the B-side recordings with Ivor Perry meant that the final two Smiths singles from *Strangeways, Here We Come* were released without fanfare. Both 'I Started Something I Couldn't Finish' and 'Last Night I Dreamt That Somebody Loved Me' reached the Top 30, but received little airplay or media interest. In the meantime, Morrissey had telephoned

Marr proposing a Smiths farewell concert, but the guitarist refused to be drawn. He was still annoyed about the circumstances surrounding the announcement of the split and saw no point in organizing a funeral just to satisfy Morrissey. "I did bear him a lot of ill feeling at the time," Johnny recalls, "right up until I joined The The really." Morrissey was similarly upset by the split. "I've learned a lot from Johnny's departure", he reflects, "and, sadly, I've kept a lot of bitterness". Marr was also disillusioned by the acerbic reactions of certain Smiths fans who were already blaming him for the break-up of the group. Steeling himself, he carried on, initially appearing onstage with A Certain Ratio and later joining The Pretenders for a short period. Sadly, there was no room in his life for Morrissey. "It was very intense and we are obviously different people, so it was inevitable that the friendship should end," he explained. "All we've got uniting us now is memories of the old days. We don't want to work together." There is a similar note of pathos in Morrissey's closing words, "I know that we will never see each other again".

EPILOGUE

The Severed Alliance

AFTER 1987, MORRISSEY AND MARR severed their alliance, each branching out into new areas that will eventually demand book treatments of their own. Morrissey's disappointment over the split was alleviated by a flurry of work as he plunged headlong into the recording of his début solo album."I wanted to make a record straightaway", Morrissey recalls, "but I was still in a state of shock, still upset and very angry. That's why I called the album *Viva Hate*." With Ivor Perry now out of contention, producer Stephen Street enlisted Durutti Column's Vini Reilly as the new guitarist. On the way to Street's Chelsea flat, Reilly was told that Morrissey could be "difficult" and he soon learned that people felt peculiarly uncomfortable in the singer's presence. "He intimidated a lot of people," Reilly observed, "especially around that period, and without intending to. He's a very powerful personality. When he walks in the room it goes very quiet. It's unusual to exude that kind of power without being aware of it, and he wasn't aware of it."

Reilly was quick to notice the pressure that Morrissey was under during this crucial period and felt sympathetic. "The first thing I decided was to be completely honest with him," he explains. "Nobody was being honest with him that I could see. People around him were so busy being nice to him, or afraid of him, and guessing the right reactions that he and I just found the whole thing frustrating. That applied to everybody. There were no exceptions. Everybody I saw speaking to him, from the manager of the studio to the engineer, spoke to him in a very unnatural way. They would talk to him as if he wasn't a human being."

Despite Morrissey's intimidating presence, the winter sessions at the Wool Hall, Bath were completed reasonably punctually. Nevertheless, an air of uncertainty surrounded the recordings, particularly for Morrissey, who no longer enjoyed the guiding influence of his former partner. "I don't think Morrissey quite knew what was going to happen," Reilly recalls. "The only thing he'd done before was The Smiths and that was a set-up that worked perfectly. They had the magical combination of Morrissey and Marr. But this was the first time he'd ever done anything without Johnny Marr. He was very confused by that, so I don't think he knew what to think of it." Opinions about the quality of the recordings changed daily, right up until, and even after, the album was released. For Vini Reilly, the major frustration came from adapting his distinctive style of playing to Stephen

Street's all too straightforward pop melodies. The constraints placed upon him in the studio left the guitarist disillusioned with the project. "As far as I'm concerned, Stephen Street, as a producer, may as well have got a very good session guitar player to do what I did," he explains. "I put lots of hook lines in, played French horn on a sampler on 'Dial-A-Cliche' and played fast and wild guitar on some tracks but, apart from that, there wasn't really anything satisfying for me. It was all too rigid, all too predictable. The only thing that salvaged those songs was Morrissey's performance."

Like Ivor Perry, Vini was intrigued both by Morrissey's ability to read a song and the unorthodox way in which he structured his vocal. "We put in these very straightforward arrangements," Reilly remembers, "and when Morrissey came in to put down his guide vocals, we suddenly realized that he was treating the middle eight as a chorus, and the chorus as a middle eight. He'd put vocals in the most peculiar places. His phrasing is weird and often you'd have to change the arrangement to fit in. But it worked. That was what really saved that album from being utterly mediocre, as far as I could see. Morrissey's musical input was huge. Everybody just thinks he sings, but the way he phrases determines how the music must be rearranged. I was always waiting for that vocal to go down because I knew that I could then put more hooks in and make it more interesting for myself."

In February 1988, a pilot single emerged from the sessions which took many people by surprise. 'Suedehead' proved an exceptionally strong A-side which allowed Morrissey to tap the immediate euphoric intensity that followed The Smiths' split. Critics and fans were quick to note that the record reached number five, thereby outstripping the success of any Smiths single. When the succeeding *Viva Hate* topped the album charts, it was generally accepted that Morrissey would benefit enormously from his association with EMI and continue to reach a wider audience. At the time of its release the album was very well received, although Morrissey himself later conceded that it was a less accomplished work than *Strangeways, Here We Come*. Without Marr, the singer lacked the distinctive melodic ingenuity that highlighted The Smiths' work, but *Viva Hate* was nevertheless a fascinating departure with some strong songs. The album was dominated by images of the Seventies, from the axed child star at the dawn of the decade ('Little Man, What Now?') to the ersatz glam rock of the sartorially inept Bengali, the allusions to the break-up of the family, the stifling world of The Ordinary Boys and the oblique references to the 1970 movie *Angel, Angel, Down We Go* and Richard Allen's cult novel *Suedehead*. Significantly, the album closed with a vitriolic swipe at the politician whose rise to power at the end of the Seventies would change the face of Britain over the next decade: Margaret Thatcher.

Musically, *Viva Hate* saw Morrissey bravely dissociating himself from The Smiths' history, as well as revealing a surprising willingness to embrace a distinctly contemporary sound, complete with drum machine. The Vini Reilly influence was particularly evident on the guitar-distorted 'Alsatian

Cousin' and the almost unbearably poignant 'Late Night Maudlin Street'. Morrissey and Street also provided some contrastingly upbeat, pop-orientated material, most notably, 'Little Man, What Now?' and 'I Don't Mind If You Forget Me'. Morrissey's grand sense of melodrama, complete with allusions to suicide, was noticeable on 'Angel, Angel, Down We Go Together' and arguably reached its apogee with the pained farewell to adolescence on Maudlin Street. For most commentators, the least successful aspects of the album were Morrissey's clumsy attempts at social and political commentary on 'Bengali In Platforms' and 'Margaret On A Guillotine'. Compared to The Smiths' forays into such areas, these songs seemed lyrically forced and musically unadventurous. Such quibbles were not quite sufficient to distract from the work's stronger moments and when the superb 'Everyday Is Like Sunday' stormed the Top 10 many were convinced that Morrissey was on the brink of Smiths-like greatness. Few could have anticipated the career problems that lay immediately ahead.

The remainder of 1988 saw the Morrissey/Marr legacy continue with the belated release of a Smiths live package, *"Rank"*. Recorded at Kilburn's National Ballroom on 23 October 1986, the work captured the group in their rockiest phase, with Gannon and Marr on twin guitars. Compiled by Morrissey, and approved by Marr, *"Rank"* emphasized the diversity of The Smiths, mixing harder rock tracks like 'London' and 'Big Mouth Strikes Again' alongside the whimsical 'Vicar In A Tutu' and plaintive 'The Boy With The Thorn In His Side'. The opening 'The Queen Is Dead' proved the *tour de force* of the set, with Marr wah-wahing his way into the stratosphere and Morrissey's breathless vocal so all over the place that he substituted animal-like noises for line-ends. The wonderfully effective segue of '(Marie's The Name) His Latest Flame' and 'Rusholme Ruffians' and a seven minute plus version of 'I Know It's Over' were among the other highlights. Morrissey could easily have spread the 21 tracks from the concert over a double album but instead he carefully compiled a striking 14-song single package. There was even a notable olive branch directed towards his partner. The surprise inclusion of 'The Draize Train' meant that Marr received an even larger slice of the publishing income from the album than Morrissey. *"Rank"* proved a timely reminder of how great a live group The Smiths were in their prime, as well as underlining their historical importance. Already, there were a growing number of teenagers who listened enviously to the live sound of this dead but never-to-be-forgotten group. Morrissey would have loved to reward them with a Smiths farewell show and partly achieved this ambition two months later.

At Wolverhampton Civic Hall on 22 December 1988, Morrissey effectively closed the curtain on his Smiths years and simultaneously opened his solo performing career by recording a show with former colleagues, Rourke, Joyce and Gannon. The event, part of which was later captured on the video *Hulmerist*, proved something of a Christmas present for Morrissey's stage-starved following, and an endurance test for others. Free admission was offered to those sporting a Smiths T-shirt, but with a 1,700 capacity it was clear that the Civic Hall would be able to house a mere fraction of the pilgrim hordes who made the journey. Those lucky enough to gain admittance witnessed scenes of fan pandemonium, as Morrissey gamely attempted to complete his seven-song set beneath the embraces of starry-eyed stage invaders. "There was a radiant feeling onstage," Morrissey recalled. "You knew where everybody was and who they were, which was astonishingly good." Although the performance served as a vehicle to introduce his new material on video, Morrissey responded to the sense of occasion by framing the set with two Smiths originals: 'Stop Me If You Think You've Heard This One Before' and 'Death At One's Elbow', followed by the encore 'Sweet And Tender Hooligan'. One of the songs premièred was his next single 'The Last Of The Famous International Playboys', which promptly hit the Top 10 one month later. Johnny Marr was sufficiently impressed by Morrissey's portrayal of gangster glamour to pen his former partner a congratulatory postcard. With Marr scribbling good will and The Smiths' rhythm section back in the Morrissey camp, observers could be forgiven for assuming that a full reunion was a distinct possibility. In reality, the opposite was the case.

Johnny Marr had long put The Smiths behind him and was enjoying the freedom offered by session work. Although he had originally intended to form his own group with James Eller and David Palmer, he was painfully aware that the new ensemble would be compared unfavourably to The Smiths. The intense media speculation that still surrounded his activities and the continued barracking from die-hard Smiths fans convinced the guitarist that it would be most sensible to maintain a low profile. Throughout this period, he remained in contact with former Smiths manager Ken Friedman, who had accepted a cheque in settlement for his services rather than prolonging any ugly litigation. Friedman had many discussions with the guitarist and encouraged his guest appearances with Bryan Ferry and The Pretenders. "I thought Chrissie only had a couple of albums left in her," he candidly observed, so Marr's presence seemed the perfect panacea. Marr's tour with The Pretenders took him as far as Brazil and initially the tie-up went well. Friedman was convinced that a Hynde/Marr writing partnership would prove ideal but, ultimately, the collaboration failed to take off. It seemed that whenever Hynde wanted Marr to travel to London for a session, he preferred to remain ensconced in his Manchester home. Conversely, by the time Johnny was again ready to tour the world and rock out, Chrissie was in favour of winding down.

In the meantime, Marr was enjoying a fruitful relationship with the UK-based Ignition Management, headed by the urbane Marcus Russell, whose other clients included the promising Latin Quarter. Friedman claims that he was responsible for hiring Russell, who supposedly took exception to "being treated like a tea boy" by the American. The upshot of that personality clash was that the undemonstrative Russell went on to become Marr's sole representative. Ignition also acquired the mercurial Matt Johnson, who had recently contacted Johnny with a view to playing on a new song, 'The Beat(en) Generation'. The duo had met at 9pm in a studio, then stayed up all night clubbing and talking. Twelve hours later, Marr found himself agreeing to become a full member of the group. "It was almost the ideal band for Johnny," Johnson claims, "and he always wanted to play with The The. I think it opened his eyes when he saw the way I worked. It does give you a lot of freedom whereas, The Smiths, towards the end, was restrictive with the politics and everything else. That doesn't occur in my situation. If somebody bums me out, they're history. There's no problems or power struggles, which I can't bear. There may be some tension and electricity but, ultimately, that should be for bearing fruit. I'm not into mind games."

During March, Marr was back on *Top Of The Pops* playing guitar and harmonica on The The's catchy, yet cynical, hit single, 'The Beat(en) Generation'. One month later, The Pretenders issued 'Windows Of The World'/'1969' with Marr featured prominently in the video. The spring Marr invasion was completed in May when The The issued the long-awaited *Mind Bomb*. Contrary to public expectation, this was not some Morrissey/Marr-like collaboration between Johnson and his celebrity guitarist. "*Mind Bomb* was mainly written before Johnny," Matt confirms, "but I gave him more freedom than the other musicians." With Johnson having written the lyrics and music, as well as producing the album, Marr's compositional credit stretched to only one song: 'Gravitate To Me'. His playing, moreover, was far removed from his Smiths work, with a greater emphasis on dense, expansive arrangements, minus those familiar but imaginative chord sequences of old.

Mind Bomb was less well received than any of Johnson's previous albums. With *Soul Mining* and *Infected*, he had produced two startling works that were rightly acclaimed as among the best of their era. The problem with *Mind Bomb* was not so much Johnson's incessant anti-religious diatribes, but the lack of memorable melodic arrangements on which to hang his lyrics. Unlike the superb *Infected*, *Mind Bomb* ranted its message and provided scant evidence of Johnson's ingenuity as a songsmith. The ambition was there in abundance, but the songs were not. Given Marr's involvement, this seemed all the more ironic. What The The provided, however, was the chance to experiment with sound textures and atmospherics. This was particularly evident on the opening track, 'Good Morning Beautiful', which Johnson presently cites as his finest work. "I was really happy about what Johnny did on that," he enthuses. "We were wielding the drugs at certain times to get the atmosphere, which is something I don't do so much anymore. But, some of the tracks we did that on, particularly 'Good Morning Beautiful'. I filled Johnny up with drugs and said: 'This is Satan meets Jesus'. What he came up with was exactly what I wanted. It was superb. I was just filling up the multi-track with sound, saying: 'Go again! Go again!' He could do all the things he wanted, without the usual confines of session work."

The bombastic nature of *Mind Bomb*, in which virtually every lyric was accompanied by copious exclamation marks, was aptly captured on the world stage, as Johnson took flight like an agent of pandemic destruction. The performances brought the album to life in many respects, especially as the new songs nestled bristlingly between inspired selections from The

The's classic earlier work. Beneath a fog of dry ice, Johnson lurked menacingly like a Victorian serial killer, while Marr stood undemonstrably on the right hand side of the stage, playing those spacious parts that contrasted so radically with his Smiths' work. With the aid of a full-time trainer, Johnson survived the rigours of life on the road and, by the end of the tour, several more songs were completed in fragmentary form. "Whenever we play together we write something," Matt exults. "We haven't scratched the surface yet. *Mind Bomb* was like a trial effort."

Even while The The's tour was in progress, however, Marr had already begun another project. Originally, he had intended merely to guest on a solo album by New Order's Bernard Sumner, but the collaboration worked so effectively that they became Electronic. With the assistance of The Pet Shop Boys, the Mancunians ended the year with a Top 10 hit, 'Getting Away With It'. Suddenly, talk of Marr's post-Smiths low profile was suspended.

While Marr was enjoying the commercial fruition of his recent projects, Morrissey was encountering old but familiar problems. After a glorious start to the year, he rapidly found himself embroiled in a series of business wrangles. In the wake of The Smiths' demise, Morrissey had at last appointed a first class manager, Gail Colson, whose presence seemed likely to relieve him of the administrative chaos that had permeated the previous five years. Colson saw precious little of Morrissey during her tenure, but that seemed relatively unimportant. The fact was she was there when needed. Unfortunately, at the very time when her advice was most required, the singer chose to terminate their agreement. What followed was a plot of Shakespearian irony, as Morrissey found himself besieged by former friends and associates demanding justice - and money.

In March 1989, another of Colson's clients, Stephen Street, hit the headlines when it was revealed that he was blocking the release of the next Morrissey single, 'Interesting Drug'. The music press was brimming with tales of money wrangles, even suggesting that Street was arguing about the financial arrangements for his production and engineering going back five years. The indignant producer attempted to pour water on the dispute the following week by stressing: "It's ridiculous to say that I'm unhappy with the financial arrangements, I've always received royalties due to me. I didn't want to hold the single back but I still haven't received a production contract for *Viva Hate* even, and I have to protect my rights. I had to put pressure on Morrissey to speed up the paperwork - he just disappears and shuts himself away and, because he has no manager, nothing gets done. I'm very disappointed... it's made me look like a money-grabbing bastard whereas, really, I'm just protecting myself legally." By the time the injunction was lifted, Street's working relationship with Morrissey was on the rocks. It would not survive the year.

By now, the press had also caught rumours of a further dispute involving Gannon, Rourke and Joyce. The fact that the three ex-Smiths had recently performed alongside Morrissey and worked with him in the studio confounded the *NME* newshounds, who speculated: "One theory is that The

Smiths musicians are seeking extra cash after signing 'bad' contracts early in the group's career and feeling hard-done-by when the money started rolling in." This was a plausible guess, but only half the story; far from signing 'bad' contracts, the subsidiary Smiths had, of course, never signed anything.

The inevitable legacy of that unfortunate early verbal agreement was a contentious legal dispute that commenced soon after The Smiths had split. While the Gannon case continued, Morrissey/Marr attempted to settle their outstanding account with Rourke/Joyce by offering them a percentage of The Smiths' royalties. The figure that the songwriting duo agreed upon was 10 per cent. According to Marr, this was the basis of their original verbal agreement back in 1982, and when Andy and Mike subsequently refused this settlement and threatened legal reparation, the guitarist felt indignant. "I didn't expect it," he innocently suggests. "They've got very short memories in that case. It's all right to remember some things, but not others. It was always understood that we could handle the headaches. Our problem was to take care of all the logistical and management situations because we were getting paid the bigger share for it. That was the understanding we all had. Let them live their much less pressurized lives. [The legal action] was very surprising. I think it's just the way of the world, it just happens. I think it's a bit tacky, but there you go... it's not going to carry on, so I'll get a bit of what's there." In conclusion, Marr still insists that Joyce and Rourke were aware of the original terms presented by himself and Morrissey and were happy with the percentage then on offer.

While Marr and Morrissey felt their partners were unfairly demanding more money after the event, the junior members questioned the very basis of the original agreement. "I never agreed to 10 per cent," Joyce sternly points out. "I was never told. That's probably what Johnny can remember, not what I remember. As far as I was concerned, if 10 per cent was put forward to me [originally] I probably would have accepted that, or said *maybe* I will accept that, but the fact is that it never was. People who know me know that I'm not stupid enough to accept a certain percentage and then, when we split up, say I want some more. I wasn't trying to reap some benefit from the fact that the band had split up - it was more of a fact that, as far as I was concerned, I was always on 25 per cent. When we split up I found out that I was on 10 per cent and I was pretty upset about it." It says much for The Smiths' lack of business sense that Joyce remained ignorant of such basics for the entire duration of the group's career. The failure to render accounts or even provide a simple written agreement for the subsidiary members was now reaping a whirlwind. The implications transcended a mere settlement of monies accruing from The Smiths' account *since* the split. As Morrissey ruefully observed: "Mike Joyce is demanding 25 per cent of *everything* The Smiths ever earned".*

Joyce and Rourke's attempt to correct what they considered to be the

* Morrissey's use of the word "everything" only extended as far as record royalties and live work. Obviously, Joyce and Rourke made no claims for any revenue from songwriting.

wrongs of Smiths' financial history initially looked very promising. "Andy and I got together because it was something that we felt quite strongly about," Joyce explains. "Morrissey and Johnny said, 'Look, it's there, accept it'. We thought it was a bit unfair and tried to speak to them, but Johnny and Morrissey were adamant that it was going to be 10 per cent." As a united front, the rhythm section could at least share the legal costs and emotional burdens resulting from the struggle but, almost two years on, Rourke lost heart and decided to accept the 10 per cent settlement. "Andy said he had to accept," Joyce recalls. "I found that hard to come to terms with. It seemed like the last couple of years had been futile. But, then again, Andy didn't realize how difficult it was going to be. I don't think people do when they enter into litigation."

Without Rourke, Joyce was left in the unenviable position of taking on Morrissey and Marr alone. Still convinced that he was in the right and confident of ultimate victory, the drummer continued the fight although, like so many others, he felt an almost irrational guilt about offending Morrissey. "I never believed that I could take legal proceedings against Morrissey and Johnny because I felt that there was a bond between us," he explains. "I felt as though I'd done something wrong by doing that. I felt sick inside... I'm sure they thought, 'What's he playing at?'" Joyce's ambivalent feelings were understandable, particularly in view of the enormous talents of Morrissey/Marr and their contribution to his life. "I looked up to them so much," he reminisces, "and they gave me a massive platform to work from." In a sense, the guilt that Joyce felt about demanding what he perceived as his rightful due made him even more frustrated and angry. It would have been much easier if he merely felt contempt for his ex-partners, but he still regarded them as old friends. The scenario resembled that of divorcees arguing over the bank balance and furnishings.

In the end, the lengthy legal process provided Joyce with more than enough time to come to terms with his confused feelings. "I've worked it through emotionally from bitterness to sadness," he now philosophizes. "It seems such a surreal situation. You read about these things and see them on television - the mythology of the music industry. You see it happening in other people's lives, and now it's happening in mine. It's something I still find difficult to come to terms with, and I'm sure Johnny and Morrissey do too." Four-and-a-half years on from The Smiths' split, the case has still to reach the High Court, but Joyce looks optimistically towards some form of settlement by the end of 1992. He still speaks of his former partners in glowing terms and infrequently socializes with Marr. When the pair last met, the friendly guitarist brushed aside their legal differences with the stoical rejoinder, "Business is business."

What with the battle royal involving Joyce, the concomitant action with Gannon and a disgruntled Stephen Street delaying his single, Morrissey could have done with some compensatory commercial or critical acclaim during 1989. Even in those areas, however, he was abruptly thwarted. His next single, 'Ouija Board, Ouija Board', was lambasted in the press and failed to emulate the Top 10 success of its predecessors, peaking at a lowly number 18. The severity of the criticism puzzled both Morrissey and his new producers, Clive Langer and Alan Winstanley, who felt the record was both amusing and chart worthy. It was another example of Morrissey turning his wit unexpectedly upon himself. Heavenly choirs sing of carnivores while Morrissey's desperate search for a lover from beyond the grave is scuppered by the surly message: "Steven - Push Off!" That response was soon reflected in certain review columns, which regarded Morrissey's light touch as evidence of encroaching superficiality. In the meantime, Manchester danced to a new beat led by The Stone Roses, Happy Mondays and The Inspiral Carpets. Morrissey's quaint pop was far removed from their psychedelic/dance orientated work and led some sarcastic critics to proclaim him an anachronism. Even his previous group now seemed part of a golden era, their memory upheld in the annual Smiths Convention, which attracted die-hard fans from all over the country, and abroad. Towards the end of 1989, Morrissey seemed to have overcome his recent spate of problems and was busily completing songs for a new album, tentatively titled *Bona Drag*. It proved a false dawn. Although at least half-a-dozen titles were completed, including the rare 'Striptease With A Difference', the sessions ended abruptly and, early the following year, the projected LP was cancelled.

Instead, Morrissey issued the outstanding cuts as singles. In April, the extraordinary 'November Spawned A Monster' was released and wasted no time in dividing critics. Its use of the wailing Mary Margaret O'Hara was perceived by some as offensively theatrical, but came as no surprise to those used to the singer's deft dramatic touches (cf the "Hindley" laugh in 'Suffer Little Children', the screaming knives and mooing cows in 'Meat Is Murder', and the thud of the blade in 'Margaret On A Guillotine'). Issued at a time of increasing debate about Morrissey's "relevance", 'November Spawned A Monster' proved his most forceful and arresting composition in several years. In its searing commentary on the plight of a disabled girl, the song reiterated Morrissey's inexhaustible interest in society's "outsiders". The dispossessed ('Interesting Drug'), the culturally alienated ('Bengali In Platforms') and the generally neurotic ('Ouija Board, Ouija Board') had all featured in his recent material, but never with such a brutal realism and taboo-removing assertiveness. The most intriguing aspect of 'November Spawned A Monster' is its point of view. Morrissey remorselessly strips away the usual condescending approach to the disabled in popular song in order to touch nerve ends. He does not merely empathize with the crippled and deformed but dramatizes a self-revulsion that brilliantly combines cruelty, mockery and sympathy, sometimes within the space of a single line. The opening couplet, "Sleep on and dream of Love/because it's the closest *you'll* get to love" is both sympathetic and mocking in its connotations. The specific vocabulary, with such phrases as "poor twisted child", "a frame of useless limbs", "so ugly" and "monster" is deliberately confrontational. Sexual black humour incongruously creeps into the line: "Could you even bear to kiss her full on the mouth, or *anywhere?*" Morrissey could never resist an element of nervously flippant humour in dealing with the harsher realities of life (cf the "inappropriate" references to murder in 'Girlfriend In A Coma'). The genuinely moving and sympathetic response to the disabled "monster" is captured most poignantly in the final lines where Morrissey champions her pathetic ambition to choose some clothes of her own. It is a resonant image that further complicates the mood of the song and ably articulates Morrissey's mixed feelings about his subject. In adopting the persona of the taunter, as well as the saviour, Morrissey forces his listeners to confront their own prejudices head on.

Given its controversial nature, 'November Spawned A Monster' did well to outsell 'Ouija Board, Ouija Board' and climb to number 12. By now, however, it was clear that Morrissey could no longer rely on automatic Top 10, or indeed Top 20, hits. His detractors were quick to note his gradual commercial slide and predicted an increasingly barren future. His continued failure to tour and the mysterious non-appearance of a new album led to ludicrously premature artistic obituaries. Following the release of the video compilation, *Hulmerist*, Morrissey returned in October with the excellent 'Piccadilly Palare'. The Madness influence, already evident via the production of Langer and Winstanley, was reinforced by the presence of guest vocalist Suggs on this poignant tale of boyish meat in Piccadilly playland.

The subject of teenage runaways and male prostitution fitted in well with Morrissey's social critiques and proved a welcome appetizer for *Bona Drag*. Having abandoned the album, Morrissey retained the title for this new compilation which, in many ways, served a similar purpose to *Hatful Of Hollow* and *The World Won't Listen*. *Bona Drag* provided a fresh perspective on Morrissey's solo career by bringing together the flip sides and apparent fragments of his work in a single collection that was astonishing in its breadth and quality. Songs that had been neatly tucked away on 12-inch singles suddenly gained new dramatic force when placed in the context of a long player. The brilliantly humorous 'Hairdresser On Fire', with its portentous opening line and dramatic orchestration, emphasized the idiosyncratic nature of the singer's satiric wit. Who else but Morrissey would wreak a bathetically affectionate vengeance on a Sloane Square hairdresser who failed to fit him on to his books? The exuberant arrangement was a joy to hear in its new context, not least because Morrissey's growls were probably the most effective heard on any recording since Roy Orbison's 'Oh Pretty Woman'.

Even without the presence of 'East West', 'I Know Very Well How I Got My Name', 'Sister, I'm A Poet', 'Michael's Bones' or 'Girl Least Likely To', *Bona Drag* gave stupendous range to Morrissey's incredible power and diversity as a singer and writer. The gloriously defiant 'Will Never Marry' and 'Such A Little Thing Makes Such A Difference' celebrated Morrissey's non-conformity and there was a very revealing autobiographical moment in 'He Knows I'd Love To See Him' in which the singer documented his brush with the police following his inflammatory comments on Margaret Thatcher. After being dismissed as a bed-ridden rebel who thinks he can change the world, Morrissey languorously intones: "I know I do". His curiously mild-mannered but acerbic defiance was never more simply, yet effectively, expressed.

With its mixture of hits and high moments, from 'Suedehead' and 'Last Of The Famous International Playboys' to 'Lucky Lisp', 'Yes, I Am Blind' and the ultimate album closer, 'Disappointed', *Bona Drag* was an unexpected triumph. Issued as a stop-gap between albums, it instantly gave the lie to those critics who had maligned Morrissey's solo work as well as providing considerable promise for the future.

Morrissey's perennial management problems were alleviated temporarily by the short-term appointment of Fachtna O'Ceallaigh, who had previously worked with The Boomtown Rats and Sinéad O'Connor. Fachtna helped Morrissey find a new writing partner in guitarist Mark Nevin, previously the principal songwriter in the chart-topping Fairground Attraction and collaborator with Kirsty MacColl. Nevin was pleased to join Morrissey at Hook End Manor to begin work on a new album. It was now approaching two years since the release of *Viva Hate* and rumours of writer's block and perpetual vacillation abounded. Few believed that a new album would be completed by early 1991.

Like Morrissey, Marr had a relatively quiet start to the new decade. With a stable and supportive management structure behind him, the guitarist was enjoying working at his own speed, minus the administrative and business wrangles that characterized his period in The Smiths. The collaboration with Bernard Sumner had evolved into a full-blown album project, which was as long in the making as a president. With deadline dates extending every quarter and expectations rising, the spectre of anti-climax beckoned. The duo remained unfazed by the pressure and played a couple of one-off gigs, supporting Depeche Mode in America and performing a brief set at the Haçienda. Finally, in the early summer of 1991, the pilot single 'Get The Message' was released to justifiable critical and commercial acclaim. It was indubitably one of the year's finest singles. The evocative guitar opening recalled the best of The Smiths, while the synthesizer and drum machine evoked late period New Order. The single was undoubtedly Marr's most exciting and spine-tingling moment since the end of The Smiths. The subsequent long-awaited album, *Electronic*, proved neither a milestone release nor a grand failure, but a solid, respectable effort, ranging from the accessible thrust of 'Tighten Up' and 'Idiot Country' to the evocative instrumental 'Soviet' and atmospheric coda 'Feel Every Beat'. The involvement of The Pet Shop Boys on 'The Patience Of A Saint' added an appropriately languid feel to the proceedings, despite the supergroup line-up. With a US tour and probable series of 12-inch singles to follow, the Electronic experiment is far from over and will no doubt serve as a launching pad for other Marr projects. Morrissey's 1991 matched Marr's in musical newsworthiness. After the indecisions surrounding the abandoned second album, many assumed that it could easily be another year before he released a new work. Instead, *Kill Uncle* appeared promptly in February, preceded by the catchy single 'Our Frank'. The album was a surprisingly lightweight affair, clocking in at a paltry 33 minutes. Moreover, the collaborations with former Fairground Attraction guitarist, Mark Nevin, sounded noticeably slight in tone and content. Morrissey's love of pure pop is demonstrated at its brilliant best on the wistful 'Sing Your Life' and attractively languorous 'Driving Your Girlfriend Home' (with Linder on backing vocals). The racist debate is reopened with 'Asian Rut', on which the singer displays his sympathies in mini-opera style, complete with raga-sounding violin. 'King Leer' reveals lapses in Morrissey's usually razor-sharp wit by featuring the worst word play of his career ("Your boyfriend, he went down on one knee/well, could it be, he's only got one knee?"). The lugubrious 'The Harsh Truth Of The Camera Eye' is one of the less impressive Morrissey songs in recent memory, despite the revealing final lines ("I don't want to be judged... I would sooner be just blindly loved"). The two closing cuts end the work on a sober note, from earthly finality to thoughts of the after life. Although the male children of his late Uncle Tom would no doubt dispute his claim to be "The End Of The Family Line", Morrissey brings a stoical air to his song of genealogical extinction. Having run short of things to complain about in this life, the singer adopts a more cosmological viewpoint in "There's A Place In Hell For Me And My Friends", where he finds the antidote to loneliness in communal damnation. Morrissey's other co-composer Clive Langer provided two contrasting melodies to the album: 'Found Found Found' broke the airy pop feel with its harder edge, while the quaint 'Mute Witness' offered an opening strikingly similar to Roxy Music's 'Virginia Plain'. Not for the first time, Morrissey's approach to the disabled proved ambiguous and a touch flippant. He makes a comedy of manners out of a deaf and dumb witness and laces the tone with benign condescension, culminating in the mockingly polite directive:"'Your taxi is here, my dear'." As with his previous compositions, Morrissey does not attempt to elevate the downtrodden through flattery but highlights their sense of defeat and troubled self-perception, then seeks to draw some form of strength from the very fact of their insularity. In that sense, at least, the mute witness, the gun-toting Asian, the sartorially suspect Bengali, the deformed monster and the hapless suitor reflect the darker aspects of his own isolated self. Ultimately, Morrissey's art is still a pyrrhic glorification of the power of isolation over integration.

While critics pored over the anti-climactic aspects of *Kill Uncle* little consideration was given to Morrissey the performer. Four years into his solo career, he had yet to tour, and it was all too easy to assume that this represented some crisis of confidence that was irreversible. It was doubly frustrating to remember that Morrissey's live work with The Smiths had brought him such intense satisfaction. His stage appearances were a vital part of his art and his full impact as a performer could never be adequately judged or appreciated without the opportunity to witness some live work. Thankfully, the stage hibernation ended in 1991, when the singer embarked on a magnificent series of gigs, culminating in a world tour. Audiences, starved of his presence for so many years, responded with predictable intensity to the live spectacle. With his rockabilly backing group, the newly-energetic Morrissey provided a dazzling selection of songs from his solo years. Even the lighter moments from *Kill Uncle* sounded arresting in live performance, and received a fresh, grittier treatment from his rocka-billy accomplices. The 1991 concerts served as Morrissey's final exorcism of The Smiths' era and a crucial new beginning in his career as a soloist.

Morrissey and Marr's return to centre stage is arguably better timed than many critics realize. At the time of writing, they have been apart almost as long as they were together, and the interim has been a period of tough adjustment. Surviving a legend is never easy, and broken songwriting part-nerships have often proven particularly vulnerable to crises of confidence. Often, there is doubt, indecision and a morbidly fallow period as the public comes to terms with a new approach. When Rodgers and Hart parted com-pany, the latter continued his downward plunge into alcoholism and shot himself. After Lennon/McCartney split, it took both fans and critics a con-siderable time before they could view the duo in a different context from The Beatles. The dissolution of the Bacharach/David partnership, which provided so many hits and standards during the Sixties, caused a scarcely believable reversal of fortune. The once gold-fingered Bacharach failed to register a single chart entry for the entire Seventies, a crazy statistic for a tunesmith of his calibre. Morrissey/Marr have had similar problems in pacing their post-Smiths careers and have laboured under the weight of a previously formidable musical output of immense quality. Like the world, they have had to wait patiently while time erodes the familiarity of The Smiths as an entity and recognizes their own importance as individuals. Irrespective of what they achieve in the future, Morrissey and Marr have already secured their place in history by producing some of the most enduring music of their era. Theirs is a body of work that has not notice-ably dated and still impresses by its sheer quality. Years after their separation, the songwriting duo are still fêted in the most unexpected of quarters. Even the mainstream American rock press voted *The Queen Is Dead* as rock's best ever album. It would be naïve to overestimate the cultural importance of the group, but there is no doubting their cult credi-bility. Like my other favourites, The Byrds, there is something ineffably special about The Smiths. They may not have been as innovative, pioneer-ing or cross-culturally significant as their Sixties counterparts, but there is that same discernible valour and timeless quality about their work which will, surely, ensure its longevity. Morrissey knows this to be the case and, despite expressing a desire to place The Smiths firmly in the history books, realizes that his present work is always likely to be compared to the best of Morrissey/Marr. Whether this still applies by the time I write the next volume in this series is debatable. The frame of reference for a detailed work on Morrissey through the 90s will no doubt be determined largely by the quality of his work and the drama of his life. Whether he will ever be allowed to transcend The Smiths' legend and wipe the slate clean is debatable, but Morrissey is clearly sceptical. "I don't think that's possible," he wearily stresses. "I don't think people will allow me to, and, without wishing to sound pompous, I don't really imagine you will either. But, you go on, and I go on."

DISCOGRAPHY

WHITE DICE

Line-up: Johnny Maher (Marr), vocals/guitar; Robin Allman (vocals/guitar); Paul Whittall (keyboards); Bobby Durkin (drums).

4/80 **F-Beat demos** *(unreleased)*
Someone Waved Goodbye; American Girl; The Hold; Makes No Sense; On The Beach; It's Over; You Made Me Cry.

FREAKY PARTY

Line-up: Johnny Maher (Marr), guitar; Andy Rourke (bass guitar); Simon Wolstencroft (drums).

/81 **Crak Therapy** *(unreleased)*

SMITHS

7-INCH SINGLES:	TITLE	LABEL	CHART POSITION

1983

5/83 Hand In Glove/Handsome Devil   *RT 132*

11/83 This Charming Man/Jeane   *RT 136*   **25**
A limited number of test pressings of the cancelled 'Reel Around The Fountain'/'Jeane' are in existence.

1984

1/84 What Difference Does It Make?/Back To The Old House
    RT 146   **12**

5/84 Heaven Knows I'm Miserable Now/Suffer Little Children
    RT 156   **19**

8/84 William, It Was Really Nothing/Please Please Please Let Me Get What I Want
    RT 166   **17**

During February 1984 a limited number of DJ-only promotional copies of 'Still Ill'/'You've Got Everything Now' (R61 DJ) were circulated in order to plug the group's début album.

1985

2/85 How Soon Is Now?/Well I Wonder	*RT 176*	**24**
3/85 Shakespeare's Sister/What She Said	*RT 181*	**26**
7/85 That Joke Isn't Funny Anymore/Meat Is Murder (Live)	*RT 186*	**49**
9/85 The Boy With The Thorn In His Side/Asleep	*RT 191*	**23**

1986

5/86 Bigmouth Strikes Again/Money Changes Everything	*RT 192*	**26**
7/86 Panic/Vicar In A Tutu	*RT 193*	**11**
10/86 Ask/Cemetry Gates	*RT 194*	**14**

1987

1/87 Shoplifters Of The World Unite/Half A Person	*RT 195*	**12**
4/87 Sheila Take A Bow/Is It Really So Strange?	*RT 196*	**10**
7/87 Girlfriend In A Coma/I Keep Mine Hidden	*RT 197*	**13**
10/87 I Started Something I Couldn't Finish/Pretty Girls Make Graves	*RT 198*	**23**
12/87 Last Night I Dreamt That Somebody Loved Me/Rusholme Ruffians	*RT 200*	**30**

12-INCH SINGLES

1983

11/83 This Charming Man (Manchester)/This Charming Man (London)/Accept Yourself/Wonderful Woman   *RTT 136*

12/83 This Charming Man (New York Mix - Vocal)/This Charming Man (New York Mix - Instrumental)   *RT 136*

1984

2/84 What Difference Does It Make?/Back To The Old House/These Things Take Time
RTT 146

5/84 Heaven Knows I'm Miserable Now/Suffer Little Children/Girl Afraid
RTT 156

8/84 William, It Was Really Nothing/Please Please Please Let Me Get What
I Want/How Soon Is Now?   *RTT 166*

1985

1/85 Barbarism Begins At Home/Barbarism Begins At Home
                                                           RTT 171
(A promotion only release in a limited edition of 500 copies)

2/85 How Soon Is Now?/Well I Wonder/Oscillate Wildly
                                                           RTT 176

3/85 Shakespeare's Sister/What She Said/Stretch Out And Wait
                                                           RTT 181

7/85 That Joke Isn't Funny Anymore/Nowhere Fast (Live)/Stretch Out And Wait
(Live)/Shakespeare's Sister (Live)/Meat Is Murder (Live)
                                                           RTT 186

9/85 The Boy With The Thorn In His Side/Asleep/Rubber Ring
                                                           RTT 191

1986

5/86 Bigmouth Strikes Again/Money Changes Everything/Unloveable
                                                           RTT 192

7/86 Panic/Vicar In A Tutu/The Draize Train   *RTT 193*

10/86 Ask/Cemetry Gates/Golden Lights   *RTT 194*

1987

1/87 Shoplifters Of The World Unite/Half A Person/London
                                                           RTT 195
*(Initial versions of 'Shoplifters Of The World Unite' were despatched with 'You Just Haven't
Earned It Yet, Baby' on the A-side).*

4/87 Sheila Take A Bow/Is It Really So Strange?/Sweet And Tender Hooligan
                                                           RTT 196

7/87 Girlfriend In A Coma/I Keep Mine Hidden/Work Is A Four Letter Word
                                                           RTT 197

10/87 I Started Something I Couldn't Finish/Pretty Girls Make Graves/Some Girls Are
Bigger Than Others   *RTT 198*
*(Cassette versions of the single included a cover version of James' 'What's The World?', recorded
live in Glasgow).*

12/87 Last Night I Dreamt That Somebody Loved Me/Rusholme Ruffians/
Nowhere Fast   *RTT 200*
(The CD version of this single featured an extra track: 'William, It Was Really Nothing').

11/88 Barbarism Begins At Home/Shakespeare's Sister/Stretch Out And Wait
                                                           RTT 171 CD

11/88 The Headmaster Ritual/Nowhere Fast (Live); Stretch Out And Wait (Live)/
Meat Is Murder (Live)   *RTT 215 CD*

Singles were repackaged in various countries, occasionally with edited versions, but the only alternate take of which I am aware is the Italian version of 'How Soon Is Now?' on the flip side of the 12-inch 'William, It Was Really Nothing' (Italy: Virgin VINX 71).

EPs

On 25 May 1984, the New Musical Express *issued a free EP (GIV 1) featuring 'What She Said'. At one point, a live EP was rumoured for release featuring 'Meat Is Murder', 'Nowhere Fast', 'What She Said', 'Stretch Out And Wait', 'William, It Was Really Nothing' and 'Miserable Lie'. The tracks later appeared on various 7-inch and 12-inch B-sides. A live version of 'Girl Afraid' was also available, by mail order only, on the* NME *Various Artistes compilation* Department Of Enjoyment.

Albums

2/84 **The Smiths***   *Rough 61*   **2**
Reel Around The Fountain; You've Got Everything Now; Miserable Lie; Pretty Girls Make Graves; The Hand That Rocks The Cradle; Still Ill; Hand In Glove; What Difference Does It Make?; I Don't Owe You Anything; Suffer Little Children.

11/84 **Hatful Of Hollow**   *Rough 76*   **7**
William, It Was Really Nothing; What Difference Does It Make?; These Things Take Time; This Charming Man; How Soon Is Now?; Handsome Devil; Hand In Glove; Still Ill; Heaven Knows I'm Miserable Now; This Night Has Opened My Eyes; You've Got Everything Now; Accept Yourself; Girl Afraid; Back To The Old House; Reel Around The Fountain; Please Please Please Let Me Get What I Want.

2/85 **Meat Is Murder***   *Rough 81*   **1**
The Headmaster Ritual; Rusholme Ruffians; I Want The One I Can't Have; What She Said; That Joke Isn't Funny Anymore; Nowhere Fast; Well I Wonder; Barbarism Begins At Home; Meat Is Murder.

6/86 **The Queen Is Dead**   *Rough 96*   **2**
The Queen Is Dead; Frankly, Mr Shankly; I Know It's Over; Never Had No One Ever; Cemetry Gates; Bigmouth Strikes Again; The Boy With The Thorn In His Side; Vicar In A Tutu; There Is A Light That Never Goes Out; Some Girls Are Bigger Than Others.

3/87 **The World Won't Listen**   *Rough 101*   **2**
Panic; Ask; London; Bigmouth Strikes Again; Shakespeare's Sister; There Is A Light That Never Goes Out; Shoplifters Of The World Unite; The Boy With The Thorn In His Side; Asleep; Unloveable; Half A Person; Stretch Out And Wait; That Joke Isn't Funny Anymore; Oscillate Wildly; You Just Haven't Earned It Yet, Baby; Rubber Ring.
(Cassette versions include the instrumental: Money Changes Everything*).*

4/87 **Louder Than Bombs**   *Rough 255/Sire 9 25569-1*   **38**
Is It Really So Strange?; Sheila Take A Bow; Shoplifters Of The World Unite; Sweet And Tender Hooligan; Half A Person; London; Panic; Girl Afraid; Shakespeare's Sister;

---

* US versions of *The Smiths* and *Meat Is Murder* featured the additional 'This Charming Man' and 'How Soon Is Now?', respectively. Smiths tracks have been packaged differently in various countries and there are a number of examples of edited tracks. Alternate takes are less rare, but the Canadian Compilation Rough Trade (RTS 1986) features an otherwise unavailable live version of 'Miserable Lie', taken from the Apollo Theatre, Oxford concert of 18 March 1985.

William, It Was Really Nothing; You Just Haven't Earned It Yet, Baby; Heaven Knows I'm Miserable Now; Ask; Golden Lights; Oscillate Wildly; These Things Take Time; Rubber Ring; Back To The Old House; Hand In Glove; Stretch Out And Wait; Please Please Please Let Me Get What I Want; This Night Has Opened My Eyes; Unloveable; Asleep.

9/87 Strangeways, Here We Come   *Rough 106*   **2**
A Rush And A Push And The Land Is Ours; I Started Something I Couldn't Finish; Death Of A Disco Dancer; Girlfriend In A Coma; Stop Me If You Think You've Heard This One Before; Last Night I Dreamt That Somebody Loved Me; Unhappy Birthday; Paint A Vulgar Picture; Death At One's Elbow; I Won't Share You.

 9/88 "Rank"   `   *Rough 126*   **2**
The Queen Is Dead; Panic; Vicar In A Tutu; Ask; Rusholme Ruffians/(Marie's The Name) His Latest Flame (Medley); The Boy With The Thorn In His Side; What She Said; Is It Really So Strange?; Cemetry Gates; London; I Know It's Over; The Draize Train; Still Ill; Bigmouth Strikes Again.

10/88 The Peel Sessions   *Strange Fruit SF PS 055*
What Difference Does It Make?; Miserable Lie; Reel Around The Fountain; Handsome Devil.

CDs

4/85 Meat Is Murder   *Rough CD 81*

12/85 Hatful Of Hollow   *Rough CD 76*

6/86 The Queen Is Dead   *Rough CD 96*

10/86 The Smiths   *Rough CD 61*

3/87 The World Won't Listen   *Rough CD 101*

5/87 Louder Than Bombs   *Sire 9 25569-2*

9/88 "Rank"   *Rough CD 126*

10/88 The Peel Sessions   *SF PS CD 055*
See Albums section for track listings.

BOOTLEGS

Live At The Electric Ballroom 19 December 1983   *TS 24681*
Hand In Glove; Still Ill; Barbarism Begins At Home; This Night Has Opened My Eyes; You've Got Everything Now; What Difference Does It Make?; Miserable Lie; This Charming Man; Back To The Old House; Reel Around The Fountain; Handsome Devil; Accept Yourself; This Charming Man.
Excellent quality recording.

The Smiths
Hand In Glove; Heaven Knows I'm Miserable Now; Girl Afraid; This Charming Man; Pretty Girls Make Graves; Still Ill; Barbarism Begins At Home; This Night Has Opened My Eyes; You've Got Everything Now; Handsome Devil; What Difference Does It

Make?; These Things Take Time; Barbarism Begins At Home.
This excellent quality bootleg was taken largely from The Smiths' performance at the Markthalle,
Hamburg on 4 May 1984, which was filmed for the television show Rockpalast.

Merry Xmas   SC 003
I Don't Owe You Anything; Reel Around The Fountain; Hand In Glove; You've Got
Everything Now; Handsome Devil; These Things Take Time; This Charming Man; Girl
Afraid; Pretty Girls Make Graves; Still Ill; This Night Has Opened My Eyes.
Very good quality recording of the Hammersmith Palais gig of 12 March 1984.

Wilde About Morrissey   *Riot City Records CITY 002*
These Things Take Time; What Difference Does It Make?; The Hand That Rocks The
Cradle; Handsome Devil; Jeane; Wonderful Woman; Hand In Glove; Miserable Lie; I
Don't Owe You Anything (featuring Sandie Shaw); Reel Around The Fountain; You've
Got Everything Now; These Things Take Time; This Charming Man; Still Ill; Pretty Girls
Make Graves.
Good quality recording taken from two sources: Haçienda (4 February 1983) and Hammersmith
Palais (12 March 1984).

Music Is Magnificent
The Headmaster Ritual; Rusholme Ruffians; I Want The One I Can't Have; What She
Said; That Joke Isn't Funny Anymore; Nowhere Fast; Shakespeare's Sister; Barbarism
Begins At Home; Meat Is Murder.
Inferior quality recording of The Smiths at the Ipswich Gaumont (11 March 1985).

Live At The Electric Ballroom
Hand In Glove; Still Ill; Barbarism Begins At Home; This Night Has Opened My Eyes;
You've Got Everything Now; What Difference Does It Make?; Miserable Lie; This
Charming Man; Back To The Old House; Reel Around The Fountain; Handsome Devil;
Accept Yourself; This Charming Man.
A re-release of Live At The Electric Ballroom 19 December 1983.

Royal Command Performance
Some Girls Are Bigger Than Others; Shoplifters Of The World Unite; Cemetry Gates;
This Night Has Opened My Eyes; Still Ill; Panic; The Queen Is Dead; William, It Was
Really Nothing; Hand In Glove; Bigmouth Strikes Again; Vicar In A Tutu; Frankly Mr
Shankly; There Is A Light That Never Goes Out; Ask; I Want The One I Can't Have; Is It
Really So Strange?; Shakespeare's Sister; Stretch Out And Wait; That Joke Isn't Funny
Anymore; Jeane (featuring Sandie Shaw); I Know It's Over; Rusholme
Ruffians/(Marie's The Name) His Latest Flame; London; Miserable Lie; The Boy With
The Thorn In His Side; Girl Don't Come (featuring Sandie Shaw).
A double album humorously credited to The Vegetarians, this above average quality recording
was taken from the G-Mex Festival, Manchester (19 July 1986) and the Brixton Academy,
London (12 December 1986).

The Rusholme Ruffians   *Neurotic Records NUT 009*
What She Said; Hand In Glove; How Soon Is Now?; Stretch Out And Wait;
Shakespeare's Sister; Still Ill; Meat Is Murder; Heaven Knows I'm Miserable Now;
Handsome Devil; Miserable Lie; You've Got Everything Now.
Fair quality recording taken from the Manchester Palace (31 March 1985).

So This Is America   *Indecency Records 102*
How Soon Is Now?; Hand In Glove; I Want The One I Can't Have; Still Ill; Frankly Mr
Shankly; Panic; Never Had No One Ever; Stretch Out And Wait; The Boy With The
Thorn In His Side; Cemetry Gates; What She Said/Rubber Ring (Medley); Is It Really So
Strange?; There Is A Light That Never Goes Out; That Joke Isn't Funny Anymore; The

Queen Is Dead; Money Changes Everything; I Know It's Over; Heaven Knows I'm Miserable Now; Bigmouth Strikes Again; What She Said.
Good quality recording from Great Woods, Mansfield, Massachusetts (4 August 1986). Strangely, the track listings on the LP are severely erroneous.

Never Had No One Ever
Ask; Bigmouth Strikes Again; London; Miserable Lie; Some Girls Are Bigger Than Others; The Boy With The Thorn In His Side; Shoplifters Of The World Unite; There Is A Light That Never Goes Out; Is It Really So Strange?; Cemetry Gates; This Night Has Opened My Eyes; Still Ill; Panic; The Queen Is Dead; William, It Was Really Nothing; Hand In Glove; Handsome Devil; That Joke Isn't Funny Anymore; Shakespeare's Sister; Rusholme Ruffians; Meat Is Murder; Heaven Knows I'm Miserable Now; This Charming Man; You've Got Everything Now.
An excellent quality double album taken from the Academy Brixton (12 December 1986) and Pasco De Camoens, Madrid (18 May 1985).

A Nice Bit Of Meat
Panic; Sheila Take A Bow; Purple Haze; How Soon Is Now?; Barbarism Begins At Home; Please Please Please Let Me Get What I Want; Asleep; Unloveable; Wonderful Woman; Reel Around The Fountain; This Night Has Opened My Eyes.
Again credited to The Vegetarians, this wryly titled work, with the famous Marilyn Monroe nude shot on the cover, is an impressive collection. A mish-mash of sources include The Tube ('Panic'; 'Sheila Take A Bow'), the Royal Albert Hall, 6 April 1985 ('Barbarism Begins At Home' featuring guest vocalist Pete Burns) and, most intriguingly, some rare soundcheck material, including Marr's trip through 'Purple Haze'.

Acid Head
Half A Person; Cemetry Gates; I Know It's Over.
This poor quality 7-inch single features the BBC John Peel session recording of Half A Person and two tracks from the National, Kilburn (23 October 1986), which later appeared on "Rank".

Brixton Academy Friday 20/10/86
The Queen Is Dead; Panic; I Want The One I Can't Have; Vicar In A Tutu; There Is A Light That Never Goes Out; Ask; Rusholme Ruffians/(Marie's The Name) His Latest Flame; Shakespeare's Sister; Frankly Mr Shankly; The Boy With The Thorn In His Side; What She Said/Rubber Ring (Medley); Is It Really So Strange?; London; Meat Is Murder; I Know It's Over; The Draize Train; How Soon Is Now?; Still Ill; Bigmouth Strikes Again.
A fine quality recording of the Brixton gig from 24 October 1986, which is wrongly dated on the sleeve.

Heavy Horses   TMQ 71103
Bigmouth Strikes Again; Panic; Vicar In A Tutu; Frankly Mr Shankly; There Is A Light That Never Goes Out; Ask; I Want The One I Can't Have; Cemetry Gates; Shakespeare's Sister; Stretch Out And Wait; That Joke Isn't Funny Anymore; The Queen Is Dead; I Know It's Over; Hand In Glove.
Inferior quality recording taken from the G-Mex Festival, Manchester (19 July 1986).

Electric Stars   TMQ 71109
Hand In Glove; Still Ill; Barbarism Begins At Home; This Night Has Opened My Eyes; Pretty Girls Make Graves; You've Got Everything Now; This Charming Man; Back To The Old House; Reel Around The Fountain; Handsome Devil; Accept Yourself.
A re-release of the first Smiths bootleg Live At The Electric Ballroom 19 December 1983.

Sorrow's Son *TMQ 71128*
Handsome Devil; Still Ill; This Charming Man; Pretty Girls Make Graves; Reel Around The Fountain; What Difference Does It Make?; Miserable Lie; This Night Has Opened My Eyes; Hand In Glove; These Things Take Time; You've Got Everything Now.
An excellent quality recording from The Old Grey Whistle Test *television broadcast of the Assembly Rooms, Derby (7 December 1983).*

Haçienda *TMQ 71129*
These Things Take Time; What Difference Does It Make?; The Hand That Rocks The Cradle; Handsome Devil; Jeane; Wonderful Woman; Hand In Glove; Miserable Lie.
Inferior version of the Haçienda concert, previously available on bootleg vinyl on Wilde About Morrissey.

Hammersmith *TMQ 72107*
Miserable Lie; Heaven Knows I'm Miserable Now; This Charming Man; Girl Afraid; Pretty Girls Make Graves; Still Ill; This Night Has Opened My Eyes; Barbarism Begins At Home; Back To The Old House; What Difference Does It Make?; I Don't Owe You Anything (featuring Sandie Shaw); Reel Around The Fountain; Hand In Glove; You've Got Everything Now; Handsome Devil; These Things Take Time.
A double album of very good quality, capturing the entire performance from the Hammersmith Palais (12 March 1984).

Smithsessions *TMQ 72112*
Accept Yourself; I Don't Owe You Anything; Pretty Girls Make Graves; Reel Around The Fountain; This Charming Man; Still Ill; This Night Has Opened My Eyes; Back To The Old House; Handsome Devil; Reel Around The Fountain; Miserable Lie; These Things Take Time; What Difference Does It Make?; You've Got Everything Now; Hand In Glove; Wonderful Woman.
Excellent quality recording of the John Peel and Kid Jensen sessions from 1983.

Headmasters *TMQ 72120*
Meat Is Murder; Hand In Glove; I Want The One I Can't Have; Nowhere Fast; Shakespeare's Sister; That Joke Isn't Funny Anymore; Stretch Out And Wait; Heaven Knows I'm Miserable Now; What She Said; Still Ill; How Soon Is Now?; Jeane; The Headmaster Ritual; Reel Around The Fountain; William, It Was Really Nothing; This Charming Man; Miserable Lie; Barbarism Begins At Home.
Excellent quality recording, taken from Irvine Meadows Amphitheater (29 June 1985).

Live In Rome 1985 *HS-01*
William, It Was Really Nothing; I Want The One I Can't Have; How Soon Is Now?; Stretch Out And Wait; The Headmaster Ritual; Hand In Glove; Still Ill; Heaven Knows I'm Miserable Now; Handsome Devil; This Charming Man.
A fair quality recording taken from Tendetrisce, Rome (14 May 1985).

...The Bad Boy From A Good Family
The Queen Is Dead; Panic; I Want The One I Can't Have; Vicar In A Tutu; There Is A Light That Never Goes Out; Ask; Rusholme Ruffians/(Marie's The Name) His Latest Flame (Medley); Frankly Mr Shankly; The Boy With The Thorn In His Side; What She Said; Is It Really So Strange?; Never Had No One Ever; Cemetry Gates; London; Meat Is Murder; I Know It's Over; The Draize Train; How Soon Is Now?; Still Ill; Bigmouth Strikes Again.
This recording, taken from the National, Kilburn, London (23 October 1986), features the complete concert from which "Rank" was adapted. Although the quality is excellent, the recording speed is disconcertingly awry.

The Playbox
Heaven Knows I'm Miserable Now; Jeane; This Charming Man; Hand In Glove.
Allegedly, only 200 copies of this rare bootleg 7-inch EP were pressed. The concert selections are taken from the Capital Theatre, Aberdeen (30 September 1985).

Goodbye To Elvis
Still Ill; Rusholme Ruffians; What She Said; What's The World.
Another 7-inch EP of fine quality, taken from the Capital Theatre, Aberdeen (30 September 1985).

Miserable Lies
Girl Afraid; This Charming Man; Barbarism Begins At Home; This Night Has Opened My Eyes; Still Ill; These Things Take Time; Miserable Lie; I Don't Owe You Anything; What Difference Does It Make?; Handsome Devil.

The Final Radio Sessions
Is It Really So Strange?; London; Sweet And Tender Hooligan; Half A Person.
A fair recording of the John Peel session from December 1986.

Spanish Sun Live Madrid 18 May 1985
How Soon Is Now?; Handsome Devil; That Joke Isn't Funny Anymore; Shakespeare's Sister; Rusholme Ruffians; Hand In Glove; Meat Is Murder; Heaven Knows I'm Miserable Now; Barbarism Begins At Home.
An Italian bootleg of excellent quality taken from an FM broadcast of the concert.

Better Live Than Dead   *TVO 1D 1038*
William, It Was Really Nothing; Nowhere Fast; What She Said; Hand In Glove; How Soon Is Now?; Stretch Out And Wait; That Joke Isn't Funny Anymore; Shakespeare's Sister; Meat Is Murder; Miserable Lie; Barbarism Begins At Home.
Excellent quality recording on CD only.

Nice Bit Of Meat 2
There Is A Light That Never Goes Out; Frankly Mr Shankly; This Charming Man; Jeane; Rusholme Ruffians; What's The World; Instrumental; How Soon Is Now?; William, It Was Really Nothing; Stop Me If You Think You've Heard This One Before; Disappointed; Interesting Drug; Suedehead; The Last Of The Famous International Playboys; Sister I'm A Poet; Death At One's Elbow; Sweet And Tender Hooligan.
Like its predecessor, A Nice Bit Of Meat, this is another mish-mash which includes selections from the National Kilburn (29 October 1986), a couple of John Peel sessions and, most interestingly, two soundcheck instrumentals, including 'How Soon Is Now?' Side two is a fair quality recording of Morrissey's first solo performance at Wolverhampton (22 December 1988).

The Smiths
Wonderful Woman (What Do You See In Him?); Jeane; What's The World?
Released in 1991, this three track single features two songs from the Haçienda concert on 4 February 1983 (erroneously dated as December 1982 on the sleeve) and the James cover 'What's The World?' The track 'What Do You See In Him?' later emerged in slightly different form as 'Wonderful Woman'. The pressing was a limited edition of 1,000.

Live At The Oxford Apollo   *Burning Bush Records*
William, It Was Really Nothing; Nowhere Fast; What She Said; Hand In Glove; How Soon Is Now?; Stretch Out And Wait; That Joke Isn't Funny Anymore; Shakespeare's Sister; Meat Is Murder; Miserable Lie; Barbarism Begins At Home.
An excellent quality recording from the BBC radio broadcast (9 May 1985) of the performance at Oxford Apollo on 18 March 1985.

Before Love
Handsome Devil; Reel Around The Fountain; Miserable Lie; These Things Take Time; Hand In Glove; Wonderful Woman; These Things Take Time; Hand In Glove; This Charming Man.
A good quality recording taken from the John Peel and Kid Jensen sessions of 1983, interspersed with interviews on the Jensen show. The last three tracks are live cuts from 1983, recorded out of time.

CONCERT TAPES

1982

4/10/82 Ritz, Manchester
The Hand That Rocks The Cradle; Suffer Little Children; Handsome Devil.

1983

6/1/83 Manhattan, Manchester

4/2/83 Haçienda, Manchester
These Things Take Time; What Difference Does It Make?; The Hand That Rocks The Cradle; Handsome Devil; Jeane; What Do You See In Him? (blueprint for Wonderful Woman); Hand In Glove; Miserable Lie.

21/2/83 Rafters, Manchester

23/3/83 Rock Garden, London

6/5/83 University of London Union, London

21/5/83 Electric Ballroom, London
You've Got Everything Now; Accept Yourself; What Difference Does It Make?; Reel Around The Fountain; These Things Take Time; I Don't Owe You Anything; Hand In Glove; The Hand That Rocks The Cradle; Handsome Devil; Miserable Lie.

2/6/83 Miners' Gala, Cannock Chase

3/6/83 Fighting Cocks, Birmingham
You've Got Everything Now; Handsome Devil; Accept Youself; What Difference Does It Make?; Reel Around The Fountain; Wonderful Woman; These Things Take Time; I Don't Owe You Anything; Hand In Glove; Miserable Lie.

4/6/83 Brixton Ace, London
You've Got Everything Now; Handsome Devil; Accept Yourself; Reel Around The Fountain; These Things Take Time; Miserable Lie.

29/6/83 Brixton Ace, London
You've Got Everything Now; Handsome Devil; Reel Around The Fountain; What Difference Does It Make?; Wonderful Woman; These Things Take Time; Hand In Glove; I Don't Owe You Anything; Miserable Lie.

30/6/83 Warwick University, Coventry

1/7/83 Midnight Express Club, Bournemouth
You've Got Everything Now; Handsome Devil; Reel Around The Fountain; What

Difference Does It Make?; Wonderful Woman; These Things Take Time; Hand In Glove;
I Don't Owe You Anything; Miserable Lie; Accept Yourself.

6/7/83 Haçienda, Manchester
You've Got Everything Now; Handsome Devil; Reel Around The Fountain; What
Difference Does It Make?; Wonderful Woman; These Things Take Time; I Don't Owe
You Anything; Hand In Glove; Miserable Lie; Accept Yourself.

7/7/83 Rock Garden, London
You've Got Everything Now; Handsome Devil; Reel Around The Fountain; What
Difference Does It Make?; Wonderful Woman; These Things Take Time; I Don't Owe
You Anything; Hand In Glove; Miserable Lie; Accept Yourself; Hand In Glove.

7/8/83 Lyceum, London
You've Got Everthing Now; Handsome Devil; What Difference Does It Make?; Reel
Around The Fountain; These Things Take Time; I Don't Owe You Anything; Hand In
Glove; Miserable Lie.

9/8/83 Dingwalls, London
You've Got Everything Now; What Difference Does It Make?; Handsome Devil;
Wonderful Woman; Reel Around The Fountain; These Things Take Time; I Don't Owe
You Anything; Hand In Glove; Miserable Lie; Accept Yourself; Hand In Glove;
Handsome Devil.

11/8/83 Warehouse, Leeds
You've Got Everything Now; What Difference Does It Make?; Handsome Devil;
Wonderful Woman; Reel Around The Fountain; These Things Take Time; I Don't Owe
You Anything; Hand In Glove; Miserable Lie; Accept Yourself; Hand In Glove.

12/8/83 Dingwalls, Hull

13/8/83 Dingwalls, Newcastle

19/8/83 Gala Ballroom, Norwich
You've Got Everything Now; What Difference Does It Make?; Handsome Devil;
Wonderful Woman; Reel Around The Fountain; These Things Take Time; I Don't Owe
You Anything; Hand In Glove; Miserable Lie; Accept Yourself; Hand In Glove;
Handsome Devil.

30/8/83 Dingwalls, London
You've Got Everything Now; What Difference Does It Make?; Wonderful Woman;
Pretty Girls Make Graves; Handsome Devil; Reel Around The Fountain; Miserable Lie;
These Things Take Time; I Don't Owe You Anything; Hand In Glove; Accept Yourself;
Hand In Glove; Handsome Devil.

3/9/83 Woods Centre, Colchester

15/9/83 Venue, London
Handsome Devil; You've Got Everything Now; These Things Take Time; This
Charming Man; Reel Around The Fountain; Miserable Lie; Still Ill; I Don't Owe You
Anything; What Difference Does It Make?; Accept Yourself; Hand In Glove;
Handsome Devil.

16/9/83 Moles Club, Bath

24/9/83 Escape Club, Brighton

25/9/83 **Lyceum Ballroom, London**
Pretty Girls Make Graves; Wonderful Woman; Miserable Lie; Reel Around The Fountain; I Don't Owe You Anything; Hand In Glove; What Difference Does It Make?; These Things Take Time; Hand In Glove.

29/9/83 **Gum Club, Blackburn**

30/9/83 **Univerity of Birmingham, Birmingham**
You've Got Everything Now; This Charming Man; Handsome Devil; Still Ill; Reel Around The Fountain; Pretty Girls Make Graves; Miserable Lie; I Don't Owe You Anything; Hand In Glove; What Difference Does It Make?; These Things Take Time; Hand In Glove; Accept Yourself.

5/10/83 **ICA, London**
You've Got Everything Now; This Charming Man; Handsome Devil; Still Ill; Reel Around The Fountain; Pretty Girls Make Graves; Miserable Lie; I Don't Owe You Anything; Hand In Glove; What Difference Does It Make?; These Things Take Time; Hand In Glove.

7/10/83 **University of Durham, Durham**

8/10/83 **Liverpool Polytechnic, Liverpool**

12/10/83 **Polytechnic of Wales, Pontypridd, Mid-Glamorgan**

14/10/83 **University of Bangor, Bangor**

21/10/83 **North East London Polytechnic, London**
Still Ill; These Things Take Time; This Charming Man; What Difference Does It Make?; This Night Has Opened My Eyes; Pretty Girls Make Graves; Miserable Lie; Reel Around The Fountain; Hand In Glove; Handsome Devil; You've Got Everything Now; Hand In Glove.

22/10/83 **Liverpool Polytechnic, Liverpool**
Handsome Devil; Still Ill; This Charming Man; What Difference Does It Make?; Pretty Girls Make Graves; This Night Has Opened My Eyes; Hand In Glove; Reel Around The Fountain; Miserable Lie; You've Got Everything Now; Hand In Glove.

27/10/83 **Kingston Polytechnic, London**

28/10/83 **Kings College, London**
Handsome Devil; Still Ill; This Charming Man; Pretty Girls Make Graves; Miserable Lie; This Night Has Opened My Eyes; What Difference Does It Make?; Reel Around The Fountain; Hand In Glove.

10/11/83 **Portsmouth Polytechnic, Portsmouth**

16/11/83 **Leicester Polytechnic, Leicester**
Handsome Devil; Still Ill; This Charming Man; What Difference Does It Make?; This Night Has Opened My Eyes; Pretty Girls Make Graves; Hand In Glove; Reel Around The Fountain; These Things Take Time; Miserable Lie; Accept Yourself; This Charming Man; You've Got Everythng Now; Hand In Glove.

17/11/83 **Westfield College, London**
Handsome Devil; Still Ill; This Charming Man; Pretty Girls Make Graves; This Night Has Opened My Eyes; What Difference Does It Make?; Hand In Glove; Reel Around

The Fountain; Miserable Lie; Accept Yourself; This Charming Man; You've Got Everything Now.

18/11/83 Edge Hill College, Liverpool
Handsome Devil; Still Ill; This Charming Man; Pretty Girls Make Graves; This Night Has Opened My Eyes; What Difference Does It Make?; Wonderful Woman; Hand In Glove; Reel Around The Fountain; Miserable Lie; You've Got Everything Now; This Charming Man.

23/11/83 Huddersfield Polytechnic, Huddersfield

24/11/83 Haçienda, Manchester
Handsome Devil; Still Ill; This Charming Man; Pretty Girls Make Graves; Reel Around The Fountain; Miserable Lie; This Night Has Opened My Eyes; What Difference Does It Make?; Hand In Glove; You've Got Everything Now; These Things Take Time; This Charming Man; Accept Yourself; Hand In Glove.

7/12/83 Assembly Rooms, Derby
Handsome Devil; Still Ill; This Charming Man; Pretty Girls Make Graves; Reel Around The Fountain; What Difference Does It Make?; Miserable Lie; This Night Has Opened My Eyes; You've Got Everything Now; These Things Take Time; Hand In Glove.

9/12/83 SFX, Dublin

19/12/83 Electric Ballroom, London
Hand In Glove; Still Ill; Barbarism Begins At Home; This Night Has Opened My Eyes; Pretty Girls Make Graves; You've Got Everything Now; What Difference Does It Make?; Miserable Lie; This Charming Man; Back To The Old House; Reel Around The Fountain; Handsome Devil; Accept Yourself; This Charming Man.

1984

1/1/84 Danceteria, New York
Although booked as a New Year's Eve gig, the group did not take the stage until after midnight.

31/1/84 University of Sheffield, Sheffield
Hand In Glove; Heaven Knows I'm Miserable Now; Girl Afraid; This Charming Man; Pretty Girls Make Graves; Still Ill; I Don't Owe You Anything; Miserable Lie; This Night Has Opened My Eyes; Barbarism Begins At Home; Back To The Old House; What Difference Does It Make?; Reel Around The Fountain; You've Got Everything Now.

1/2/84 North Staffordshire Polytechnic, Stoke-on-Trent

2/2/84 University of Warwick, Coventry

12/2/84 Lyceum, London
Hand In Glove; Heaven Knows I'm Miserable Now; Girl Afraid; This Charming Man; Pretty Girls Make Graves; Still Ill; This Night Has Opened My Eyes; Barbarism Begins At Home; Back To The Old House; What Difference Does It Make?; You've Got Everything Now.

14/2/84 University of East Anglia, Norwich
Hand In Glove; Heaven Knows I'm Miserable Now; Girl Afraid; This Charming Man; Pretty Girls Make Graves; Still Ill; This Night Has Opened My Eyes; Barbarism Begins At Home; Back To The Old House; What Difference Does It Make?;

You've Got Everything Now.

15/2/84 Rock City, Nottingham
Hand In Glove; Heaven Knows I'm Miserable Now; Girl Afraid; This Charming Man; Pretty Girls Make Graves; Still Ill; This Night Has Opened My Eyes; Barbarism Begins At Home; Back To The Old House; What Difference Does It Make?; You've Got Everything Now; Reel Around The Fountain; Hand In Glove.

16/2/84 University of Leicester, Leicester
Hand In Glove; Heaven Knows I'm Miserable Now; Girl Afraid; This Charming Man; Pretty Girls Make Graves; Still Ill; This Night Has Opened My Eyes; Barbarism Begins At Home; Back To The Old House; What Difference Does It Make?; You've Got Everything Now.

18/2/84 University of Essex, Colchester
Hand In Glove; Heaven Knows I'm Miserable Now; Girl Afraid; This Charming Man; Pretty Girls Make Graves; Still Ill; This Night Has Opened My Eyes; Barbarism Begins At Home; Back To The Old House; What Difference Does It Make?; You've Got Everything Now; Reel Around The Fountain; Hand In Glove.

21/2/84 Town Hall, Bournemouth
Hand In Glove; Heaven Knows I'm Miserable Now; Girl Afraid; This Charming Man; Pretty Girls Make Graves; Still Ill; This Night Has Opened My Eyes; Barbarism Begins At Home; Back To The Old House; What Difference Does It Make?; Reel Around The Fountain; You've Got Everything Now; Handsome Devil.

22/2/84 University of Reading, Reading
Hand In Glove; Heaven Knows I'm Miserable Now; Girl Afraid; This Charming Man; Pretty Girls Make Graves; Still Ill; This Night Has Opened My Eyes; Barbarism Begins At Home; Back To The Old House; What Difference Does It Make?; You've Got Everything Now.

23/2/84 University of Swansea, Swansea
Hand In Glove; Heaven Knows I'm Miserable Now; Girl Afraid; This Charming Man; Pretty Girls Make Graves; Still Ill; This Night Has Opened My Eyes; Barbarism Begins At Home; Back To The Old House; What Difference Does It Make?; Reel Around The Fountain; You've Got Everything Now; Handsome Devil.

24/2/84 University of Bristol, Bristol
Hand In Glove; Heaven Knows I'm Miserable Now; Girl Afraid; This Charming Man; Pretty Girls Make Graves; Still Ill; This Night Has Opened My Eyes; Barbarism Begins At Home; Back To The Old House; What Difference Does It Make?; Reel Around The Fountain; You've Got Everything Now.

25/2/84 Brighton Polytechnic, Brighton
Hand In Glove; Heaven Knows I'm Miserable Now; Girl Afraid; This Charming Man; Pretty Girls Make Graves; Still Ill; This Night Has Opened My Eyes; Barbarism Begins At Home; Back To The Old House; What Difference Does It Make?; Reel Around The Fountain; You've Got Everything Now; Handsome Devil.

27/2/84 University of Kent at Canterbury, Canterbury
Hand In Glove; Heaven Knows I'm Miserable Now; Girl Afraid; This Charming Man; Pretty Girls Make Graves; Still Ill; This Night Has Opened My Eyes; Barbarism Begins At Home; Back To The Old House; What Difference Does It Make?; Reel Around The Fountain; You've Got Everything Now; Handsome Devil.

28/2/84 Hanley Victoria Hall, Stoke-on-Trent
Hand In Glove; Heaven Knows I'm Miserable Now; Girl Afraid; This Charming Man;
Pretty Girls Make Graves; Still Ill; This Night Has Opened My Eyes; Barbarism Begins
At Home; Back To The Old House; What Difference Does It Make?; Reel Around The
Fountain; You've Got Everything Now; Handsome Devil.

29/2/84 University of Leeds, Leeds
Hand In Glove; Heaven Knows I'm Miserable Now; Girl Afraid; This Charming Man;
Pretty Girls Make Graves; Still Ill; This Night Has Opened My Eyes; Barbarism Begins
At Home; Back To The Old House; What Difference Does It Make?; Reel Around The
Fountain; You've Got Everything Now; Handsome Devil.

2/3/84 Queen Margaret Hall, University of Glasgow, Glasgow
Hand In Glove; Heaven Knows I'm Miserable Now; Girl Afraid; This Charming Man;
Pretty Girls Make Graves; Still Ill; This Night Has Opened My Eyes; Barbarism Begins
At Home; Back To The Old House; What Difference Does It Make?; Reel Around The
Fountain; You've Got Everything Now; Handsome Devil.

3/3/84 University of Dundee, Dundee
Hand In Glove; Heaven Knows I'm Miserable Now; Girl Afraid; This Charming Man
(instrumental); This Charming Man; Pretty Girls Make Graves; Still Ill; This Night Has
Opened My Eyes; Barbarism Begins At Home; Back To The Old House; What
Difference Does It Make?; Reel Around The Fountain; You've Got Everything Now;
Handsome Devil.

4/3/84 Fusion Club, Aberdeen
Hand In Glove; Heaven Knows I'm Miserable Now; Girl Afraid; This Charming Man;
Pretty Girls Make Graves; Still Ill; This Night Has Opened My Eyes; Barbarism Begins
At Home; Back To The Old House; What Difference Does It Make?; Reel Around The
Fountain; You've Got Everything Now; Handsome Devil.

5/3/84 Coasters, Edinburgh
Hand In Glove; Heaven Knows I'm Miserable Now; Girl Afraid; This Charming Man;
Pretty Girls Make Graves; Still Ill; This Night Has Opened My Eyes; Barbarism Begins
At Home; Back To The Old House; What Difference Does It Make?; Reel Around The
Fountain; You've Got Everything Now.

7/3/84 Mayfair, Newcastle-upon-Tyne
Hand In Glove; Heaven Knows I'm Miserable Now; Girl Afraid; This Charming Man;
Pretty Girls Make Graves; Still Ill; This Night Has Opened My Eyes; Barbarism Begins
At Home; Back To The Old House; What Difference Does It Make?; Reel Around The
Fountain; You've Got Everything Now; Handsome Devil.

8/3/84 Town Hall, Middlesbrough
Hand In Glove; Heaven Knows I'm Miserable Now; Girl Afraid; This Charming Man;
Pretty Girls Make Graves; Still Ill; This Night Has Opened My Eyes; Barbarism Begins
At Home; Back To The Old House; What Difference Does It Make?; Reel Around The
Fountain; You've Got Everything Now; Handsome Devil.

9/3/84 University of Lancaster, Lancaster
Hand In Glove; Heaven Knows I'm Miserable Now; Girl Afraid; This Charming Man;
Pretty Girls Make Graves; Still Ill; This Night Has Opened My Eyes; Barbarism Begins
At Home; Back To The Old House; What Difference Does It Make?; Reel Around The
Fountain; You've Got Everything Now; Handsome Devil.

10/3/84 Coventry Polytechnic

12/3/84 Hammersmith Palais, London
Miserable Lie; Heaven Knows I'm Miserable Now; This Charming Man; Girl Afraid; Pretty Girls Make Graves; Still Ill; This Night Has Opened My Eyes; Barbarism Begins At Home; Back To The Old House; What Difference Does It Make?; I Don't Owe You Anything (featuring Sandie Shaw); Reel Around The Fountain; Hand In Glove; You've Got Everything Now; Handsome Devil; These Things Take Time.

13/3/84 Free Trade Hall, Manchester
Hand In Glove; Heaven Knows I'm Miserable Now; Girl Afraid; This Charming Man; Pretty Girls Make Graves; Still Ill; This Night Has Opened My Eyes; Barbarism Begins At Home; Back To The Old House; What Difference Does It Make?; Reel Around The Fountain; You've Got Everything Now; Handsome Devil; These Things Take Time.

14/3/84 University of Liverpool, Liverpool
Hand In Glove; Still Ill; Heaven Knows I'm Miserable Now; This Charming Man; Girl Afraid; Pretty Girls Make Graves; This Night Has Opened My Eyes; Barbarism Begins At Home; Back To The Old House; What Difference Does It Make?; Reel Around The Fountain; You've Got Everything Now; Handsome Devil.

15/3/84 University of Hull, Hull
Hand In Glove; Still Ill; Heaven Knows I'm Miserable Now; This Charming Man; Girl Afraid; Pretty Girls Make Graves; This Night Has Opened My Eyes; Barbarism Begins At Home; Back To The Old House; What Difference Does It Make?; Reel Around The Fountain; You've Got Everything Now; Handsome Devil.

17/3/84 University of Loughborough, Loughborough

18/3/84 De Montfort Hall, Leicester
Hand In Glove; Still Ill; Heaven Knows I'm Miserable Now; This Charming Man; Girl Afraid; Pretty Girls Make Graves; This Night Has Opened My Eyes; Barbarism Begins At Home; Back To The Old House; What Difference Does It Make?; Reel Around The Fountain; You've Got Everything Now; Handsome Devil; These Things Take Time.

19/3/84 City Hall, Sheffield

20/3/84 Tower Ballroom, Birmingham
Hand In Glove; Still Ill; Heaven Knows I'm Miserable Now; This Charming Man; Girl Afraid; Pretty Girls Make Graves; This Night Has Opened My Eyes; Barbarism Begins At Home; What Difference Does It Make?; I Don't Owe You Anything; You've Got Everything Now; Handsome Devil; These Things Take Time.

21/4/84 *Vinyl* Party, De Meervaart, Amsterdam
Hand In Glove; Heaven Knows I'm Miserable Now; Girl Afraid; This Charming Man; Barbarism Begins At Home; This Night Has Opened My Eyes; Miserable Lie; Still Ill; I Don't Owe You Anything; What Difference Does It Make?; Handsome Devil; You've Got Everything Now; These Things Take Time.

22/4/84 Brecon Festival, Bree, Belgium
Hand In Glove; Heaven Knows I'm Miserable Now; Girl Afraid; This Charming Man; Barbarism Begins At Home; This Night Has Opened My Eyes; Still Ill; Handsome Devil; What Difference Does It Make?; You've Got Everything Now; These Things Take Time.

4/5/84 Markthalle, Hamburg
Hand In Glove; Heaven Knows I'm Miserable Now; Girl Afraid; This Charming Man; Pretty Girls Make Graves; Still Ill; Barbarism Begins At Home; This Night Has Opened My Eyes; Miserable Lie; You've Got Everything Now; Handsome Devil; What

Difference Does It Make?; These Things Take Time; This Charming Man; Barbarism Begins At Home; Pretty Girls Make Graves; This Night Has Opened My Eyes; Still Ill; You've Got Everything Now; Handsome Devil; Miserable Lie; These Things Take Time; What Difference Does It Make?; Barbarism Begins At Home; Hand In Glove.

9/5/84 The Theatre, El Dorado, Paris
Hand In Glove; Heaven Knows I'm Miserable Now; Girl Afraid; This Charming Man; Barbarism Begins At Home; Pretty Girls Make Graves; This Night Has Opened My Eyes; Still Ill; You've Got Everything Now; Handsome Devil; Miserable Lie; These Things Take Time; What Difference Does It Make?; Barbarism Begins At Home; Hand In Glove.

17/5/84 Ulster Hall, Belfast

18/5/84 SFX Centre, Dublin
Hand In Glove; Still Ill; This Charming Man; This Night Has Opened My Eyes; Heaven Knows I'm Miserable Now; Miserable Lie; I Don't Owe You Anything; Barbarism Begins At Home; Reel Around The Fountain; What Difference Does It Make?; These Things Take Time; Hand In Glove; You've Got Everything Now; Handsome Devil.

19/5/84 SFX Centre, Dublin
Still Ill; Hand In Glove; Pretty Girls Make Graves; This Charming Man; This Night Has Opened My Eyes; Heaven Knows I'm Miserable Now; Miserable Lie; I Don't Owe You Anything; Barbarism Begins At Home; Reel Around The Fountain; What Difference Does It Make?; Jeane; These Things Take Time; Hand In Glove; You've Got Everything Now; Handsome Devil.

20/5/84 Savoy, Cork
Still Ill; Hand In Glove; Pretty Girls Make Graves; This Charming Man; This Night Has Opened My Eyes; Heaven Knows I'm Miserable Now; Miserable Lie; I Don't Owe You Anything; Barbarism Begins At Home; Reel Around The Fountain; What Difference Does It Make?; Jeane; These Things Take Time; Hand In Glove; You've Got Everything Now; What Difference Does It Make?

2/6/84 Provinssi Rock Festival, Seinajoki, Finland
Heaven Knows I'm Miserable Now; This Charming Man; This Night Has Opened My Eyes; Still Ill; I Don't Owe You Anything; Barbarism Begins At Home; Miserable Lie; You've Got Everything Now; Handsome Devil; Jeane; What Difference Does It Make?; These Things Take Time.

10/6/84 GLC "Jobs For A Change" Festival, London
Nowhere Fast; Girl Afraid; This Charming Man; William, It Was Really Nothing; Heaven Knows I'm Miserable Now; I Don't Owe You Anything; Still Ill; Jeane; Barbarism Begins At Home; Hand In Glove; What Difference Does It Make?; You've Got Everything Now; Pretty Girls Make Graves; Miserable Lie.

12/6/84 Market Hall, Carlisle
Nowhere Fast; Girl Afraid; Handsome Devil; This Charming Man; William, It Was Really Nothing; Heaven Knows I'm Miserable Now; Still Ill; I Don't Owe You Anything; Jeane; Barbarism Begins At Home; Hand In Glove; What Difference Does It Make?; You've Got Everything Now; Pretty Girls Make Graves; Miserable Lie; These Things Take Time.

13/6/84 Barrowlands, Glasgow
Nowhere Fast; Girl Afraid; Handsome Devil; William, It Was Really Nothing; This Charming Man; Heaven Knows I'm Miserable Now; Still Ill; I Don't Owe You Anything;

Jeane; Barbarism Begins At Home; Hand In Glove; Pretty Girls Make Graves; Miserable Lie; What Difference Does It Make?; You've Got Everything Now.

14/6/84 Caley Palais, Edinburgh
Nowhere Fast; Girl Afraid; Handsome Devil; William, It Was Really Nothing; This Charming Man; Heaven Knows I'm Miserable Now; Still Ill; I Don't Owe You Anything; Jeane; Barbarism Begins At Home; Hand In Glove; Pretty Girls Make Graves; Miserable Lie; What Difference Does It Make?; You've Got Everything Now.

15/6/84 Caird Hall, Dundee
Nowhere Fast; Girl Afraid; Handsome Devil; William, It Was Really Nothing; This Charming Man; Heaven Knows I'm Miserable Now; Still Ill; I Don't Owe You Anything; Jeane; Barbarism Begins At Home; Hand In Glove; Pretty Girls Make Graves; Miserable Lie; What Difference Does It Make?; You've Got Everything Now.

16/6/84 Capital Theatre, Aberdeen
Nowhere Fast; Girl Afraid; Handsome Devil; William, It Was Really Nothing; This Charming Man; Heaven Knows I'm Miserable Now; Still Ill; I Don't Owe You Anything; Jeane; Barbarism Begins At Home; Hand In Glove; Pretty Girls Make Graves; Miserable Lie; What Difference Does It Make?; You've Got Everything Now.

17/6/84 Eden Court, Inverness
Nowhere Fast; Girl Afraid; Handsome Devil; William, It Was Really Nothing; Heaven Knows I'm Miserable Now; Still Ill; I Don't Owe You Anything; Jeane; Barbarism Begins At Home; Hand In Glove; Pretty Girls Make Graves; Miserable Lie; Handsome Devil; You've Got Everything Now.

20/6/84 Opera House, Blackpool
Nowhere Fast; Girl Afraid; Handsome Devil; This Charming Man; William, It Was Really Nothing; Heaven Knows I'm Miserable Now; Still Ill; I Don't Owe You Anything; Jeane; Barbarism Begins At Home; Hand In Glove; Pretty Girls Make Graves; Miserable Lie; What Difference Does It Make?; You've Got Everything Now.

22/6/84 Cornish Coliseum, St Austell, Cornwall

23/6/84 CND Festival, Glastonbury
Nowhere Fast; Girl Afraid; Handsome Devil; This Charming Man; William, It Was Really Nothing; Heaven Knows I'm Miserable Now; Still Ill; Jeane; Barbarism Begins At Home; Hand In Glove.

24/9/84 Leisure Centre, Gloucester
William, It Was Really Nothing; Handsome Devil; Nowhere Fast; How Soon Is Now?; Barbarism Begins At Home; Rusholme Ruffians; This Charming Man; Reel Around The Fountain; Jeane; You've Got Everything Now; Girl Afraid; Heaven Knows I'm Miserable Now; Still Ill; These Things Take Time; Please Please Please Let Me Get What I Want; Hand In Glove; Miserable Lie.

25/9/84 University of Cardiff, Cardiff
William, It Was Really Nothing; Handsome Devil; Nowhere Fast; How Soon Is Now?; Barbarism Begins At Home; Rusholme Ruffians; This Charming Man; Reel Around The Fountain; Jeane; You've Got Everything Now; Girl Afraid; Heaven Knows I'm Miserable Now; Still Ill; These Things Take Time; Please Please Please Let Me Get What I Want; Hand In Glove; Miserable Lie.

26/9/84 Mayfair, Swansea
William, It Was Really Nothing; Handsome Devil; Nowhere Fast; How Soon Is Now?;

Barbarism Begins At Home; Rusholme Ruffians; This Charming Man; Reel Around The Fountain; Jeane; You've Got Everything Now; Girl Afraid; Heaven Knows I'm Miserable Now; Still Ill; These Things Take Time; Please Please Please Let Me Get What I Want; Hand In Glove; Miserable Lie.

12/11/84 Savoy, Waterford
Please Please Please Let Me Get What I Want; William, It Was Really Nothing; What She Said; Nowhere Fast; Pretty Girls Make Graves; Reel Around The Fountain; Heaven Knows I'm Miserable Now; This Night Has Opened My Eyes; How Soon Is Now?; Still Ill; I Want The One I Can't Have; Miserable Lie; This Charming Man; Hand In Glove; Jeane; These Things Take Time; What Difference Does It Make?

13/11/84 SFX, Dublin
Please Please Please Let Me Get What I Want; William, It Was Really Nothing; What She Said; Nowhere Fast; Reel Around The Fountain; Heaven Knows I'm Miserable Now; Rusholme Ruffians; This Charming Man; How Soon Is Now?; Still Ill; Barbarism Begins At Home; I Want The One I Can't Have; Miserable Lie; Hand In Glove; What Difference Does It Make?; Jeane; These Things Take Time.

14/11/84 SFX, Dublin
Please Please Please Let Me Get What I Want; William, It Was Really Nothing; What She Said; Nowhere Fast; Reel Around The Fountain; Heaven Knows I'm Miserable Now; Rusholme Ruffians; This Charming Man; How Soon Is Now?; Still Ill; Barbarism Begins At Home; I Want The One I Can't Have; Miserable Lie; Hand In Glove; What Difference Does It Make?; Jeane; These Things Take Time.

16/11/84 Savoy, Limerick
William, It Was Really Nothing; What She Said; Nowhere Fast; Reel Around The Fountain; Rusholme Ruffians; This Charming Man; How Soon Is Now?; Still Ill; Barbarism Begins At Home; I Want The One I Can't Have; Miserable Lie; Hand In Glove; What Difference Does It Make?; Jeane; These Things Take Time; Handsome Devil.

17/11/84 Leisureland, Galway
Please Please Please Let Me Get What I Want; William, It Was Really Nothing; What She Said; Nowhere Fast; Pretty Girls Make Graves; Reel Around The Fountain; Heaven Knows I'm Miserable Now; This Night Has Opened My Eyes; How Soon Is Now?; Still Ill; I Want The One I Can't Have; Miserable Lie; This Charming Man; Hand In Glove; These Things Take Time; What Difference Does It Make?

18/11/84 Savoy, Cork
Please Please Please Let Me Get What I Want; William, It Was Really Nothing; What She Said; Nowhere Fast; Reel Around The Fountain; Heaven Knows I'm Miserable Now; Rusholme Ruffians; How Soon Is Now?; Still Ill; I Want The One I Can't Have; Miserable Lie; Hand In Glove; What Difference Does It Make?

20/11/84 Leisure Centre, Letterkenny, Donegal
How Soon Is Now?; Still Ill; This Charming Man; I Want The One I Can't Have; Handsome Devil; Hand In Glove; What Difference Does It Make?; Jeane; You've Got Everything Now.

21/11/84 University of Coleraine, Coleraine

22/11/84 Ulster Hall, Belfast

1/12/84 Versailles, Paris

William, It Was Really Nothing; Shakespeare's Sister; Nowhere Fast; Reel Around The Fountain; Heaven Knows I'm Miserable Now; How Soon Is Now?; Still Ill; Rusholme Ruffians: This Charming Man; Barbarism Begins At Home; I Want The One I Can't Have; Hand In Glove; What Difference Does It Make?; Handsome Devil; Miserable Lie.

1985

27/2/85 Golddiggers, Chippenham, Wiltshire
William, It Was Really Nothing; I Want The One I Can't Have; What She Said; Handsome Devil; How Soon Is Now?; Shakespeare's Sister; Heaven Knows I'm Miserable Now; That Joke Isn't Funny Anymore; Reel Around The Fountain; Rusholme Ruffians; Hand In Glove; The Headmaster Ritual; Nowhere Fast; Still Ill; Meat Is Murder; Miserable Lie.

28/2/85 Civic Hall, Guildford, Surrey
William, It Was Really Nothing; I Want The One I Can't Have; What She Said; Handsome Devil; How Soon Is Now?; Shakespeare's Sister; Heaven Knows I'm Miserable Now; That Joke Isn't Funny Anymore; Rusholme Ruffians; Hand In Glove; The Headmaster Ritual; Nowhere Fast; Stretch Out And Wait; Miserable Lie; Still Ill; Meat Is Murder; Barbarism Begins At Home.

1/3/85 Brixton Academy, London
William, It Was Really Nothing; I Want The One I Can't Have; What She Said; Handsome Devil; How Soon Is Now?; Shakespeare's Sister; Heaven Knows I'm Miserable Now; That Joke Isn't Funny Anymore; Stretch Out And Wait; Rusholme Ruffians; Hand In Glove; The Headmaster Ritual; Nowhere Fast; Still Ill; Meat Is Murder; Miserable Lie; Barbarism Begins At Home; You've Got Everything Now; These Things Take Time.

3/3/85 Guildhall, Portsmouth
William, It Was Really Nothing; I Want The One I Can't Have; What She Said; Handsome Devil; How Soon Is Now?; Shakespeare's Sister; Heaven Knows I'm Miserable Now; That Joke Isn't Funny Anymore; Reel Around The Fountain; Rusholme Ruffians; Hand In Glove; The Headmaster Ritual; Nowhere Fast; Still Ill; Meat Is Murder; Miserable Lie; Barbarism Begins At Home; You've Got Everything Now.

4/3/85 Hexagon, Reading
William, It Was Really Nothing; I Want The One I Can't Have; What She Said; Handsome Devil; How Soon Is Now?; Shakespeare's Sister; Heaven Knows I'm Miserable Now; That Joke Isn't Funny Anymore; Reel Around The Fountain; Rusholme Ruffians; Hand In Glove; The Headmaster Ritual; Nowhere Fast; Still Ill; Meat Is Murder; Barbarism Begins At Home; Miserable Lie.

6/3/85 Arts Centre, Poole, Dorset
William, It Was Really Nothing; I Want The One I Can't Have; What She Said; Handsome Devil; How Soon Is Now?; Shakespeare's Sister; Heaven Knows I'm Miserable Now; That Joke Isn't Funny Anymore; Reel Around The Fountain; Rusholme Ruffians; Hand In Glove; The Headmaster Ritual; Nowhere Fast; Still Ill; Meat Is Murder; Miserable Lie.

7/3/85 Dome, Brighton
William, It Was Really Nothing; I Want The One I Can't Have; What She Said; Handsome Devil; How Soon Is Now?; Shakespeare's Sister; Heaven Knows I'm Miserable Now; That Joke Isn't Funny Anymore; Reel Around The Fountain; Rusholme Ruffians; Hand In Glove; The Headmaster Ritual; Nowhere Fast; Meat Is Murder; Still Ill; Miserable Lie.

8/3/85 Winter Gardens, Margate
Nowhere Fast; Barbarism Begins At Home; Still Ill; How Soon Is Now?; Shakespeare's Sister; Handsome Devil; The Headmaster Ritual; Reel Around The Fountain; That Joke Isn't Funny Anymore; Hand In Glove; Rusholme Ruffians; I Want The One I Can't Have; What She Said; William, It Was Really Nothing; Meat Is Murder; Miserable Lie.

11/3/85 Gaumont, Ipswich
William, It Was Really Nothing; Nowhere Fast; I Want The One I Can't Have; What She Said; How Soon Is Now?; Stretch Out And Wait; Heaven Knows I'm Miserable Now; That Joke Isn't Funny Anymore; Handsome Devil; The Headmaster Ritual; Shakespeare's Sister; Rusholme Ruffians; Hand In Glove; Still Ill; Meat Is Murder; Barbarism Begins At Home; Miserable Lie.

12/3/85 Royal Centre, Nottingham
William, It Was Really Nothing; Nowhere Fast; I Want The One I Can't Have; What She Said; How Soon Is Now?; Shakespeare's Sister; Heaven Knows I'm Miserable Now; Stretch Out And Wait; That Joke Isn't Funny Anymore; Rusholme Ruffians; Hand In Glove; The Headmaster Ritual; Still Ill; Meat Is Murder; Barbarism Begins At Home; Miserable Lie.

16/3/85 Victoria Hall, Hanley, Stoke-on-Trent
William, It Was Really Nothing; Nowhere Fast; I Want The One I Can't Have; Handsome Devil; What She Said; How Soon Is Now?; Heaven Knows I'm Miserable Now; Stretch Out And Wait; That Joke Isn't Funny Anymore; Shakespeare's Sister; Rusholme Ruffians; The Headmaster Ritual; Still Ill; Hand In Glove; Meat Is Murder; Miserable Lie; Barbarism Begins At Home.

17/3/85 Hippodrome, Birmingham

18/3/85 Apollo Theatre, Oxford
William, It Was Really Nothing; Nowhere Fast; What She Said; Hand In Glove; How Soon Is Now?; Stretch Out And Wait; That Joke Isn't Funny Anymore; Shakespeare's Sister; The Headmaster Ritual; Still Ill; Meat Is Murder; Miserable Lie; Barbarism Begins At Home; You've Got Everything Now.

22/3/85 City Hall, Sheffield
William, It Was Really Nothing; Nowhere Fast; I Want The One I Can't Have; What She Said; Hand In Glove; How Soon Is Now?; Stretch Out And Wait: That Joke Isn't Funny Anymore; Shakespeare's Sister; Rusholme Ruffians; The Headmaster Ritual; Still Ill; Meat Is Murder; Miserable Lie; Barbarism Begins At Home; You've Got Everything Now; Handsome Devil.

23/3/85 Town Hall, Middlesbrough
William, It Was Really Nothing; Nowhere Fast; I Want The One I Can't Have; What She Said; Hand In Glove; How Soon Is Now?; Stretch Out And Wait: That Joke Isn't Funny Anymore; Shakespeare's Sister; Rusholme Ruffians; The Headmaster Ritual; Still Ill; Meat Is Murder; Miserable Lie; Barbarism Begins At Home; You've Got Everything Now.

24/3/85 City Hall, Newcastle-upon-Tyne
William, It Was Really Nothing; Nowhere Fast; I Want The One I Can't Have; What She Said; Hand In Glove; How Soon Is Now?; Stretch Out And Wait: That Joke Isn't Funny Anymore; Shakespeare's Sister; Rusholme Ruffians; The Headmaster Ritual; Still Ill; Handsome Devil; Meat Is Murder; Miserable Lie; Heaven Knows I'm Miserable Now; Barbarism Begins At Home.

27/3/85 Royal Court, Liverpool
William, It Was Really Nothing; Nowhere Fast; I Want The One I Can't Have; What She Said; Hand In Glove; How Soon Is Now?; Stretch Out And Wait: That Joke Isn't Funny Anymore; Shakespeare's Sister; Rusholme Ruffians; The Headmaster Ritual; Still Ill; Meat Is Murder; Heaven Knows I'm Miserable Now; Barbarism Begins At Home; Miserable Lie.

28/3/85 St George's Hall, Bradford
William, It Was Really Nothing; Nowhere Fast; I Want The One I Can't Have; What She Said; Hand In Glove; How Soon Is Now?; Stretch Out And Wait: That Joke Isn't Funny Anymore; Shakespeare's Sister; Rusholme Ruffians; The Headmaster Ritual; Still Ill; Heaven Knows I'm Miserable Now; Meat Is Murder; Handsome Devil; Barbarism Begins At Home; Miserable Lie.

29/3/85 Derngate Centre, Northampton
William, It Was Really Nothing; Nowhere Fast; I Want The One I Can't Have; What She Said; Hand In Glove; How Soon Is Now?; Stretch Out And Wait: That Joke Isn't Funny Anymore; Shakespeare's Sister; Rusholme Ruffians; The Headmaster Ritual; Still Ill; Meat Is Murder; Heaven Knows I'm Miserable Now; Miserable Lie; This Charming Man; Handsome Devil.

31/3/85 Palace, Manchester
William, It Was Really Nothing; Nowhere Fast; I Want The One I Can't Have; What She Said; Hand In Glove; How Soon Is Now?; Stretch Out And Wait: That Joke Isn't Funny Anymore; Shakespeare's Sister; Rusholme Ruffians; The Headmaster Ritual; Still Ill; Meat Is Murder; Heaven Knows I'm Miserable Now; Handsome Devil; Barbarism Begins At Home; Miserable Lie; You've Got Everything Now.

1/4/85 De Montfort Hall, Leicester
William, It Was Really Nothing; Nowhere Fast; I Want The One I Can't Have; What She Said; Hand In Glove; How Soon Is Now?; Stretch Out And Wait: That Joke Isn't Funny Anymore; Shakespeare's Sister; Rusholme Ruffians; The Headmaster Ritual; Still Ill; Meat Is Murder; Heaven Knows I'm Miserable Now; Handsome Devil; Barbarism Begins At Home; Miserable Lie; Barbarism Begins At Home.

4/4/85 Hippodrome, Bristol
William, It Was Really Nothing; Nowhere Fast; I Want The One I Can't Have; What She Said; Hand In Glove; How Soon Is Now?; Stretch Out And Wait; That Joke Isn't Funny Anymore; Shakespeare's Sister; Rusholme Ruffians; The Headmaster Ritual; Still Ill; Meat Is Murder; Heaven Knows I'm Miserable Now; Handsome Devil; Miserable Lie.

6/4/85 Royal Albert Hall, London
How Soon Is Now?; Nowhere Fast; I Want The One I Can't Have; What She Said; Hand In Glove; Stretch Out And Wait; That Joke Isn't Funny Anymore; Shakespeare's Sister; Rusholme Ruffians; The Headmaster Ritual; You've Got Everything Now; Handsome Devil; Still Ill; Meat Is Murder; William, It Was Really Nothing; Heaven Knows I'm Miserable Now; Barbarism Begins At Home (featuring guest vocalist Pete Burns); Miserable Lie.

14/5/85 Tendetrisce, Rome
William, It Was Really Nothing; Nowhere Fast; I Want The One I Can't Have; What She Said; How Soon Is Now?; Stretch Out And Wait: That Joke Isn't Funny Anymore; Shakespeare's Sister; Rusholme Ruffians; The Headmaster Ritual; Hand In Glove; Still Ill; Meat Is Murder; Heaven Knows I'm Miserable Now; Handsome Devil; This Charming Man; Miserable Lie; You've Got Everything Now.

18/5/85 Paseo De Camoens, Madrid
William, It Was Really Nothing; Nowhere Fast; I Want The One I Can't Have; What She Said; How Soon Is Now?; Handsome Devil; That Joke Isn't Funny Anymore; Shakespeare's Sister; Rusholme Ruffians; The Headmaster Ritual; Hand In Glove; Still Ill; Meat Is Murder; Heaven Knows I'm Miserable Now; Miserable Lie; Barbarism Begins At Home; This Charming Man; You've Got Everything Now.

7/6/85 Aragon Ballroom, Chicago
William, It Was Really Nothing; Nowhere Fast; I Want The One I Can't Have; What She Said; How Soon Is Now?; Handsome Devil; That Joke Isn't Funny Anymore; Stretch Out And Wait; Shakespeare's Sister; Rusholme Ruffians; The Headmaster Ritual; Hand In Glove; Still Ill; Meat Is Murder; Please Please Please Let Me Get What I Want; Heaven Knows I'm Miserable Now; This Charming Man; Miserable Lie.

8/6/85 Royal Oak Theatre, Detroit
William, It Was Really Nothing; Nowhere Fast; I Want The One I Can't Have; What She Said; Handsome Devil; How Soon Is Now?; That Joke Isn't Funny Anymore; Stretch Out And Wait; Shakespeare's Sister; Rusholme Ruffians; The Headmaster Ritual; Hand In Glove; Still Ill; Meat Is Murder; Please Please Please Let Me Get What I Want; Heaven Knows I'm Miserable Now; This Charming Man; Miserable Lie.

9/6/85 Kingswood Theatre, Toronto
William, It Was Really Nothing; Nowhere Fast; I Want The One I Can't Have; What She Said; Handsome Devil; How Soon Is Now?; That Joke Isn't Funny Anymore; Stretch Out And Wait; Shakespeare's Sister; Rusholme Ruffians; The Headmaster Ritual; The Hand That Rocks The Cradle; Still Ill; Meat Is Murder; Heaven Knows I'm Miserable Now; This Charming Man; Please Please Please Let Me Get What I Want; Miserable Lie.

11/6/85 Warner Theater, Washington
William, It Was Really Nothing; Nowhere Fast; I Want The One I Can't Have; What She Said; Handsome Devil; How Soon Is Now?; That Joke Isn't Funny Anymore; Stretch Out And Wait; Shakespeare's Sister; Rusholme Ruffians; The Headmaster Ritual; Hand In Glove; Still Ill; Meat Is Murder.

12/6/85 Tower Theater, Philadelphia

14/6/85 Opera House, Boston

17/6/85 Beacon Theater, New York
William, It Was Really Nothing; Nowhere Fast; I Want The One I Can't Have; What She Said; How Soon Is Now?; That Joke Isn't Funny Anymore; Stretch Out And Wait; Shakespeare's Sister; Rusholme Ruffians; The Headmaster Ritual; Hand In Glove; Still Ill; Meat Is Murder; Heaven Knows I'm Miserable Now; This Charming Man; Please Please Please Let Me Get What I Want; Miserable Lie; Jeane; Barbarism Begins At Home.

18/6/85 Beacon Theater, New York
Meat Is Murder; The Headmaster Ritual; Reel Around The Fountain; Shakespeare's Sister; Nowhere Fast; I Want The One I Can't Have; This Charming Man; That Joke Isn't Funny Anymore; Stretch Out And Wait; Heaven Knows I'm Miserable Now; What She Said; Still Ill; How Soon Is Now?; William, It Was Really Nothing; Hand In Glove; Please Please Please Let Me Get What I Want; Rusholme Ruffians; Miserable Lie; Jeane; Barbarism Begins At Home.

21/6/85 Kaiser Auditorium, Oakland

25/6/85 State University Open Air Theater, San Diego
Meat Is Murder; The Headmaster Ritual; Shakespeare's Sister; Hand In Glove; Nowhere Fast; I Want The One I Can't Have; This Charming Man; That Joke Isn't Funny Anymore; Stretch Out And Wait; Heaven Knows I'm Miserable Now; What She Said; Still Ill; How Soon Is Now?; William, It Was Really Nothing; Jeane; Please Please Please Let Me Get What I Want; Rusholme Ruffians; Miserable Lie; Barbarism Begins At Home.

27/6/85 Palladium Theater, Los Angeles
Meat Is Murder; Hand In Glove; Shakespeare's Sister; The Headmaster Ritual; Nowhere Fast; I Want The One I Can't Have; This Charming Man; That Joke Isn't Funny Anymore; Stretch Out And Wait; Heaven Knows I'm Miserable Now; How Soon Is Now?; William, It Was Really Nothing; Jeane; Barbarism Begins At Home.

28/6/85 Palladium Theater, Los Angeles
Meat Is Murder; Hand In Glove; I Want The One I Can't Have; Nowhere Fast; Shakespeare's Sister; That Joke Isn't Funny Anymore; Stretch Out And Wait; Heaven Knows I'm Miserable Now; What She Said; Still Ill; How Soon Is Now?; Jeane; The Headmaster Ritual; Reel Around The Fountain; William, It Was Really Nothing; This Charming Man; Miserable Lie.

29/6/85 Irving Meadows Amphitheater, Laguna Hills
Meat Is Murder; Hand In Glove; I Want The One I Can't Have; Nowhere Fast; Shakespeare's Sister; That Joke Isn't Funny Anymore; Stretch Out And Wait; Heaven Knows I'm Miserable Now; What She Said; Still Ill; How Soon Is Now?; Jeane; The Headmaster Ritual; Reel Around The Fountain; William, It Was Really Nothing; This Charming Man; Miserable Lie; Barbarism Begins At Home.

22/9/85 Magnum Leisure Centre, Irvine
Shakespeare's Sister; I Want The One I Can't Have; What She Said; What's The World?; Nowhere Fast; The Boy With The Thorn In His Side; Frankly Mr Shankly; Bigmouth Strikes Again; That Joke Isn't Funny Anymore; Stretch Out And Wait; Still Ill; Rusholme Ruffians/(Marie's The Name) His Latest Flame (Medley); How Soon Is Now?; The Headmaster Ritual; Meat Is Murder; Heaven Knows I'm Miserable Now; Hand In Glove; William, It Was Really Nothing; Miserable Lie.

24/9/85 Playhouse, Edinburgh
Shakespeare's Sister; I Want The One I Can't Have; What She Said; What's The World?; Nowhere Fast; The Boy With The Thorn In His Side; Frankly Mr Shankly; Bigmouth Strikes Again; That Joke Isn't Funny Anymore; Stretch Out And Wait; Still Ill; Rusholme Ruffians/(Marie's The Name) His Latest Flame (Medley); How Soon Is Now?; The Headmaster Ritual; Meat Is Murder; Heaven Knows I'm Miserable Now; Hand In Glove; William, It Was Really Nothing; Miserable Lie.

25/9/85 Barrowlands, Glasgow
Shakespeare's Sister; I Want The One I Can't Have; What She Said; What's The World?; Nowhere Fast; The Boy With The Thorn In His Side; Frankly Mr Shankly; Bigmouth Strikes Again; That Joke Isn't Funny Anymore; Stretch Out And Wait; Still Ill; Rusholme Ruffians/(Marie's The Name) His Latest Flame (Medley); Heaven Knows I'm Miserable Now; Meat Is Murder; This Charming Man; Hand In Glove; William, It Was Really Nothing; Miserable Lie.

26/9/85 Caird Hall, Dundee
Shakespeare's Sister; I Want The One I Can't Have; What She Said; What's The World?; The Boy With The Thorn In His Side; Nowhere Fast; That Joke Isn't Funny Anymore; Stretch Out And Wait; Frankly Mr Shankly; Bigmouth Strikes Again; Still Ill; Heaven

Knows I'm Miserable Now; Meat Is Murder; This Charming Man; Hand In Glove; William, It Was Really Nothing; Miserable Lie.

28/9/85 Clickerman Centre, Lerwick, Shetland Isles
Shakespeare's Sister; I Want The One I Can't Have; What She Said; Nowhere Fast; What's The World?; The Boy With The Thorn In His Side; That Joke Isn't Funny Anymore; Stretch Out And Wait; Frankly Mr Shankly; Bigmouth Strikes Again; Still Ill; Rusholme Ruffians/(Marie's The Name) His Latest Flame (Medley); Heaven Knows I'm Miserable Now; Meat Is Murder; This Charming Man; Hand In Glove; Miserable Lie.

30/9/85 Capital Theatre, Aberdeen
Shakespeare's Sister; I Want The One I Can't Have; What She Said; What's The World?; Nowhere Fast; The Boy With The Thorn In His Side; That Joke Isn't Funny Anymore; Stretch Out And Wait; Frankly Mr Shankly; Bigmouth Strikes Again; How Soon Is Now?; Still Ill; Rusholme Ruffians/(Marie's The Name) His Latest Flame (Medley); Heaven Knows I'm Miserable Now; Jeane; Meat Is Murder; This Charming Man; Hand In Glove; William, It Was Really Nothing; Miserable Lie.

1/10/85 Eden Court, Inverness
Meat Is Murder; Shakespeare's Sister; I Want The One I Can't Have; What She Said; What's The World?; Nowhere Fast; The Boy With The Thorn In His Side; That Joke Isn't Funny Anymore; Stretch Out And Wait; Heaven Knows I'm Miserable Now; Frankly Mr Shankly; Bigmouth Strikes Again; Asleep; Hand In Glove; This Charming Man; William, It Was Really Nothing; Miserable Lie.

1986

31/1/86 City Hall, Newcastle-upon-Tyne
Shakespeare's Sister; I Want The One I Can't Have; The Boy With The Thorn In His Side; Bigmouth Strikes Again.

8/2/86 Royal Court, Liverpool
Shakespeare's Sister; I Want The One I Can't Have; Vicar In A Tutu; Frankly Mr Shankly; Rusholme Ruffians; The Boy With The Thorn In His Side; Cemetry Gates; Nowhere Fast; What She Said; There Is A Light That Never Goes Out; Bigmouth Strikes Again; William, It Was Really Nothing; Meat Is Murder; Stretch Out And Wait.

10/2/86 National Stadium, Dublin
Shakespeare's Sister; I Want The One I Can't Have; Vicar In A Tutu; Rusholme Ruffians/(Marie's The Name) His Latest Flame (Medley); Cemetry Gates; Still Ill; Stretch Out And Wait; That Joke Isn't Funny Anymore; Nowhere Fast; What She Said; The Boy With The Thorn In His Side; There Is A Light That Never Goes Out; Bigmouth Strikes Again; Meat Is Murder; William, It Was Really Nothing; Heaven Knows I'm Miserable Now; Miserable Lie.

11/2/86 Fairways Hotel, Dundalk
Shakespeare's Sister; I Want The One I Can't Have; Vicar In A Tutu; Rusholme Ruffians/(Marie's The Name) His Latest Flame (Medley); Cemetry Gates; Still Ill; Stretch Out And Wait; That Joke Isn't Funny Anymore; Nowhere Fast; What She Said; The Boy With The Thorn In His Side; Bigmouth Strikes Again; Hand In Glove.

12/2/86 Whitla Hall, Queens University, Belfast
Shakespeare's Sister; I Want The One I Can't Have; Vicar In A Tutu; Rusholme Ruffians/(Marie's The Name) His Latest Flame (Medley); Cemetry Gates; Still Ill; Stretch Out And Wait; That Joke Isn't Funny Anymore; Nowhere Fast; What She Said; The Boy With The Thorn In His Side; There Is A Light That Never Goes Out; Bigmouth

Strikes Again; Meat Is Murder; William, It Was Really Nothing; Heaven Knows I'm Miserable Now; Hand In Glove.

16/7/86 Barrowlands, Glasgow
Bigmouth Strikes Again; Panic; Vicar In A Tutu; Frankly Mr Shankly; There Is A Light That Never Goes Out; Ask; I Want The One I Can't Have; Never Had No One Ever; Cemetry Gates; The Boy With The Thorn In His Side; Is It Really So Strange?; Shakespeare's Sister; What She Said; That Joke Isn't Funny Anymore; The Queen Is Dead; I Know It's Over; Rusholme Ruffians/(Marie's The Name) His Latest Flame (Medley); William, It Was Really Nothing.

17/7/86 Mayfair, Newcastle-upon-Tyne
Bigmouth Strikes Again; Panic; Vicar In A Tutu; Frankly Mr Shankly; There Is A Light That Never Goes Out; Ask; I Want The One I Can't Have; Never Had No One Ever; Cemetry Gates; The Boy With The Thorn In His Side; Is It Really So Strange?; Shakespeare's Sister; Stretch Out And Wait; That Joke Isn't Funny Anymore; The Queen Is Dead; I Know It's Over; Rusholme Ruffians/(Marie's The Name) His Latest Flame (Medley); Hand In Glove.

19/7/86 G-Mex Festival, Manchester
Bigmouth Strikes Again; Panic; Vicar In A Tutu; Frankly Mr Shankly; There Is A Light That Never Goes Out; Ask; I Want The One I Can't Have; Cemetry Gates; The Boy With The Thorn In His Side; Is It Really So Strange?; Shakespeare's Sister; Stretch Out And Wait; That Joke Isn't Funny Anymore; The Queen Is Dead; I Know It's Over; Rusholme Ruffians/(Marie's The Name) His Latest Flame (Medley); Hand In Glove.

20/7/86 University of Salford, Salford
Panic; Shakespeare's Sister; Frankly Mr Shankly; Vicar In A Tutu; Ask; I Want The One I Can't Have; Cemetry Gates; Never Had No One Ever; Is It Really So Strange?; The Boy With The Thorn In His Side; There Is A Light That Never Goes Out; That Joke Isn't Funny Anymore; What She Said/Rubber Ring (Medley); The Queen Is Dead; Money Changes Everything; I Know It's Over; Bigmouth Strikes Again; Rusholme Ruffians/(Marie's The Name) His Latest Flame (Medley); Hand In Glove.

30/7/86 Centennial Hall, London, Ontario
Panic; Still Ill; I Want The One I Can't Have; Vicar In A Tutu; Frankly Mr Shankly; Is It Really So Strange?; Cemetry Gates; What She Said/Rubber Ring (Medley); There Is A Light That Never Goes Out; The Boy With The Thorn In His Side; That Joke Isn't Funny Anymore; Ask; Shakespeare's Sister; William, It Was Really Nothing; How Soon Is Now?; Heaven Knows I'm Miserable Now; The Queen Is Dead; Money Changes Everything; Please Please Please Let Me Get What I Want; Bigmouth Strikes Again; Hand In Glove.

31/7/86 Kingswood Music Theatre, Toronto

2/8/86 Capital Congress Centre, Ottawa

3/8/86 Centre Sportif, Université de Montreal

5/8/86 Great Woods Performing Arts Center, Mansfield, Massachusetts
How Soon Is Now?; Hand In Glove; I Want The One I Can't Have; Still Ill; Frankly Mr Shankly; Panic; Never Had No One Ever; Stretch Out And Wait; The Boy With The Thorn In His Side; Cemetry Gates; What She Said/Rubber Ring (Medley); Is It Really So Strange?; There Is A Light That Never Goes Out; That Joke Isn't Funny Anymore; The Queen Is Dead; Money Changes Everything; I Know It's Over; Heaven Knows I'm Miserable Now; Bigmouth Strikes Again.

6/8/86 **Pier 84, New York**
How Soon Is Now?; I Want The One I Can't Have; Still Ill; Frankly Mr Shankly; Panic; Never Had No One Ever; Stretch Out And Wait; The Boy With The Thorn In His Side; Cemetry Gates; What She Said/Rubber Ring (Medley); Hand In Glove; Is It Really So Strange?; There Is A Light That Never Goes Out; That Joke Isn't Funny Anymore; The Queen Is Dead; Money Changes Everything; I Know It's Over; Heaven Knows I'm Miserable Now; Bigmouth Strikes Again.

8/8/86 **Smith Center, Washington**

11/8/86 **Music Hall, Cleveland**

12/8/86 **Fulton Theater, Pittsburg**
Still Ill; I Want The One I Can't Have; There Is A Light That Never Goes Out; How Soon Is Now?; Frankly Mr Shankly; Panic; Stretch Out And Wait; The Boy With The Thorn In His Side; Is It Really So Strange?; Cemetry Gates; Never Had No One Ever; What She Said/Rubber Ring (Medley); That Joke Isn't Funny Anymore; Meat Is Murder; The Queen Is Dead; Money Changes Everything; I Know It's Over; Hand In Glove; Bigmouth Strikes Again.

14/8/86 **Fox Theater, Chicago**
Still Ill; I Want The One I Can't Have; There Is A Light That Never Goes Out; How Soon Is Now?; Stretch Out And Wait; The Boy With The Thorn In His Side; Is It Really So Strange?; Cemetry Gates; Never Had No One Ever; What She Said/Rubber Ring (Medley).

15/8/86 **Aragon Ballroom, Chicago**
Still Ill; I Want The One I Can't Have; There Is A Light That Never Goes Out; How Soon Is Now?; Frankly Mr Shankly; Panic; Stretch Out And Wait; The Boy With The Thorn In His Side; Is It Really So Strange?; Cemetry Gates; Never Had No One Ever; What She Said/Rubber Ring (Medley); That Joke Isn't Funny Anymore; Meat Is Murder; The Queen Is Dead; Money Changes Everything; I Know It's Over; Hand In Glove; Bigmouth Strikes Again.

16/8/86 **Performing Arts Center, Milwaukee**

22/8/86 **Arlington Theater, Santa Barbara**
Still Ill; I Want The One I Can't Have; There Is A Light That Never Goes Out; How Soon Is Now?; Frankly Mr Shankly; Panic; Stretch Out And Wait; The Boy With The Thorn In His Side; Is It Really So Strange?; Cemetry Gates; Never Had No One Ever; What She Said/Rubber Ring (Medley); That Joke Isn't Funny Anymore; Meat Is Murder; The Queen Is Dead; Money Changes Everything; I Know It's Over; Hand In Glove.

23/8/86 **Greek Theater, San Francisco**

25/8/86 **Universal Amphitheater, Studio City, Los Angeles**
Still Ill; I Want The One I Can't Have; There Is A Light That Never Goes Out; How Soon Is Now?; Frankly, Mr Shankly; Panic; Stretch Out And Wait; The Boy With The Thorn In His Side; Is It Really So Strange?; Cemetry Gates; Never Had No One Ever; What She Said/Rubber Ring (Medley); That Joke Isn't Funny Anymore; Meat Is Murder; Rusholme Ruffians/(Marie's The Name) His Latest Flame (Medley); Heaven Knows I'm Miserable Now; The Queen Is Dead; Money Changes Everything; I Know It's Over; Hand In Glove; Bigmouth Strikes Again.

26/8/86 **Universal Amphitheater, Studio City, Los Angeles**
Please Please Please Let Me Get What I Want; Still Ill; I Want The One I Can't Have;

There Is A Light That Never Goes Out; How Soon Is Now?; Frankly Mr Shankly; Panic; Stretch Out And Wait; The Boy With The Thorn In His Side; Is It Really So Strange?; Cemetry Gates; Never Had No One Ever; What She Said/Rubber Ring (Medley); That Joke Isn't Funny Anymore; Meat Is Murder; Heaven Knows I'm Miserable Now; Reel Around The Fountain; The Queen Is Dead; Money Changes Everything; I Know It's Over; Hand In Glove; Bigmouth Strikes Again.

28/8/86 **Irving Meadows, Laguna Hills**

29/8/86 **Open Air Theater, San Diego**
Panic; I Want The One I Can't Have; There Is A Light That Never Goes Out; How Soon Is Now?; Frankly Mr Shankly; Still Ill; Stretch Out And Wait; The Boy With The Thorn In His Side; Is It Really So Strange?; Cemetry Gates; Never Had No One Ever; What She Said/Rubber Ring (Medley); That Joke Isn't Funny Anymore; Meat Is Murder; Heaven Knows I'm Miserable Now; The Queen Is Dead.

31/8/86 **MESA Amphitheater, Phoenix, Arizona**

3/9/86 **Events Center, Boulder, Colorado**
Still Ill; I Want The One I Can't Have; There Is A Light That Never Goes Out; How Soon Is Now?; Frankly Mr Shankly; Panic; Stretch Out And Wait; The Boy With The Thorn In His Side; Is It Really So Strange?; Cemetry Gates; Never Had No One Ever; What She Said/Rubber Ring (Medley); That Joke Isn't Funny Anymore; Meat Is Murder; Rusholme Ruffians/(Marie's The Name) His Latest Flame (Medley); The Queen Is Dead.

5/9/86 **Cullen Auditorium, Houston, Texas**
The Queen Is Dead; Panic; I Want The One I Can't Have; Rusholme Ruffians/(Marie's The Name) His Latest Flame (Medley); There Is A Light That Never Goes Out; Still Ill; William, It Was Really Nothing; Cemetry Gates; Stretch Out And Wait; Never Had No One Ever; Is It Really So Strange?; That Joke Isn't Funny Anymore; Meat Is Murder; What She Said/Rubber Ring (Medley); I Know It's Over; Money Changes Everything; How Soon Is Now?; Hand In Glove; Bigmouth Strikes Again.

6/9/86 **Bronco Bowl, Dallas, Texas**

8/9/86 **McAlister Auditorium, New Orleans**

10/9/86 **Bay Front Theater, Tampa, Florida**

13/10/86 **Sands Centre, Carlisle**
The Queen Is Dead; Panic; I Want The One I Can't Have; Vicar In A Tutu; There Is A Light That Never Goes Out; Rusholme Ruffians/(Marie's The Name) His Latest Flame (Medley); Frankly Mr Shankly; The Boy With The Thorn In His Side; What She Said/Rubber Ring (Medley); Ask; Is It Really So Strange?; That Joke Isn't Funny Anymore; Never Had No One Ever; Cemetry Gates; London; Meat Is Murder; I Know It's Over; The Draize Train; How Soon Is Now?; Still Ill; Bigmouth Strikes Again.

14/10/86 **Town Hall, Middlesbrough**
The Queen Is Dead; Panic; I Want The One I Can't Have; Vicar In A Tutu; There Is A Light That Never Goes Out; Ask; Rusholme Ruffians/(Marie's The Name) His Latest Flame (Medley); Frankly Mr Shankly; The Boy With The Thorn In His Side; What She Said/Rubber Ring (Medley); Is It Really So Strange; Never Had No One Ever; Cemetry Gates; London; Meat Is Murder; I Know It's Over; The Draize Train; How Soon Is Now?; Still Ill; Bigmouth Strikes Again.

15/10/86 Civic Hall, Wolverhampton
The Queen Is Dead; Panic; I Want The One I Can't Have; Vicar In A Tutu; There Is A Light That Never Goes Out; Ask; Rusholme Ruffians/(Marie's The Name) His Latest Flame (Medley); Frankly Mr Shankly; The Boy With The Thorn In His Side; What She Said/Rubber Ring (Medley); Is It Really So Strange?; Never Had No One Ever; Cemetry Gates; London; Meat Is Murder; I Know It's Over; The Draize Train; How Soon Is Now?; Still Ill; Bigmouth Strikes Again.

17/10/86 Coliseum, St Austell, Cornwall
The Queen Is Dead; Panic; I Want The One I Can't Have; Vicar In A Tutu; There Is A Light That Never Goes Out; Ask; Rusholme Ruffians/(Marie's The Name) His Latest Flame (Medley); Frankly Mr Shankly; The Boy With The Thorn In His Side; What She Said/Rubber Ring (Medley); Is It Really So Strange?; Never Had No One Ever; Cemetry Gates; London; Meat Is Murder; I Know It's Over; The Draize Train; How Soon Is Now?; Still Ill; Bigmouth Strikes Again.

18/10/86 Leisure Centre, Gloucester
The Queen Is Dead; Panic; I Want The One I Can't Have; Vicar In A Tutu; There Is A Light That Never Goes Out; Ask; Rusholme Ruffians/(Marie's The Name) His Latest Flame (Medley); Frankly Mr Shankly; The Boy With The Thorn In His Side; What She Said/Rubber Ring (Medley); Is It Really So Strange?; Never Had No One Ever; Cemetry Gates; London; Meat Is Murder; I Know It's Over; The Draize Train; How Soon Is Now?; Still Ill; Bigmouth Strikes Again.

19/10/86 Leisure Centre, Newport, Wales
The Queen Is Dead; Panic; I Want The One I Can't Have; Vicar In A Tutu; There Is A Light That Never Goes Out; Ask; Rusholme Ruffians/(Marie's The Name) His Latest Flame (Medley); Frankly Mr Shankly; The Boy With The Thorn In His Side; The Draize Train.

21/10/86 Royal Concert Hall, Nottingham
The Queen Is Dead; Panic; I Want The One I Can't Have; Vicar In A Tutu; There Is A Light That Never Goes Out; Ask; Rusholme Ruffians/(Marie's The Name) His Latest Flame (Medley); Frankly Mr Shankly; The Boy With The Thorn In His Side; What She Said/Rubber Ring (Medley); Is It Really So Strange?; Never Had No One Ever; Cemetry Gates; London; Meat Is Murder; I Know It's Over; The Draize Train; How Soon Is Now?; Still Ill; Bigmouth Strikes Again.

23/10/86 National Ballroom, Kilburn
The Queen Is Dead; Panic; I Want The One I Can't Have; Vicar In A Tutu; There Is A Light That Never Goes Out; Ask; Rusholme Ruffians/(Marie's The Name) His Latest Flame (Medley); Shakespeare's Sister; Frankly Mr Shankly; The Boy With The Thorn In His Side; What She Said/Rubber Ring (Medley); Ask; Is It Really So Strange?; Never Had No One Ever; Cemetry Gates; London; Meat Is Murder; I Know It's Over; The Draize Train; How Soon Is Now?; Still Ill; Bigmouth Strikes Again.

24/10/86 Brixton Academy, London
The Queen Is Dead; Panic; I Want The One I Can't Have; Vicar In A Tutu; There Is A Light That Never Goes Out; Ask; Rusholme Ruffians/(Marie's The Name) His Latest Flame (Medley); Shakespeare's Sister; Frankly Mr Shankly; The Boy With The Thorn In His Side; What She Said/Rubber Ring (Medley); Is It Really So Strange?; Cemetry Gates; London; Meat Is Murder; I Know It's Over; The Draize Train; How Soon Is Now?; Still Ill; Bigmouth Strikes Again.

26/10/86 Palladium, London
The Queen Is Dead; Panic; I Want The One I Can't Have; Vicar In A Tutu; There Is A

Light That Never Goes Out; Ask; Rusholme Ruffians/(Marie's The Name) His Latest Flame (Medley); Shakespeare's Sister; Frankly Mr Shankly; The Boy With The Thorn In His Side; What She Said/Rubber Ring (Medley); Is It Really So Strange?; Never Had No One Ever; Cemetry Gates; London; Meat Is Murder; I Know It's Over; The Draize Train; How Soon Is Now?; Still Ill; Bigmouth Strikes Again.

27/10/86 Guildhall, Preston
The Queen Is Dead *(set terminated)*.

30/10/86 Free Trade Hall, Manchester
Ask; The Queen Is Dead; Panic; How Soon Is Now?; Vicar In A Tutu; Rusholme Ruffians/(Marie's The Name) His Latest Flame (Medley); Frankly Mr Shankly; The Boy With The Thorn In His Side; There Is A Light That Never Goes Out; Cemetry Gates; Is It Really So Strange?; What She Said/Rubber Ring (Medley); That Joke Isn't Funny Anymore; London; Meat Is Murder; Still Ill; The Draize Train; I Know It's Over; Bigmouth Strikes Again.

12/12/86 Brixton Academy, London
Ask; Bigmouth Strikes Again; London, Miserable Lie; Some Girls Are Bigger Than Others; The Boy With The Thorn In His Side; Shoplifters Of The World Unite; There Is A Light That Never Goes Out; Is It Really So Strange?; Cemetry Gates; This Night Has Opened My Eyes; Still Ill; Panic; The Queen Is Dead; William, It Was Really Nothing; Hand In Glove.

1987

7/2/87 San Remo Festival, Italy
Shoplifters Of The World Unite; There Is A Light That Never Goes Out; The Boy With The Thorn In His Side; Panic; Ask.

VIDEOGRAPHY

4/11/83 *The Tube*
This Charming Man.

7/11/83 *Riverside*
This Charming Man.

24/11/83 *Top Of The Pops*
This Charming Man.

9/12/83 *The Old Grey Whistle Test*
Handsome Devil; Still Ill; This Charming Man; Pretty Girls Make Graves; Reel Around The Fountain; What Difference Does It Make?; Miserable Lie; This Night Has Opened My Eyes; Hand In Glove; These Things Take Time; You've Got Everything Now.

26/1/84 *Top Of The Pops*
What Difference Does It Make?

6/2/84 *YES*
What Difference Does It Make?; This Night Has Opened My Eyes.

10/2/84 *Oxford Road Show*
What Difference Does It Make?

9/3/84 **Backstage Footage** of The Smiths at Middlesbrough Town Hall and Lancaster University, including soundchecks.

16/3/84 *The Tube*
Hand In Glove; Still Ill; Barbarism Begins At Home.

18/3/84 *Elektron Pop* (Belgium)
What Difference Does It Make?

7/4/84 *Datarun*
This Charming Man.

26/4/84 *Top Of The Pops*
Hand In Glove.

/5/84 *Formel Eins* (Germany)
Hand In Glove.

4/5/84 *Rockpalast* (Germany). **Live at Markthalle, Hamburg**
Hand In Glove; Heaven Knows I'm Miserable Now; Girl Afraid; This Charming Man; Pretty Girls Make Graves; Still Ill; Barbarism Begins At Home; This Night Has Opened My Eyes; Miserable Lie; You've Got Everything Now; Handsome Devil; What Difference Does It Make?; These Things Take Time; This Charming Man; Hand In Glove; Barbarism Begins At Home.

18/5/84 *Les Enfants Du Rock* (France)
Girl Afraid; Still Ill; Barbarism Begins At Home.

31/5/84 *Top Of The Pops*
Heaven Knows I'm Miserable Now.

7/6/84 *Earsay*
Heaven Knows I'm Miserable Now.

14/6/84 *Top Of The Pops*
Heaven Knows I'm Miserable Now.

30/8/84 *Top Of The Pops*
William, It Was Really Nothing.

12/2/85 *Whistle Test*
Nowhere Fast, edited songs.

14/2/85 *Top Of The Pops*
How Soon Is Now?

22/2/85 *Oxford Road Show*
Shakespeare's Sister; The Headmaster Ritual.

18/5/85 *Edad de Oro* (Spain). **Paseo De Cameons, Madrid.**
William, It Was Really Nothing; Nowhere Fast; I Want The One I Can't Have; What She Said; How Soon Is Now?; Handsome Devil; That Joke Isn't Funny Anymore; Shakespeare's Sister; Rusholme Ruffians; The Headmaster Ritual; Hand In Glove; Still Ill; Meat Is Murder; Heaven Knows I'm Miserable Now; Miserable Lie; Barbarism Begins At Home; This Charming Man; You've Got Everything Now.

24/5/85 *Studio One*
Still Ill; Meat Is Murder; Barbarism Begins At Home.

22/9/85 **Home Video. Irvine Magnum Leisure Centre, Irvine**
Shakespeare's Sister; I Want The One I Can't Have; What She Said; What's The World?;
Nowhere Fast; The Boy With The Thorn In His Side; Frankly Mr Shankly; Bigmouth
Strikes Again; That Joke Isn't Funny Anymore; Stretch Out And Wait.

8/10/85 *Top Of The Pops*
The Boy With The Thorn In His Side *(promotional video)*.

25/10/85 *The Tube*
*Morrissey in conversation with Margi Clarke at Glasgow Barrowlands with live songs
interspersed from the previous night's show in Edinburgh.*

27/10/85 *The Cutting Edge* (US)
The Boy With The Thorn In His Side (promotional video).

/10/85 *Arsenal* (Spain)
Includes live footage and promotional videos/interviews.

20/5/86 *Whistle Test*
Bigmouth Strikes Again; Vicar In A Tutu.

5/7/86 *Euro-Tube*
There Is A Light That Never Goes Out; Panic.

19/7/86 **Home Video, G-Mex Festival, Manchester**
Bigmouth Strikes Again; Panic; Vicar In A Tutu; Frankly Mr Shankly; There Is A Light
That Never Goes Out; Ask; I Want The One I Can't Have; Cemetry Gates; The Boy With
The Thorn In His Side; Is It Really So Strange?; Shakespeare's Sister; Stretch Out And
Wait; That Joke Isn't Funny Anymore; The Queen Is Dead; I Know It's Over; Rusholme
Ruffians/(Marie's The Name) His Latest Flame (Medley); Hand In Glove.

20/7/86 **Home Video. Maxwell Hall, University of Salford.**
Panic; Shakespeare's Sister; Frankly Mr Shankly; Vicar In A Tutu; Ask; I Want The One I
Can't Have; Cemetry Gates; Never Had No One Ever; Is It Really So Strange?; The Boy
With The Thorn In His Side; There Is A Light That Never Goes Out; That Joke Isn't
Funny Anymore; What She Said/Rubber Ring (Medley); The Queen Is Dead; Money
Changes Everything; I Know It's Over; Bigmouth Strikes Again; Rusholme
Ruffians/(Marie's The Name) His Latest Flame (Medley); Hand In Glove.

7/8/86 *Top Of The Pops*
Panic *(promotional video)*.

20/9/86 *Rock Around The Clock*
Promotional videos of: The Queen Is Dead; There Is A Light That Never Goes Out; Panic.

15/10/86 **Home Video, Civic Hall, Wolverhampton**
The Queen Is Dead; Panic; I Want The One I Can't Have; Vicar In A Tutu; There Is A
Light That Never Goes Out; Ask; Rusholme Ruffians/(Marie's The Name) His Latest
Flame (Medley); Frankly Mr Shankly; The Boy With The Thorn In His Side; What She
Said/Rubber Ring (Medley); Is It Really So Strange?; Never Had No One Ever; Cemetry
Gates; London; Meat Is Murder; I Know It's Over; The Draize Train; How Soon Is
Now?; Still Ill; Bigmouth Strikes Again.

17/10/86 *The Chart Show*
Ask *(promotional video)*.

21/10/86 **Home Video, Royal Concert Hall, Nottingham**
The Queen Is Dead; Panic; I Want The One I Can't Have; Vicar In A Tutu; There Is A Light That Never Goes Out; Ask; Rusholme Ruffians/(Marie's The Name) His Latest Flame (Medley); Frankly Mr Shankly; The Boy With The Thorn In His Side; What She Said/Rubber Ring (Medley); Is It Really So Strange?; Never Had No One Ever; Cemetry Gates; London; Meat Is Murder; I Know It's Over; The Draize Train; How Soon Is Now?; Still Ill; Bigmouth Strikes Again.

23/10/86 **Home Video, National Ballroom, Kilburn**
The Queen Is Dead; Panic; I Want The One I Can't Have; Vicar In A Tutu; There Is A Light That Never Goes Out; Ask; Rusholme Ruffians/(Marie's The Name) His Latest Flame (Medley); Shakespeare's Sister; Frankly Mr Shankly; The Boy With The Thorn In His Side; What She Said/Rubber Ring (Medley); Ask; Is It Really So Strange?; Never Had No One Ever; Cemetry Gates; London; Meat Is Murder; I Know It's Over; The Draize Train; How Soon Is Now?; Still Ill; Bigmouth Strikes Again.

24/10/86 **Home Video, Brixton Academy, London**
The Queen Is Dead; Panic; I Want The One I Can't Have; Vicar In A Tutu; There Is A Light That Never Goes Out; Ask; Rusholme Ruffians/(Marie's The Name) His Latest Flame (Medley); Shakespeare's Sister; Frankly Mr Shankly; The Boy With The Thorn In His Side; What She Said/Rubber Ring (Medley); Is It Really So Strange?; Cemetry Gates; London; Meat Is Murder; I Know It's Over; The Draize Train; How Soon Is Now?; Still Ill; Bigmouth Strikes Again.

26/10/86 **Home Video, Palladium, London**
The Queen Is Dead; Panic; I Want The One I Can't Have; Vicar In A Tutu; There Is A Light That Never Goes Out; Ask; Rusholme Ruffians/(Marie's The Name) His Latest Flame (Medley); Shakespeare's Sister; Frankly Mr Shankly; The Boy With The Thorn In His Side; What She Said/Rubber Ring (Medley); Is It Really So Strange?; Never Had No One Ever; Cemetry Gates; London; Meat Is Murder; I Know It's Over; The Draize Train; How Soon Is Now?; Still Ill; Bigmouth Strikes Again.

12/12/86 **Home Video, Brixton Academy, London**
Ask; Bigmouth Strikes Again; London; Miserable Lie; Some Girls Are Bigger Than Others; The Boy With The Thorn In His Side; Shoplifters Of The World Unite; There Is A Light That Never Goes Out; Is It Really So Strange?; Cemetry Gates; This Night Has Opened My Eyes; Still Ill; Panic; The Queen Is Dead; William, It Was Really Nothing; Hand In Glove.

27/1/87 *Top Of The Pops*
Shoplifters Of The World Unite.

13/2/87 *Megamix* (Eire)
Shoplifters Of The World Unite.

15/2/87 *San Remo Festival* (Italy)
Ask; Ask.

10/4/87 *The Tube*
Sheila Take A Bow; Shoplifters Of The World Unite.

23/4/87 *Top Of The Pops*
Sheila Take A Bow.

9/5/87 *Rock Arena* (Australia)
Promotional videos: Ask; The Queen Is Dead; Panic; There Is A Light That Never Goes Out.

25/5/87 *San Remo Festival* (Italy)
Shoplifters Of The World Unite; There Is A Light That Never Goes Out; The Boy With The Thorn In His Side; Panic; Ask.

13/10/87 *The Roxy*
The Right Stuff *(Bryan Ferry; featuring Johnny Marr)*.

18/10/87 *The South Bank Show*
Documentary, including live footage.

MORRISSEY SOLO RECORDINGS

7-INCH SINGLES:	TITLE	LABEL	CHART POSITION

2/88 Suedehead/I Know Very Well How I Got My Name
HMV POP 1618   5

6/88 Everyday Is Like Sunday/Sister I'm A Poet
HMV POP 1619   9

2/89 The Last Of The Famous International Playboys/Lucky Lisp
HMV POP 1620   6

4/89 Interesting Drug/Such A Little Thing Makes Such A Big Difference
HMV POP 1621   9

11/89 Ouija Board, Ouija Board/Yes, I Am Blind
HMV POP 1622   18

4/90 November Spawned A Monster/He Knows I'd Love To See Him
HMV POP 1623   12

10/90 Piccadilly Palare/Get Off The Stage   *HMV POP 1624*   18

2/91 Our Frank/Journalists Who Lie   *HMV POP 1625*   26

3/91 Sing Your Life/That's Entertainment   *HMV POP 1626*   33

7/91 Pregnant For The Last Time/Skin Storm
HMV POP 1627   25

10/91 My Love Life/I've Changed My Plea To Guilty
HMV POP 1628   29

12-INCH SINGLES/CD SINGLES:

2/88 Suedehead/I Know Very Well How I Got My Name/Hairdresser On Fire
HMV 12 POP 1618
(CD version CD POP 1618 includes 'Oh Well, I'll Never Learn')

6/88 Everyday Is Like Sunday/Sister I'm A Poet/ Disappointed
                                                HMV 12 POP 1619
(CD version CD POP 1619 includes 'Will Never Marry')

2/89 The Last Of The Famous International Playboys/Lucky Lisp/Michael's Bones
                                                HMV 12 POP 1620/CD POP 1620

4/89 Interesting Drug/Such A Little Thing Makes Such A Big Difference/
Sweet And Tender Hooligan (Live)   HMV POP 1621/CD POP 1621

11/89 Ouija Board, Ouija Board/Yes, I Am Blind/East West
                                                HMV 12 POP 1622/CD POP 1622

4/90 November Spawned A Monster/He Knows I'd Love To See Him/
Girl Least Likely To   HMV 12 POP 1623/CD POP 1623

10/90 Piccadilly Palare/Get Off The Stage/At Amber
                                                HMV 12 POP 1624/CD POP 1624

2/91 Our Frank/Journalists Who Lie/Tony The Pony
                                                HMV 12 POP 1625/CD POP 1625

3/91 Sing Your Life/That's Entertainment/The Loop
                                                HMV 12 POP 1626/CD POP 1626

7/91 Pregnant For The Last Time/Skin Storm/Cosmic Dancer (Live)/
Disappointed (Live)   HMV 12 POP 1627/CD POP 1627

10/91 My Love Life/I've Changed My Plea To Guilty/There's A Place In Hell For Me
And My Friends   HMV 12 POP 1628/CD POP 1628

ALBUMS/CDs

3/88 **Viva Hate**   HMV (CD) CSD 3787   **1**
Alsatian Cousin; Little Man, What Now?; Everyday Is Like Sunday; Bengali In
Platforms; Angel, Angel, Down We Go Together; Late Night, Maudlin Street;
Suedehead; Break Up The Family; The Ordinary Boys; I Don't Mind If You Forget Me;
Dial A Cliche; Margaret On A Guillotine.

10/90 **Bona Drag**   HMV (CD) CSD 3788   **9**
Piccadilly Palare; Interesting Drug; November Spawned A Monster; Will Never Marry;
Such A Little Thing Makes Such A Big Difference; The Last Of The Famous
International Playboys; Ouija Board, Ouija Board; Hairdresser On Fire; Everyday Is Like
Sunday; He Knows I'd Love To See Him; Yes, I Am Blind; Lucky Lisp; Suedehead;
Disappointed.

3/91 **Kill Uncle**   HMV (CD) CSD 3789   **8**
Our Frank; Asian Rut; Sing Your Life; Mute Witness; Found Found Found; Driving
Your Girlfriend Home; The Harsh Truth Of The Camera Eye; (I'm) The End Of The
Family Line; There's A Place In Hell For Me And My Friends.

EPs

10/10/91 **Morrissey At KROQ**   *Sire 940184-2*

There's A Place In Hell For Me And My Friends; My Love Life; Sing Your Life.

VIDEOS

5/90 **Hulmerist** *HMV MVP 9912183*
The Last Of The Famous International Playboys; Sister I'm A Poet; Everyday Is Like Sunday; Interesting Drug; Suedehead; Ouija Board, Ouija Board; November Spawned A Monster.

GUEST APPEARANCES

Morrissey, unlike his former songwriting partner, is not known for appearing on other artistes' discs. One exception, however, is the humorous Viva Hate *outtake, 'I Know Very Well How I Got My Note Wrong' credited to Vincent Gerard and Steven Patrick. This seven-inch single came free with initial copies of Durutti Column's* Vini Reilly. *Another, as yet unissued, track from the same sessions, features Reilly on lead vocal attempting 'Hairdresser On Fire', complete with hilarious Morrissey-style inflexions.*

JOHNNY MARR Post-Smiths Recordings

PRETENDERS

4/89 Windows Of The World/1969 *Polydor PRE 69*

THE THE

SINGLES

3/89 The Beat(en) Generation/Angel/Soul Mining
(Marr plays on A-side only) *Epic EMU (CD) 8*

7/89 Gravitate To Me/The Violence Of Truth
Epic EMU (CD) 9

ALBUMS

5/89 **Mind Bomb** *Epic 463319 1/2*
Good Morning Beautiful; Armageddon Days Are Here (Again); The Violence Of Truth; Kingdom Of Rain; The Beat(en) Generation; August & September; Gravitate To Me; Beyond Love.

ELECTRONIC

SINGLES

12/89 Getting Away With It/Getting Away With It
Factory FAC (CD) 757

4/91 Get The Message/Free Will
Various remixes of the single were also available Factory FAC (D) 287(R)

9/91 Feel Every Beat, 7" remix/ Feel Every Beat, DNA Mix/Second To None/
Lean To The Inside   *Factory FACT D 328*

ALBUMS

6/91 **Electronic**   *FACD 290*
Idiot Country; Reality; Tighten Up; The Patience Of A Saint; Gangster; Soviet; Get The
Message; Try All You Want; Some Distant Memory; Feel Every Beat.

JOHNNY MARR Session Appearances

QUANDO QUANGO

6/84 Atom Rock/Triangle   *Factory FAC 102*

EVERYTHING BUT THE GIRL

9/84 Native Land/River Bed Dry   *Blanco Y Negro NEG6*
(Marr appears on A-side only).

IMPOSSIBLE DREAMERS

9/85 August Avenue   *RCA PB 40349*
(Marr appears on A-side only).

BILLY BRAGG

SINGLES

6/86 Levi Stubbs Tears/Walk Away Renee (Version)
                                                      Go! Discs GOD 12
(Marr appears on B-side only credited as Duane Tremelo).

12/86 Greetings To The New Brunette/Deportees/The Tatler/Jeane/There Is Power In
The Union (Instrumental)   *Go! Discs GOD X15*
(Marr appears on 'Greetings To The New Brunette' only).

7/91 Sexuality/One Good Thing/Sexuality *Go! Discs GOD X56*

ALBUMS

9/86 **Talking With The Taxman About Poetry**
                                                      Go! Discs AGOLP 6
(Marr appears on 'Greetings To The New Brunette' and 'The Passion').

9/91 **Don't Try This At Home**   *Go! Discs 828 279-2*
(Marr appears on 'Cindy Of A Thousand Lives', and 'Sexuality').

BRYAN FERRY

SINGLES

9/87 The Right Stuff/The Right Stuff (Brooklyn Mix)
(Various mixes were issued).   Virgin VS 940

2/88 Kiss And Tell/Zamba   Virgin VS 1034
(Marr plays on A-side only. Various mixes were issued).

6/88 Limbo (Latin Mix)/Limbo (Brooklyn Mix)
                                   Virgin VS 1066

ALBUMS

11/87 **Bete Noir**   Virgin 7424
(Marr plays on 'Limbo'; 'Kiss And Tell'; 'The Right Stuff'; 'Seven Deadly Sins').

TALKING HEADS

3/88 **Naked**   EMI (CD) EMD 1005
*(Marr appears on 'Ruby Dear'; '(Nothing But) Flowers'; 'Mommy, Daddy, You And I'; '
Cool Water').*

KIRSTY MACCOLL

SINGLES

2/89 Free World/Closer To God/You Just Haven't Earned It Yet Baby
                                   Virgin KMAT 1

6/89 Days/Happy   KMA(T) 2

6/91 Walking Down Madison/One Good Thing/Walking Down Madison
                                   Virgin VST 1348

ALBUMS

4/89 **Kite**   Virgin KMLP 1
*(Marr plays on 'Mother's Ruin'; 'Days'; 'No Victims'; 'Tread Lightly'; 'What Do Pretty Girls
Do'; 'The End Of A Perfect Day'; 'You And Me Baby'; 'You Just Haven't Earned It Yet, Baby';
'Complainte Pour Ste Catherine').*

6/91 **Electric Landlady**   Virgin 211640/CDV 2663
(Marr plays on 'Walking Down Madison' and 'Children Of The Revolution').

ANDREW BERRY

7/90 Kiss Me I'm Cold/That's My Business
(Released in multi-mix format).   Fontana BERRY 1

PET SHOP BOYS

10/90 **Behaviour**   *Parlophone PCSD 113*
(Marr appears on 'My October Symphony' and 'This Must Be The Place').

STEX

1/91 Still Feel The Rain/Still Feel The Rain (alternate mix)
                                                         Some Bizzare SBZ 002
(Marr appears on A-side; released in various formats).

BANDERAS

SINGLES

2/91 This Is Your Life/It's Written All Over My Face
(Marr appears on A-side only).   *London LON 290*

9/91 May This Be Your Last Sorrow/Smith And Mighty/This Is Your Life
(Marr appears on 'This Is Your Life').   *London LONX 306*

ALBUMS

3/91 **Ripe**   *London 828-24-1/7-2*
(Marr appears on 'This Is Your Life')

INDEX